CRYSTALS, MOTHER EARTH
AND THE FORCES OF LIVING NATURE

Adventures Unlimited Press

Crystals, Mother Earth and the Forces of Living Nature

ISBN 978-1-948803-63-2

Published by:
Adventures Unlimited Press
One Adventure Place
Kempton, Illinois 60946 USA
auphq@frontiernet.net

AdventuresUnlimitedPress.com

Acknowledgement

This book would be incomplete without extending an enormous thank you to my dear friend of nearly fifty years, Nelson Cavendish. You taught me that things are truly never what they seem and your blessings for this project are no exception. You have walked with me every step of the way and for that I can never thank you enough.

CRYSTALS,
MOTHER EARTH
AND THE FORCES OF
LIVING NATURE

Nigel Graddon

Adventures Unlimited Press

Other Books by Nigel Graddon:

PYTHAGORAS OF SAMOS
THE GODS IN THE FIELDS
JACK THE RIPPER'S NEW TESTAMENT
THE LANDING LIGHTS OF MAGONIA
U-33: HITLER'S SECRET ENVOY
OTTO RAHN AND THE QUEST FOR THE HOLY GRAIL

Other Books of Interest:

VIMANA
ARK OF GOD
THE LOST WORLD OF CHAM
OBELISKS: TOWERS OF POWER
ANCIENT TECHNOLOGY IN PERU & BOLIVIA
THE MYSTERY OF THE OLMECS
PIRATES AND THE LOST TEMPLAR FLEET
TECHNOLOGY OF THE GODS
A HITCHHIKER'S GUIDE TO ARMAGEDDON
LOST CONTINENTS & THE HOLLOW EARTH
ATLANTIS & THE POWER SYSTEM OF THE GODS
THE FANTASTIC INVENTIONS OF NIKOLA TESLA
LOST CITIES OF NORTH & CENTRAL AMERICA
LOST CITIES OF CHINA, CENTRAL ASIA & INDIA
LOST CITIES & ANCIENT MYSTERIES OF AFRICA & ARABIA
LOST CITIES & ANCIENT MYSTERIES OF SOUTH AMERICA
LOST CITIES OF ANCIENT LEMURIA & THE PACIFIC
LOST CITIES OF ATLANTIS, ANCIENT EUROPE & THE MEDITERRANEAN
LOST CITIES & ANCIENT MYSTERIES OF THE SOUTHWEST
YETIS, SASQUATCH AND HAIRY GIANTS
THE ENIGMA OF CRANIAL DEFORMATION
THE CRYSTAL SKULLS

CONTENTS

The earth is not a dead body but is inhabited by a spirit that is its life and soul. All created things, minerals included, draw their strength from the earth spirit. This spirit is life; it is nourished by the stars, and it gives nourishment to all living things it shelters in its womb. Through the spirit received from on high, the earth hatches the minerals in her womb as the mother the unborn child. This invisible spirit is like the reflection in a mirror, intangible, yet it is at the same time the root of all the substances necessary to the alchemical process or arising therefrom.

—15th century alchemist, Basilius Valentinus

Rock crystal (from the author's collection)

Crystal points, obelisks and pyramids pictured by a model of Alice
"Wonderland" Liddell's holiday home in Penmorfa, North Wales
(author's collection)

Introduction

Be thou the tenth Muse, ten times more in worth
Than those old nine which rhymers invocate.

William Shakespeare
Sonnet XXXVIII

In a recent book for AUP ,[1] I introduced the fictional character of Brad Pulaski and his visit to a very unusual Flying A gas station and its equally unusual proprietor. At the time of his adventure, Brad was a twenty -six-year-old lumberjack in a Montana logging camp, a job from whi ch he derived little enjoyment. He got a buzz from wor king in a nature environment but he regarded the work as somewhat boring and unrewardingly repetitive. He wanted more from life but could not put his finger on precisely what it was that he was looking for.

Brad, of course, was a thinly disguised version of myself when I began my search for the "meaning of life" back in the sixties. Little did I know back then that answers are more likely to be found in the little things in life rather than in some mystical "revelation" that is sought at the cost of missing the delights that d'one step, one day at a time' attitude brings our way. Ignorant of this simple but beautiful truth, by the mid - seventies my quest to find waymarkers to my personal Grail Castle was proceeding with increasing vigour.

One evening in December 197 6 I was attending my father's office Christmas party in a London hotel by the Thames. Two of his employees had had to drop out of the celebration and so Dad asked if I would like to come along with my girlfriend.   Naturally, we were delighted for the opportunity to enjoy a free spread. Seated opposite me that evening was a man who was a few years my senior. Quickly (and heaven knows how we got onto such rarified topics at an office party) we got to talking about all the subjects that fascinated me —the Mystery Schools of antiquity, Ancient Egypt, Stone henge and Avebury, Merlin, Arthur and Camelot, the Druids, the Knights Templar, Carroll and Alice, and much more. The evening flew by because I was so engrossed in tal king with this quietly

---

[1] Graddon, N., *Pythagoras of Samos: First Philosopher and Magician of Numbers*, AUP, 2021

spoken and unusually informed man.

Eventually, my conversation partner mentioned that he was planning to attend in the coming week an evening meeting that might interest me. All manner of topics were to be covered in what was to be the first in a series of workshops dedicated to inner life learning and the western metaphysical tradition. Might this, I wondered, be another step in my search for hidden answers?

To cut a long story short, my subsequent participation in the metaphysics workshops in London's Notting Hill in 1976-7 was the beginning of my esoteric studentship in the company of remarkable teachers. Gradually, I was exposed to the power and the beauty of the "perennial philosophy," as exemplified by the teachings of the Hermetic Mysteries and, later, of Pythagoras.

The ancient Masters taught that it is within nature that humans discover their immortality. Earth, without man, is a natural balance. The mineral, plant and animal kingdoms are a natural force on this plane. Without man there would be perfect equilibrium. A planet without humans would be so positive that there would be no difficulties, no sadness, no sorrow, no over-population, and no destruction other than that needed. To redress the imbalance brought about by man's presence on Earth, humans must learn to revere nature, not just Mother Earth and her outer forms and diverse modes of expression, but one's personal Nature-Self, which, in quieter moments, reminds us that we are innately connected to a magnificent, infinite power.

Irish mystic George William Russell (pen name "AE") described the magical essence of this power in *The Candle of Vision*:

> ...one warm summer day lying idly on the hillside, not then thinking of anything but the sunlight, and how sweet it was to drowse there... suddenly, I felt a fiery heart throb, and knew it was personal and intimate, and started with every sense dilated and intent, and turned inwards, and I heard first a music as of bells going away, away into that wondrous underland whither, as legend relates, the Danaan gods withdrew; and then the heart of the hills was opened to me, and I knew there was no hill for those who were there, and they were unconscious of the ponderous mountain piled above the palaces of light, and the winds were sparkling and diamond clear, yet full of colour as an opal, as they glittered through the valley, and I knew the Golden Age was all about me, and it was we who had been blind to it but that it had never passed away from the world.

In my seventy-one years there have been four occasions when I have caught a glimpse of Russell's "wondrous underland," twice as a child and twice in adulthood. The brevity of the occasions was more than compensated by the powerful impressions they etched into my consciousness, which is where they remain, ready and inspirational reminders of a power that exists beyond the visible, and accessible by anyone.

One of the Notting Hill teachers, Nelson, an American with whom I developed a lasting friendship until his death a few years ago was closely acquainted with a man named Frank Dorland. In his day, Dorland was one of the world's most accomplished biocrystallographers. Before he began to work with crystals, Dorland was employed in the engineering division of Consolidated Aircraft at Lindbergh Field in San Diego. Later as an art conservator, he researched and produced the first scientifically formulated artists' wax for painting and preserving art pieces, sculptures, and archaeological artefacts.

In 1964, when a human-sized quartz crystal skull was brought to Dorland from England, his life changed considerably. The more Dorland studied the Mitchell-Hedges Crystal Skull, the more it demanded further research. Having been entrusted with the magnificent crystal skull for six years, including taking responsibility for the important examinations conducted at the Hewlett-Packard Laboratory, Dorland's work evolved into a new category: biocrystallography, the study of the interchange of energies between the human mind and quartz crystal.

Frank Dorland pictured alongside the Mitchell-Hedges Crystal Skull

Nelson had brought to the London workshops a handful of Dorland's hand-crafted crystal items. I was immediately drawn to a beautiful clear quartz Latin cross, which became mine. Worn daily, suspended on a double silver chain, it has for forty-six years been a treasured friend and companion, cut and polished by a master craftsman from one of the finest and most powerful materials that may be found in nature. A few months later, I acquired more Dorland pieces: two small, perfectly shaped crystal balls.

Having three cherished quartz treasures carved by Dorland has brought not only lifelong pleasure and an enhanced sense of a deep personal relationship with the natural world but, also, a lasting connection to the traditions of the mysterious Crystal Skulls, aspects of which will be explored in later pages.

The author's crystal Latin Cross, carved by Frank Dorland, 1977

My retirement from "9 -5" work eight years ago coincided with a greatly increased personal interest in crystals. Until then I had no idea that there was so much variety in the quartz kingdom. Subsequently, I have built a significant collection of crystals, photographs of many of which I have placed throughout this work. Handling or simply observing them in quiet moments gives me enormous pleasure. Equally, they are a constant reminder of Mother Earth's munificence, a gift that keeps on giving provided we treat her with the love and respect that is her due.

When I confessed to David Childress that since writing my book on Pythagoras, my sixth for AUP, I had run out of ideas for further projects, he said straightaway that he felt sure I had another one in me. Up to that point, chewing over possible ideas, I had considered "something about crystals" but quickly abandoned the idea because there is no shortage of well-written, informative books on the topic in the marketplace. But as soon as David put his faith in me, I soon realised that I could write something that put crystals front and centre but was contextualised alongside a study of the western metaphysical tradition and, especially, its teachings concerning humankind's relationship with Nature.

This new book, although bearing three distinct motifs in its title — Crystals, Mother Earth, and the Forces of Living Nature—has a single focus that unites all three: essentially, the opening of one's heart to She who, over countless millennia, created us; who, despite our evident disdain, ignorance and selfishness, cares for us, feeds, clothes and shelters us even while we do our upmost to destroy her: Nature.

Simply, I invite readers to similarly reflect on what we can all do better to reconnect our ties with Mother Earth so that she may heal the wounds made by our hands since humanity, relatively recently in its existence, cast out the goddess from its daily devotions.

For countless millennia, goddess worship was a critical component of mankind's daily spiritual devotions. Not a thought was formed, a word spoken, or an action taken that did not, as its prime purpose, seek to express profound gratitude for the life -enriching gifts that Nature gives so bounteously and freely. To our modern-day ears, "goddess worship" must smack of primitive, tribalistic behaviour that is beneath the dignity of our smartworld conceptions of what counts as important in our unceasing quest to gather more "stuff" into already overbrimming and, ultimately, ever emptier lives. But let us not be fooled into believing that the development of a personal, intimate relationship with Nature (personified in myth and legend as the goddess) was for uneducated, unskilled savages.

5

Life in the Neolithic era (c. 10,000 BC to 5,500 BC), for example, has been revealed to have been a great age of discovery, which led mankind to forge no less than a brand-new relationship with the universe, with love and care for the goddess—Mother Nature—being heart and centre of this new and more profound bonding with the cosmological orders of Creation.

A development of a personal, day-to-day relationship with the goddess is more important now than at any other time in mankind's history if we are to give Mother Nature a fighting chance to heal. The consequences of failing to do so are evident in Earth's historic record. The story of a great Flood, for example, is told in many cultures and is an ever-present reminder of what can happen if Mother Nature decides that enough is enough. Nature is neutral, devoid of sentiment. Humans are not a biological necessity to ensure the continuance of life on Earth; we are tolerated, no less, no more.

There is something uniquely powerful about the forces of Nature. Those who seek enlightenment have only to look about them to find the signs and symbols by which to facilitate their personal journey to Nature's inner realm, where resides Mother Earth and her magical company.

The key to finding in nature a door to a Secret Garden is to tend one's positive qualities: unswerving belief, courage, insight, wisdom, patience, humour, a healthy sense of quest adventure, and, of course, a deep respect for Mother Earth and her abundant gifts.

The lock is the subconscious mind whose chaotic nature, without the necessary training, prohibits the development of those instinctual and intuitive qualities by which to find Mother Nature's secret entrances.

Possessing the key and having the faculties to access the lock will enable one to find these doors, which admit one to the companion planes of the earth, those enchanted realms of finer ethers that are located just within our own "solid" world.

They can be anywhere: a waterfall, a cave, a bluebell wood, a rabbit hole, even a Paris Café or an old ramshackle gas station. In fact, any place can become an entrance to something sublime and magical when commanded by an "open sesame" from a person in tune with their own nature self. What follows is a work in three parts in celebration of Mother Nature's powers and her amazing gifts. Long may they continue.

Part 1, Physical Crystal, addresses crystal (the material that form's the Earth's endocrine system which circulates planetary "chi") and its appearance during the formation of the Earth after billions of years in the evolution of the Universe.

Part 2, Amazing Crystal, looks at some of the incredible stories associated with crystal in history, legend and folklore, and also highlights its many and varied present and future technological and scientific applications.

Crystal Treasures comprises a gallery of photos of favourite crystals from my own personal collection.

Part 3, Living Crystal, examines crystals in the context of Mother Earth and "the forces of living nature ," which includes a study of crop circles, the UFO phenomenon, nature's invisible gardeners (the Nature Spirits), mankind's esoteric relationship with the four elements of antiquity, the healing power of crystals and the colours associated with them, metaphysical crystal in the context of the Earth's Gaia consciousness, and a beguiling story about a mysterious post-cataclysm crystal skulls community in ancient Chile.

In those sections of the text in Part 3 that focus on UFOs, crop circles and the elemental spirits as critical aspects of Mother Earth's forces of living nature, I draw and enlarge upon material first presented in two former books for Adventures Unlimited Press: *The Landing Lights of Magonia* and *The Gods in the Fields*.

We begin with a brief study of the formation of the Universe, of our Solar System, planet and moon, and of the Earth's rocks, minerals and crystals.

It is difficult for many to realise that they [humans] are actual universes; that their physical bodies are a visible nature through the structure of which countless waves of evolving life are unfolding their latent potentialities. Yet through man's physical body not only are a mineral, a plant, and an animal kingdom evolving, but also unknown classifications and divisions of invisible spiritual life. Just as cells are infinitesimal units in the structure of man, so man is an infinitesimal unit in the structure of the universe.

—Manly P. Hall, *The Secret Teachings of All Ages*

PART 1
PHYSICAL CRYSTAL

Aphrodite, Goddess of love, fertility and beauty

Chapter 1

Formation of the Universe
and the Earth

THE UNIVERSE

When we look at the world around us it is very difficult to imagine a time when it did not exist: a time when there were no chemical elements from which rocks, minerals and crystals are made. In fact, our planet is a very late addition in the evolution of the physical Universe. Astronomers tell us that 13.8 billion years ago, the entire Universe comprised one tiny blob of primordial energy that existed in a highly compressed state and at an extremely high temperature. In an instant, this period of stasis was brought to an end by the "Big Bang." The ensuing lightning expansion of this point of energy resulted in a rapid drop in its density and temperature and, in a few seconds, formed a number of elementary particles such as electrons, neutrons, photons and protons.

In the first few billionths of a second after the Big Bang, the Universe consisted of a "soup" of enormously varied particles and radiation. In the next seconds quarks began binding to form protons and neutrons. One "down" and two "up" quarks made a proton, while one "up" and two "down" quarks made a neutron. Between 1 and 180 seconds after the event, collisions between protons and neutrons formed the nuclei of light elements, chiefly helium, though they did not yet capture electrons. The expanding energy was still far too hot to form atoms.

Gradually, as denser matter generated ever-stronger gravitational pull, gas was drawn into these regions, which, in turn, created vast, coalescing clouds or nebulae of hydrogen. In these clouds even denser areas formed, each drawing more gas into itself. Eventually, 300,000 years after the Big Bang, in the centre of these dense gaseous regions, temperatures and pressures increased to such a point that hydrogen atoms began to fuse together to form helium, and protons captured one electron each to form hydrogen atoms. This process of nuclear fusion generated light and yet more heat, thereby creating the first stars to light the newly formed universe, each cloud of newborn stars creating a galaxy.

Recent investigations give a twist to this traditional scientific account of the genesis of the Universe. Approximately 300,000 years after the blazingly bright Big Bang, the expanding universe cooled sufficiently for its remaining radiation to shift to longer, invisible wavelengths and travel freely into space. The Universe's brilliant beginning ended, giving way to an era of blackness and the onset of the Cosmic Dark Ages. In fact, even in the darkness the tiny fluctuations in the density of matter were growing bigger. Supercomputer simulations undertaken at Massachusetts Institute of Technology and University of California, San Diego, of the early universe assume the existence of cold dark matter (CDM). According to the CDM scenario, small objects formed first and then coalesced into galaxy-size bodies.

The simulation begins 13 million years after the Big Bang, when CDM started to clump and form invisible halos in regions that contained slightly higher-than-average concentrations of matter. After about 100 million years, CDM halos weighing about 100,000 times as much as the sun had begun to form, a watershed in the Universe's formation because CDM halos this massive are the first to pull in and confine small amounts of hydrogen and helium gas—the stuff of which the first stars were made.

That was no mean feat because gravity had firstly to overcome the outward pressure exerted by the gases, which became ever more compressed and hot as they were jammed into a smaller volume. To make stars, compressed gas must grow even denser. To do so, it must cool down to a few degrees above absolute zero. But in order to cool, the gas must first become relatively hot. Because these first halos of matter were not very massive, they compressed the trapped gas only slightly and so the material therefore never reached a temperature much greater than 1,000 kelvins. At that temperature, the gas has enough energy to excite molecular hydrogen but not atomic hydrogen. The excited molecules cool the gases by converting their heat into radiation, which escapes into space. Nevertheless, molecular hydrogen is a much poorer coolant than atomic hydrogen.

The simulations show that the clouds of gas within each of the CDM halos weigh as much as 1,000 times the sun: an early, lightweight version of the giant molecular clouds that would later give birth to thousands of stars in the Milky Way and countless other galaxies. At the very core of each cloud, a chunk of material about as massive as the sun rapidly condensed. But before this small, relatively dense bit of material had a chance to turn into a relatively lightweight star, gas as massive as one hundred suns piled on top of it. It, too, was cooled by molecular hydrogen. The entire process, from first halo to first star, happened so rapidly—in no more than about 10,000 years—that there was no time for the material to fragment. Instead, a single massive star was born. As similar stars flashed into existence across the universe a few hundred million years after the Big Bang, the Cosmic Dark Ages ended.

New stars are created from material dispersed throughout space resulting from the explosion of other stars. Stars may be visualised as factories that make elements from hydrogen. In the cores of stars , temperatures and pressures are so high that nuclei can collide with such force that they fuse together to become heavier elements, which, in turn, can fuse with more hydrogen to forge heavier nuclei. In this way, oxygen, carbon and most of the other elements up to the mass of iron are formed.

It is not until towards the end of the lives of larger stars that elements heavier than iron can be made by a process of adding neutrons to nuclei and radioactive decay. At the end of its life a star will explode, creating a supernova. Minerals are found in meteorites that formed in the otflows of Red Giant stars (a luminous giant star of low or intermediate mass in a late phase of stellar evolution), others around supernovae.

Our own Sun is a third-generation star. A first-generation star is one made from primordial Big Bang material. A second-generation star is made solely from the detritus of dying first -generation stars , while a third-generation star contains atoms, nuclei and elements that have been cycled through at least two other stages of star -death. Although, like all stars, second-generation stars are composed main ly of hydrogen, they incorporate elements formed in the first generation of stars and can use these as building blocks for new isotopes and elements. We can identify these second -generation elements and isotopes in the Sun and in the planets that circle it, including Earth. Our Solar System—the Sun, planets, moons, asteroids, comets and assorted debris —located towards the edge of the Milky Way galaxy, was formed out of a rotating cloud of interstellar gas and dust, known as the Solar Nebula, which was the remnant of two earlier generations of stars. Approximately 4.6 billion years ago, the nebula collapsed, possibly due to shockwaves created by a nearby exploding supernova. This collapse caused the rate of rotation of the nebula to increase and the collapsing material to flatten into what is termed the protoplanetary disc. Matter continued to be drawn from this disc towards its centre. Meanwhile, energy from the collapse caused the temperature in the centre to rise and its density to increase. Event ually, both temperature and density became high enough for hydrogen nuclei to begin fusing to form helium and hence to give off energy in the form of heat and light. Thus was born our own star, the Sun.

Not all of the material in the Solar Nebula was dragged by gravity into the formation of our Sun. Some gas and dust remained in the protoplanetary disc. Gradually, dust particles stuck together or *accreted* to form larger and larger agglomerations. Some of these dust balls melted to form tiny rocks smaller than marbles, known as "chondrules."

In turn, these tiny rocks accreted, sticking together in ever-larger bodies, "planetesimals," until gravitational forces were able to take over and keep them from breaking apart. Once the planetesimals had grown to around a kilometre in size, some started to attract similar sized bodies, at which point the process of accretion grew in efficiency.

At this stage many planetesimals continued to coalesce to form bodies the size of Mercury or the Earth. The entire process from collapse of the nebula through to formation of our Sun's planets may have taken about 10 million years. Those planetesimals that did not achieve ever-larger coalescence became frozen in size between one kilometre and tens of kilometres, many preserved as asteroids between Mars and Jupiter.

The protoplanetary disc became hotter nearer the Sun than further out. In the hotter parts, ices evaporated and gas was driven out towards the outer parts of the Solar System, an action that was assisted by the solar wind, a stream of energetic particles from the Sun. Consequently, planets in the inner Solar System, known as the terrestrial planets, are relatively small and rocky. In the cold outer regions, the rocky bodies accreted ice, which, because of the extreme cold and their greater mass, could also hold on to other gases such as ammonia, methane, hydrogen and helium. The result was the formation of massive gassy planets.

Pluto, regarded by some astronomers as non-planetary and simply one of many icy bodies beyond Neptune, formed much further out, along with many other similar frozen bodies that remained small because they were sparsely distributed and therefore could not accrete efficiently.

(Despite the evidence of starry skies, the Universe is a rather empty void. From its mapping of Cosmic Microwave Background radiation at the extreme edges of Creation, the Atacama Cosmology Telescope in Chile estimates: 5% normal matter, atoms; 27% dark matter, unseen directly and defying description; 68% dark energy, the mysterious component accelerating cosmic expansion. A thought—might these unseen but mighty forces possess cosmic intelligence, a "Universal Mind," a Godforce? David Bohm, late visionary and influential quantum physicist, believed it. In describing his notion of the Implicate Order and the "Plenum," a "holomovement" consciousness at the depths of existence, scientist Bohm dubbed this all-pervasive Cosmic Energy, "The Player.")

THE EARTH

Formation

The Earth's rocks and minerals are the result of a series of processes that began with our planet's formation from the Solar Nebula over 4.5 billion years ago, and which are estimated will continue for at least as long in the future.

Just as with the other planets in our Solar System, the Earth formed through a process of accretion. Matter from the Solar Nebula was drawn together to form asteroid-size bodies. These objects then accreted to form ever larger bodies. As this process repeated over time, the Earth's mass increased, so did its gravity which attracted ever larger planetisimals and other meteorite debris.

At first, the accreting planet consolidated loosely, not forming a coherent whole. This period was relatively shortlived because the successive impacts of collisions with meteorites and planetisimals brought about the development of a differentiated structure.

The shock of the impacts generated heat, causing rocks to melt. The molten Earth separated into liquid iron and silicate melt . The less dense silicate material floated on top of the higher density material core that consisted of iron and other heavy elements.   Subsequently, the silicate portion and other lighter elements also started to separate out into the higher density mantle and the lower density crust on the top. Accretion is not a thing from Earth's far distant past. The process continues as the planet sweeps up tonnes of space debris every year.

The first accurate estimate of the age of the Earth was carried out by physicist Claire Patterson, who in 1956 arrived at an age of 4.55 billion years after comparing radioisotope measurements from meteorites and Earth minerals. More recently, the Earth's age has been revised slightly to 4.6 billion years.

The Moon

According to current theory, the Moon was formed as the result of a massive collision early in the Earth's history It is thought that also around 4.5 billion years ago, a very large planetisimal, probably an object about the size of Mars, hit the Earth, penetrating far below   the surface and ejecting huge amounts of debris.

This material, together with debris from the planetisimal itself, went into orbit around the Earth was held in place by its gravity and gradually cooled and coalesced. This process of accretion then formed into the Earth's natural satellite . Studies of trace elements in lunar rocks show results similar to those obtained from the Earth's mantle. This strongly implies that at the time of the collision the Earth must have already differentiated into a denser core and a lighter mantle, only the latter splashing out into orbit.

Because lunar rocks have been dated to around the time of the Earth's formation, scientists have concluded that planet formation must be a relatively rapid process, lasting less than a hundred million years. In the case of the Earth, this period, a blink of an eye in astronomical terms, saw our planet form, its mantle develop, the awesome collision take place, and the ejected material accrete to form the Moon.

The Core

The Earth has three distinct layers: i) a core consisting of a solid inner core and a liquid outer core, which together make up more than half of the planet's diameter; ii) the mantle comprising a layer of dense minerals that makes up most of the rest of the diameter; and iii) a thin crust composed of rocks and minerals that are chemically distinct from those that make up the core and mantle. Like the Moon, the Earth's core was also formed early in the planet's development as heavier elements sank towards the centre. Various ingenious ways are used to study its composition, including analysis of the Earth's magnetic field, earthquake waves as they pass through the Earth, rock density and meteorites.

The solid inner core, beginning 6,370km below the Earth's surface, is probably composed chiefly of iron combined with a small percentage of nickel and a lighter element, thought to be sulphur. The liquid nickel-iron outer core is 5,150km below the surface. Refinements of the core's composition are still taking place as a result of chemical interactions with the lower mantle. The inner core's temperatures are estimated to be approximate to those on the surface of the Sun. Precisely which minerals might form at such temperatures and pressures is not known.

Mantle and Crust Minerals

The extreme heat in the Earth's forming interior encouraged chemical reactions at the iron-rich core and the surrounding material. Elements that readily combine with iron formed denser minerals which accumulated in a thick shell around the core, creating the lower mantle. The lower mantle reaches 2,900km below the surface.

Lighter minerals were formed from elements with a greater affinity for oxygen than for iron. These combined as oxide compounds, mostly silicates. Being lighter, these silicon rich compounds rose upwards to form the upper mantle and the crust, in effect floating on the denser inner mantle. The upper mantle, solid and predominantly composed of peridotite, reaches 660km below the surface. The earth's land surface, a solid continental crust composed of igneous, metamorphic and sedimentary rocks, extends down to 70km, while the solid oceanic crust, of which the sea floor is made and composed mostly of basalt, reaches down to just 7km below the surface.

The Atmosphere and the Oceans

The formation of the atmosphere and the oceans was directly connected to the formation of the Earth's crust. During the intense period of accretion while the Earth melted and re -crystallised, water vapour and other gases were released toadd to the gasesthat were accumulating from the Solar Nebula, resulting in the formation of the Earth's first atmosphere.

This process started 4 billion years ago when the material forming Earth coalesced and melted; it organized itself into layers with dense materials at the core and less dense compounds closer to the surface.

Subsequently, the Earth and Moon were subjected to sustained meteorite bombardment, a process that is believed to have stripped away the first atmosphere. Thereafter, volcanic activity released nitrogen, carbon dioxide and water vapour, which, in turn, were broken down by the sun's ultraviolet light into hydrogen, oxygen and ozone.

By 3.8 billion years ago, the water vapour had collected to form oceans where salts dissolved, increasing salinity. As steam condensed into water, the atmospheric pressure of Earth became lower, and the water started dissolving gases such as ammonia, removing them from the atmosphere and creating ammonium compounds, amines, and other nitrogen-containing substances suitable for the origin of life.

The condensation of water with gases, such as sulphur dioxide, produced acid rain that created new minerals on Earth's surface. Microfossils of sulphur-metabolizing cells have been found in rocks 3.4-billion-years-old. The first aquatic photosynthetic orga nisms originated around 3.5 billion years ago.

The Earth's Crust

A conspicuous feature of the Earth's surface is its division between ocean basins and continents. Both the oceanic and continental crust lie on top of the mantle but the two types of crust a re significantly different. The continental crust, lighter and thicker than the denser and thinner oceanic crust, floats higher in the mantle. About two-thirds of the Earth's surface is oceanic crust but the continental crust has a much wider variety of rocks.

The oceanic crust is much younger than its continental counterpart; even the oldest parts of the ocean floor are only 200-million-years-old. This is because it is continually being recycled. The oceanic crust forms from mantle material rising within rifts and ocean ridges and spreading to either side of the ridge. This material returns to the mantle at the same rate in areas called subduction zones.

In the 1960s, Canadian geophysicist John Wilson (1908-93) became an advocate of the theory that the sea floor is spreading from the ocean ridges. He became a leading exponent of the theory when he advanced the notion that volcanic mid-ocean island chains, such as Hawaii, form as a result of the sea floor moving slowly over the top of a "hotspot," a fixed point where magma (molten rock) wells up inside the mantle.

The oceanic crust is composed of several layers, the topmost being one of sediments, which are primarily very fine muds overlying a layer of basalt. The lower layers are primarily gabbro, with increasing olivine content as the depth increases. Gabbro is coarse-grained intrusive igneous rock formed from the slow cooling of magnesium-rich and iron-rich magma into a holocrystalline mass deep beneath the Earth's surface.

Continental Crust

The continental crust covers approximately one third of the Earth's surface, constituting the planet's main landmasses and the beds of the shallow seas that surround them. The crust varies in thickness from 25km to 70km, its geatest thickness being under the mountain ranges.

At the heart of each continent is a stable mass of crystalline rocks dating from the Precambrian period (4,560 million to 545 million years ago), covering thousands of of square kilometres known as the continental shield. Other rocks of the continental crust have more recently been subjected to the processes of erosion, metamorphism and sedimentation. It is this process of transformation over billions of years that accounts for Earth's immense variety of rocks.

The Earth's crust acts as if it were floating on the underlying dense, flexible rock of the mantle, a concept known as "isostasy." The crust can be visualised as resembling an iceberg floating on water, similarly, extending downwards into the medium on which it floats.

Because the crust is not uniformly dense or thick, different parts protrude into the mantle to different depths. It extends deeper under mountain ranges, such as the Himalayas, because it requires a deeper "root" to buoy up the mountains' additional weight compared with that needed in low-lying areas. About two-thirds of the thickness of the continental crust forms the root that supports the rest.

Plate Tectonics, Boundaries and Faults

"Tectonics" refers to the ongoing building and movements of the Earth's crust. According to the principles of plate tectonics, the solid brittle lithosphere, which constitutes the hard and rigid outer vertical layer of the Earth rests on and is carried along by the underlying layer of hot and flowing mantle rock, the asthenosphere, which is the weaker, hotter, and deeper part of the upper mantle.

The lithosphere is made up of both continents and ocean basins. It is divided into relatively rigid sections known as "plates." The movements of these plates relative to one another   result in the formation and the modification of the Earth's principal surface features.   The lithosphere remains rigid for very long periods of geologic time in which it deforms elastically and through brittle failure.

The asthenosphere, which deforms viscously and accommodates strain through plastic deformation, is almost solid but a slight amount of melting contributes to its mechanical weakness. More extensive decompression melting of the asthenosphere takes place where it wells upwards, and this is the most important source of magma on Earth.

There are about a dozen large tectonic plates   , some consisting of both continental and oceanic crust, others made up exclusively of oceanic crust. The forces that drive the lithospheric plates across the Earth's surface are not wholly understood but heat rising from the planet interior is thought to be the principal factor involved.

As the plates move relative to each other, diverging, converging or moving past, major geological interactions occur along their boundaries. This is where many of the principal processes that shape the Earth's surface take place such as earthquakes, volcanic activity and the deformation of the Earth's crust that builds mountain ranges.

Where plates are moving away from each other along a divergent boundary—typically a mid-ocean ridge—magma wells up from below as the release of pressure produces partial melting of the underlying mantle. Chiefly basalt in composition, the magma solidifies to create new, primarily oceanic crust. The accompanying plate movements generate a great deal of minor earthquake activity as the crust repeatedly undergoes cycles of fracturing and healing.

Plates moving towards each other create a convergent boundary. Where oceanic crust meets oceanic crust, one of the plates descends beneath the other in a process called subduction. The subducted crust is then recycled into the mantle, compensating for the new crust being created continually at divergent plate boundaries. Subduction also takes place where the oceanic crust of one plate meets the continental plate of

19

another. The greater buoyancy of the continental crust prevents it from being subducted, so it is the plate carrying the oceanic crust that dives underneath. The subducted oceanic crust triggers melting at depth and molten rock rises up through the crust, erupting to form explosive volcanoes. The volcanoes along the upper Pacific coast of the USA such as Mount Saint Helens, are formed in this manner. If both plates meet along a continental edge, then neither can be subducted. The consequent collision causes the crust to crumple, pushing mountain ranges upwards.

In addition to divergent and convergent boundaries, there is a third type, a transform boundary, where two plates move past each other without creating or destroying crust material. Sizeable earthquakes are caused by the continuous build-up and release of tensions where the plates meet. California's San Andreas Fault and the Norther Anatolian fault system in Turkey are prime examples of transform boundaries.

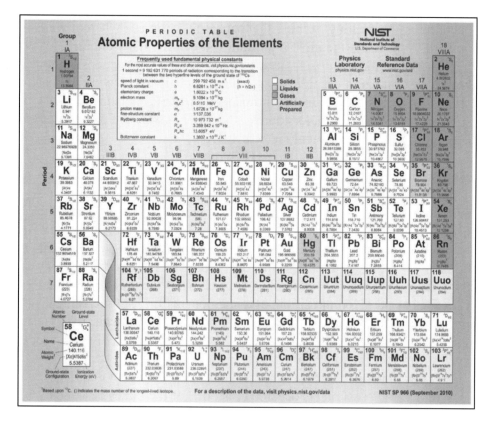

The Periodic Table

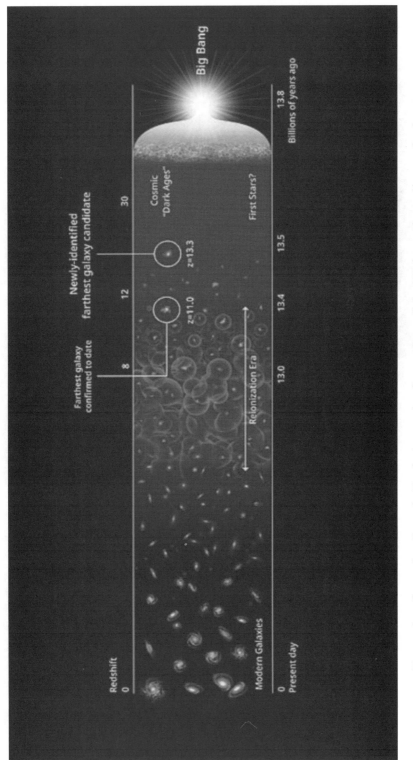

Emerging from the Cosmic Dark Ages, the formation of the Universe's earliest galaxiess

Orion Nebula

Galaxy discovered by Swiss astronomer, Fritz Zwicky in the 1940s

Chapter 2

Rocks

"Some run uphill and down dale, knappin' the chucky stones to pieces like sa' many roadmakers run daft. They say it is to see how the warld was made!"

—Sir Walter Scott on "daft" rock hunters

On any beach or stream where water has exposed sand and grave l, one will see stones lying there. They will probably look dull and grey at first, but if one looks closer one will gradually see subtle differences in colour. One might be pale cream, another mottled brown, yet another slightly stripy.

To an experienced rock hunter their id entification will be revealed. The pale cream stone could be limestone, its crystals of calcite precipitated out of tropical oceans hundreds of millions of years ago , revealing themselves under a microscope. One might be lucky enough to see embedded in these stones fossils of the creatures that swam in those ancient seas. The mottled brown stone could be granite, a stone that reveals under the microscope three different minerals: tiny black flecks of mica, glassy quartz grains and yellow feldspar, all forged in the extreme heat of the Earth's interior millions of years ago.

The stripy stone could be schist, a rock formed when other rocks came under such intense pressure from earth movements that the crystals in them broke down and were made anew in differe nt forms, squeezed into stripes by the pressure. A magnifying glass might show tiny red spots embedded in the rock. An experienced rock hunter might identify these spots as garnets, even rubies.

Rocks have long played a part in human history. In millennia past, our ancestors were chipping the edges of hand -sized pebbles to make tools and weapons. Even then, finding the right stones required a certain practical knowledge of geology. Few people today would know where to find flint, yet our Stone Age brethren knew and even dug mines to extract them from the depths.

Copper and gold were first used about 10,000 years ago but it required skill and knowledge to know where to find these precious commodities. Both minerals are too soft to make tools from but the discovery that an addition of tin to copper makes a tough alloy, initiated about 5,000 years ago the first great age of metal use, the Bronze Age; the age also when the first great civilisations, such as that of Ancient Egypt, appeared.

Tin only occurs in the ore cassiterite, which has to be melted to extract the tin. Some cassiterite was found in river gravels but these deposits only occur where there is granite nearby, so to find more cassiterite deep mines had to be dug to get to the ore-bearing veins, such as those in Cornwall and the Austrian Tyrol.

It was not until the 18th century that geology emerged as a science in its own right, pioneered by the great Scottish geologist James Hutton (1726-97). In his day, people still believed in the Biblical record that the age of the Earth was just a few thousand years old. Hutton realized that it is far, far older, and that the slow processes one sees acting on the landscape today are quite enough to shape it without invoking great catastrophes. Hutton demonstrated that landscapes are worn away by rivers and that sediment washed into the sea forms new sedimentary rocks. He also saw how the Earth's heat could transform rocks, lifting and twisting them to create new mountains. He understood how the world is shaped by countless cycles of erosion, sedimentation and uplift; each new beginning often clearly marked by breaks in the rock sequence called unconformities: breaks in time in an otherwise continuous rock record.

Inspired by Hutton's work and ideas, more and more geologists arived on the scene. Geology became a popular pastime for Victorian gentlemen, who ventured out in stout boots with just a hammer and a sturdy bag for specimens. These included Charles Darwin, who brought his knowledge of geological history to bear in formulating his theory of evolution.

Rock Formation

Compared to the lifespan of a human to eonian geological time, rocks may appear permanent and unchanging. But rocks and old minerals are constantly breaking down and new ones being formed. What we see around us today are rocks and minerals in the process of the "rock cycle."

Rocks are either igneous, sedimentary or metamorphic. Igneous rock is formed as magma rises and cools. It is called extrusive if is disgorged by volcanoes and intrusive if instead it solidifies below ground. Weathering and erosion lead to the formation of sedimentary rocks, which can turn into metamorphic rock if the temperature and/or pressure conditions change.

Although the processes of the rock cycle are acting all at once, and can occur in more than one order, the cycle can be regarded as starting with magma rising from the crust or upper man tle. Magma solidifies to form either intrusive or extrusive igneous rocks.

If intrusive rock solidifies deep in the crust, it requires uplift and erosion to bring it to the surface before the next stage of the cycle can began. If the intrusion is near th e surface, the erosion of overlying rock may expose it without uplift.

Extrusive volcanic rocks begin to undergo weathering and erosion immediately, whether extruded on land or in water. The impressive Giant's Causeway in Northern Ireland is an example of extrusive rock. A flow of lava cooled down slowly, developing cracks (known as joints) that created the basalt columns.

Uplift is an upward vertical movement of the earth's lithosphere. The action can be slow and gentle, involving a broad up-warping over a long period of time, or sudden and dramatic as when a fault snaps. When uplift takes place buried igneous, sedimentary and metamorphic rocks are brought to the surface and exposed to weathering and erosion. Uplift can be related to the pressures of plate tectonics or it can occur as a response to the removal of a large weight, as through erosion or the retreat of glaciers.

Sediments created by weathering and erosion are deposited in layers, which gradually become compacted to form sedimentary rocks. Because the Earth's crust moves downwards as well as upwards, great thicknesses of these sedimentary rocks can in some cases become buried deep inside the Earth, accumulating in the lower regions of the crust. Faulting and folding may eventually return these rocks from their deep locations and transport them back to the Earth's surface.

Weathering occurs when rocks are exposed to the atmosphere, water or living organisms at the Earth's surface. In the process, rocks may break apart without significant change to their chemical structure, for example when rock is shattered by freezing water. This is known as physical weathering.

Chemical weathering occurs when some of the minerals within the rock break down. They may be dissolved outright or combine with water over millennia to become new, easily eroded minerals.

Biological weathering occurs when living organisms directly attack the rock or the growth of plants in joints and seams and break them apart. Erosion involves the movement of rock debris away from the site where weathering has taken place. Without it, the debris would accumulate where it formed.

Wind, water, glaciers and gravity are the primary agents of erosion, between them constantly reshaping the landscape. Overall, the net effect of erosion is to lower the earth's elevations.

Once rock has been eroded or dissolved, the products of these actions are usually transported and deposited elsewhere to become new rock (that is, to be "lithified"). An exception is breccia, whch is composed of shattered rock fragments that accumulate and lithify near their place of origin. Particles transported by the wind form dunes on land or fall into water.

Waterborne rock fragments are deposited in lakes, oceans or old river channels. Rock material dissolved in the water is also deposited, filtering through other sediments to become cementing material for lithification. Glaciers carry rock debris in or on their ice. Also, volcanoes spew out ash and dust that may be deposited far away.

Deeply buried sedimentary or igneous rocks may be subjected to tectonic forces that change their structure. Sometimes they are baked at high temperatures. Alternatively, they may be squeezed or folded by immense pressures, or maybe subjected to both high temperature and extreme pressure. In response, rocks begin to reform, without melting, creating metamorphic rocks and new minerals that are stable under the new conditions. If the heat and pressure increase sufficiently, melting takes place amd the whole rock cycle starts again, although not every rock particle is destined to undergo the full cycle.

Types of Rock

A rock is a naturally occurring and coherent aggregate of one or more minerals, although there a few rocks composed of other substances such as the decayed vegetation of which coal is formed. The three classes of rocks—igneous, sedimentary and metamorphic—are further subdivided into groups and types, principally based on differences in their mineral composition and texture.

Igneous rocks vary in texture, depending on how quickly the magma cooled. Rapid cooling creates tiny crystals and freezes the liquid to glass, while slower cooling forms coarse-grained rocks. The oceanic crust is primarily composed of igneous rocks, including volcanic basalts and underlying gabbros. Igneous rocks are defined as intrusive or extrusive, depending on whether or not the molten magma from which they were formed emerged at the earth's surface before crystallising. If the magma flows solidly underground, it will create intrusive rocks such as granite. Intrusive rocks are termed plutonic if formed deep inside the crust and hypabyssal if formed at shallow depths. Granite, diorite, peridotite, syenite and gabbro are all plutonic igneous rocks.

Plutonic intrusive rocks are characterised by their large crystals, which occur as batholiths, plutons and laccoliths. Batholiths are a mass of intrusive igneous rock larger than 100 square kilometres. They are almost always made mostly of felsic or interme diate rock types, such as granite, quartz, monzonite or diorite . A striking example of batholithic structures are the peaks of the Sierra Nevada in California.

The term pluton is poorly defined and can variously be described as an intrusion emplaced at g reat depth , as a general term for intrusions whose size or character are not well determined , or for a crystallized magma chamber.

A laccolith is a body of intrusive rock with a dome -shaped upper surface and a level base, fed by a conduit from below. It forms when magma rising through the Earth's crust begins to spread out horizontally, prying apart the host rock strata. Over time, erosion can expose the solidified laccolith, which is typically more resistant to weathering than the host rock. The exposed laccolith then forms a hill or mountain. Examples are the Henry Mountains of Utah , and the Devil's Marbles, a dome of red granite in Australia's Northern Territory.

Hypabyssal intrusive rocks are found at shallow depths and are characterised by fine crystallisation. They are found in dykes, sills, volcanic plugs and in other relatively small formations. A dyke is a sheet like body that cuts vertically or at a steep angle to the surrounding rocks. Dykes range from less than a centimetre to many metres in thickness and can be many hundreds of kilometres in length. A sill is a tabular sheet intrusion that has intruded between older layers of sedimentary rock, beds of volcanic lava or tuff Volcanic plugs are formed from magma that solidified inside volcanic ven ts. The Devil's Tower in Wyoming, instantly familiar to fans of Steven Spielberg's *Close Encounters of the Third Kind*, is a plug of rock that cooled within a volcano and was subsequently exposed by erosion.

If the molten magma flows onto the surface of the land or ocean bed it will form extrusive rocks (also known as volcanic rocks). The principal extrusive rock types include basalt (the commonest igneous rock, forming the floor of most oceans), rhyolite, trachyte, andesite and obsidian (Dr. Dee's magical obsidian scrying mirror will feature in later pages). All of these extrusive types generally form from lava, molten magma that has flowed onto the surface, either on land or underwater.

A distinctive example of extrusive rock formed from lava are those on the Keanae Peninsula of Hawaii. Other extrusive rocks such as tuff and pumice are formed as a result of explosive volcanic eruptions. These pyroclastic rocks are porous because of the frothing expansion of volcanic gases when they formed.

Examples of igneous rocks are: i) Granite, the most common intrusive rock in the earth's continental crust. Coarse to medium grained, granite's three main minerals are feldspar, quartz and mica; ii) Pegmatite, the name given to very coarse-grained igneous rocks. Most have the same major constituents—quartz and feldspar. The crystals in pegmatite can be huge, metres long, but the average size is 8-10cm. They are a major source of gemstones, including tourmaline, aquamarine, emerald, rock crystal, smoky quartz, rose quartz, topaz, moonstone and garnet. Pegmatites are also the source of important minerals, including those that contain beryllium, tungsten, lithium, tin, molybdenum, tantalum and other rare elements; iii) Granodiorite, a medium to coarse grained rock, its hornblende and biotite constituents give it a speckled appearance. Hard and durable, and one of the stones sold as "black granite," granodiorite is quarried, cut and crushed for use as road ballast and kerbstones. It is also sawn and polished to create flooring, worktops and facing for buildings; iv) Dolerite (or microgabbro), a fine to medium grained calcium-rich rock, is equivalent to basalt and gabbro in composition and intermediate between them in grain size. Extremely hard and tough, it occurs in dykes and sills intruded into fissures in other rocks. The dolerite "bluestones" of the inner circle of Stonehenge were transported 385km from the Carn Meini Quarry in the Preseli hills of Wales to Wiltshire; v) Kimberlite, a form of peridotite, is a major source of diamonds. It is mica rich. Its other abundant minerals include chromium- and pyrope-rich garnet and chrome-bearing diopside. Lesser amounts of serpentine, pyroxene, calcite, rutile, perovskite, magnetite and ilmenite can also be present. Kimberlite is found in pipes, intrusive igneous bodies roughly circular in cross section with vertical sides, and generally less than 1km in diameter. It appears that the kimberlite was injected into zones of weakness in the crust as a relatively cool "mush" of crystals, rather than as a liquid magma that crystallized within the pipes themselves.

Sedimentary rocks are generally made of deposits laid down on the Earth's surface by water, wind or ice. They make up between 80%-90% of the rock exposed at the Earth's surface, yet they amount to no more than about 8% by volume of the entire crust, which is predominantly composed of igneous and metamorphic rock. Sedimentary rock is formed at or near t he Eart h's surface by either accumulation of grains or   by precipitation of dissolved material.

Sedimentary deposits are almost always deposited in layers or strata. The stratification survives compaction and   cementation and   is a distinguishing feature of sedimentary rocks. They are also characterised by the presence of fossils, which are rarely found in other rock types. The distinctive sandstone in Utah's Zion National Park displays typical sedimentary layering.

The formation of sedimentary rock begins with the   weathering of other rocks that in some   ways have been cemented together. Physical weathering is the breakdown of rock into smaller fragments. Such rocks are described as clastic.   Clastic rocks range in size from boulders to microscopic particles. Clastic sedimentary rocks can be grouped according to the size of the clasts from which they were formed. Larger clasts such as pebbles, cobbles and boulder size gravels form breccia and conglomerate, the most coarse -grained sedimentary rocks consisting of grains the size of pebbles, or even larger, which typically contain a matrix of finer-grained sediments such as sand, silt, or clay; sand becomes sandstone; and finer silt and clay particles form siltstone, claystone, mudstone and shale.

The mineral composition of clastic rock can be subject to considerable changes over time. Chemical reactions may take place between clasts of different minerals, between clasts and cementing agents, or between clasts, cement and ground water. Minerals in the rock may also be disolved and redistributed. At the Grand Canyon in Arizona water erosion by th e Colorado River has cut through 1.6km of accumulated sedimentary rock.

Additionally, there is the process of weathering by chemical origin, in which the dissolved rock material is transported in solution and precipitated in a new location. In some cases, the dissolved chemical constituents are directly precipitated as solid r   ock. Examples include banded iron formations, some limestones and bedded evaporite deposits rocks and mineral deposits of soluble salts such as halite, gypsum and anhydrite, resulting from the evaporation of water.

In the formation of other sedimentary rocks, the solid material precipitates into particles, which are then deposited and lithified. Limestones and cherts are mostly formed in this manner. There are also sedimentary rocks tof biochemical origin , composed mainly of calcium carbonate. Lastly, there are organic deposits such as coal, derived from the breakdown of the organic tissue of dead plants and animals.

The process of lithification often requires a cementing agent to bind grains together, especially in the case of sandstone and conglomerates, The cementing agent is generally precipitated from solutions filtering through the sediment, although in some cases it is created at least partly by the breakdown of some of the rock particles of the sediment itself. The most common cementing material is silica, usually in the form of quartz, but other carbonates also form cements, as do iron oxides, baryte, anhydrite, zeolites, and clay minerals. In some cases, clasts can also be formed by simple compaction, in which the grains are forced to combine together under exttreme pressure.

Lithification can sometimes take place almost immediately after the grains have been deposited as sediment. In other cases, hundreds or even millions of years go by before the process occurs. It therefore follows that at any one time there are large amounts of sedimentary fragments produced by weathering that have not yet been subject to lithification.

Examples of sedimentary rocks: i) White, grey, pink limestone is an abundant rock which occurs in thick, extensive, multiple layers. It generally forms in warm, shallow seas from the precipitation of calcium carbonate from sea water or the accumulation of the shells and skeletons of calcareous marine organisms. Its main constituent is calcite but can also contain lesser amounts of aragonite, dolomite, siderite, quartz and pyrite. It is an important rock commercially and has a number of different uses ranging from building stone, as a raw material in the manufacture of glass, as a flux in metallurgical processes, and in agriculture; ii) Chalk, a soft, fine-grained white to greyish variety of limestone, is composed of calcite shells of minute marine organisms. Other minerals that can be present include glauconite, apatite and clay minerals. Chalk deposits can be rich in fossils. Commercially, it is used for making lime and cement, and as a fertiliser. It is also used as a filler or pigment in a wide variety of materials, such as ceramics, putty, cosmetics, crayons, plastics, rubber, paper, paints and linoleum; iii) Tufa, the name given to two different sedimentary rocks that precipitate from water. Calcareous tufa is composed principally of calcium carbonate that precipitates from hot springs, lake water and ground water. It is often stained red by the presence of iron oxides. Siliceous tufa is a deposit of opaline or amorphous silica, which forms, at least partly, by the action of algae in the heated water of hot springs and geysers. The variety of tufa that occurs around active geysers is called geyserite, where it forms as terraces and cones around their mouths. Major locations for geyserite include Yellowstone Park in Wyoming, Steamboat Springs in Colorado, New Zealand and Iceland.

Metamorphic rocks are formed when an existing rock (a protolith) is subjected to temperatures or pressures , or both, very different to those under which it originally formed. This causes its atoms and molecules to rearrange themselves into new minerals while still in the solid state, without melting taking place. For example, quartzite is metamorphosed sandstone, while slate is metamorphosed mudstone or shale. Such changes typically occur deep within the crust and may result from the deformation caused by the actions of plate tectonics. Metamorphism can also form very clos e to the surface of the Earth under the impact of meteorites or near igneous intrusions, which create zones of high temperature around them.

Metamorphic rocks include schists (medium-grained metamorphic rock composed of mineral grains easily seen with a l ow-power hand lens), and gneisses (widely distributed metamorp hic rock that form at higher temperatures and pressures than schist and which are nearly always characterised by showing a banded texture of alternating darker and lighter coloured bands). The coastal rocks near Cape Breton in Nova Scotia are mainly schists and gneisses, but marked with pink granite that has been forced into cracks in the metamorphic rocks.

There are three different ways in which metamorphic rocks are formed: dynamic metamorphism, contact metamorphism (or thermal metamorphism), and regional metamorphism.

Dynamic metamorphism results from large -scale movements in the Earth's crust, especially along fault plates and at continen tal margins where tectonic plates are colliding. The rocks that are produced in this manner range from angular fragments to fine-grained, granulated or powdered rocks, such as mylonite. Rocks formed by dynamic metamorphism are characterised by foliation: he alignment of of mineral grains in parallel plates. They are often distorted as a result of the stresses to which they have been subjected.

Contact metamorphism takes place mainly as a result of increases in temperature with little or no accompanying pr essure changes. It is common in rocks near an igneous intrusion. Heat from the intrusion alters rocks in the surrounding area to produce an "aureole" of metamorphic rock. Since the rocks nearest to the intrusion are subjected to higher temperatures than those farther away, they exhibit different characteristics. Consequently, the temperature gradient, from high to low, creates concentric zones of distinctive metamorphic rocks. The new minerals that form due to contact metamorphism depend on the composition of the host rocks. For example, aluminium-bearing minerals such as the feldspar in arkosic sandstones are changed to micas and garnets, but when carbonate minerals, such as calcite, are present, hornblende, epidote, and diopside are formed. Garnet can grow as large, eye-shaped grains called "augens."

It is often not obvious that a rock is metamorphic. The quartzose mica schists at Kintyre, Scotland, for example, could easily be confused for sandstone.

The formation of regional metamorphic rocks is associated with the processes of mountain-building through the collision of tectonic plates, during which occur increases in temperature and pressure that may extend over many thousands of square kilometres, producing widespread metamorphism. The most important rocks produced in this manner include slates, schists and gneisses. Slates are produced in areas of relatively low temperature and pressure. High temperatures and pressures produce gneisses, while schists are formed in intermediate zones.

Metamorphism is described as low grade if it occurs at relatively low temperature and pressure, and high grade at the intense end of the scale.

The assemblages of minerals in rocks are affected differently depending on the grade of metamorphism and the relative importance of pressure and temperature in the reaction. In some low-grade reactions, the components of existing mineral assemblages are simply redistributed. For example, the iron-rich garnet almandine and magnesium-biotite may be metamorphosed into the magnesium-rich garnet pyrope and iron-biotite. The iron from the almandine garnet migrates to the biotite, and the magnesium from the biotite migrates to the garnet.

In other reactions at higher temperatures and pressures, the biotite and garnet may disappear entirely, their chemical components combining with other materials present in the rock to form an entirely new set of minerals or a liquid.

Some metamorphic reactions are more dependent on pressure than temperature. For example, undergoing the high pressures found in subduction zones, albite breaks down to form jadeite and quartz. Jadeite is much denser that albite, reflecting the closer packing of atoms under pressure.

The number of possible reactions found in metamorphism is vast because of the chemical and mineralogical complexity of the Earth's crust.

A striking example of metemorphic rock is marble. Marbles are formed under the the influence of heat and pressure and consist of a mass of interlocking calcite or dolomite grains. The impressive, folded rocks in Antarctica's Royal Society Range began as beds of limestone and have been subsequently deformed and recrystallised to form metamorphosed marble. Pure marble is nothing but calcite. Materials in the original limestone often recrystallize during metamorphism to give mineral impurities in the marble. The most common of these impurities are quartz, mica, graphite, iron oxides, and small pyrite crystals. Silicates of lime or magnesia are found in other marbles and can include tremolite, diopside, labradorite, albite, anorthite, g arnet, vesuvianite, epidote, tourmaline and sphene.

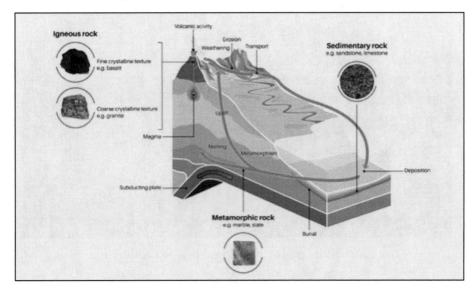

The Rock Cycle

Marble

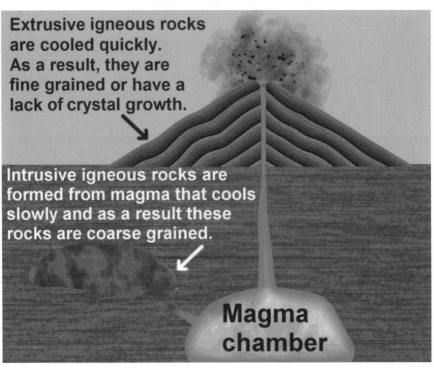

Extrusive and Intrusive Igneous Rocks

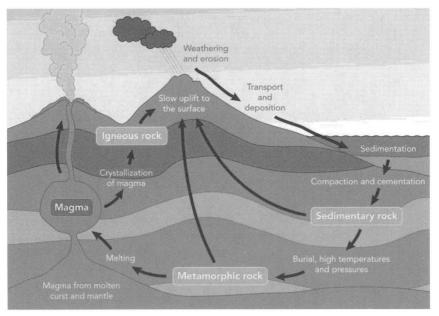

Igneous, Metamorphic and Sedimentary Rocks formation

Mushroom Sedimentary Rocks, Northen Kenya

Granite

Val Verzasca Metamorphic Rocks

Sedimentary Rocks in Makhtesh Ramon, Israel

Chapter 3

Minerals

There are 4,000 to 5,000 different minerals in the Earth's crust, yet only thirty or so are widespread. Most of the others are only present in rocks in minute traces and only easy to see when they become concentrated in certain places by geological processes. It is concentrations like these that give us the ores from which many metals are extracted.

Minerals, the stuff of which the Earth's rocks are made, are defined as naturally occurring solids with a specific chemical composition and an instinctive internal crystal structure that occurs naturally in pure form.

The geological definition of mineral normally excludes compounds that occur only in living organisms. Howeve r, some minerals are often biogenic (such as calcite) or are organic compounds in the sense of chemistry (such as mellite). Moreover, living organisms often synthesize inorganic minerals (such as the hydroxylapatite present in teeth and bones) that also occur in rocks.

The concept of mineral is distinct from rock, which is any bulk solid geologic material that is relatively homogeneous at a large enough scale. A rock may consist of one type of mineral or may be an aggregate of two or more different types o f minerals, spacially segregated into distinct phases.

Some natural solid substances without a definite crystalline structure, such as opal, obsidian and glass, are more properly called mineraloids. If a chemical compound occurs naturally with different crystal structures, each structure is considered a different mineral species. Thus, for example, quartz and stishovite are two different minerals consisting of the same compound, silicon dioxide.

Large crystals of even common minerals are very rare in nature. Big, spectacular specimens need both time and space to grow, together with a steady supply of precisely the right ingredients. Such a perfect combination is extraordinarily rare.

Mineral crystals form in four main ways . Some form as hot, molten magma cools and crystallizes; some from chemicals dissolved in watery liquids; some when existing minerals are altered chemically; and some form when existing minerals are squeezed or superheated as rocks are subjected to metamorphism.

Minerals from magma

As magma cools, groups of atoms begin to come together and form crystals. These grow as more atoms attach themselves to the initial structure, just as icicles grow as more water freezes on them. Minerals with the highest melting points form first and as they crystallize out the composition of the remaining melt changes. Chemicals that slot easily into crystal structures are removed from the melt first, and it is bigger, more unusual atoms that are left behind. It is these 'late-stage' magmas, the last portion of the melt to crystallize, that give the most varied and interesting minerals. Just what these minerals are depends on the original ingredients in the magma and the way it cools. Large crystals tend to form in magmas that have cooled slowly. The biggest and most interesting often form in what are called pegmatites, which form from the fraction of melt left over after the rest has crystallized. Pegmatites typically collect in cracks in an intrusion or ooze into joints in the country rock, forming sheets of rock called dykes. The residual fluids in the late-stage magmas are rich in exotic elements such as fluorine, boron, lithium, beryllium, niobium and tantalum. These can combine to form giant crystals of tourmaline, topaz, beryl, and other rare minerals.

Minerals from water

Water can only hold so much dissolved chemicals. When the water becomes saturated, the chemicals precipitate out as solids. Typically, this happens when water evaporates or cools down. When sodium, chlorine, borax and calcium are dissolved from rocks, they may be carried by rivers to inland seas and lakes, which then evaporate, leaving mineral deposits such as salt, gypsum and borax. Many other minerals form from the cooling of hydrothermal solutions: hot water rich in dissolved chemicals. Sometimes the water is rainwater that seeps down through the ground (meteoric water) and is then heated by proximity to either the mantle or a hot igneous intrusion. Hydrothermic solutions also come from late-stage magmas, and so are rich in unusual chemicals. Such solutions ooze up through cracks in the intrusion and cool to form thin, branching veins.

Alteration minerals

Although some minerals such as gold and diamond seem to last forever, most have a limited lifespan. As soon as minerals are formed, they begin to interact with their environment, some very slowly, others very rapidly.

During these reactions they form different minerals. Metal minerals often oxidise when. exposed to air or oxygen -rich water. When water containing dissolved oxygen seeps into the ground into rocks and veins containing metals, it creates an oxidation zone in the upper layers as the metals are altered. For example, cuprite, goethite, anglesite, chalcanthite, azurite and many other minerals form this way. Some sulphide minerals are oxidised to sulphates that dissolve in water. These sulphates may be washed down through the rock to be deposited lower down as different minerals which become valuable ores such as chalcocite.

Definition, Nomenclature and Composition
The International Mineralogical Association (IMA) is the generally recognized standard body for the definition and nomenclature of mineral species. Currently, the IMA recognizes 5,863 official mineral species , only about a hundred of which are common.

Silicon and oxygen are by far the most abundant elements in the Earth's crust, making up about three -quarters of the crust by weight. Correspondingly, silicates such as quartz, feldspar and olivine are the most common minerals inrocks, making up about 90 per cent of the rocks at the Earth's surface.

Carbonates are important in forming sedimentary rocks such as limestone. Many sulphides, including pyrite and galena, and oxides such as hematite are also relatively common, as are some of the native elements, like copper.

Most minerals are chemical compounds consisting of two or more chemical elements, although copper, sulphur, gold, silver and few others occur as single "native" elements.

Minerals are defined by their chemical formula and by the atomic arrangement of its crystallization. For example, iron sulphide has the chemical formula FeS_2 (where F is iron, and S is sulphur). It can crystallize in two different ways, either according to the cubic crystal system to form pyrite, or in the orthorhombic crystal system to form marcasite.

The chemical composition of a named mineral species may vary somewhat by the inclusion of small amounts of impurities. Specific varieties of a species someti mes have conventional or official names of their own. For example, amethyst is a purple variety of the mineral species quartz.

A mineral compound is based on an electrical balance between a positively charged part, often a metal, and a negatively charged p art. These charged particles are known as ions. In many minerals the negative electrical charge is carried by a "radical," which is a combination of atoms, rather than by a single atom. For example, the sulphur in pyrite is present as the disulphide (S2) group with two sulphur atoms, which has a negative charge the same as the positive charge of an iron (Fe) ion. The sulphur radical balances the iron ion and the formula for pyrite is FeS2.

The element or elements that carry the negative electrical charge determine which chemical group a mineral is assigned to. For example, minerals formed with two sulphur atoms are known as sulphides, while those with oxygen are oxides, those made with carbon and oxygen are called carbonates, and those formed with silicon and oxygen are silicates.

Classification

Minerals are classified by key chemical constituents; the two dominant systems are the Dana classification and the Strunz classification. Silicate minerals comprise approximately 90% of the Earth's crust. Other important mineral groups include the native elements, sulfides, oxides, halides, carbonates, sulfates and phosphates.

Besides the essential chemical composition and crystal structure, the description of a mineral species usually includes its common physical properties such as habit, hardness, lustre, diaphaneity, colour, streak, tenacity, cleavage, fracture, parting, specific gravity, magnetism, fluorescence and radioactivity, as well as its taste or smell and its reaction to acid. The IMA has established certain requirements for a substance to be considered a distinct mineral:

i) It must be a naturally occurring substance formed by natural geological processes, on Earth or on other extraterrestrial bodies. This excludes compounds directly and exclusively generated by human activities (anthropogenic), such as laboratory-synthesized emeralds, rubies and diamonds, or in living beings (biogenic), such as tungsten carbide, urinary calculi, calcium oxalate crystals in plant tissues, and seashells. However, substances with such origins may qualify if geological processes were involved in their genesis (as is the case of evenkite, derived from plant material; or taranakite from bat guano; or alpersite from mine tailings). Hypothetical substances are also excluded, even if they are predicted to occur in inaccessible natural environments, like the Earth's core or other planets.

ii) It must be a solid substance in its natural occurrence. A major exception to this rule is native mercury, which is still classified as a mineral by the IMA, even though it crystallizes only below −39°C, because it was included before the current rules were established. Water and carbon dioxide are not considered minerals, even though they are often found as inclusions in other minerals, but water ice is considered a mineral.

iii) It must have a well -defined crystallographic structure or, more generally, an ordered atomic arrangement.

iv) It must have a fairly well-defined chemical composition.

The IMA is reluctant to accept minerals that occur naturally only in the form of nanoparticles a few hundred atoms across, but it has not defined a minimum crystal size Although called a "mineral" in economic terms, crude oil is classed as a hydrocarbon. Equally, the "minerals" related to foodstuffs are also not minerals in the geological sense, as they refer to single elements such as calcium, iron or zinc.

Minerals' Chemical Groups

Mineralogists classify minerals into groups according to their chemical composition. Within chemical groups, minerals are further classified into sub-groups, which take their name from their most characteristic mineral. The major chemical groups are:

Native Elements

Native elements are minerals formed of a single chemical element. They include metals such as gold, silver, platinum and copper, but they are also classified as part of the gold group of minerals because they have an identical arrangement of th eir atoms. Also, the native elements group includes non-metals such as sulphur and carbon.

Oxides

When oxygen alone combines with a metal or semi -metal, an oxide mineral is formed. For example, aluminium oxide is corundum, the red variety of which is called ruby.

Hydroxides

Hydroxide minerals contain a hydroxyl (hydrogen and oxygen) radical combined with a metallic element, an example being manganese in the case of brucite.

Sulphides

The sulphides are formed when a metal or semi -metal combines with sulphur. In chalcocite, for example, the metal element is copper.

Carbonates

The carbonate radical (carbon and oxygen) combines with a metal or semi-metal to form carbonate material. In smithsonite the metal is zinc.

Silicates

In this group, silicon and oxygen form a tetrahedral silica radical that combines with various metals or semi-metals. Silica also occurs on its own as quartz.

Halides

A halogen element (chlorine, bromine, fluorine or iodine) combined with a metal or semi-metal makes a halide. For example, sylvite is a compound of chlorine and potassium.

Borates and Nitrates

These minerals contain respectively, radicals of boron and oxygen. For example, colemanite is a borate in which boron and oxygen combine with calcium and water.

Arsenates, Phosphates and Vanadates

In these minerals a radical of oxygen and either arsenic, phosphorus or vanadium combines with a metal or semi-metal. For example, apatite is a phosphate.

Sulphates, Chromates, Tungstates and Molybdates

Sulphur, molybdenum and chromium or tungsten form a radical with oxygen that combines with a metal or semi-metal. For example, celestine is a sulphate.

Organic Minerals

Organic compounds with well-defined crystal structures are classified as minerals. However, amber, which originates as a resin and is amorphous, is not a mineral.

Solid Solutions

Some minerals do not have specific chemical composition but are homogenous mixtures of two mineral species. These homogenous mixtures are known as solid solutions. For example, the olivine group of silicates includes the minerals forsterite and fayalite, both formed in igneous rocks. Forsterite is magnesium silicate, while fayalite is an iron silicate. In fact, both of these minerals are rare in their pure state. Most specimens are homogenous mixtures of the two, with the relative content of magnesium and iron varying from specimen to specimen.

Primary and Secondary Minerals

A primary mineral is one that has crystallised directly through some igneous, sedimentary or metamorphic process, while a secondary mineral has been produced through the alteration of a primary mineral after its formation. For example, when copper -bearing primary minerals come into contact with carbonated water they can be turned into bright blue azurite or bright green malachite, both secondary minerals.

Identifying Minerals

Minerals contain certain physical properties, determined by crystalline structure and chemical composition, that can help with the often-tricky task of identification without involving the use of expensive equipment.

Colour

Some minerals have characteristic colours. For example, the bright blue of azurite, the green of malachite and the yellow of su lphur allow for almost immediate identification. Wher eas fluorite can be found in virtually all colours so has to be identified by taking note of its other properties.

Colour in minerals is caused by the absorption or refraction of light of particular wavelengths. This can happen because of several factors. One is the presence in the crystal structure of foreign atoms that are not an intrinsic part of the minera l's chemical makeup. As few as thr ee or four atoms per million can absorb enough of certain parts of the visible light spectrum to give colour to a mineral.

The colour produced by a n element varies accor ding to the specific mineral which it inhabits. For example, chromium is the colouring element in both red ruby and green emerald. Colour can also result from the absence of an atom or radical from a point that it would normally occupy in a crystal. These types of defects are called vacancies, and their result is called a colour centre. The violet colour of some fluorite is produced by a vacancy.

The structure of the minera l itself, without any defects or foreign constitiuents, may also cause colour. For example, opal is is composed of minute spheres of silica that diffract light, while the colour and sheen of moonstone is determined by the thin interlaying of two different feldspars. In some crystals, light vibrates in different planes within the crystal, with the result that whatever the initial cause of its colour may be, it appears as different colours when observed along different axes. This phenomenon is called pleochroism.

Lustre

A mineral's lustre is the general appearance of its surface in reflected light. There are two main types of lustre: metallic and nonmetallic. Metallic lustre is that of an untarnished metal surface such as gold, copper or steel. Minerals with metallic lustre are opaque to light, even on thin edges.

In contrast, minerals with nonmetallic lustre are generally lighter in colour and show some degree of transparency or translucency, even though this may only be on a thin edge. A number of terms are used to describe nonmetallic lustre: vitreous, having the lustre of a piece of broken glass; adamantine, having the brilliant lustre of diamond; resinous, having the lustre of a piece of resin; pearly, having the lustre of pearl or mother-of-pearl; greasy, appearing to be covered with a thin layer of oil; and earthy, having the nonlustrous appearance of raw earth.

Diagnostic Streak

A streak is the colour of the powder produced when a mineral specimen is drawn across a surface such as a piece of unglazed porcelain, the reverse side of a bathroom or kitchen tile, for example.

This means of identification is a very useful diagnostic because a mineral's streak is far more consistent than its colour, which tends to vary from specimen to specimen. It can allow one to distinguish between minerals that are otherwise easily confused. For example, the iron oxide hematite gives a red streak, while magnetite, another oxide of iron, gives a black streak. If a mineral is too hard to mark a streak plate, the colour of its powder can be determined by filing or crushing a small sample.

Cleavage

Cleavage is the ability of a mineral to break along flat, planar surfaces. It occurs at places within the mineral's crystal structure where the forces that bond atoms are weakest. Cleavage surfaces are generally smooth and reflect light evenly. Cleavage is a consistent property and thus useful for identification.

Cleavage is described by its direction relative to the position of crystal faces (employing the terms cubic, prismatic and basal) and by the ease with which it is produced. If cleavage easily produces smooth, lustrous surfaces it is called perfect. Terms for lesser degrees of ease include distinct, imperfect and difficult, while some minerals have no cleavage at all. A mineral can have cleavages in different directions, each of which may be of different quality. For example, one may be perfect, another may be imperfect.

Fracture

Some minerals will break in directions other than along cleavage planes. Such breaks are known as fractures and may also assist the task of identification. For example, hackly fractures with jagged edges, are often found in metals, while shell-like conchoidal fractures are typical of quartz. Other terms for fractures include even (rough but more or less flat), uneven (rough and completely irregular), and splintery (with partially separated fibres).

Tenacity

Tenacity is a term used for a set of physical properties, such a s malleability, ductility or brittleness that depend on the cohesive force between atoms in mineral structures. Gold, silver and copper are good examples of malleable minerals, capable of being flattened without breaking or crumbling. Acanthite is sectile, meaning able to be smoothly cut with a knife. Talc is flexible, bending easily and staying bent after the pressure on it is removed. Other terms used include ductile (capable of being drawn into a wire), brittle (showing little resistance to breakage), and elastic (capable of being pulled out of shape but returning to its original form when relieved).

Hardness

The hardness of a mineral is the relative ease or difficulty that it can be scratched. A harder mineral will scr atch a softer one but not vice versa. A mineral can be allotted a number on the Mohs Scale, which measures hardness relative to ten minerals of increasing hardness, from 1 (as soft as talc) to 10 (as hard as diamond). Hardness should not be cnfused with strength or toughness. Very hard minerals (including diamond) can actually be quite brittle. However, there is a general link between hardness and chemical composition. Most hydrous minerals (minerals containing water molecules) are relatively soft, as are sulphates, halides, phosphates, carbonates and most sulphides. Most anhydrous oxides (those containing no water molecules) and silicates are relatively hard (above 5 on the Mohs Scale).

Refractive Index

When light passes through a transparent or tra nslucent mineral, it changes direction and velocity. These changes are measured by the refractive index: the ratio of the velocity of light in air to its velocity in the crystal. A high refractive index is linked to the dispersion of light into its component colours, which gives minerals such as diamond their fire.

Specific Gravity

Specific gravity (SG) is a measure of the density of a substance and is calculated as the ratio of the substance to the mass of an equal volume of water. A mineral with an SG of 2 is twice as heavy as water of the same volume. With experience, one will find that the "feel" of a specimen begins to relate instinctively to its SG measure. For example, quartz, with an SG of 2.6 feels "normal," while galena, SG 7.6, feels "very heavy."

Fluorescence

Some minerals are characterised by fluorescence, which means that they emit visible light of various colours when subjected to ultraviolet radiation. Fluorescence is generally one of the less reliable indicators of a mineral's identity because it lacks consistency. Some specimens of a mineral will exhibit fluorescence while others may not, even when the mineral specimens are from the same location and appear identical.

THE MOHS SCALE OF HARDNESS		
Hardness	**Mineral**	**Other materials for hardness testing**
1	Talc	Very easily scratched by a fingernail
2	Gypsum	Can be scratched by a fingernail
3	Calcite	Just scratched with a copper coin
4	Fluorite	Easily scratched with a knife but not as easily as calcite
5	Apatite	Scratched with a knife with difficulty
6	Orthoclase	Cannot be scratched with a knife but scratches glass with difficulty
7	Quartz	Scratches glass easily
8	Topaz	Scratches glass very easily
9	Corundum	Cuts glass
10	Diamond	Cuts glass

Mineral Associations and Assemblages

Normally, minerals are found together in grouped "associations." Just as fossils are a record of life on Earth, mineral associations offer a record of the Earth's geological history. Patterns of association or assemblage can also help with identification of minerals. Some minerals are consistently found together over large areas because they are found in the same rock type. Other associations occur less extensively in veins, cavities, encrustations or thin layers. Most local associations have built up over geological time, the associated minerals not forming simultaneously.

For example, within a hollow left by a gas bubble in solidified lava (a geode), one may find agate, amethyst and calcite. First, dissolved silica was deposited as an agate lining on the inside of the bubble. Later, other manganese-bearing silica solutions deposited the layer of amethyst, followed at yet another time by carbonate -rich waters, which deposited the calcite.

The fact that certain minerals are likely to be found togeher can help with both the discovery and identification of minerals. For those seeking particular metals, it is useful to know , for example, that lead, and zinc ore minerals are often associated with calcite and baryte, while gold is frequently found in association with quartz.

Additionally, if one is having difficulty identifying a mineral but recognizes another that it is associated with it, this can provide a valuable clue to its identity. For example, bertrandite is an obscure silicate, often difficult to identify, but is found in association with the more familiar beryl.

Important mineral ores, such as the copper deposits at Bingham in Utah, are often discovered through their associated minerals. In the case of copper, the primary ore minerals, for example, chalcopyrite, are oxidised near or at the earth's surface into secondary mineral s, such as malachite or azurite. When prospectors find these secondary minerals on the surface, they know they will lead to a rich concentration of copp er ore below the surface. Similarly, vivianite forms near or at the surface from the alteration of iron or manganese ores and indicates their presence at greater depths.

An association of minerals that forms more or less simultaneously and is usually present in a specific type of rock is called an assemblage. For example, the association of orthoclase, albite, quartz and biotite is a mineral assemblage for granite ; while plagioclase, augite, olivi ne and magnetite is an assemblage for gabbro.

The minerals present in any specific rock vary according to the forces present when it was formed. A shale formed at rel atively low temperature, for example, will have the assemblage muscovite, kaolin, dolomite, quartz and feldspar; while another shale formed at high temperature will be characterised by the assemblage garnet, sillimanite, biotite and feldspar. This effect i s especially striking in metamorphic rocks. For example, a basalt that is metamorphosed at high pressures and low temperaures recrystallizes into a rock containing glaucophane and albite. These minerals have a bluish colouration, and the resulting rocks are known as blueschist. The same rock metamorphosed at more moderate pressures and temperatures would contain an abundance of chlorite and actinolite, both of which are green, giving this rock the name greenschist.

An impressive ammonite fossil found in 2023 in a cliff-face by 9-year-old Eli Morris in the South Wales town of Llantwit Major, a renowned coastal location for Jurassic treasures.

Chapter 4

Crystals

What is a crystal?

All minerals are crystalline, a solid in which the component atoms are arranged in a particular, repeating, three -dimensional pattern. This is expressed externally as flat faces arranged in geometric forms. Some crystals are large enough to see, even attainin g dimensions measured in metres, while others are so small they can only be seen with the most powerful microscopes. From the smallest to the largest, crystals of the same mineral are composed of the same atomic patter ns. Crystallography, the study of the geometric properties and internal structure of crystals, is a fundamental aspect of minerology.

Atomic Structure

A crystal is built up of individual, identical, structural units of atoms and molecules called unit cells. A crystal can consist of just a few unit cells or billions of them. The unit cell is reproduced over and over in three dimensions, constructing the larger scale internal structure of the crystal, whch is called the lattice. The shape of the unit cell and the symmetry of the lattice determine the position and shape of the crystal's faces.

The crystals of many different minerals have unit cells that are of the same shape but are made of different chemical elements. The final development of the faces that appear on any given crystal is dete rmined largely by the geological conditions at the time that the crystal is forming. Certain faces may be emphasised, while others disappear altogether. A crystal's final form is known as its habit.

Crystal Systems

Because a crystal consists of repeating geometric patterns, all crystals exhibit symmetry. These patterns fall into six main groups, called crystal systems, according to to the maximum symmetry of their faces . These systems are cubic, tetragonal, hexagonal and trigonal (regarded as a single system), monoclinic, orthorhombic and triclinic.

Each system is defined by the relative lengths and orientation of its three crystallographic axes, imaginary lines that pass through the centre of an ideal crystal and which are indicated by the letters a, b and c if they are all of different lengths. Crystal systems, and subgroups called classes, are also defined by crystals' axes of symmetry.

Cubic

Cubic crystals have three crystallographic axes at right angles of equal length, and four threefold axes of symmetry. The main forms within this system (also known as the isometric system) are cube, octahedron and rhombic dodecahedron. Minerals that crystallize in this system include halite, copper, gold, silver, platinum, iron, fluorite, leucite, diamond, garnet, spinel, pyrite, galena and magnetite.

Tetragonal

Tetragonal crystals have three crystallographic axes at right angles; two are equal in length and the third is shorter or longer. They have one principal, fourfold axis of symmetry. Tetragonal crystals have the appearance of square prisms. Among the minerals that crystallize in the tetragonal system are rutile, calomel, cassiterite, zircon, chalcopyrite and wulfenite.

Hexagonal and Trigonal

Some mineralogists consider that there are seven crystal systems rather than six, separating the hexagonal from the trigonic crystals. Both hexagonal and trigonal crystals have three crystallographic axes of equal length, set at 120° to one another, and a fourth perpendicular to the place of the other three axes. They differ from one another in that trigonal crystals have only threefold symmetry, while hexagonal crystals have sixfold symmetry. Minerals that crystallize in the hexagonal system include beryl (emerald and aquamarine) and apatite; and among those that crystallize in the trigonal system are calcite, quartz and tourmaline.

Monoclinic

Monoclinic ("one incline") crystals have three crystallographic axes of unequal length. One is at right angles to the other two, these latter two not being perpendicular to each other although they are in the same plane. The crystals have twofold symmetry. More crystals crystallize in the monoclinic system than in any other, including gypsum, borax, orthoclase, muscovite, clinopyroxene, jadeite, azurite, malachite, orpiment and realgar.

Orthorhombic ("perpendicular parallelogram")

Crystals in this system have three crystallographic axes at right angles, all of which are unequal in length. The crystals have three twofold axes of symmetry. Minerals that crystallize in this system include olivine, aragonite, topaz, marcasite and baryte.

Triclinic

Triclinic crystals have the least symmetrical shape of all crystals. They have three crystallographic axes of unequal length, which are inclined at angles of less than 90° to one another. The orientation of a triclinic crystal is arbitrary. Minerals in this system include albite, anorthite, kaolin, kyanite and microcline.

Crystal Habits

A description of the external shape of a crystal is known as its habit. It includes all of the crystal's visible characteristics, incorporating the names of its faces, for example pyramidal or prismatic, and the name of its form, for example octahedral or cubic . It also includes more general descriptive terms such as bladed or dendritic. A habit's description may relate to a single crystal or to an assemblage of intergrown crystals known as aggregate.

Crystal Faces

There are three types of crystal face: prism, pyramid and pinacoid, each determined by their relationship to the crystallographic axes. Prism faces are those parallel to the c axis; pyramid faces cut through the c axis at an angle; and pinacoid faces are at right angles to the c axis. A crystal may have numerous sets of pyramid faces, each at a different angle to the c axis, as well as major and minor prism faces with edges parallel to each other. However, in most crystals so me faces are more developed than others. As a crystal grows, the faces that grow most rapidly eventually eliminate themselves, while those that grow more slowly become prominent. Where prism faces predominate in a crystal, the habit may be described as pri smatic; where pyramid faces predominate, it may be described as pyramidal; and where pinacoid faces predominate, the habit is described as platy. A face at the end of a crystal is called a termination face.

Crystal Forms

Some crystal habits derive their names purely from their forms: for example, cubic, crystallizing in the form of cubes , and do decahedron, crystallizing in the forms of dodecahedrons. However, if crystals of one system crystallize in forms that appear to be the crystals of another system, the habit name is preceded by "pseudo." For example, if cyclic twins of orthorhombic aragonite appear to form hexagonal prisms, they are decribed as pseudohexagonal. If the terminations (end faces) of the crystal are different from each other, the habit is known as hemimorphic.

Aggregates

Aggregates are groups of intimately associated crystals. They differ from clusters in that in crystal clusters there are a number of individuals growing together but there is not an intimate intergrowth as in aggregates. The type of aggregation is often typical of the particular mineral species. Terms used to describe aggregates include granular, fibrous, radiating, botryoidal, stalactitic, concentric, geode, oolitic and massive.

Crystal Appearance (Habit)

Some crystal habits are descriptive of their general appearance: i) tabular is used to describe a crystal with predominantly large, flat, parallel faces; ii) bladed describes elongated crystals such as kyanite, flattened like a knife blade; iii) stalactitic describes a crystal aggregate that has grown in the shape of a stalactite; iv) lenticular, as in a selenite rose crystal, form in lens shapes; v) dendritic, such as copper, form in slender, divergent, plant-like branches; vi) acicular, which features needle-like crystals such as in slender, radiating mesolite; and vii) lamellar, where, such as in mica, the individual crystals are flat and plate-like and arranged in layers.

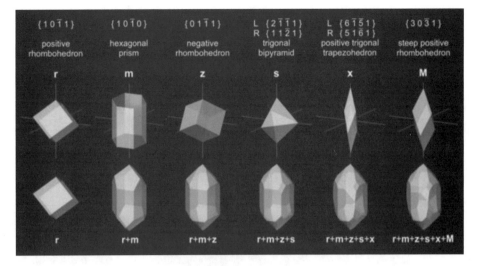

Crystal Morphology

Macrocrystalline Crystal

Microcrystalline Crystal

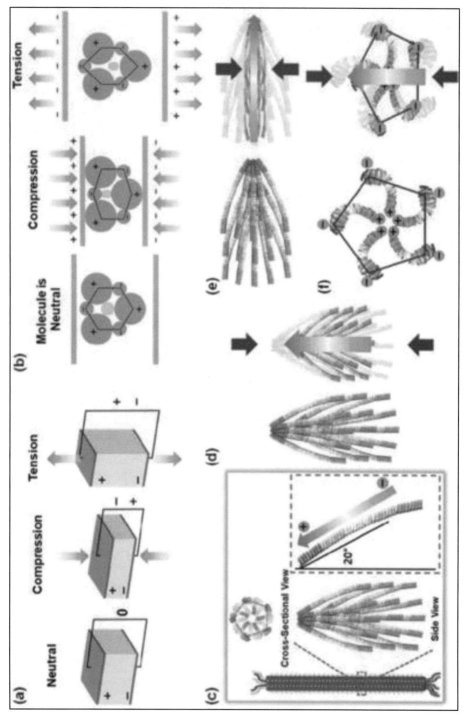

The Piezo-Electric Effect

Chapter 5

Quartz Crystal

Pure quartz, traditionally called rock crystal or clear quartz, is colourless and transparent or translucent, and has often been used for hardstone carvings, such as the Lothair Crystal.Common coloured varieties include citrine, rose quartz, amethyst, smoky quartz and milky quartz. These colour differentiations arise from the presence of impurities which change the molecular orbitals, causing some electronic transitions to take place in the visible spectrum, resulting in different colours. Quartz is one of the most common minerals found in the Earth 's crust. If pure, quartz forms colourless, transparent, very hard crystals with a glass-like lustre.

Quartz has always been known and admired. The most ancient name known is recorded by Theophrastus in about 300-325 BC as κρύσταλλος (kristallos). Varietal names such as rock crystal and bergcrystal preserve the ancient usage. The root words κρύοσ signifying ice cold and στέλλειυ to contract, or solidify, suggest that kristallos was once believed to be permanently solidified ice.

The earliest printed use of "querz" was anonymously published in 1505 and attributed to Ulrich Rülein von Kalbe, a Freiberg physician.

Agricola used the spelling "quarz um," as well as "querze" but also referred to it as "crystallum," "silicum," "silex," and "silice."

Saxon miners called small cross veins of ores "Querklüfte" and metallic minerals as a whole " Erz" or "Ertz." In 1941 Tomkeieff suggested as an etymology for quartz that it arose from a condensed form of the Saxons' clumsy conflation of these two words into "Querkluftertz." Eventually, it became "Quarz" in German, "quarzum" in Latin and "quartz" in English. As the preferred specific term for silic on dioxide crystal, the name quartz became established in the second half of the 18th century.

The most important distinction between types of quartz is that of macrocrystalline (individual crystals visible to the unaided eye) and the less common microcrystalline or cryptocrystalline varieties (aggregates of crystals visible only under high magnification). The cryptocrystalline varieties are either translucent or mostly opaque, while the transparent varieties tend to be macrocrystalline.

Examples of macrocrystalline quartz are rock crystals, the grains in sandstone, and also massive quartz that is made of large crystallites without any crystal faces like vein quartz. In thin sections macrocrystalline quartz appears clear and homogeneous, with blue grey to white or bright yellow interference colours and a low relief.

Examples of microcrystalline quartz are chert, agate and chalcedony, which is a cryptocrystalline form of silica that consists of fine intergrowths of quartz and its monoclinic polymorph morganite. Other opaque gemstone varieties of quartz, or mixed rocks including quartz, often including contrasting bands or patterns of color, are carnelian or sard, onyx, heliotrope and jasper.

Quartz crystals or aggregates that share certain peculiar physical properties have been classified as quartz varieties with specific "trivial names." The best-known examples are the coloured varieties of quartz, like amethyst or smoky quartz, but there are also trivial names for specific crystal shapes, aggregates and textures, like sceptre quartz, gwindel or quartzine.

Because there are no formal rules on naming or defining quartz varieties, the definitions of some are precise and generally accepted, while the definitions of others vary considerably.

Quartz crystals show about one hundred different crystallographic forms in nature. The structure of quartz was deciphered by Bragg and Gibbs in 1925. Its basic building block is the SiO_4 group, in which four oxygen atoms surround a central silicon atom to form a tetrahedron. Since each oxygen atom is a member of two SiO_4 groups, the formula of quartz is SiO_2. Many mineralogy textbooks classify quartz as a network silicate or a tectosilicate.

Quartz can be thought of as being made of threefold and sixfold helical chains of SiO_4 tetrahedra that run parallel to the c-axis. Six of such helices are connected to form a ring that surrounds a central channel which runs parallel to the c-axis, sometimes called "c-channel." The large channels are an important structural feature of quartz because they may be occupied by small cations (positively charged ions). A helix is either turning clockwise (right-handed) or counterclockwise (left-handed). Due to the helical arrangement of the SiO_4 tetrahedra, the atomic lattice of quartz possesses the symmetry properties of a helix, thus, quartz forms left- and right-handed crystals, whose crystal structure and morphology are mirror-images of each other.

Quartz is optically active: the polarization of a light ray passing through a crystal parallel to the c-axis will be rotated either to the left or the right, depending on the handedness of the crystal.

Quartz is found as individual crystals and as crystal aggregates. Well crystallized quartz crystals are typically six-sided prisms with steep pyramidal terminations. They can be stubby ("short prismatic") or elongated and even needle-like. In most environments, quartz crystals are attached to the host rock and only have one tip but double   -terminated crystals are also found.

As a rock -forming mineral, quartz commonly occurs as sub - millimeter to centimet re-sized anhedral (having no plane faces) grains; well-formed crystals are uncommon. Secondary vein -fillings of quartz are typically massive.

The crystallographic form of quartz that is characteristic for its symmetry properties is the trigonal trapezohedron. The position of   the faces of the positive trigonal trapezohedra on the crystal reflects the handedness of the structure of the crystal. Quartz belongs to the trigonal-trapezohedral crystal class.

Of the seven basic crystallographic forms of the trigonal trapezohedron class, the hexagonal prism and trigonal rhombohedra are very common and determine the overall shape of the crystals. The trigonal bipyramids and trigonal trapezohedra are frequently fo und but typically only as relatively small faces. The trigonal prisms, the basal pinacoid and, in particular, ditrigonal prisms are very rare.

Consequent to defects in their lattice and the circumstances of growth conditions, quartz crystals may develop two very distinct and mutually exclusive types of internal structure: Macromosaic Structure, sometimes called "Friedlaender Quartz," and Lamellar Structure, sometimes called "Bambauer Quartz." Individual crystals may possess both structural types, but the se respective parts of the crystal grew at different developmental stages. It is sometimes claimed incorrectly, that all quartz occurs either as macromosaic or as lamellar structural type.

Macromosaic quartz crystals are composed of slightly tilted and radially arranged wedge-shaped sectors. They are recognized by the presence of sutures on the crystal faces , which are often confused with twin boundaries. Crystals with such a structure are found in pegmatite , in miarole pockets, and in high-temperature alpine-type fissures. Layers of quartz with a   lamellar structure show an optical anomaly: they are biaxial. The layers are stacked parallel to the crystal faces in an onion - like manner and are associated with a relatively high hydrogen and aluminium content.

In addition to crystallographic forms and habits, many quartz crystals are characterized by certain morphological features that reflect different modes of growth during their development. Some of these "growth forms" are found at many different localities and, like habits, have been given "trivial names" (for example, "cactus quartz"). Among the more common and important growth forms are:

> Sceptre quartz: crystals with syntaxial overgrowth of a second-generation tip.

> Faden quartz: crystals and crystal aggregates with a white thread running through the crystals. The thread is caused by repetitive cracking of the crystal during growth and consists of fluid inclusions.

> Window or Skeleton or Frame or Fenster quartz: crystals with frame-like, elevated edges of the crystal faces, usually with parallel grown blades that grow from the edges to the centre of the faces in a window-glass-like manner.

> Phantom quartz: crystals in which outlines of the shape of earlier developmental stages of the crystal are visible because of inclusions or colour zones.

> Sprouting quartz ("Sprossenquarz"): crystals on which split growth causes sub-parallel daughter crystals to sprout from the crystal faces.

> Artichoke quartz: a form of split-growth resulting in specimens with composite artichoke-like crystal tips.

> Gwindel: crystals elongated and twisted along an a-axis.

> Cactus quartz or spirit quartz: crystals whose prism faces are covered by small, roughly radially grown second-generation crystals.

Compared to many other minerals, quartz is chemically very pure; most crystals contain more than 99.5% $SiO2$. Nevertheless, varieties coloured by impurities occur. These can be divided into two groups:

i) Quartz coloured by trace elements built into the crystal lattice. Only a few elements can replace silicon in the lattice or are small enough to occupy its free spaces. In natural quartz crystals, the most common ones to replace Silicon are Aluminium (Al), Iron (Fe), Germanium (Ge) and Titanium (Ti). There are only a handful of quartz varieties coloured by trace elements built into the lattice, the more common ones being: smoky quartz, amethyst, citrine, pink quartz / euhedral[2] rose quartz, and

---

[2] A euhedral quartz is a crystal in a rock bounded by faces corresponding to its regular crystal form and not constrained by adjacent minerals.

prasiolite. With the possible exception of some prasiolites and some citrines, the colour of these varieties is based on colour centres whose formation requires high energy irradiation from radioactive elements in the surrounding rocks. Quartz varieties based on colour centres are pleochroic, and their colour centre can be destroyed by heat treatment.

ii) Quartz coloured by inclusions of separate phases, for example minerals or fluids. Because quartz crystals grow in many geological environments, they embed many different minerals during growth and assume the colours of the included minerals. Colours may also be caused by light scattering at finely distributed but colourless inclusions. There are also trivial names for varieties coloured by inclusions that have been found at many localities, like "prase," "ferruginous quartz" or "rose quartz." However, the definitions of these varieties are often rather fuzzy, and different authors use different definitions.

Occurrence of Quartz

Quartz can only form where silica is present in excess of what is consumed in the formation of other silicate minerals. Quartz may also be consumed during the formation of new silicate minerals, in particular at higher temperatures and pressures. Certain geological environments are "incompatible" with free silica and hence are quartz-free.

Silica has been enriched in the continental Earth's crust to about 60% by processes like magmatic differentiation and the formation of silica -rich igneous rocks (mainly driven by plate tectonics), and the accumulation of the physically and chemically stable quartz in sediments and sedimentary rocks. The oceanic crust's silica content of about 50% in its igneous rocks is too low for quartz to form in them.

Quartz is a defining constituent of granite and other felsic igneous rocks. It is very common in sedimentary rocks such as sandstone and shale. It is a common constituent of schist, gneiss, quartzite and other metamorphic rocks.

Quartz has the lowest potential for weathering in the Goldich dissolution series, a method of predicting the relative stability or weathering rate of igneous minerals. Consequently, it is very common as a residual mineral in stream sediments and residual soils. Generally, a high presence of quartz suggests a "mature" rock, since it indicates the rock has been heavily reworked and quartz was the primary mineral that endured heavy weathering.

The largest amount of quartz is found as a rock -forming mineral in silica-rich igneous rocks, namely granite -like plutonic rocks, and in the metamorphic rocks that are derived from them. Under conditions at or near the surface, quartz is generally more stable than most other rock-forming minerals and its accumulation in sediments leads to rocks that are highly enriched in quartz, like sandstones.

Quartz is also a major constituent of sedimentary rocks whose high quartz content is not immediately obvious, like slates, as well as in the metamorphic rocks derived from such quartz-bearing precursor rocks.

At higher temperatures and pressures quartz is easily dissolved by watery fluids percolating the rock. When silica-rich solutions penetrate cooler rocks, the silica will precipitate as quartz in fissures, forming thin white seams as well as large veins which may extend over many kilometers. In most cases, the quartz in these veins will be massive, but they may also contain well-formed quartz crystals.

Phyllites[3] and schists often contain thin lenticular or regular veins of so-called "segregation quartz" that run parallel to the bedding and are the result of local transport of silica during metamorphism. Silica-rich fluids are also driven out of solidifying magma bodies. When these brines enter cooler rocks, the solution gets oversaturated in silica, and quartz forms.

Along with the silica, metals are also transported with the brines and precipitate in the veins as sometimes valuable ore minerals. The association of gold and quartz veins is a well-known example. Quartz is the most common gangue mineral[4] in ore deposits.

Quartz crystals typically grow in fluids at elevated temperatures between 150°C and 600°C, but they also grow at ambient conditions. Quartz is best known for the beautiful crystals it forms in all sorts of cavities and fissures. The greatest variety of shapes and colours of quartz crystals comes from hydrothermal ore veins and deposits, reflecting large differences in growth conditions in these environments (chemistry, temperature and pressure).

Splendid, large crystals grow from ascending hot brines in large fissures, from residual silica-rich fluids in cavities in pegmatites, and from locally mobilized silica in Alpine-type fissures. An economically important source of amethyst for the lapidary industry are cavities of volcanic rocks. Small, but well-formed quartz crystals are found in septarian nodules,[5] and in dissolution pockets in limestones.

Well-formed quartz crystals that are fully embedded in sedimentary

---

[3] A phyllite is a type of foliated metamorphic rock formed from slate, which is further metamorphosed so that very fine-grained white mica achieves a preferred orientation.

[4] In mining, gangue is the commercially worthless material that surrounds, or is closely mixed with, a wanted mineral in an ore deposit.

[5] A sedimentary rock that was formed during the time of the dinosaurs. It is a combination of several minerals, including Aragonite, Barite, Betonite and Calcite.

rocks and grew during diagenesis[6] (so-called authigenic quartz crystals) are occasionally found in limestones, marls and evaporites.

Euhedral quartz crystals that are embedded in igneous rocks are uncommon. Quartz is among the last minerals that form during the solidification of a magma, and because the crystals fill the residual space between the older crystals of other minerals they are usually irregular. Euhedral, stubby bipyramidal quartz crystals are occasionally found in rhyolites. Only rarely are euhedral quartz crystals seen embedded in metamorphic rocks.

Elemental impurity incorporation strongly influences the ability to process and utilize quartz. Naturally occurring quartz crystals of extremely high purity, necessary for the crucibles and other equipment used for growing silicon wafers in the semiconductor industry, are expensive and rare. These high-purity quartz are defined as containing less than 50 ppm of impurity elements. A major mining location for high purity quartz is the Spruce Pine Gem Mine in North Carolina. Quartz is also found in Caldoveiro Peak in Spain. The largest documented single crystal of quartz was found near Itapore in Brazil; it measured approximately 6m × 1.5m × 1.5m and weighed 39,916 kilograms.

Quartz is extracted from open pit mines. Miners occasionally use explosives to expose deep pockets of quartz. More frequently, bulldozers and backhoes are used to remove soil and clay and expose quartz veins, which are then worked using hand tools. Care must be taken to avoid sudden temperature changes that may damage the crystals.

Almost all the industrial demand for quartz crystal (used primarily in electronics) is met with synthetic quartz produced by the hydrothermal process. However, synthetic crystals are less prized for use as gemstones. The popularity of crystal healing has increased the demand for natural quartz crystals, which are now often mined in developing countries using primitive mining methods, sometimes involving child labour.

Identification

In most cases quartz is easy to identify by its combination of the following properties:

➢ hardness (easily scratches glass, also harder than steel)

➢ glass-like lustre

➢ poor to indistinct cleavage

---

[6] Refers to the physical and chemical processes that affect sedimentary materials after deposition and before metamorphism, and between deposition and weathering.

> conchoidal fracture in crystals; in massive specimens the fracture often looks irregular to the naked eye but still conchoidal at high magnification.

Note that in macrocrystalline quartz the fracture surfaces have a vitreous to resinous lustre, whereas in cryptocrystalline quartz fractured surfaces are dull. Crystals are very common, and their usually six-sided shape and six-sided pyramidal tips are well-known. Intergrown crystals without tips can often be recognized by the presence of the characteristic striation on the prism faces.

Quartz as a rock-forming mineral, in particular as irregular grains in the matrix, occasionally poses problems and may require additional means of identification. It may be confused with cordierite (pleochroic, tendency to alteration) and nepheline (lower hardness, geological environment incompatible with quartz).

Handling Quartz

Quartz normally does not require special attention when handled or stored. At ambient conditions, quartz is chemically almost inert, so it does not suffer from the problems seen in many other minerals. Crystals do not disintegrate or crumble, they do not oxidize or dissolve easily in water and they do not mind being touched. The only problem for the collector is dust.

Quartz crystals that contain large fluid or gas inclusions may crack when heated; skeleton quartz is the most sensitive variety in this respect, but most quartz specimens can take some heat, such as cleaning in warm water, without being damaged.

Quartz is hard but quite brittle, and with some effort one can damage a crystal even with things that are much softer. The edges of the crystals are very often slightly damaged because crystals were not kept separate from each other.

Coloured quartz varieties can pale in sunlight, the most sensitive variety being euhedral rose quartz/pink quartz, which should be kept in the dark. Amethyst, smoky quartz and natural citrine will also pale, but it takes a very long time.

Varieties according to colour

Amethyst is a form of quartz that ranges from a bright vivid violet to a dark or dull lavender shade. The world's largest deposits of amethysts can be found in Brazil, Mexico, Uruguay, Russia, France, Namibia and Morocco. Sometimes amethyst and citrine are found growing in the same crystal. It is then referred to as ametrine. Amethyst derives its color from traces of iron in its structure.

Blue quartz, more formally known as Dumortierite quartz, contains inclusions of fibrous magnesio-riebeckite or crocidolite. Inclusions of the mineral dumortierite within quartz pieces often result in silky-appearing splotches with a blue hue. Shades of purple or grey sometimes also are present. Dumortierite will sometimes feature contrasting light and dark color zones across the material. "Blue quartz" is classed as a minor gemstone.

Citrine is a variety of quartz whose colour ranges from pale yellow to brown due to a submicroscopic distribution of colloidal ferric hydroxide impurities. Natural citrines are rare; m ost commercial citrines are heat - treated amethysts or smoky quartz. However, a heat-treated amethyst will have small lines in the crystal, as opposed to a natural citrine's cloudy or smoky appearance.

It is nearly impossible to differentiate between cut citrine and yellow topaz visually, but they differ in hardness. Brazil is the leading producer of citrine, with much of its production coming from the state of Rio Grande do Sul.

The name is derived from the Latin word citrina which means "yellow" and is also the origin of the word "citron ." Citrine has been referred to as the "merchant's stone" or "money stone ," due to a superstition that it would bring prosperity. Citrine was first appreciated as a golden-yellow gemstone in Greece between 300 and 150 BC, during the Hellenistic Age. Yellow quartz was used prior to that to decorate jewelry and tools but it was not highly sought after.

Milk quartz or milky quartz is the most common variety of crystalline quartz. The white colour is caused by minute fluid inclusions of gas, liquid, or both, trapped during crystal formation, making it of little value for optical and quality gemstone applications.

Rose quartz is a type of quartz that exhibits a pale pink to rose red hue. The colour is usually considered as due to trace amounts of titanium, iron, or manganese in the material. Some rose quartz contains microscopic rutile needles that produce asterism in transmitted light. Recent X -ray diffraction studies suggest that the colour is due to thin microscopic fibres of possibly dumortierite within the quartz.

Additionally, there is a rare type of pink quartz (also called crystalline rose quartz) with colour that is thought to be caused by trace amounts of phosphate or aluminium. The colour in crystals is apparently photosensitive and subject to fading. The first crystals were found in a pegmatite near Rumford, Maine, U.S., and in Minas Gerais, Brazil.

Smoky quartz is a grey, translucent quartz. It ranges in clarity from almost complete transparency to a brownish-grey crystal that is almost opaque. Some can also be black. The translucency results from natural irradiation acting on minute traces of aluminum in the crystal structure.

Prasiolite (not to be confused with Praseolite), also known as vermarine, is a variety of quartz that is green in colour. Since 1950, almost all natural prasiolite has come from a small Brazilian mine but it is also seen in Lower Silesia in Poland. Naturally occurring prasiolite is also found in the Thunder Bay area of Canada. Rare in nature, most green quartz is heat-treated amethyst.

Synthetic and artificial treatments
Not all varieties of quartz are naturally occurring. Some clear quartz crystals can be treated using heat or gamma-irradiation to induce colour where it would not otherwise have occurred naturally. Susceptibility to such treatments depends on the location from which the quartz was mined. Although citrine occurs naturally, the majority is the result of heat-treating amethyst or smoky quartz. Carnelian has been heat-treated to deepen its colour since prehistoric times. Because natural quartz is often twinned, synthetic quartz is produced for use in industry. Large, flawless, single crystals are synthesized in an autoclave via the hydrothermal process. Like other crystals, quartz may be coated with metal vapours to give it an attractive sheen.

Varieties of Quartz (source: Mindat.org)

"Herkimer-style" Quartz	This is a collective name to group together the many different local names for transparent, lustrous quartz crystals, usually doubly terminated, often associated with inclusions of petroleum and/or associated with oil or coal deposits within sedimentary rocks.
Agate	A distinctly banded fibrous chalcedony. Originally reported from Dirillo river, Ragusa Province, Sicily, Italy. The banding in agate is based on periodic changes in the translucency of the agate substance.

Agate-Jasper	A variety of agate consisting of Jasper veined with Chalcedony
Agatized coral	A variety of agate/chalcedony replacing coral.
Alladinite	A name given to a jasper found in Wabuska, Nevada. Also, unrelatedly, a name for a synthetic casein resin and possibly as a marketing name for gem diopside.
Amarillo Stone	A figured variety of chalcedony. May be the same as Alibates flint.
Amberine	Yellow to yellow-green chalcedony variety found in Death Valley, Inyo Co., California, USA.
Amethyst	A violet to purple variety of quartz that owes its colour to gamma irradiation and the presence of traces of iron built into its crystal lattice.
Ametrine	Ametrine crystals are made of alternating sectors of purple and yellow to orange colour. Slabs cut perpendicular to the c axis of the crystal look a bit like a pinwheel.
Apricotine	Reddish-yellow waterworn apricot-coloured quartz pebbles.
Aquaprase	A bluish green chalcedony, coloured by chromium and nickel, is marketed under the trade name "Aquaprase."
Arkansas Candle	A cluster of clear Quartz crystals in a candle-like formation. Also, single crystals that show a greater than 7 to 1 length to width ratio.
Aventurine	A variety of quartz containing glistening fragments (usually mica, such as fuchsite, but also hematite, which can be cut and polished as a gemstone. Most commonly when the general public encounter this stone it is in the form of green stone beads.
Azurchalcedony	Chalcedony coloured by Chrysocolla, from Arizona.
Babel-Quartz	A historical name given for a variety of quartz named for the fancied resemblance of the crystals to the successive tiers of the Tower of Babel.
Ball Jasper	Jasper showing concentric red and yellow bands. Jasper occurring in spherical masses.
Bayate	A local name for a brown ferruginous variety of Jasper. Originally described from Cuba.
Beekite	A name given to Chalcedony pseudomorphs after coral or shells. Originally described from Devon, England, UK.
Bergerit	Local name for a net-like jasper.
Binghamite	Binghamite refers to a diverse group of lapidary materials from the mines on the Cuyuna North Iron

	Range in Crow Wing County, Minnesota. It is related to Minnesota silkstone and Minnesota tigers' eye.
Bird's Eye Agate	A variety of eye agate where the eyes are supposed to resemble the eyes of a bird.
Blue Chalcedony	Blue colour caused by the Tyndall effect (light scattering by colloid sized particles). Transmitted light looks yellowish or reddish rather than blue.
Blue Lace Agate	A pale blue banded variety of Chalcedony.
Blue Quartz	An opaque to translucent, blue variety of quartz, owing its colour to inclusions, commonly of fibrous magnesioriebeckite or crocidolite or of tourmaline. The colour may be caused by the colour of the included minerals or by scattering of light.
Botswana Agate	A variety of agate from Botswana, banded with fine, parallel lines, often coloured pink blending into white.
Brecciated Agate	A naturally cemented matrix of broken agate fragments.
Buhrstone	A cellular flinty material used for millstones.
Bull Quartz	Milky to greyish, massive.
Burnt amethyst	Heated amethyst; the heating results in a yellow-orange, yellow-brown, or dark brownish colour. Often incorrectly sold as citrine.
Cactus Quartz	Quartz crystals encrusted by a second generation of smaller crystals grown on the prism faces. The small second-generation crystals point away from the prism.
Cape May Diamond	Waterworn transparent quartz pebbles. A locally applied marketing name/ploy to clear, colourless quartz beach pebbles occurring along the Delaware Bay beaches of Cape May County, New Jersey, USA.
Capped Quartz	Quartz crystals made of loosely connected or easily separable parts that correspond to different growth phases. This is caused by the deposition of thin continuous layers of, for example, clay minerals, on the crystal during growth.
Carnelian	A reddish variety of Chalcedony.
Catalinite	No information yet entered in Mindat.org database.
Chalcedony	A more general term for all varieties of quartz that are made of microscopic or submicroscopic crystals, the so-called microcrystalline varieties of quartz.
Chrome-Chalcedony	A variety of chalcedony coloured deep green by Cr compounds.
Chrysojasper	A variety of jasper coloured by chrysocolla.
Citrine	A yellow to yellow-orange or yellow-green variety of

	quartz. Quartz coloured by inclusions, or coatings, of any kind is not called citrine. Iron-stained quartz should not be mistaken for citrine.
Clear Lake Diamond	Quartz crystals from the Manke Ranch, Lake County, California.
Cloud Agate	Greyish agate with patches of blurry, foggy inclusions.
Cotterite	A variety of quartz with "metallic pearly lustre" coating normal quartz crystals. Originally described from Rock Forest, Mallow, Co. Cork, Ireland.
Crazy Lace Agate	An agate composed of multicoloured twisting and turning bands.
Creolite	A red-and-white banded jasper. Originally reported from California, USA.
Cubosilicite	Pseudomorphs of Chalcedony after Fluorite - small blue cubes.
Dallasite	A variety of jasper from Vancouver Island, British Columbia, Canada.
Damsonite	Trade name for a light violet to dark purple chalcedony from Arizona.
Darlingite	Local name for a variety of Jasper. A kind of lydian stone. Originally reported from Victoria, Australia.
Dendritic Agate	Chalcedony containing dendritic inclusions.
Diackethyst	A local name for translucent wine and amethystine coloured chalcedony pebbles. Originally described from Craig, Montrose, Tayside (Angus), Scotland,
Dotsero Diamond	Fanciful local name for quartz crystals enclosed in a geologically recent basalt flow. Being incompatible with basaltic lava, the quartz crystals are rounded by reaction with the surrounding lava.
Dragonite	A rounded quartz pebble representing a quartz crystal that has lost its brilliancy and angular form; in gravels, once believed to be a fabulous stone obtained from the head of a flying dragon.
Egyptian Jasper	A brown variety (brown alternating with black stripes - Egypt) or red (blood-red, flesh red, yellow, brown - found in Baden), originally described from Egypt.
Eisenkiesel	A quartz that is coloured red, orange or brown by hematite inclusions. Translucent to almost opaque. The term "eisenkiesel" is sometimes also used in a wider sense, as a synonym of ferruginous quartz for any quartz with iron oxides and hydroxide mineral .
El Doradoite	Trade name for blue quartz or chalcedony. Originally described from El Dorado Co., California.

Ema egg	A river-tumbled pebble of transparent quartz with a frosted exterior resembling an eggshell, originally collected from rivers in Brazil, with one side sawn flat and polished as a window to view the interior.
Enhydro Agate	An agate nodule partly filled with water.
Eye Agate	Agate with concentric ring pattern looking like an eye.
Faden Quartz	"Faden quartz" is the anglicized version of the German "Fadenquarz." "Faden" (pronounced "fah-den") means "thread" and refers to a white line that runs through the crystal. In French, these are called " quartz à l'âme."
Fairburn Agate	A unique and rare variety of Fortification Agate from Fairburn, Custer Co., South Dakota, USA.
Fensterquarz	Literally "window quartz." Skeletal quartz which has rhombohedral faces appearing like windows.
Ferruginous Quartz	A variety of quartz coloured red, brown, or yellow by inclusions of hematite or limonite and usually massive and opaque.
Fire Agate	Chalcedony containing inclusions of goethite or limonite, producing an iridescent effect or "fire."
Fortification Agate	Agate with sharp-angled bands which resemble the outlines of fortifications of a castle.
Fossil Agate	Agate as a replacement material in fossils.
Haema-ovoid-agates	Name proposed for a reddish agate with ovoidal patches of cacholong, etc.
Hair Amethyst	A name for acicular crystals of Amethyst.
Haytorite	Although the original specimens from Haytor Mine were pseudomorphs of quartz after datolite, the name has been frequently used in Cornwall also for quartz pseudomorphs after a veriety of other minerals, including calcite dolomite and siderite.
Herbeckite	A variety of Agate or Jasper impregnated with Iron Hydrate. Originally described from Hrbek Mine, Svatá Dobrotivá (St Benigna), Beroun (Beraun), Central Bohemia Region, Bohemia (Böhmen; Boehmen), Czech Republic.
Iris Agate	An iridescent variety of agate: when sliced into a thin section it exhibits all the colours of the spectrum when viewed in transmitted light.
Iris Quartz	Quartz crystals displaying internal spectral colours under minor rhombohedral faces, interference due to reflection and refraction processes.
Irnimite	Very special multicolour black-blue-brown-white local variety of jasperor microquartzite associated with

	manganese ores of Taikan range in Eastern Siberia. Its colouration is caused by black manganese oxides (very often braunite), and blue alkali amphibole.
Jacinto de Compostela	In Spanish mineralogical literature, the name is traditionally used for the red "floater" variety of authigenic quartzes from continental gypsum-bearing marls of the Triassic Keuper formation.
Jasper	Geologically the name has long been used for an opaque to slightly translucent, generally red or brown to variably coloured, impure chalcedony or microcrystalline chert.
Keystonite Chalcedony	A local trade name for Chalcedony coloured blue by Chrysocolla.
Kinradite	An orbicular jasper originally observed in the San Francisco area and named for lapidary J.J. Kinrade.
Laguna Agate	A colourful agate variety. Originally described from Ojo Laguna, Chihuahua, Mexico.
Lake Superior Agate	Believed to be the world's oldest agates, over 1 billion years old, these are found throughout the northern US having been spread from the original Lake Superior region by glaciation. It has generally pale colouring.
Landscape Agate	A variety of chalcedony with inclusions giving the appearance of a landscape scene.
Lithium Quartz	A name in common trade use for a pink/purple translucent to opaque variety of quartz, possibly containing inclusions of a lithium-rich mineral such as lepidolite.
Mexican Lace Agate	Lacy or wavy agate from Mexico.
Milky Quartz	A semi-transparent to opaque, white-coloured variety of quartz.
Mocha Stone	A variety of agate containing inclusions of pyrolusite. Originally described from Mocha, Saudi Arabia.
Moss Agate	A variety of Chalcedony frequently containing green mineral inclusions (e.g. Chlorite, Hornblende, etc.) or brown to black dendrites of iron or manganese oxides.
Mutzschen Diamonds	Clear variety of rock crystal from Mutzschen, Saxony. Occurs in voids of Permian volcanic rocks (rhyolites).
Myrickite	Local name for chalcedony with grey ground and red inclusions of cinnabar). Originally described from Myrick Spring, San Bernardino Co., California.
Nipomo Agate	Chalcedony with inclusions of Marcasite. Originally described from Nipomo, San Luis Obispo

	Co., California, USA.
Oil Quartz	A variety of Quartz from Tyrol, Austria, which contains yellow stains in cracks.
Onyx	In correct usage, the name refers to a (usually) black and white banded variety of Agate, or sometimes a monochromatic agate with dark and light parallel bands (brown and white for example).
Owyhee Jasper	No information yet entered in Mindat.org database
Pastelite	Variety of jasper exhibiting pastel colours.
Pecos Diamonds	Colourful, doubly terminated quartz crystals that occur in the Permian Seven Rivers Formation along the Pecos River valley in southeastern New Mexico.
Phantomquartz	A variety of quartz that shows one or more phantoms.
Pietersite	Chalcedony with embedded fibers of amphibole minerals with varying degrees of alteration. Blue-gray, brown and yellow colours. The fibers cause a chatoyancy similar to that seen in tiger's eye, but tiger's eye is not made of chalcedony, it is macrocrystalline in form.
Pigeon Blood Agate	A blood-red and white variety of agate from Utah.
Plasma	A microgranular or microfibrous form of chalcedony coloured in various shades of green by disseminated silicate particles (variously attributed to celadonite, chlorite, amphibole, etc.).
Plume Agate	A variety of chalcedony with contrasting coloured, plume-like structures within the material.
Prase	Originally, the varietal name "prase" was applied to a dull leek-green coloured quartzite (a rock, not a mineral); but over the years it has been also applied to other materials, particularly a green coloured jasper of similar colour.
Prase-malachite	A term for Prase enclosing Malachite.
Prasiolite	A green transparent variety of macrocrystalline quartz. Compare with prase and plasma. Not to be confused with prasolite.
Pseudocubic Quartz	Crystals with a (pseudo)cubic appearance that are dominated by a single rhombohedral form.
Quartz Gwindel	Quartz crystals that grew along and are slightly rotated around a single a-axis. This results in twisted and tabular crystals. The twist reflects the handedness of the quartz crystals.
Quartzine	A fibrous variety of chalcedony. It is also called

	"length-slow chalcedony" and is usually intergrown with another, more common type of fibrous chalcedony, "length-fast chalcedony", that comprises most of the different varieties of chalcedony.
Quetzalitztli	Translucent, emerald, green jasper from Guatemala, coloured by inclusions of Cr-muscovite.
Riband Agate	A banded agate.
Riband Jasper	A banded Jasper.
Rock Crystal	A transparent colourless variety of quartz.
Rose Quartz	Two varieties, 1. Found in translucent masses made of intergrown anhedral crystals. It occurs in different hues of pink, sometimes bluish, sometimes more reddish; irradiation may cause the formation of smoky quartz colour centers and add a grey tone. Rose quartz is always showing a hazy to translucent character due to microscopic fibrous inclusions of a pink borosilicate mineral related to dumortierite These inclusions are probably the result of an exsolution from an initially homogeneous material. 2. this variety occurs in well-formed crystals of similar colour, found as a late formation in pegmatite pockets, often overgrowing smoky quartz crystals in groups of parallel-grown crystals. The colour is caused by irradiation-induced colour centers based on aluminum, Al, and phosphorous.
Rutilated Quartz	Quartz shot through with needles of rutile.
Sard	A brown to brownish-red translucent variety of chalcedony. Pliny the Elder stated that it was named after Sardis, in Lydia, where it was first discovered; but the name probably came with the stone from Persia (Persian sered = yellowish red).
Sardonyx	A variety of Agate with reddish-brown and either black or white bands.
Sceptre Quartz	Crystals in which a second-generation crystal tip grew on top of another quartz crystal.
Schwimmstein	Earthy quartz, as nodular to mamillary masses, as coating on flint. Specific weight < 1, therefore floating on water.
Seftonite	A translucent, moss green variety of chalcedony.
Shocked Quartz	Quartz shocked under intense pressure (but limited temperature). During the pressure shock, the crystalline structure of quartz will be deformed along planes inside the crystal.

Smoky Quartz	A smoky-grey, brown to black variety of quartz that owes its colour to gamma irradiation and the presence of traces of aluminum built into its crystal lattice. Smoky quartz is dichroic (from darker yellow brown to lighter red brown) when viewed in polarized light.
Snakeskin Agate	Chalcedony with snakeskin-like surface pattern.
Star Quartz	Refers to the shape of an aggregate of radiating crystals; not to be confused with the optical property "asterism". Star quartz usually grows at low temperature, often around a core of chalcedony.
Suttroper Quarz	Name used for bi-terminated, milky quartz crystals originally described from Suttrop, Warstein, Sauerland, North Rhine-Westphalia, Germany.
Vogelaugenjaspis	No information yet entered in Mindat.org database.
Watercolour jasper	Very special multicolour black-blue-brown-white local variety of Jasper or microquartzite associated with manganese ores of Taikan range in Eastern Siberia.
Wilkite	A yellow, purple, pink, and green jasper from Willow Creek, Ada County, Idaho, USA.
Youngite	Local name for agate or jasper coated by druzy quartz crystals. Found near Guernsey, Platte Co., Wyoming, USA, in limestone rocks.

Crystal Systems and Examples

PART 2
AMAZING CRYSTAL

Hebe, Goddess of Eternal Youth

Chapter 6

Crystal Skulls

One can buy crystal skulls very easily. There are scores to be bought on platforms such as eBay and Etsy, for example. Here's a batch from a seller in China , each under an inch in size and under $10 in price, description: *"Wholesale! A Lot Natural quartz crystal mini Skull Carved Crystal Skull Healing... 100% Natural quartz crystal rock."*

Quartz's unique properties: its latticeof "silica tetrahedra" that ideally forms into a six-sided prism terminating with six-sided pyramids at each end; the ability of q uartz crystals to grow together; and its underlying structure in which internal patterns of molecules are regular, repeated and geometrically arranged, enables the mineral to serve as an excellent retainer of information. David Childress[7] suggests that these properties make it possible for one to believe that crystal skulls may be the depositories of ancient wisdom. I agree.

The crystal skulls that generate so much controversy are, of course, the life-size ones that are purported to originate in Mesoamerica. These crystal skulls are defined in Wikipedia as 'human skull hardstone carvings made of clear or milky white quartz ("rock crystal"), whose finders claim them to be pre-Columbian Mesoamerican artefacts.'

Theories abound. Some believe the skulls are the handiwork of the Maya or Aztecs , while others insist that they originated on a sunken continent or in outer space. The alien explanation , or rather an exotic inter-dimensional version of it, was successfully exploited in the fourth outing in the Indiana Jones franchise, *Indiana Jones and the Kingdom of the Crystal Skull*, 2008.

---

[7] Childress, D; Mehler, S., *The Crystal Skulls, Astonishing Portals to Man's Past*, Adventures Unlimited Press, Illinois, 2008

But what about the question of authenticity? This really does divide opinion. The scientific consensus, however unpopular this may be with those that believe these artefacts have magical powers, is that the crystal skulls offered up for scientific study are not of ancient origin. The type of crystal examined to date under the microscope has been determined by examination of chlorite inclusions. It is only found in Madagascar and Brazil, and therefore unobtainable or unknown within pre-Columbian Mesoamerica.

Mesoamerican art has numerous representations of skulls, but none of the skulls in museum collections come from documented excavations.

One of the problems that "finders" of crystal skulls and those that believe in their reputed supernatural characteristics have to face is the fact that legends of crystal skulls with mystical powers do not figure in genuine Mesoamerican or other Native American mythologies and spiritual accounts. However, in this book's final chapter one reads the account of one man's dog-walking trip in the San Francisco headlands, which, although necessarily presented as an extraordinary but unverifiable adventure, may suggest to the intuitive reader that there may be a very different perspective on the subject.

The scientific studies carried out to date suggest that crystal skulls examined were crafted in the 19th century in Germany, quite likely at workshops in the town of Idar-Oberstein, which was renowned for crafting objects made from imported Brazilian quartz in the late 19th century. Moreover, research carried out on several crystal skulls at the British Museum in 1967, 1996 and 2004 shows that the indented lines marking the teeth (for these skulls had no separate jawbone, unlike the famed Mitchell-Hedges skull) were carved using jewellers' rotary tools not developed until the 19th century, making a pre-Columbian origin appear untenable in scientific opinion. Museums began collecting rock-crystal skulls during the second half of the nineteenth century, when no scientific archaeological excavations had been undertaken in Mexico and knowledge of real pre-Columbian artefacts was scarce.

It was also a period that saw a burgeoning industry in faking pre-Columbian objects. When Smithsonian archaeologist W.H. Holmes visited Mexico City in 1884, he saw "relic shops" on every corner filled with fake ceramic vessels, whistles and figurines. Two years later, Holmes warned about the abundance of fake pre-Columbian artefacts in museum collections in an article for the journal Science titled "The Trade in Spurious Mexican Antiquities."

The first Mexican crystal skulls appeared on the scene just before the 1863 French intervention, when Louis Napoleon's army invaded the country and installed Maximilian von Hapsburg of Austria as emperor. Mostly, these items were small, not taller than 1.5 inches. The earliest specimen seems to be a British Museum crystal skull about an inch high that may have been acquired in 1856 by British banker Henry Christy.

Two other examples were exhibited in 1867 at the Exposition Universelle in Paris as part of the collection of Eugène Boban, a most mysterious figure in the h istory of the crystal skulls , who operated in Mexico City between 1860 and 1880. Boban served as the official "archaeologist" of the Mexican court of Maximilian He was also a member of the French Scientific Commission in Mexico, whose work was highlighted at the Paris Expo. Boban arrived in Mexico in his teens and was soon conducting his own archaeological expeditions and collecting exotic birds. Boban fell in love with Mexican culture , becoming fluent in Spanish and Nahuatl, the Aztec language Eventually, Boban began to make his living selling archaeological artefacts and natural history specimens through a family business in Mexico City.

After returning to France in the 1870s, Boban opened an antiquities shop in Paris and sold a large part of his original Mexican archaeological collection to Alphonse Pinart, a French explorer and ethnographer. In 1878, Pinart donated the collection, which included three crystal skulls, to the Trocadéro, the precursor of the Musée de l'Homme.

The British Museum's "Aztec" Crystal Skull
The British Museum's crystal skull appeared in Boban's shop in 1881. Its origin was not stated in his catalogue at the time. He is said to have tried to sell it to Mexi co's national museum as an Aztec artefact but was unsuccessful.

In July 1886, Boban moved his museum business and collection to New York City . In December of that year Boban held an auction of archaeological artefacts, colonial Mexican manuscripts and a large library of books in New York. The catalogue listed almost two thousand objects. According to Smithsonian anthropologist Jane MacLaren Walsh,[8] the "Aztec" skull was bought at the auction for $950 by someone named Ellis on behalf of Tiffany's. A jeweller named J.L. Ellis had been a partner at Tiffany & Co., although he had retired from the firm by 1886. George Kunz, a gemologist and vice president of Tiffany's, was acting as an intermediary between Boban and a buyer named George Sisson. Possibly, Ellis had been sent by Kunz to make the sale for Tiffany's on behalf of Sisson.

---

[8] *Features*, Volume 61 Number 3, May/June 2008

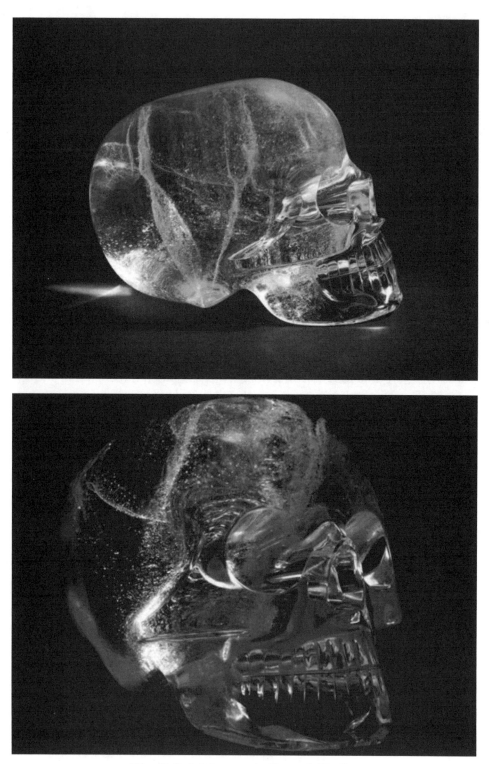

The Britsh Museum's Crystal Skull

As recorded by Kunz in his book, *Gems and Precious Stones*, George H. Sisson, who made a fortune in mining ventures in Colorado and Arizona, owned the skull in 1890. In the mid-1890s Sisson either sold the skull back to Tiffany's or asked Kunz to sell it for him. The British Museum bought it at the original purchase price from Tiffany's, through Kunz, in 1897. The skull is very similar to the Mitchell-Hedges skull, although it is less detailed and does not have a movable lower jaw. The British Museum catalogues the skull's provenance as "probably European, 19th century AD" and describes it as "not an authentic pre-Columbian artefact."

Also referenced in the British Museum's catalogue card is Kunz's book, which was published in 1890. In *Gems and Precious Stones*, Kunz enumerated several rock crystal artefacts then known to him. "Small skulls are in the Blake Collection at the United States National Museum [Smithsonian Institution], the Douglas Collection New York, the British Museum and the Trocadéro Museum. A large skull, now in the possession of George H. Sisson of New York, is very remarkable.. Little is known of its history and nothing of its origin. It was brought from Mexico by a Spanish Officer sometime before the French occupation of Mexico, and was sold to an English collector, at whose death it passed into the hands of E. Boban, of Paris, and then became the property of Mr. Sisson."

Between 1970 and 1997, the British Museum's crystal skull was exhibited at the Museum of Mankind, which occupied the original University College London building at Burlington Gardens in London's Mayfair. In 1997, the exhibits in Mayfair were re-housed in the British Museum's main site in Bloomsbury. The crystal skull can be seen today in the Museum's Wellcome Trust Gallery, Room 24.

In the late 1980s I visited the Museum of Mankind to see the crystal skull. It occupied a beautiful glass case which allowed one to examine the skull close up and all around. I found the experience beautiful and a little eerie. Rather like Indie's experience when, in *Indiana Jones and the Kingdom of the Crystal Skull*, he is forced by baddie Irinia Spalko (Cate Blanchett) to stare at an "alien" crystal skull, I do believe I sensed something in the beautifully carved artefact: a power, a feeling, an ancient intelligence? I don't know what but obviously I was "mistaken" because, years later, scientists pronounced it as relatively recently made, arriving at this assumption because Mesoamerican society did not have the requisite tools to make such an item. Or may it have been the case that scientists had not considered other "outside-the-box" possibilities, and, therefore, had not gone back in history as far as is necessary?

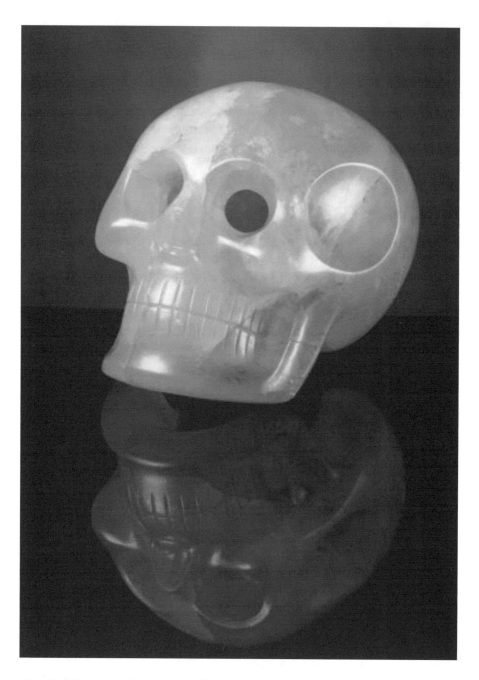

<u>The Smithsonian Crystal Skull (pictured above)</u>
The rock crystal "Smithsonian Skull," Catalogue No. A562841-0 in the collections of the Department of Anthropology, National Museum of Natural History, was mailed in 1992 to the Smithsonian Institution anonymously. The package had gone to the National Museum of

American History. A handwritten note accompanying it said that it was an Aztec skull purchased in Mexico in 1960. The note also said that the skull had belonged to Porfirio Díaz, the dictator of Mexico from the late 1870s until 1910.

It is the largest among the British Museum, Smithsonian and Paris skulls, weighing 31 pounds (14kg) and is 15 inches (38cm) high. It was carved using carborundum, a modern abrasive. It has been displayed as a modern fake at the National Museum of Natural History.

Richard Ahlborn, a colleague at the National Museum of American History, contacted Jane MacLaren Walsh in her capacity as primary researcher on Mexican pre-Columbian archaeology in the Smithsonian's Museum of Natural History. The next day, Ahlborn had the skull delivered to Walsh for scrutiny. It was surprisingly large, about the size of a football helmet, and heavy. It had been carved and hollowed out from milky white quartz. It had prominent teeth, deep eye sockets and circular depressions at the temples. Walsh asked for a cart to move it from the loading dock to her office. An archivist standing nearby jokingly warned, 'Don't look it in the eye! It might be cursed.' Once it was upstairs in her office, Walsh examined it carefully. It was an impressive and interesting artefact but to her eye it did not look at all Aztec, or even preColumbian. It was much too big, the proportions were off, the teeth and circular depressions at the temples did not look right, and overall, it seemed too rounded and polished. Walsh put it into a locked cabinet and forgot about it for a while.

Paris Skull

The Paris skull, about 10cm (4in) high and with a hole drilled vertically through its centre, is the largest of the three sold by Eugène Boban to Alphonse Pinart. It is part of a collection held at the Musée du Quai Branly and was subjected to scientific tests carried out in 2007 –08 by France's national Centre de Recherche et de Restauration des Musées de France (C2RMF). After a series of analyses carried out over three months, C2RMF engineers concluded that it was "certainly not pre-Columbian, it shows traces of polishing and abrasion by modern tools." Particle accelerator tests also revealed occluded traces of water that were dated to the 19th century. The Musée du Quai Branly released a statement that the tests "seem to indicate that it was made late in the 19th century."

In 2009 the C2RMF researchers published results of further investigations to establish when the Paris skull had been carved. Scanning Electron Microscopy (SEM) analysis indicated the use of lapidary machine tools in its carving. The results of a new dating technique known as Quartz Hydration Dating (QHD) demonstrated that the Paris skull had been carved later than a reference quartz specimen artefact, known to have been cut in 1740. The researchers concluded that the SEM and QHD results, combined with the details of the skull's known provenance, indicated it was carved in the 18th or 19th century.

Joint studies of the British Museum and Smithsonian skulls

Later, when a colleague asked Walsh to write a book chapter about an unusual or problematic object of her own choosing in the Department of Anthropology's collection, she recalled the crystal skull delivered from Ahlborn and selected this for the subject topic.

The Porfirio Díaz provenance was anecdotal, and the Aztec attribution seemed unlikely to Walsh since no crystal skull had ever been found in an archaeological excavation in Mexico. She began researching crystal skulls, first investigating the archival and published history of a two-inch crystal skull in the Smithsonian's collections. It had come to the museum from Mexico in the nineteenth century as part of the Wilson Wilberforce Blake Collection, but it disappeared sometime in the 1970s after it was taken off exhibit.

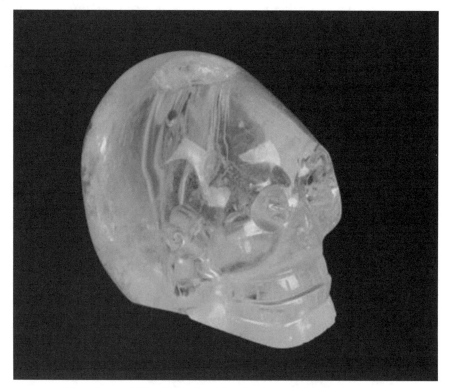

The Crystal Skull in the Musée du Quai Branly, Paris

The collection accession file contained a sheaf of letters that Blake had written to the Smithsonian curator, William Henry Holmes. Blake's letters were filled with journalistic details discussing archaeological questions and general goings -on in Mexico City. One letter from 1886 referred to a "Frenchman named Boban, " who had tried to sell a fake crystal skull to Mexico's Museo Nacional in partnership with Leopoldo Batres, the Mexican government's inspector of archaeological monuments. This was the first time that Walsh had come across Boban's name.

Knowing that both the British Museum in London and the Musée de l'Homme in Paris had a large crystal skull in their collections, Walsh contacted Elizabeth Carmichael at the British Museum and Daniel Levine at the Musée de l'Homme , requesting information about their respective skulls. Carmichael's response was full of interesting notes about the acquisition history of the British Museum crystal skulls—they had two—as well as comments on scientific studies performed on them since the 1960s. A copy of the original registration slip for the smaller skull indicated it might have been purchased in the 1860s, and that the larger skull was purchased in November 1897 from Tiffany & Co. of New York, through George F. Kunz.

Daniel Levine's letter informed Walsh that he believed the Musée de l'Homme's crystal skull was one of the most important artefacts in its pre-Columbian holdings. A copy of the object's catalogue card indicated that the skull was part of the Alphonse Pinart Collection, which had arrived in 1878 when the Musée d'Ethnographie du Trocadéro, France's national ethnographic museum and the Musée de l'Homme's predecessor, first opened to the public.

The opportunity for Walsh to determine scientifically the authenticity of the skulls came when an independent producer of documentaries contacted her and spoke of a television programme about crystal skulls that was planned for the British BBC. Eventually, this led to plans for a joint study of the crystal skulls in the British Museum, the Smithsonian Institution, the Musée de l'Homme, and possibly in a few private collections, the whole process to be filmed.

Because the project team needed an example of carved rock crystal that was known to be definitively pre -Columbian as a basis of comparison with the skulls, Walsh suggested that the documentary's producers contact the Instituto Nacional de Antropología e Historia (INAH) in Mexico City to request the loan of a rock crystal g oblet that had been recovered from excavations at Monte Albán in Oaxaca, to use in the study. It would provide an unquestionable example of pre -

Columbian materials, procedures and carving techniques to use as a yardstick for evaluating the crystal skulls to be examined.

After completing a couple days of filming at the Smithsonian, the production crew moved on to London to continue at the British Museum. Arriving at the Department of Scientific Research in Russell Square, Walsh met with Elizabeth Carmichael and Margaret Sax, a specialist in prehistoric stone carving. Together, they would examine the two British Museum skulls and the large Smithsonian skull, which had been brought to London for the studies. Mexican archeologist Arturo Oliveros had brought the rock crystal goblet from Monte Albán. The goblet, insured for a million dollars, was placed on a long table in the centre of the room next to the British Museum skulls and the Smithsonian skull, which dwarfed the other artefacts.

Margaret Sax had developed a method using SEM for studying tool marks left on carved stone from her work examining Mesopotamian cylinder seals dating from 3,500 BC to 400 BC. She concluded that the two British Museum skulls and the Smithsonian skull had been carved with rotary cutting tools. By analyzing the impressions of the tool marks replicated on the molds used in the SEM tests, Sax could demonstrate to her satisfaction that all three crystal skulls had been carved and polished using modern technology. The remnant marks on the skulls did not resemble those found on the pre-Columbian crystal goblet from Monte Albán. None of these skulls could possibly be Aztec, they concluded.

The next task was to examine the crystal skulls Boban had sold to Alphonse Pinart. Since the Musée de l'Homme had refused to lend its skulls for the study, Walsh flew to Paris after the team's work at the British Museum to have a close look at them. Disappointingly, at the Musée de l'Homme Walsh was only able to examine the larger crystal skull through the glass of its exhibition case.

The results of further research on the British Museum and the Smithsonian skulls, was published in the *The Journal of Archaeological Science* in 2008. Using electron microscopy and X-ray crystallography, British and American researchers found that the British Museum skull was worked with a harsh abrasive substance such as corundum or diamond and shaped using a rotary disc tool made from some suitable metal, while the Smithsonian specimen had been worked with a different abrasive, namely the silicon-carbon compound carborundum (silicon carbide), which is a synthetic substance manufactured using modern industrial techniques. Since the synthesis of carborundum dates only to the 1890s and its wider availability to the 20th century, the researchers concluded that the Smithsonian specimen was made in the 1950s or later.

Mitchell-Hedges Crystal Skull

Perhaps the most famous and enigmatic of the known life-size crystal skulls, the "Mitchell-Hedges" artefact was, allegedly, discovered in 1924 at an archaeological dig at Lubaantun in British Honduras (now Belize) by Anna Mitchell -Hedges, adopted daughter of British adventurer and popular author, F.A. "Mike" Mitchell-Hedges. Anna claimed she found the upper skull buried beneath an altar which had been covered by fallen rocks; the detachable jaw, she said, was found nearby three months later. She claimed that in addition to her father   Dr. Thomas K. Gann, Lady Richmond Brown and Captain T.A. Joyce witnessed the find.

By 1988, Anna's story had changed. She was then saying that on her seventeenth birthday she found the upper skull just sitting partially exposed in the dirt, and no great moving of stones was necessary for her to uncover it. Up until her death, Anna swore this was the true story even though she had signed an affidavit to Frank Dorland in 1968 stating she found the skull in 1926 and never mentioned the fact about her birthday.

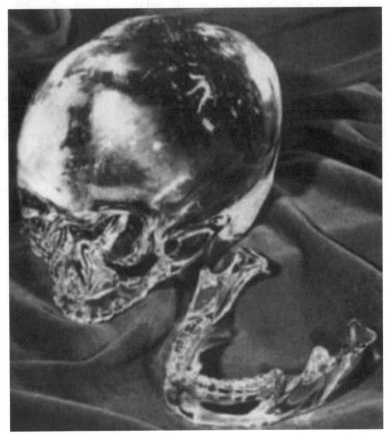

Mitchell-Hedges skull showing detachable jaw.

85

Lubaantun is a pre-Columbian ruined city of the Maya civilization in southern Belize. It is located in the Toledo District. The city dates from the Maya Classic era, flourishing from the 730s to the 890s AD, after which it seems to have been completely abandoned. The architecture is somewhat unusual compared to classical central lowlands Maya sites.

Lubaantun's structures are mostly built of large stone blocks laid with no mortar, primarily black slate, rather than the limestone typical of the region. Several structures have distinctive "in-and-out masonry"; each tier is built with a batter, every second course projecting slightly beyond the course below it. Corners of the step-pyramids are usually rounded and lack stone structures atop the pyramids. The centre of the site is on a large artificially raised platform between two small rivers; it has often been noted that the situation is well-suited to military defence. The ancient name of the site is currently unknown. "Lubaantun" is a modern Maya name meaning "place of fallen stones."

At the start of the 20th century, inhabitants of various Kekchi and Mopan Maya villages in the area mentioned the large ruins to inhabitants of Punta Gorda. British medical doctor and gifted amateur archaeologist Dr. Thomas K. Gann came to investigate the site in 1903 and published two reports about the ruins in 1905. Dr. Gann had a long history of archaeological work in Belize, having directed investigations of Xunantunich in 1894 and 1895. The next expedition was led in 1915 by R.E. Merwin of Harvard University's Peabody Museum, who cleared the site of vegetation, made a more detailed map, took measurements and photographs, and made minor excavations.

In 1924, Gann revisited the ruins and then led adventurer F.A. Mitchell-Hedges to the site. In his typical fashion, Mitchell-Hedges published an article in the *Illustrated London News* in which he claimed to have "discovered" the site. The following year Mitchell-Hedges returned to Lubaantun as a reporter for the *Illustrated London News*, accompanied by his companion Lady Richmond Brown. The team returned for more digs in Lubaantun in subsequent years.

Anna Mitchell-Hedges would later claim that she not only accompanied her father, but also that it was she who found there the now infamous crystal skull. However, there is no evidence that Anna was ever in Belize. Moreover, if the impressive skull actually had been excavated at Lubaantun it would be hard to explain why none of the official reports mention it, why other expedition members deny that it was found there, why no other members of the dig recalled Anna being present, and why the publicity-loving Mike Mitchell-Hedges did not publish even a single mention of the skull before the 1950s.

Anna le Guillon Mitchell-Hedges with the Crystal Skull reportedly found in 1924 at Lubaantun in Belize (formerly British Honduras)

Gann listed all the finds in the expedition. Not one of his reports mentioned the find of a crystal skull or Anna Mitchell-Hedges's presence at the digs. Lady Richmond Brown, who financed the expedition, and Captain T.A. Joyce, who led the treks, both wrote books about the expedition in later years and, like Dr. Gann, neither of them ever mentioned the find of a crystal skull or Anna Mitchell-Hedges either being a part of the team or being at the site. It would have been expected that if an item as sensational as a life-size crystal skull had been discovered at Lubaantun, this would have generated huge interest and produced many written and photographic accounts, none of which appeared at the time or later.

The "Lubaantun" crystal skull was examined and described by Smithsonian researchers as "very nearly a replica of the British Museum skull – almost exactly the same shape, but with more detailed modeling of the eyes and the teeth."

In 2010, *Archaeology*, a publication of the Archaeological Institute of America, published an article that described the acquisition history of the Mitchell-Hedges crystal skull. The article makes no mention of the skull having been owned by Anna Mitchell-Hedges prior to her father's death in 1959. It states that the Mitchell-Hedges skull was first publicly known in 1936, when its existence was made known in the journal *Man* after London art dealer Sydney Burney brought it to the British Museum for study. Burney obtained his crystal skull in early 1933, as attested in a letter he wrote on Burney Gallery stationery to the director of the American Museum of Natural History in February of that year: 'I have just acquired a life-size rock crystal skull with separate jaw, from Mexico, and I shall be glad to know if it is of interest to you or your museum.' It is not known from whom Burney acquired the skull. In his letter he writes that he acquired it from Mexico so he either obtained it while he was in the country, or elsewhere from a Mexican vendor, or from another who said it was from Mexico, or Burney supposed it was of Mexican origin because he had seen the British Museum skull and was struck by its similarities. Burney owned the skull from 1933 until 1943, all this while attempting to find a buyer.

(Significantly, Burney never mentioned Mike or Anna Mitchell-Hedges in published references to the skull. It was only Anna's word when she declared that Burney had either obtained the skull from her father for collateral on a loan or that her father had left it with him for "security" reasons while he went back to Central America. Burney never corroborated these statements and Anna never presented any paperwork or documents as proof of these alleged transactions.)

The British Museum photographed, measured and compared the Burney skull, as it was then called with its own "Aztec" crystal skull [the one I saw in the Museum of Mankind]. The Burney skull is very nearly a replica of the British Museum skull —almost exactly the same shape, but with more detailed modelling of the eyes and the teeth. It also has a separate mandible.

In 1943 Burney asked Sotheby's to auction the skull. The 1943 Sotheby's catalogue gave this description of the skull, a photograph of which was used as the frontispiece: "A superb life -size crystal Carving of a Human Skull, the lower jaw separate, the details are correctly rendered and the carver has given the orbits, zygomatic arches and mastoid processes the similitude of their natural forms."   Burney first asked the British Museum if it was interested in purchasing it at the auction. It certainly did want it for their collection but, missing from the *Archaeology* acquisition account but known from contemporary notes at the British Museum, the employee which it sent to Sotheby's to make the purchase was only authorised to spend up to £340. Because of this budgetary constraint, *Archaeology* states that Mitchell-Hedges succeeding in outbidding the Museum and securing the skull for £400. He announced this purchase to his brother in a letter written in December 1943, which includes perhaps the first mention of a date for the   skull's manufacture:

> The "Collection" grows and grows and grows. You possibly saw in the papers that I acquired that amazing Crystal Skull that was formerly in the "Sydney Burney Collection." It is fashioned from a single block of transparent rock crystal, exactly life size; scientists put the date at pre-1800 B.C., and they estimate it took five generations passing from Father to son, to complete. It is anthropologically perfect in every detail, a superb piece of craftsmanship. There is only one other in t he world known like it, which is in the British Museum and it is acknowledged to be not so fine as this.

However, this account of how the skull came into Mitchell -Hedges' possession in 1943 is challenged by Stephen Mehler   , who states [9] that Mitchell-Hedges did not bid for the lot at Sotheby's. If his adopted daughter's assertions that her father had temporarily passed the skull to Burney for loan or security purposes were true, this would have been a great opportunity for Mike to re-acquire his cherished artefact. Mitchell-

---

[9] ibid

Hedges is known to have been in London at the time of the sale, but Mehler says that Burney withdrew the skull when the bids were not what he wanted (presumably unimpressed with the British Museum's £340 maximum purchase price, and also with not getting any better bids from other interested parties, including from Mitchell-Hedges).

Contrary to what has been written elsewhere, it was not until the following year, 1944, that Mitchell-Hedges bought the crystal skull from Burney for £400, at which point the item becomes the "Mitchell-Hedges Crystal Skull." The crystal skull remained with Mike Mitchell-Hedges until his death in 1959, and then with his adopted daughter until her death in April 2007.

It is interesting that Mitchell-Hedges' letter to his brother refers to scientists' belief that the skull was made pre-1800 BC and that it was the product of five generations of work by the same family. One wonders which scientists he was referring to and when they did their tests (considering that all those carried out since his death have declared the skull to be a recent construction), and how he came to the conclusion about the five generations carrying out the work.

After allegedly procuring the skull from Sotheby's, Mike Mitchell-Hedges mentioned it only briefly in the first edition of his autobiography,[10] without specifying where or by whom it was found. He merely claimed that "it is at least 3,600 years old and according to legend it was used by the High Priest of the Maya when he was performing esoteric rites. It is said that when he willed death with the help of the skull, death invariably followed." All subsequent editions of *Danger My Ally* omitted mention of the skull entirely.

F.A. Mitchell-Hedges (1882-1959) left for America in 1899 when he was 17 years old, worked in New York and Montreal, played poker with J.P. Morgan and his friends, and then went to Mexico to "ride with Villa."

After his adventure in Mexico with Pancho Villa in 1914, Mitchell-Hedges returned first to England and next to Canada where he found and adopted young Anna. They journeyed to California where he put Anna in a boarding school, and he went on to Mazatlan and Honduras. For the next several years Mitchell-Hedges travelled in Central America. He says in *Danger My Ally*, "I now set out the task of discovering Central America. During the next two years I travelled from Spanish Honduras to Guatemala into Nicaragua, and also into the tiny country of San Salvador."

---

[10] Mitchell-Hedges, F., *Danger My Ally*, Elek Books Ltd., London, 1954

By about 1920 he returned to England and visited his ailing friend and mistress, the wealthy Lady Richmond Brown, whose doctors had told her not to travel but rest. She refused and bought a yacht, *Cara*, for the two of them and they set sail for the Caribbean.

Starting in 1921, the pair, plus crew and Mitchell-Hedges' Secretary, Jane Harvey Houlson, cruised and explored the Bay Islands off Honduras, the San Blas Islands off Panama and the area around Jamaica. He and, apparently, Lady Richmond, believed that artefacts which he had found in the Bay Islands pointed to a highly advanced civilization that was now beneath the water, which they equated with Atlantis.

The Atlantis peoples are reputed to have been well versed in the advanced utilisation of crystal power. The renowned psychic Edgar Cayce first mentioned Atlantis in a reading in 1923. He stated that Atlantis was an ancient, now-submerged, highly evolved civilization with ships and aircraft powered by a mysterious form of energy crystal , which gathered solar, lunar, stellar, atmospheric and Earth energies , as well as other, unknown elemental forces. Cayce believed that the Atlanteans used the crystal initial ly to rejuvenate their bodies , with the effect that bodies several hundreds of years old kept a youthful appearance. He said also that the energy was used to power crafts and vehicles that could travel on land, in the sky , and under the sea at the speed of sound.

In the early 1970s this theory became popular again, when Dr . Ray Brown, a naturopathic practitioner from Arizona, allegedly found a mysterious crystal in a pyramid when he was separated from friends whilst diving from the edge of a submarine drop -off called The Tongue of the Ocean. Although he was not carrying a torch , Brown entered the pyramid as it was well lit, though there was no direct light source. Inside he found a metallic rod bearing a red gem and a crystal sphere in a pair of metal bron ze-coloured life -sized hands. As Brown departed, he reportedly felt a presence and heard a voice telling him never to return. Dr. Brown did not tell authorities about the find or his experience until 1975, when he exhibited the crystal for the first time.

One theory in circulation concerning the origin of the Mitchell-Hedges crystal skull is that it is indeed a 12,000 -year-old relic from Atlantis, which somehow came into the possession of the Knights Templar and, much later, was obtained by inner circle members of the Masons. The theory speculates that Mitchell-Hedges, a Freemason, may have somehow acquired the skull either through the secret society or as part of a gambling debt. He then introduced it to the world through the ingenious device of a lost city.

In 1924, three years after the Bay Islands explorations, Mitchell-Hedges and Lady Richmond Brown were in British Honduras at Lubaantun to join Dr. Gann for excavation work at the site.

The Mitchell-Hedges crystal skull is made from a block of clear quartz, measuring 5 inches (13cm) high, 7 inches (18cm) long and 5 inches wide. It closely corresponds in size to a small male human cranium, with near perfect detail, made with such skill that the maker(s) accurately rendered the skull without the globular prominence or superciliary ridges, which are characteristics of a female. As noted earlier, the lower jaw is detachable. In 1970, Anna Mitchell-Hedges agreed to put the skull into the temporary care of art conservator and restorer Frank Dorland for study. Dorland said of the skull in Holy Ice:[11]

> The supranatural properties of the skull are puzzling, of course, but they are very much in existence and are demonstrable to any sensitive person. The skull exhibits and transmits to the human brain all the five senses: taste, touch, smell, sight and hearing. The skull changes visibly in color and transparency, it exhibits its own unmistakable odor when it cares to, it plants thoughts in viewers' minds, it makes people thirsty, it impresses audible sounds on the ears of viewers. To those in meditation before the skull, they feel all this, and they also feel physical pressures on their faces and bodies. When a sensitive person places his hands near the skull, distinct feelings of vibrations and energy are felt and the senses of both heat and cold depending on where the hands are held. As far as sight is concerned, the skull seems to be constantly in a state of flux, exhibiting changes of mood, clarity and colour. The front part of the skull has been observed to turn cloudy like soft cotton candy. The very center of the skull sometimes turns so absolutely clear it seems to disappear into a vast void. The skull itself in total has changed in color from clear crystal to shades of green, violet, purple, amber, red, blue, etc. The visual study of the skull has strong tendencies to exert hypnotic effects on the majority of viewers. On at least one occasion, the skull developed a radiating aura that was in existence and very evident for at least a time of six minutes, allowing not lengthy, but quite accurate studies of its appearance.

---

[11] Dorland, F., *Holy Ice: Bridge to the Subconscious*, Galde Press Inc., St. Paul, MN, 1992.

Numerous sounds have been heard by many observers; the most usual sounds so far have been rhythmic tinkling of high-pitched chimes or bells and a polyphonia-like chorus of what sounds to be many soft human voices. There have been unexplained thumps, cracking and snapping noises and various other sounds which may or may not have any relation at all to the presence of the skull.

(As for) touch or physical feel or sensation, not necessarily in the fingertips as very few individuals have ever been allowed to go so far as the actual fingertip exploration of the skull, most sensations have been reported as the pulling of the eyes or a sensation in the back of the eye sockets, a tightness through the chest area, a tightening of the arm and leg muscles or tendons. Observations have shown that these feelings have frequently been accompanied by an accelerated pulse and rise in blood pressure, usually noticeable in pulsing at both sides of the throat. On occasions, there has been a most distinctive and elusive perfume or odor, with a velvety smooth heavy earth-type muskiness with a high accent note that is both bitter and acid. Taste, the last of the five senses, has not been in particula evidence so far. Probably the most important thing the skull did while it was in my care was to show me that most living things and many material things are surrounded by a halo or aura or whatever you want to call it.

While in Dorland's care the skull came to the attention of writer Richard Garvin, at the time working at an advertising agency where he supervised Hewlett-Packard's advertising account. In 1970, Garvin made arrangements for the Mitchell-Hedges skull to be examined at Hewlett-Packard's crystal laboratories in Santa Clara, California.

From these tests, and from careful studies done by Dorland himself, the skull revealed a whole array of anomalies. Dorland reported being unable to find any tell-tale scratch marks, except for traces of mechanical grinding on the teeth. From tiny patterns in the quartz near the carved surfaces, he speculated that it was first chiseled into rough form, probably using diamonds. The finer shaping, grinding and polishing, Dorland believed, was done by applying innumerable applications of solutions of water and silicon-crystal sand over a period of 150 to 300 years. He said it could be up to 12,000 years old. Although various claims have been made over the years regarding the skull's physical properties, such as an allegedly constant temperature of 70°F (21°C), Dorland reported that there was no difference in properties between it and other natural quartz crystals.

The testers immersed the skull in a bath of benzyl alcohol, which closely matches the refractive index of quartz crystal. The tank had glass sides to allow light projection and viewing. The skull was barely visible, because when quartz is immersed in a matching refractive liquid it tends to become invisible. Polarised light was then projected through the tank and skull, and viewing was done through a polarised screen.

What was astounding to the testers is that they found that the skull and jaw had been carved with total disregard to the natural crystal axis in the quartz. In modern crystallography, the first procedure is always to determine the axis before commencing work to prevent fracturing and breakage during the subsequent shaping process. Yet, the skull's maker(s) appears to have employed methods which eliminated such concerns.

In the polarised light one could easily see wavy stress lines throughout the face of the skull and jawbone. The wavy lines reminded Dorland of moiré patterns. The lines went from the skull to the jaw piece in a perfect continuation of pattern without the slightest flaw or mismatch. There was no possible doubt: the jaw piece was once an integral part of the skull and had subsequently been cut out to make a separate piece. This was an amazing discovery because the cutting loose of the section of the skull and then carving it to form a perfect fit of a corresponding jawbone would have been exponentially more difficult than merely shaping a separate jawbone from another chunk of crystal. Dorland reflected on the implications and concluded that the skull was a vital religious or ceremonial object shaped from a specially selected specimen of pure rock crystal that required the utmost care and skill regardless of time, cost or effort.

The tests also showed that the unknown artist(s) used no metal tools. Dorland was unable to find signs of any tell-tale scratch marks on the crystal, under high-powered microscopic analysis. Indeed, most metals would have been ineffectual for the crystal has a specific gravity of 2.65, and a Mohs hardness factor of 7. In other words, even a modern penknife cannot make a mark on it.

The enigma of the skull, however, does not end with just its making. The zygomatic arches (the bone arch extending along the sides and front of the cranium) are accurately separated from the skull piece and act as light pipes, using principles similar to modern optics, to channel light from the base of the skull to the eye sockets. The eye sockets in turn are miniature concave lenses that also transfer light from a source below into the upper cranium. Finally, in the interior of the skull is a ribbon prism and tiny light tunnels, by which objects held beneath the skull are magnified and brightened.

Garvin, who authored a book about the Mitchell-Hedges Skull (*Crystal Skull*), believes it was designed to be placed over an upward shining beam. The result, with the various light transfers and prismatic effects, would illuminate the entire skull and cause the sockets to become glowing eyes. Dorland performed experiments using this technique and reported the skull 'lights up like it was on fire.'

Still another finding reveals knowledge of weights and fulcrum points. The jaw piece fits precisely onto the skull by two polished sockets, which allow the jaw to move up and down. The skull itself can be balanced exactly where two tiny holes are drilled on each side of its base, which probably once held suspending supports. So perfect is the balance at these points that the slightest breeze causes the skull to nod back and forth, the jaw opening and cl osing as a counterweight. The visual effect is that of a living skull, talking and articulating.

Observers have reported that the skull will change colour. Sometimes the frontal cranium clouds up and resembles white cotton, while at other times it turns perfectly clear as if the space within has vanished into an empty void. Over a period from 5 to 6 minutes, a dark spot often begins forming on the right side and slowly blackens the entire skull, then recedes and disappears as mysteriously as it came. Other observers have seen strange scenes reflected in the eye sockets, scenes of buildings and other objects even though the skull is resting against a black background. Still others have heard ringing noises emanating from within, and at least on one occasion a distinct glow from no known light source surrounded the skull like an aura for up to six minutes. Photographs have been taken of "pictures" which sometimes form within the skull, including images of "UFO" forms, and of what appears to be the Caracol observatory at the Toltec-Mayan site of Chichen Itza.

Dorland was of the opinion that what is happening in all these phenomena is that the 'crystal stimulates an unknown part of the brain, opening a psychic door to the absolute.' He remarked that , 'Crystals continuously put out electric -like radio waves. Since the brain does the same thing, they naturally interact.' He found, too, that periodic happenings in the crystal skull are due to the positions of the sun, moo n and planets in the sky.

Researcher Marianne Zezelic agrees that the skull was primarily used to stimulate and amplify the psychic abilities in its handlers. She observes: 'Crystal serves as an accumulator of terrestial magnetism. By gazing at the crystal, the eyes set up a harmonic relation stimulating the magnetism collected in that portion of the brain known as the cerebellum. The cerebellum therefore becomes a reservoir of magnetism which influences the quality of the magnetic outflow through the eyes, thus setting up a continuous flow of magnetism between gazer and crystal. The amount of energy entering the brain eventually increases to such a proportion as to affect the poles of the brain, a region extending just above the eyes, contributing to psychic phenomena.'

In their 2008 collaboration,[12] Childress and Mehler suggest that the amazing properties of quartz crystal: its tetrahedral lattice structure, its internal repeating and geometrically aranged molecular patterns, its axis of rotation allowing perfect polarization of light, and its piezoelectrical faculty makes it entirely possible that crystal skulls may be the depositories of ancient wisdom. They note also that these qualities make quartz crystal an ideal material for "psychic" experiments and "light" experiments, suggesting that, in theory, a piece of crystal quartz, or a crystal skull, could and would react to what was around it, including light, electricity, pressure, sound, vibrations of all sorts, and probably human thought waves and the human electrical field.

Going a step further, Tom Bearden, an expert in the field of psychotronic studies, believes that in the hands of a skilled meditator and mental focaliser, the Mitchell-Hedges crystal skull also serves as a vehicle to transform life-force energy into electromagnetic energy and other physical effects. He also claims that the skull aids in healing through the altering of its crystalline resonance to match that of a patient's mind and body frequencies, and affects curing energies on the skull that will manifest in the patient's auric field.

In 1986, Dorland received a letter from historical writer Frank Joseph, author of such books as *Crystals of Atlantis* and *The Lost Pyramid of Rock Lake,* who expressed an interest in making a facial reconstruction of the Mitchell-Hedges skull. Dorland was receptive because he had often received questions from people who were curious about what the model for the skull carving might have looked like. Also, in his personal meditations on the skull, Dorland would inwardly see a young woman's face and had mentioned this to people. Joseph told Dorland that he knew of a well-known physical anthropologist, Dr. Clyde Snow at the University of Oklahoma. Joseph asked if it would be possible to show one of the molds that Dorland had made from the skull to Dr. Snow to see what he thought about the viability of a forensic reconstruction. Dorland agreed and shipped a plaster mold to Joseph.

---

[12] ibid

Dr. Snow was impressed with the mold and concluded that the skull was not just an artist's conception of a human skull but was a copy made of an actual skull of a young female, a finding that contradicts previous observations that the Mitchell-Hedges skull closely corresponds in size and form to that of a small male human cranium.

Consequently, Joseph became more encouraged and was eventually led to the team of Peggy C. Caldwell, a collaborator with the anthropology department of the Smithsonian Institute, and detective Frank Domingo, a composite artist with the New York police department. Joseph sent the forensic team the mold, and Dorland sent some glossary photographs he had taken of the skull. The reconstruction team came up with the image below left as the face of the person who had modelled the Mitchell-Hedges Skull. The image on the right is the one that Dorland sketched from his meditations. There is no denying the similarities. A few days after the Hewlett-Packard tests, Anna Mitchell-Hedges took the skull from Dorland and travelled by bus to Ontario, where she lived off and on for the next thirty years. The skull resided there with her in Kitchener, Ontario, and then later in England.

In a 1970 letter Anna Mitchell-Hedges stated that she was "told by the few remaining Maya that the skull was used by the high priest to will death." For this reason, the artefact is sometimes referred to as "The Skull of Doom." Of, course, Anna could equally have learned of this purported characteristic from her father who described this grisly quality of the skull in *Danger My Ally* in 1954. Anna toured with the skull occasionally up to 1990, charging a fee for viewings. She continued to grant interviews about the artefact until her death in 2007. In her last eight years, Anna lived in Chesterton, Indiana, with Bill Homann, whom she married in 2002. She died on April 11, 2007, aged a hundred. Since that time the Mitchell-Hedges Skull has been owned by Homann (despite claims to ownership by a small tribe of nieces and nephews), who continues to believe in its mystical properties. Known as the Skull of Doom, the Skull of Love, or simply the Mitchell-Hedges Skull, it is said to emit blue lights from its eyes and has reputedly crashed computer hard drives. In November 2007, Homann took the skull to the office of Jane MacLaren Walsh in the Smithsonian's National Museum of Natural History for

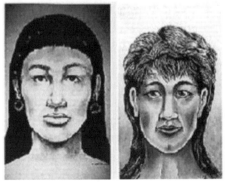

Mitchell-Hedges skull reconstructions

examination. Walsh carried out a detailed examination of the skull using ultraviolet light, a high-powered light microscope and computerized tomography. Homann took the skull to the museum again in 2008 so it could be filmed for a Smithsonian Networks documentary, *Legend of the Crystal Skull*, and on this occasion, Walsh was able to take two sets of silicone molds of surface tool marks for SEM analysis. The SEM micrographs reportedly revealed evidence that the crystal had been worked with a high speed, hard metal rotary tool coated with a hard abrasive such as diamond. Walsh's extensive research on artefacts from Mexico and Central America showed that artisans carved stone by abrading the surface with stone or wooden tools, and in later pre-Columbian times with copper tools in combination with a variety of abrasive sands or pulverized stone. These examinations led Walsh to the conclusion that the skull was probably carved in the 1930s and was most likely based on the British Museum "Aztec" skull, which had been exhibited fairly continuously from 1898.

In a National Geographic documentary, "The Truth Behind the Crystal Skulls," forensic artist Gloria Nusse performed a facial reconstruction over the skull. According to Nusse, the resulting face had female and European characteristics. As it was hypothesized that the Crystal Skull was a replica of an actual human skull, the conclusion was that it could not have been created by ancient Americans.

The Mitchell-Hedges skull and the British Museum skull were in 1936 the subject of a series of articles in *Man* in which British Museum archaeology curator Adrian Digby and physical anthropologist G.M. Morant debated whether the two were based on the same original skull, which Digby posited was revered as a Mesoamerican "death god." Interestingly, Digby added to his remarks in a commentary on the articles when he suggested that the 'British Museum skull was copied from an original skull, and that at a later date [echoing Walsh's conclusions] the Burney skull was a sort of composite copy relying for its proportions on the skull now in the Museum and for its anatomical detail on some human skull in the possession of the carver.' Digby's remarks cast significant doubts on the claims made by F.A. Mitchell-Hedges and his adopted daughter that the Lubaantun find was of great antiquity.

The Aztecs believed in thirteen heavens and nine levels of the underworld. In their belief system, the manner in which one dies dictates the nature of the soul's journey in the hereafter; but souls on all levels are obligated to perform duties to maintain life on Earth, working with the Elementals to ensure sufficient rainfall, curing diseases, the sewing of seeds for new growth, and so on. Several legends attributed to various

American Indian cultures address these beliefs. One concerns the legend that thirteen life-size crystal skulls exist that will be activated by being brought together, comparable to combining all the parts to build a quantum supercomputer. One version of this story says that the thirteen skulls were manufactured by an advanced civilisation that lived in the Earth's interior, the skulls containing information on the history of their race, their relationship with humanity and humanity's future. These supposed inner earth "aliens" scattered the thirteen skulls around the Earth, to be found and reunited at a later date. Some claim this race was extraterrestrial in origin. In this scenario, one can envisage it as a likely source for Spielberg's *Indiana Jones and the Kingdom of the Crystal Skull*, in which the thirteen enthroned, super-intelligent "aliens" hail from an inner-Earth dimension. In the movie Indy asks John Hurt's character, Oxley, about the crystal skull visitors' startling mode of departure. 'Where did they go? Space?' Oxley, who had it figured all along, replies, 'Not into space. Into the space between spaces' revealing his insight that the supremely advanced beings were not "aliens" but a natural component of Mother Earth's companion forces of living nature, which occupy a higher dimension of creation that interlaces our physical plane.

Another version of the story may be traced to the Quiche Mayan tale of creation, the Popol Vuh, in which the thirteen skulls were hidden by Mayan shamans to be rediscovered at a time of great need. As in the other legend, they contain vital information about the origin of mankind, our true purpose in creation, and our destiny. When we are ready to receive this wisdom, the skulls will be found and decoded, enabling the further advancement of the human race. Taking the legend further east, in a 1988 work[13] the authors contend that thirteen crystal skulls were kept beneath the Potala Palace in Tibet. However, they claim that these were originally created to be used in the "Thirteen Healing Temples of Atlantis." Like Dorland, they believe that certain crystal skulls are from 10,000 to 30,000 years old. One date given for the Mitchell-Hedges Skull is 17,000 years.

Stephen Mehler suggests that Anna Mitchell-Hedges may have engaged in a deliberate fraud. She had her father's autobiography republished in 1995 (first published in 1954). In this American version there is a photo, not present in the original, of Anna and a boy. Its caption states that the girl is Anna Mitchell-Hedges at age eleven and a half, that the other figure is a Mayan boy with hookworm disease, and that Anna had lived with the Maya. Upon examination, this photo could not

[13] Bowen, S; Nocerino, F; Shapiro, J., *Mystery of the Crystal Skulls Revealed*, J & S Pacifica, 1988

possibly have been of Anna Mitchell-Hedges. In 1918, when aged eleven, she was in Canada and could not have lived with the Maya before she was adopted by Mitchell-Hedges. Mehler believes this was a fraud perpetrated by Anna to create the fantasy that she had been at Lubaantun, had lived with the Maya, and found the crystal skull in the 1920s.

Today, one of the principal gemstone centres is Idar-Oberstein in southwest Germany. In the 1850s Oberstein was the leading region in the world for sources of agate and jasper, and modern quartz crystal carving. New markets opened up subsequent to increasing Prussian explorations into Brazil in the 19th century. Great quantities of all varieties of quartz crystal flowed into Idar and Oberstein for carving into many different objects. May the region's history and expertise in crystal workmanship be connected with a very curious account concerning Heinrich Himmler's "Grailhunter," Otto Rahn, the medievalist scholar and philologist who was the subject of my first book for AUP,[14] and who was born and raised in Michelstadt, just 100 miles from Oberstein? In 2011, the *Bild* newspaper described Rahn as having possessed a crystal skull. In the article, "*Kristallschädel von SS-Führer Heinrich Himmler entdeckt?*", *Bild* reports on a newly discovered list, which states: "35 valuable art treasures that should be transported on the orders of... Adolf Hitler and Heinrich Himmler... can be found on the... four-page paper, including... 263-2 FRSS collection Rahn, no. 25592, leather, Crystal Skull, colonies, South America." *Bild*'s source was Luc Bürgin, editor of *Mysteries* magazine, who reports finding hidden in an old wooden box in an attic in a Bavarian residence the list and the crystal skull: 12-kilos in weight, 17.5cm high and 21cm deep. Bürgin describes the skull as the so-called 13th skull of the Mayans (but does not explain why he arrived at the description), adding that the legend foretold that all thirteen together would on 21 December 2012 create a new age of light to prevent the Apocalypse. It is an extraordinary story, tantalisingly short on detail, but illustrates that the legend of the Crystal Skulls of Mesoamerica is far from simple, most certainly not complete, and has many more questions than answers.

Eugène Boban

[14] Graddon, N., *Otto Rahn and the Quest for the Holy Grail*, Adventures Unlimited Press, illinois, 2008

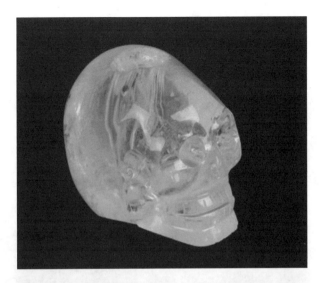

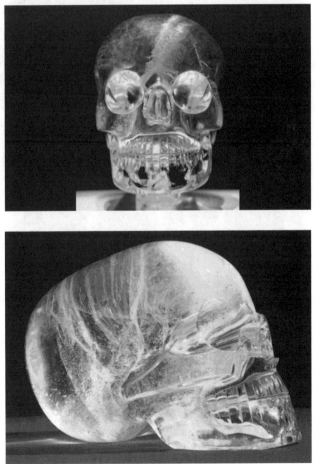

Paris skull top, British Museum skull bottom two

"Mike" Mitchell-Hedges

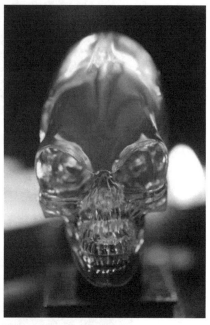

Skull from the 4th Indiana Jones movie

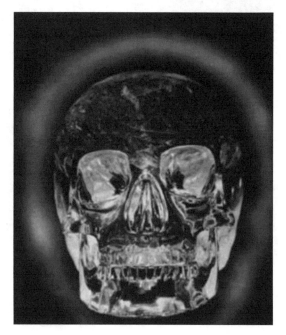

Mitchell-Hedges Skull with the observed "halo" effect

Chapter 7

The Head of God

The esoteric record, consisting largely of stories told and handed down through the generations, describes a very different narrative concerning the nature of Jesus' death than that told in the Gospels. The record was supported by a Catholic priest, who, in the weeks before the death of Pope Pius X and the commencement of the Great War, found deep in the Vatican archives a letter written by Mary Magdalene while she was travelling by boat to Gaul after the Crucifixion. Gifted in languages, the young priest was a member of Pius' inner circle of confidential advisers. Pius had asked him to go to the Archives to find a particular item of scripture.

In 1977, the priest described the letter's contents to friends in his native Tuscan village. He wanted to share its contents with those he could trust before he died. At the time, my American friend Nelson was staying as a guest of these Italian friends for a few days vacation. They vouched for Nelson's integrity, allowing him to share in the priest's confidential disclosures.

The letter explained that before he commenced his three-year Ministry beginning with his baptism by John the Baptist and ending in Crucifixion in Jerusalem, the young Jesus came to a special place above Qumran called the Caves of Zohar. Here he received instructions and insight from Zohar, an unusual teacher steeped in the mysteries of the Qabbalah and who used crystal balls to illustrate his lessons.

It was to this place, years earlier, that the three Persian Magi had come. They had discovered a phenomenon in the heavens for which their knowledge and ancient charts had no explanation. Here, Zohar told the Magi that there would shortly be born a special child who would be the catalyst for mystics and metaphysicians through years to come. He would eventually create the curtain or shroud for the Ancient Truths, which had existed from the beginnings of time. Zohar told Gaspar, Melchior and Balthazar that what the child would eventually teach he would learn in this cave during four occasions that he would visit. Those who followed him would create a religion that would be full of attempts to control humanity by spiritual manipulation. As the religion grew, it would spread throughout the world. Wars would be fought because of it; and much anger and hatred would arise from its contacts with other world religions. Behind these chaotic actions, esoteric mysticism would continue working through disciplined individuals who were aligned to Mother Nature and their "Inner Journey." The child would die in his forty-first year.

Jesus' mother was Mary of Nazareth. Mary had entered the Temple of Ishtar in Jerusalem at the age of thirteen. Her qualifications were of the highest for she was a direct descendent of four previous high priestesses of the Temple: Tamar, Ruth, Bathsheba and Rahab. In her fifteenth year. Mary was chosen to lay with Joseph and, for the first time in 2,500 years of the Goddess tradition, an initiate conceived.

As the High Priestess of the Temple, Mary Magdalene summoned Joseph to the high altar to notify him of the miracle. Somewhat embarrassed, Joseph humbly asked if he could take Mary as his wife. Approval was given under two conditions. He was to take Mary to the Mother Temple in Alexandria for sanctification ceremonies, and he must swear to keep this information secret.

However, rumours of this potential high birth began to circulate throughout Jerusalem just as Joseph was preparing to take Mary to Egypt. Mary Magdalene soon became aware of the concern that the Temple of Solomon's inner council had regarding these rumours. If it was true that one of the Ishtar temple initiates had conceived, something that had never happened before, then the child of the birth would be a definite threat to the masculine god of the Jews. In fact, the times were so harsh and cruel in Roman occupied Jerusalem that people might even be calling this child the Messiah.

After the birth, Joseph and Mary returned to Jerusalem with the baby and moved into quarters near the Temple of Ishtar. As the child grew, he played in the Temple, learning of the power and subtleties of women. At the age of thirteen, Jesus was sent by Mary Magdalene and her priestesses to the Caves of Zohar for the first of the four occasions that he would visit for further initiation and the highest teaching. Afterwards, Jesus travelled to Egypt and studied in the Mother Temple of Isis to gain further understanding of feminine power. Subsequently, Mary Magdalene was called to Alexandria by the High Council of Ishtar to be told that she was to return with Jesus to Jerusalem where they would wed. Mary was twenty-three years the young man's senior and at first protested. Jesus answered Mary's concern, saying that love was ageless and that its power would produce a child who would be trained in a far-off land by a Master of Light.

Another that found their way to Zohar's unusual place of learning was a middle-aged woman, Celicia, who had fled from powerful enemies in Rome. Zohar seated her at a loom and asked her to weave from a special yarn a cloth two lengths and one width of her body. Its warp had to be perfect. Thirty years later, after unravelling the cl oth and starting over more times than she could remember, Celecia finished the cloth. The completion of the cloth took place just before the Crucifixion.

Pontius Pilate had given two members of the Sanhedrin, disguised as simple Jews, permission to remove Jesus from the cross and entomb him. Celicia and two helpers from the cave overpowered the two men as they were making their way with the body through an olive grove. They took Jesus, barely alive, to a waiting cart. One of the helpers applied a herbal salve on his wounds and gave him an elixir to slow the bleeding and allow him to enter a state of suspended animation.

The specially woven cloth was wrapped around his body to prevent infection and keep him warm. Jesus was put in the cart, covered in hay and taken to Zohar's cave. In this healing place Jesus, laid upon an altar, in coma and wrapped in the magical shroud, remained alive, thus allowing his astral form to travel beyond the confines of the cave. He appeared to his mother, Mary Magdalene, his disciples, and to others who would eventually create Christianity. The Bible refers to these appearances:

Mark 16:9
Now when Jesus was risen early the first day of the week, he appeared first to Mary Magdalene, out of whom he had cast seven devils.

John 20:17
Jesus said to her, "Touch me not, lest I ascend to the father."

Finally, he returned to his body one last time and Zohar conducted a special Qabbalah ceremony with his magical crystal balls. In addition to those who had helped Jesus to stay alive so that his astral energy could make its appearances, also present was Mary Magdalene. Suddenly, three bolts of lightning pierced the walls of the cavern and entered the crystal balls. One concentrated bolt projected into the crystal ball that was positioned directly behind Jesus' head. A beam of electricity travelled from one ball to the other and the cavern lit up like brilliant sunshine. In one final flash the cavern went dark:

Matthew 27:50, 51

Jesus, when he had cried again with a loud voice, yielded up the ghost. And behold, the veil of the temple was rent in twain from the top to the bottom; and the earth did quake, and the rocks rent.

The shroud lay limp upon the altar; the body had vanished. The only visible sign that one had been there was the image that was left on the shroud, an imprint made indelibly by the chemicals in the cloth combined with the massive electrical charge. The weaver folded the cloth carefully and walked out of the cave.

Mary Magdalene, High Priestess of the Temple of Ishtar, knew that she and Jesus' young son had to flee Jerusalem. The night before they were due to sail to France, Mary returned to the Great Mother Temple in Jerusalem to pass on the leadership power to her first assistant.

While in meditation, there was a blinding flash of light which filled the inner sanctuary. She opened her eyes and there in front of her was the most beautiful crystal she had ever seen. It was in the shape of a skull. From somewhere deep within the skull came these words:

Before you is the skull that represents your husband and the priesthood of the Ancient Wisdoms. It is a symbol of him and his death on Golgotha, the Skull. You must take it from this land and protect it with your life for it is the clear, pure link to all that is true, powerful and holy. It is through your son that the link of the Ancient Wisdoms, Jesus, the Mother Goddess and the future will be made.

Mary Magdalene and her son, assisted by Bartholomew, took the skull by a rudderless ship to France, a land new to her but one in whose deeper recesses she knew would unfold a new Goddess tradition. She knew that the world will always want a natural belief system which does not strain credulity or insult intelligence. Such is the story handed down; make of it what you will.

Where is the crystal skull of Jesus today? It is rumoured that the Jesus skull is safely secured in a special nature place beyond the reach of human hands, protected by Mother Earth.

As for the Shroud, it is also rumoured that it was destroyed by command of Alexander VI because the Borgia Pope thought that the image magically etched into the cloth was not sufficiently masculine in appearance and, therefore, unsuitable as a symbol of a misogynist, male Church. The story goes that the Pope's son, Cesar Borgia, ordered Leonardo da Vinci to make a replacement, which is the shroud that is to be seen today in the Cathedral of St. John the Baptist in Turin.

Salvator Mundi, Leonardo da Vinci

The Penitent Magdalen, George de la Tour

Mary Magdalene in Prayer, Annibale Caracci

"Noli me Tangere", Hans Holbein the Younger

Chapter 8

The Black Stone and Goddess Worship

In 1993, *Mercian Mysteries* No.14 published Bob Trubshaw's article, *The Black Stone-the Omphalos of the Goddess,* concerning the history of Goddess worship and its association with the mysteri ous legend of the Black Stone. Later, Alby Stone made an additional contribution to the topic in her article, *Goddess of the Black Stone.*

Trubshaw spoke of "omphali," sacred centres that a number of civilisations created or adopted at various times in history. He points out that many of these centres inv olved ceremonial placement of special stones, some of which were black. These Black Stones are reputed in legend to have fallen from the stars. Clearly, meteorites the size of these large boulders would explode into tiny fragments on impact, but the literal truth is unimportant when compared to the stones' symbolism as serving as an integral aspect of the Cosmic Axis and a link between this world and the heavens.

Perhaps the best-known Black Stone, and the most revered, is the Ka'bah at Mecca. Ka'bah means "cube," and this describes the shape of the black stone structure on a marble base , which stands in the centre court of the Great Mosque, Masjidul Haram, at the centre of Mecca. It stands about 50 feet high by about 35 feet wide. Set into the eastern corner is the sacred stone, covered by an elaborately embroidered black drape. This stone is shrouded i n mystery but photographs taken surreptitiously by pilgrims (the taking of photos in the Ka-bah is strictly forbidden) reveal a polished black stone , of which less t han two feet is visible. It is s et in a large solid silver mount. Trubshaw remarks on its close resemblance to the vulva of the goddess.

Tradition holds that it was a meteorite , white in colour when it first landed and then gradually blackened. The faithful attribute this change in colour to the belief that the stone absorbs the sins of the pilgrims, but it is consistent with known meteorites which are white at first but oxidise over a period of time.

Rufus Camphausen[15] has theorized that the Moslem religion has its origins in goddess worship and suggests that Allah is a revamped version of the ancient goddess Al'Lat, and that it is her shrine which has continued as the Ka'bah. Al'Lat is a triple goddess, similar to the Greek lunar deity Kore/Demeter/Hecate. Each aspect of this trinity corresponds to a phase of the moon. In the same way, Al'Lat has three names known to the initiate: Q're, the crescent moon or the maiden (Mohammed was from a tribe of the Quraysh that not only worshipped the goddess Q're but were the sworn guardians of her shrine); Al'Uzza, literally "the strong one" who is the full moon and the mother aspect; and Al'Menat, the waning but wise goddess of fate, prophecy and divination. Islamic tradition continues to recognise these three but labels them "daughters of Allah."

Al'Lat's full moon aspect, Al'Uzza, was especially worshipped at the Ka'bah where she was served by seven priestesses. Her worshippers circled the holy stone seven times, once for each of the ancient seven planets, and did so in total nudity. Near the Ka'bah is the ever-flowing well, Zamzam, which cools the throats of the countless millions of pilgrims. Today, the *tawaf*, the sevenfold counterclockwise circuit of the *Ka'bah*, is a memory of that ancient practice.

The older practice is a strong echo of the descent of the Sumerian goddess Inanna (and her Babylonian and Roman equivalents, Ishtar and Venus) through the seven gates of the underworld, the gatekeepers demanding the removal of a garment at each gate until she stands naked before her elder sister, Ereshkigal, "Queen of the Great Earth," the goddess of death and the underworld.

Another name for Ereshkigal is *Allatu*, "the goddess," which is clearly an earlier form of *Al'Lat/Alilat*. This suggests that, far from being a moon-goddess, *Al'Lat* is actually the goddess of the underworld, who could indeed be fittingly described as the "Old Woman." The present-day priests of the sacred shrine are still known as Beni Shaybah or "Sons of the Old Woman," Shaybah being the famous Queen Sheeba of Solomon's time. Sheeba appears under the guise of Lilith in the Near East and as Hagar ("the Egyptian") in the Hebrew mythology of the Old Testament.

Stone points out that the Hebrew word *sheba* can mean either "seven" or "oath." The Biblical place-name *Beer-sheba* is literally "the well of seven," the well in question being dug by Abraham and where he made a peace-treaty with Abimelech. Abraham gave seven ewe-lambs to seal the pact, and the place was named to commemorate the event.

---

[15] Rufus C. Camphausen, *'The Ka'bah at Mecca'*, Bres (Holland) No.139, 1989

Stone remarks on the tradition that the Queen of Sheba was black and of *djinn* ancestry; in other words, she was a divine being in her own right, possibly even a hypostasis of *Al'Lat* herself. On the whole, Stone observes, the pattern presented here suggests that *Al'Lat* is essentially a chthonic mother-goddess, a deity of the underworld associated with fidelity and covenants, a later form of Ereshkigal, who has retained many of her older attributes, albeit in a slightly distorted form.

Q're (or Qure), the maiden aspect of Al'Lut, seems to be the origin of the Greek "Kore." Camphausen suggests that the holy Koran (qur'an in Arabic) is the "Word of Qure." Legend has it that it was copied from a divine prototype, *Mother of the Book*, that appeared in heaven at the beginning of time.

Returning to the geomantic significance of the *Ka'bah*, Gerald Hawkins (*Stonehenge Decoded*) has argued that it is exceedingly accurately aligned on two heavenly phenomena: the cycles of the moon and the rising of Canopus, the brightest star after Sirius.

In a thirteenth-century Arabic manuscript by Mohammed ibn Abi Bakr Al Farisi, it is stated that the alignment is set up for the setting crescent moon, an ancient symbol of the virgin-goddess. The Egyptian city known as Canopus seems also have been a goddess temple; the Greek historian Strabo (63 BC-21 AD) considered the place to be notorious for wild sexual activities, indicating that he was referring to a temple where sacred "prostitution" was practised in celebration of the goddess.

Deities of other cultures known to have been associated with stones include Aphrodite at Paphos, Cybele at Pessinus and later Rome, Astarte at Byblos, famous Artemis/Diana of Ephesus, and, in Petra, the betyls culture of the ancient Nabataeans.

After Mecca and Medina, the third most holy site of Islam is the Dome of the Rock on Temple Mount in Jerusalem. One reason for its high significance is probably the fact that in the Dome of the Rock is the *Eben Shetiyyah*, a flat, yellow-brown, asymmetrical rock believed by many Jews to be, as its name implies, the "Stone of Foundation," around which God built the world, and which was used as the pedestal of the Ark of the Covenant. The Ark was a symbol of the Hebrews' communal pact with God; it was also used as a weapon in the destruction of Jericho, an event replete with sevens. It also contained the two stone tablets engraved with the Law, and sometimes presumed to have been of meteoric origin. Beneath the *Eben Shetiyyah* is a deep hollow known to Muslims as *Bir-el-Arweh*, the Well of Souls. In Jewish lore, the *Eben Shetiyyah* rests upon and keeps in place the waters of the Abyss (that is, *abzu*).

One Jewish tradition has it that David dug the foundations of the Temple at Jerusalem and discovered the *Eben Shetiyyah* during his excavations. When he tried to remove the stone, the waters of the Abyss began to well up.

This parallels the Islamic tradition that has Mohammed casting down an idol that stood in the sacred complex at Mecca. According to the tradition, this idol was blocking a well inside the *Ka'bah*, and the waters began to flow from that moment. Supposedly, the idol represented a deity named *Hubal*, which seems to be a version of the name of the goddess who was known elsewhere as *Kybele*, and who was venerated in Phrygia in the form of a stone, a black aerolite that was presented to Rome in 204 BC by King Attalus. Considering that the Arabs habitually worshipped stones as representations of their divinities, Alby Stone suggests that the idol *Hubal* was a stone of celestial provenance.

Interestingly, the goddess *Na'ila*, one of a host of divinities venerated at the Meccan site, supposedly appeared in the form of a black woman at the time Mohammed destroyed the idols and ran screaming from the sacred place.

Robert Wenning's research[16] into the Nabataean culture investigates the presence in Petra in Jordan of many rock-cut votive niches containing betyls (aniconic stone slabs).[17] These betyls are often explained as representations of Dushara, the main deity of the Nabataeans. The Nabataeans were an ancient Aramaic-speaking Arab people who inhabited northern Arabia and then Levant. Their chief settlement was the assumed capital city of Raqmu (present-day Petra).

The Nabateans emerged as a distinct civilization and political entity between the 4th and 2nd centuries BC. Described as fiercely independent by contemporary Greco-Roman accounts, the Nabataeans were annexed into the Roman Empire by Emperor Trajan in 106 AD.

Philo of Byblos in the second century AD explains that betyls were invented by the god Ouranos when he managed to create animated stones, which fell from the heavens and possessed magical power. The features described indicate round or spherical, red or black meteorites that were especially venerated as sacred stones in the Roman East. The two most famous of these betyls are the meteor of Kybele from Pessinus in Asia Minor and the omphaloid Elagabal-Ammudates from Emesa, both of which were transferred to Rome.

---

[16] '*The Betyls of Petra*'

[17] Aniconism is the use of symbolic forms such as standing stones as objects of worship, rather than using figural images.

A sacred place to the Nabataeans was a gorge called Qattar ad-Dayr, where water is dripping from the rock. Here archaeologist found a votive hewn in the rock with an inscription that has been translated as "the betyl of the goddess Bosra," or alternatively, "the betyl of mother goddess AI-Uzza [or Allat], the goddess of Bosra."

Alby Stone explains that the name of Allat's son Dusura in the Nabataeans' system is a version of Tammuz/Dumuzi/Du'uzi, the vegetation god characterised by a seasonal death and resurrection who dwells in the underworld for half the year. His full name in Sumerian is *Dumu-zi-abzu*, "faithful son of the abyssal waters ," a rough but appropriate rendering of *abzu*, which denotes the spaces below the earth as well as the primal waters.

Dumuzi/Tammuz, of course, was the reason for Inanna/Ishtar/Venus descending to Allatu's realm. Once there, Ishtar lies about the reason for her visit, so breaking the "law of the underworld which must be fulfilled" and is sentenced to death by the *Anunnaki*, the seven judges of the underworld.

Abzu (later *Apsu*) was the natural home of the   *Sebettu*, the seven sages associated by Babylonians with the foundation of culture and the seven major cities of the region.

Wenning speaks of a different kind of Nabataean betyl , the "eye betyl." Here the high, rectangular plain slab is represented with square "eyes" and a straight "nose," which in votive inscriptions seem to refer to female deities, AI-Kutba and AI-Uzza, although some authorities suggest they are commemorative to Isis. The betyls' star -shaped eyes have been interpreted as the morning and the evening stars, the two aspects of the planet Venus.

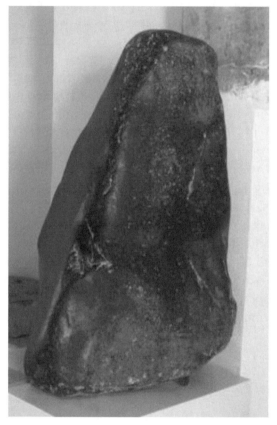

Sanctuary of Aphrodite at Palaepafos, Cyprus

Chapter 9

The Golden Tip

The apex of the Great Pyramid at Giza was once adorned with a pyramidion (plural, pyramidia), a common practice of the Egyptians who often added a capstone upon structures such as pyramids and obelisks.

During Egypt's Old Kingdom, pyramidia were generally made of diorite, granite or fine limestone. In the Middle Kingdom period through to the end of the pyramid-building era, they were built from granite . In the case of pyramid capstones, the pyramidion was often covered with gold or electrum (a naturally occurring alloy of gold and silver, with trace amounts of copper and other metals or gold) to reflect the rays of the sun. Middle Kingdom pyramidia were often inscribed with royal titles and religious symbols.

Very few pyramidia have survived into modern times. Most that remain are made of polished black granite and inscribed with the name of the pyramid's owner. Four pyramidia , the world's largest collection , are housed in the main hall of the Egyptian Museum in Cairo. Among them are the pyramidia from the so-called Black Pyramid of Amenemhat III at Dahshur and of the Pyramid of Khendjer at Saqqara.

The Egyptians associated such pyramidia with the Benben Stone. The Benben in Egyptian mythology is a stone with a conical shape and, according to some theorists, may be of extraterrestrial origin. It represented the cycle of the seasons and was a symbol of the Phoenix. As such, it was an important feature of the Temple of the Phoenix, which was within the precinct of the Great Sun Temple of Heliopolis.

In the mythology of ancient Egypt, there are several accounts of the creation of the world. One of these is centred on the god Atum who brought the universe into being. In the beginning, there was nothing but darkness and chaos. Subsequently, it was out of the primordial waters of Nu that the primordial hill, known as the Benben stone, arose, on top of which stood Atum. As the Benben stone rose from the primeval waters, it has been suggested that this word is associated with the verb 'weben,' which is the Egyptian hieroglyph for "to rise."

In another verion of the myth, the Benben stone was the primeval hill on which Atum first landed. The god looked around and realised that there was nothing around him but darkness and chaos. He was all alone. Desiring companionship, Atum began the work of creation. In some versions of the myth, Atum masturbated and through this act created Shu (the god of air) and Tefnut (the goddess of moisture). In other variations of the story, these deities were created by Atum's copulation with his own shadow.

Shu and Tefnut left Atum on the Benben stone and went away to create the rest of the world. After some time, Atum is said to have grown worried about his children. Removing his eye, he sent it in search of them. Shu and Tefnut returned with their father's eye, and Atum, seeing his children return, shed tears of joy. These teardrops, which fell on the Benben stone on which Atum was standing, transformed into human beings.

The Benben stone is also recorded to have been a sacred object that was once kept in the special shrine known as the "hwt benben," which translates as "House of the Benben." This sacred relic was in the innermost sanctuary of the temple in Heliopolis where Atum once served as its chief deity. The original cult object is said to have been lost at some point in history. Nevertheless, based on pictorial evidence, it has been suggested that this was an upright stone with a rounded top. Other solar temples would also have their own Benben stones. For example, the temple of Aten in El-Amarna that was built by the Pharaoh Akhenaten during the 14th century BC is recorded to have possessed a Benben stone, as did the 12th Dynasty Pyramid of Amenemhat III, which is today displayed in the Egyptian museum in Cairo.

Apart from being the name of a cult object, the Benben stone is also used to describe a type of ancient Egyptian architectural element, a characteristic that brings one to the connection between the Ancient Egyptian pyramidion and quartz crystal.

While most researchers believe that capstones were put in place to show off a Pharaoh's riches, others suggest that there was a deeper purpose at work. In this theory, the relatively tiny pyramidion compared with the length, breadth and height of the mighty edifice on which it sat became the key component of the entire structure. The material from which the pyramidion was made absorbed the sun's energies, thus enabling the capstone to serve as a cosmic key much like the key to a machine. In the case of the Great Pyramid, the whole structure was covered with polished limestone, which, enhanced by its golden capstone, shone at night like a terrestrial bright star visible from space.

According to the Egyptian authorities, there is no doubt about the matter. They claim that the Great Pyramid was built as a tomb for the pharaoh Cheops and the capstone was looted by thieves who also stole many other relics and treasures from the pyramids.

However, New Age theorists believe that the Great Pyramid was not built as a tomb and is far older than the 2,500 years put forward by the Egyptian authorities. Many believe that the structure is a machine and that it was its capstone that switched it on.

There appears to be little doubt that the Great Pyramid is encoded with many scientific and metaphysical laws and formulae. It has been suggested that one of the reasons for these incorporations is so th at the Great Pyramid can accumulate and transmit cosmic energies. The idea is supported by the occurrence of "magical" numbers and series in its dimensions.

Those who are concerned with the challenging question of the Pyramid's precise measurements find themselves drawn to the matter of its apex. Peter Lemesurier[18] claimed that the dimensions of the Pyramid's internal spaces foretell the collapse of our present civilisation, an event that would be followed by a Messianic return and the birth of a new order. According to those that study Pyramid prophecy, this would be the time that the "stone that the builders rejected ," the missing capstone of the Pyramid, will be restored to its apex.

This all-important capstone would have sat on the flat top of the pyramid, 480 feet above its base. In his 2016 work,[19] ancient metrology expert John Neal describes how the full height of the pyramid, reaching to its natural apex, would have been just over 481 feet. Like other pyramid capstones, its pyramidion would have repeated the form of the larger pyramid, making it a perfect scale model. In the case of the Great Pyramid, exactly 441/440th of its natural apex is missing, and this is because it is missing its pyramidion. 441/440 is an important ratio due the Earth's spin, which deforms it from the spherical. Consequently, it reduces the Earth's polar radius and expands its equatorial radius to make the mean radius of the Earth 441/440 of the polar radius. It is believed that the pyramidion would have had something to do with th is ratio, possible adding 1/440 to reach the true apex of its geometry.

The late and great authority on ancient and sacred mysteries, John Michell, wrote that the numerical patterns within the structure's

[18] Lemesurier, P., *The Great Pyramid Decoded,* Element, 1996.
[19] Neal, J., *All Done with Mirrors*, Secret Academy, 2016

dimensions imply that its capstone consisted of not just one pyramidion but a series of diminishing size, each one forming the tip of the one underneath it. Michell speculated that the top one was fashioned out of solid gold, 5-inches in volume.

Yet, as Michell astutely pointed out, if this 5-inch gold capstone is to represent the whole structure in miniature, it must itself have had a separate tip. Michell believed that this tiny object could only have been some form of quartz crystal.

There are many traditions that describe how crystals were used in antiquity for attracting and transmitting cosmic energies. Edgar Cayce, the "Sleeping Prophet" of America, described his visions of Atlantis' crystal technology which empowered the pre-Flood civilisation but which, finally, by its abuse precipitated the cataclsym. Other channeling sources have described the iniquitous process in the latter years of Atlantis in which newborn infants had a programmed quartz crystal implanted in the base of the spine, so that the State had the ability to control behaviour throughout the individual's life.

The means by which the crystal pyramidion could have been held in place at the top of the Great Pyramid is suggested by the investigative findings of Moses Cotsworth.[20] He visited Egypt in 1900 to observe the shadows cast by the Great Pyramid at certain seasons. During the visit Cotsworth identified a strange Egyptian hieroglyph showing a truncated pyramid topped by a staff or *gnomon* as an apparatus for refining the shadow from a pyramid's peak, thereby permitting measurements to be made of the length of the year. A metal rod of that description, set into the truncated pyramid, would also serve to house the parts of the capstone, securing them in place through holes drilled down their centres. A diamond or quartz crystal point on that rod, appearing at the apex of the golden tip, would cast the finest possible shadow and might also serve, like the "cat's whisker" fine wire in a crystal set used to detect radio signals, to concentrate energies for the Pyramid's principle cosmic function.

---

[20] Cotsworth, M., *The Need of a Rational Almanac*, Forgotten Books (reprint), 2018

Pyramidion of pyramid for Khendjer

The Benben Stone

Cybele, the Phrygian Mother Earth

Chapter 10

Dr. Dee's Crystal Talismans

In 1558, John Dee (1527-1698/09), became scientific advisor and astrologer to Queen Elizabeth I. Between c. 1550 and 1570, he advised on English voyages of discovery to the New World and showed great interest in accounts of Spain's initial experiences in the region. As well as serving as an advisor in the court of the 16th-century queen, Dee was an accomplished alchemist, astrologer, cartographer and mathematician. It is thought he may have been the model for Prospero, the mag ician in Shakespeare's *The Tempest*. Tales abound of Dee's occult exploits, which included conjuring angels and spirits through clairvoyant tools such as crystals and mirrors.

An archetypal Renaissance scholar who wrote on diverse subjects, Dee straddled the fine line between natural "magic," which in his day was considered a science, while the exercise of demonic magic, considered a perversion of religion, could lead one to the stake.

Dee, well connected with European intellectuals and who travelled extensively in Europe, amassed a vast library and collected a variety of navigational equipment, as well as glass mirrors that he used to demonstrate optical illusions. By the 1580s, Dee had become increasingly involved with the supernatural and utilised a number of mediums, or skryers, into his service, most notably Edward Kelley (1555–1597/8), as intermediaries between himself and the angels to communicate with spirits through the use of mirrors or crystals. It is for this period of his life that he is best known in the public imagination and was probably also the time that he acquired an obsidian mirror by which to aid these occult activities.

As a material, obsidian is often regarded as sp ecial and its use for making mirrors has often added to its allure and symbolic nature. Obsidian mirrors were first made in the seventh millennium BC in the Near East, although many were of Aztec origin. Exactly how Dee obtained his mirror is uncertain. Mirrors feature in several lists of early shipments of artefacts to Hapsburg Europe following the Spaniards' conquest of Mexico. Records show that mirrors were shipped from Mexico to Europe soon after Hernán Cortés and his troops took the Aztec capital of Tenochtitlan in 1521. Dee would have had the opportunity to acquire one of these mirrors as he mixed in courts and diplomatic circles during his visits to Europe. He may have obtained the mirror during his studies at Louvain during 1548–1550 or, possibly, while he lived in Bohemia in the early 1580s, in which period Dee maintained extensive contacts in Hapsburg circles when New World objects were increasingly being displayed in the Kunstkammer of Europe.

Many of Dee's possessions passed to the merchant, John Pontois, following supernatural advice in one of Dee's final attempts to converse with angels. In a 1624 lawsuit after Pontois's death, a deposition made by Thomas Hawes records seeing in Pontois's house "a certain round flat stone like Cristall which Pountis said was a stone which an Angell brought to doctor dye [sic] wherein he did worke and know many strange things." By c. 1770, the mirror was certainly in the possession of the politician and antiquarian Horace Walpole. A hand-written label on the case, written by Walpole himself, states: "The Black Stone into which Dr Dee used to call his Spirits... This Stone was mentioned in the Catalogue of the Collection of the Earls of Peterborough from whom it came to Lady Elizabeth Germaine." Walpole further noted in 1784 that, in the now lost catalogue of the Earls of Peterborough, the object was described as "the black stone into which Dr Dee used to call his spirits."

The mirror changed hands several times after Walpole's collection was dispersed, and it was auctioned at least four times before its acquisition by the British Museum in 1966 where it immediately became a popular exhibit. Notably, the British Museum categorises the mirror by its association with Dee, placing it in the Department of Britain, Europe and Prehistory, rather than by its likely origin. It has often been loaned to other museums for exhibitions on medicine, science and magic.

In 2021 Cambridge University Press published an article that summarises research into the obsidian mirror's provenance and geological origins. The investigations were undertaken jointly by the University of Manchester, the Sobolev Institute of Geology and Mineralogy, and the University of Missouri. The Cambridge team's research found support regarding the question of the mirror's provenance in a near-contemporary source. The investigators wanted to explore the mirror's wider context, rather than focus exclusively on the connection with Dee. The researchers examined the mirror, together with a group of related objects in the British Museum. John Dee's mirror is almost circular, measuring 195× 185mm, with a short, square, perforated tab or handle. Both the front and back surfaces have been finely ground and highly polished, with no pitting visible under low magnification. The mirror's well-preserved state may be because it was kept in a case   ; at least, by the time it was in Walpole's possession. Chipping around the perforation may have been caused by the mirror's suspension. Researchers used a portable x-ray fluorescence scanner to examine Dee's mirror, as well as three other obsidian objects two almost-identical circular mirrors, and a polished rectangular slab , both acquired by the British Museum from collectors in Mexico in the 18 00s. Because chemical elements glow differently under X-rays, the scanner was able to determine a geochemical "fingerprint" for each obsidian object based on the proportions of titanium, iron, strontium and other substances that each contained. The results show the obsidian in John Dee's mirror and in one of the other mirrors could only have come from the Pachuca region of central Mexico.

Both regions were ruled by the Aztecs, who had a tradition of making obsidian mirrors for magical purposes Circular obsidian mirrors are depicted in Aztec codices written soon after the time of the Spanish conquest in the early 16th century, and   also in depictions of the deity Tezcatlipoca ("Smoking Mirror"), who had powers of divination. The Aztecs believed the mirrors could show smoke, which would then clear to reveal a distant time or place. Ancient Mesoamericans believed mirrors were spirit doorways to alternate worlds,   "much like Alice in *Through the Looking Glass*," anthropologist Karl Taube of the University of California Riverside has remarked.

Much of the information about obsidian mirrors in the Aztec world comes from Fray Bernadino de Sahagún (c. 1499–1590), the Franciscan missionary and ethnographer who compiled the *General History of the Things of New Spain* in the early colonial period. Mirrors, he wrote, were made by specialists (tezcachiuhqui): "The mirror stone-seller [...] (is the one who makes them), a lapidary, a polisher. He abrades [... with] abrasive sand; he cuts; he carves; he uses glue [...] polishes with a fine cane, makes it shiny. He sells mirror-stones—round, circular; pierced on both sides [translucent]; two -faced, single-faced, concave [...] Mirrors are seldom used nowadays."

Writer and academic, Joscelyn Godwin, has suggested that the Thule Society, a German occultist and Völkisch group founded in Munich shortly after World War I, is linked with the work of Dr. Dee . He refers to Dee's belief that specially constructed mirrors could be use d to draw magical power from the sun to transmit messages and objects to the stars and distant planets. Dee said that a mirror propelled into space at a speed faster than light would reveal to man all the events of the past by reflection. Dee also believed in multitude planes of existence that occupy the same space but do not interferw with one another.

John Dee also wore a personal crystal, a clear, carved purple crystal attached to a chain and a ring. Dee claimed that the crystal was given to him by the angel Uriel in 1582, who instructed him and Kelley on how to make the Philosopher's Stone—the ultimate goal of alchemists. This crystal was passed down to Dee's son, Arthur (1597–1651), who gave it to Nicholas Culpeper (1616–1654) as a reward for curing his liver illness. Culpeper was a physician and alchemist who used the crystal to cure illnesses until 1651, when he claimed a demonic ghost emerged from it, which "exercised itself to lewdness and other depravity with women and girls." The Wellcome Historical Medical Museum, now the Wellcome Trust, brought the crystal into their collection in 1936. A facsimile of a statement about John Dee's crystal, written by Nicholas Culpeper on the back of a deed, is also on display. It was written on 7 March 1651 in Latin and gives a historical insight into the crystal and how Culpeper acquired it. Museum records show that the manuscript was bought at an auction for the Wellcome collection in 1922.

Dee's amethyst pendant

Tezcatlipoca and smoking obsidian mirrors

Chapter 11

Crystals in Today's Technologies

<u>Piezoelectric Effect</u>
The unique properties of quartz also allow it to exibit the piezoelectric effect. The word "piezoelectric" is derived from the word πιέζειν ("piezein"), which means to squeeze or press, and ἤλεκτρον("ēlektron"), which means amber, an ancient source of electric charge . Piezoelectric materials can turn mechanical st ress into electricity, and electricity into mechanical vibrations—the piezoelectric effect.

Quartz is an example of a naturally occurring piezoelectric crystal. Its crystals are made of silicon and oxygen atoms in a repeating pattern. In quartz, the sili con atoms have a positive charge and oxygen atoms have a negative charge. Normally, when the crystal is not under any external stress, the charges are dispersed evenly in the molecules throughout the crystal. But when quartz is stretched or squeezed, the arrangement of the atoms changes slightly. This change causes negative charges to build up on one side and positive charges to build up on the opposite side. When one makes a circuit that connects one end of the crystal to the other , one can use this potent ial difference to produce current. The more one squeezes the crystal, the stronger the electric current generated. Conversely, sending an electric current th rough the crystal changes its shape.

The piezoelectric effect is very useful within many applicati ons that require the production and detection of sound, generation of high voltages, electronic frequency generation, microbalances, and ultra fine focusing of optical assemblies , for example . It is also the basis of a number of scientific instrumental techniques with atomic resolution such as scanning probe microscopes.

The piezoelectric phenomenon was discovered in 1880 by Pierre and Jacques Curie. Their experiment measured surface changes on prepared crystals subjected to mechanical stress. The first serious applications of devices powered by piezoelectric methods did not take place until World War I. SONAR incorporated the piezoelectric effect through transducers extracted from quartz crystals crudely glued between two steel plates. A high frequency "chirp" was produced underwater; submariners would measure depth by clocking the return echo. Since then, crystals have been used in a substantial number of devices, materials and systems.

The piezoelectrical properties of quartz are useful as a standard of frequency: a stable oscillator used for frequency calibration or reference. A frequency standard generates a fundamental frequency with a high degree of accuracy and precision. Harmonics of this fundamental frequency are used to provide reference points. Moreover, since time is the reciprocal of frequency, it is relatively easy to derive a time standard from a frequency standard. For example, quartz clocks employ a crystal oscillator made from a quartz crystal that uses a combination of both direct and converse piezoelectricity to generate a regularly timed series of electrical pulses that is used to mark time. The quartz crystal has a precisely defined natural frequency (caused by its shape and size) at which it prefers to oscillate, and this is used to stabilize the frequency of a periodic voltage applied to the crystal. The same principle is used in some radio transmitters and receivers, and in computers where it creates a clock pulse.

Present day applications reliant on crystal's properties

Crystals as Actuators

As very high electric fields correspond to only tiny changes in the width of the crystal, this width can be changed with extremely high precision, making piezo crystals the most important tool for positioning objects with extreme accuracy, hence their use as actuators. An actuator is a component of a machine that is responsible for moving and controlling a mechanism or system such as by opening a valve. They are used, for example, in multilayer ceramics using extremely thin layers, which allow attainment of high electric fields with low voltages (less than 150V). They are used in many applications, including:

➢ Loudspeakers—voltage is converted to mechanical movement of a metallic diaphragm.

➢ Ultrasonic cleaning usually uses piezoelectric elements to produce intense sound waves in liquid.

➢ Motors, in which piezoelectric elements apply a directional force to an axle, causing it to rotate.

➢ Piezoelectric elements used in laser mirror alignment, where their ability to move a large mass (the mirror mount) over microscopic distances is exploited to electronically align some laser mirrors.

- Acousto-optic modulators, a device that scatters light off soundwaves in a crystal generated by piezoelectric elements, useful for fine-tuning a laser's frequency.
- Atomic force microscopes and scanning tunneling microscopes employ converse piezoelectricity to keep the sensing needle close to the specimen.
- Diesel engines—high-performance common rail diesel engines use piezoelectric fuel injectors, instead of the more common solenoid valve devices.
- i) Piezoelectric actuators used for fine servo positioning in hard disc drives; ii) Active vibration control using amplified actuators.
- X-ray shutters.
- XY stages for micro scanning used in infrared cameras.
- Moving a patient precisely inside active CT and MRI scanners, where the strong radiation or magnetism precludes electric motors.
- High-intensity focused ultrasound for localized heating or creating a localized cavitation, for example in a patient's body or in an industrial chemical process.
- Refreshable braille display —a small crystal is expanded by a current that moves a lever to raise individual braille cells.

Record players

Although an old technology, record players have seen recent increases in sales, mainly due to the hobby market boosted during the   Covid era. Created by Thomas Edison in 1877, the fundamentals behind the turntable have remained relatively the same: grooved vinyl meets needle and projects sound vibrations. The device is powered by crystal technology.

Crystals are powerful conductors of energy, generating electricity following temperature change. Modern stylus crystals are usually composed of sapphire or diamond attached to a flexible piece of metal, converting sonic vibrations into electromagnetic signals. These days record players produce sounds far louder and sonically superior to the older models. The player's stylus is affixed to an electromagnetic device called a cartridge that contains a piezoelectric crystal. Pressure is applied via a metal bar against the crystal, resulting in an outputted electric signal.

Clocks

Unlike pendulum models, quartz clocks are much more sustainable, requiring minimal electricity. As a result, the clock batteries last for many years. The battery sends electricity to a quartz crystal wired to electrodes via an electronic circuit. The rock absorbs the energy, outputs vibrations at a precise frequency of 32,768 times per second, and the circuit counts the number of vibrations, resulting in a single-second tick that stimulates the motor powering the gears.

Microphones

Microphone cartridges are transducers converting sound into electrical energy by the piezoelectric effect, which is prompted by pressurized crystals. The result is an electric signal through mechanical coupling. Crystals are cut in such a way as to produce the desired voltage output whenever they are bent, stretched, or compressed. Used primarily for voice work and acoustic instrumentation, crystal microphones do not require external power sources.

Inkjet Printers

The inkjet printer was invented in the 1980s and has contnuously grown in popularity, while simultaneously decreasing in price. (Except for the ink—why on earth do printer manufacturers have to charge so much for ink cartridges? A gallon of printer ink can cost $12,000; in cartridge form it's more expensive than vintage Champagne!)

The printer heads contain piezoelectric crystals to which electric current is applied and deformed. These crystals are located at the rear reservoir of each 300-600 ink nozzles. The tiny electric charge hits the rock and causes it to vibrate inward. The crystals then expand. As a result of the crystals expanding, the ink droplets are forced onto the document. When the current is removed, the crystal shrinks, at which point the ink is retracted back into the printer head, discontinuing the flow from the nozzle.

Barbecue Grills

When one presses the igniter button and sparks the BBQ grill, one is activating crystals. BBQs use the piezoelectrical system to set expelled gas aflame. The ignition button is connected to a long tube that collides a hammer at the end to a crystal, generating a spark. The deformation of the crystal then produces a high voltage and an electrical discharge. This same ignition method is found in fireplaces, stoves, burners and push-button lighters.

Reduction of vibrations and noise
Different teams of researchers have been investigating ways to reduce vibrations in materials by attaching piezo elem ents to them. When the material is bent by a vibration in one direction, the vibration -reduction system responds to the bend and sends electric power to the piezo element to bend in the other direction. Future applications of this technology are expected in cars and houses to reduce noise. Piezoelectric ceramic fibre technology is also being used as an electronic damping system on some tennis rackets.

Infertility treatment
In people with previous total fertilization failure, piezoelectric activation of oocytes, together with intracytoplasmic sperm injection seems to improve fertilization outcomes.

Surgery
Piezosurgery is a minimally invasive technique that aims to cut a target tissue with little damage to neighbouring tissues. It has the ability to cut mineralized tissue without cutting neurovascular and other soft tissue, thereby maintaining a blood -free operating area, better visibility and greater precision.

Liquid Crystals
Liquid crystal (LC) is a state of matter whose properties are between those of conventional liquids and those of solid crystals. For example, a liquid crystal may flow like a liquid, but its molecules may be oriented in a crystal-like way.

Liquid crystals are true liquids but also have some solid properties. Their internal order is very delicate and can be changed by a weak electrical field, magnetism, or even by temperature variations.

It is an assembly of molecules that is partly ordered —for example, its molecules can be ordered (rigid) like a crystal along a vertical direction, while remaining unordered (flowing) like a liquid in a horizontal one. It may have several possible orderings, called "phases."

The melting point of a pure crys talline substance is very precise ; in some cases, the crystalline properties of a solid crystal carry over into the liquid state. There are many compounds that will do this. Their atomic structure remains quite orderly even while taking on the other characteristics of typical liquids such as pouring or taking on the shape of its container. Selective reflection of white light into its various spectral components by these liquid crystals can be directed and controlled by thermal, acoustical, electrical, magnetic and even mechanical means.

There are two kinds of liquid crystals: those that undergo phase changes due to temperature (thermotropics), and those that undergo phase changes due to the density of a liquid, such as water (lyotropics).

Liquid crystals are everywhere. They are used in all kinds of display devices including computer monitors and laptop screens, televisions, clocks, visors and navigation systems.

Each pixel in a monitor is an assembly of liquid crystals controlled by its own electromagnetic field. The field changes the orientation of the liquid crystals, affecting how much light can be transmitted through them, in turn producing the images one sees on the screen.

Liquid crystals can also be found someplace one might not expect living things! Our bodies are 98% water, and water determines most of the processes that occur in them. Therefore, it is not surprising to encounter lyotropic liquid crystal phases in the wall of the cells of all living things. These phases allow the cells to remain flexible and perform different tasks.

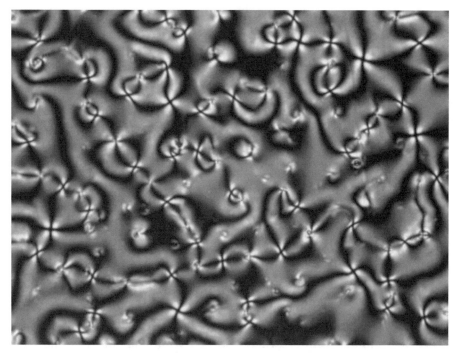

Schlieren texture of a classical nematic liquid crystal
(Credit: Nerea Sebastián and Alenka Mertelj, 2020)

Chapter 12

Crystals in Future Techologies

Organic Crystals and Smart Engineering

Research by a team at the NYU Abu Dhabi (NYUAD) Smart Materials Lab published in the journal Nature Communications (May 2022), demonstrates that organic crystals, a new class of smart engineering materials, can serve as efficient and sustainable energy conversion materials for advanced technologies such as robotics and electronics.

While organic crystals were previously thought to be fragile, the NYUAD researchers have discovered that some organic crystals are mechanically very robust. They developed a material that establishes a new world record for its ability to switch between different shapes by expansion or contraction over half of its length, without losing its perfectly ordered structure.

In the study, "Exceptionally High Work Density of a Ferroelectric Dynamic Organic Crystal around Room Temperature," the team, led by NYUAD Professor of Chemistry Pance Naumov, presents the process of observing how the organic crystalline material reacted to different temperatures. The researchers found that the organic crystals were able to reversibly change shape in a similar manner to plastics and rubber.

Specifically, this material could expand and contract over half of its length repeatedly over thousands of cycles, without any deterioration. It was also able to both expand and contract at room temperature, as opposed to other materials that require a higher temperature to transform, creating higher energy costs for operation.

Unlike traditional materials that are silicon- or silica-based, and inevitably stiff, heavy and brittle, the materials that will be used for future electronics will be soft and organic in nature. These advanced technologies require materials that are lightweight, resilient to damage, efficient in performance, and also have added qualities such as mechanical flexibility and ability to operate sustainably, with minimal consumption of energy. The results of this study have demonstrated, for the first time, that certain organic crystalline materials meet the needs of these technologies and can be used in applications such as soft robotics, artificial muscles, organic optics, and organic electronics (electronics created solely from organic materials).

This latest discovery from NYUAD builds on previous discoveries about the untapped potential of this new class of materials, which includes adaptive crystals, self-healing crystals, and organic crystalline materials with shape memory. The research has shown that organic crystals can not only meet the needs of emerging technologies, but in some cases can also surpass the levels of efficiency and sustainability of other, more common materials.

Crystals within crystals

Researchers at the Pritzker School of Molecular Engineering at the University of Chicago and Argonne National Laboratory have developed an innovative way to sculpt a liquid "crystal within a crystal."

Because such crystals-within-crystals can reflect light at certain wavelengths that others cannot, they could be used for better display technologies. They also can be manipulated with temperature, voltage or added chemicals, which would make them valuable for sensing applications. Changes in temperature, for example, would result in colour changes. Because such changes would require only slight temperature variations or small voltages, the devices would consume very little energy.

Exploiting Ripples and Imperfections in Crystals

Two researchers, Žiga Kos at the University of Ljubljana in Slovenia and Jörn Dunkel at M.I.T., have found that ripples and imperfections in liquid crystals, like those found in LCD televisions, could be used to build a new type of computer. According to the article published in the journal Science Advances (August 2022), the computer would be built using the orientation of the liquid crystal molecules to store data, with calculations expected to look like "ripples" through the liquid.

If successful, the computer design made by the researchers would provide an alternative to electronics for the building of computers. Liquid crystals consist of rod-shape molecules that slosh around like a fluid. In the case of nematic[21] liquid crystals, these molecules are mostly parallel to each other, to the point of the odd molecule that faces the wrong way having to be removed for the development of TV screens. This uniformity is, however, key for building a liquid crystal computer.

---

[21] Nematic crystals have fluidity similar to that of ordinary (isotropic) liquids but they can be easily aligned by an external magnetic or electric field.

Time Crystals

Crystals are amazing th ings. Physicists have taken a significant step towards the making of quantum devices that sound like something out of science fiction. In 2017 *Science News* reported that p hysicists at the University of Maryland had succeeded in making crystals such as those that power "Doctor Who's" TARDIS, using ytterbium ions.

A time crystal is a structure that repeats in time as well as in space. Normal crystals exhibit broken translation symmetry—they have repeated patterns in space and remain unchanged as t ime passes. A time crystal is periodic in time in the same sense that the pendulum in a pendulum-driven clock is periodic in time. Unlike a pendulum, a time crystal "spontaneously" self-organizes into robust periodic motion (breaking a temporal symmetry). The discovery could be incredibly useful in quantum computing.

Time crystals were once thought to be physically impossible. They are a phase of matter very similar to normal crystals but for one additional, peculiar and very special property. In regular crystals, the atoms are arranged in a fixed, three-dimensional grid structure like the atomic lattice of a diamond or quartz crystal. These repeating lattices can differ in configuration but any movement they exhibit comes exclusively from external pushes. In time crystals, the atoms behave a bit differently. They exhibit patterns of movement in time that cannot be so easily explained by an external push or shove. These oscillations, referred to as "ticking," are locked to a regular and particular frequency.

A discrete time crystal never reaches thermal equilibrium, as it is a type (or phase) of non -equilibrium matter. Breaking of time symmetry can only occur in non-equilibrium systems. An example of a time crystal that demonstrates non-equilibrium, broken time symmetry is a constantly rotating ring of charged ions in an otherwise lowest-energy state.

Time crystals were first proposed theoretically by Frank Wilczek in 2012 as a time -based analogue to common crystals . Whereas the atoms in crystals are arranged periodically in space, the atoms in a time crystal are arranged periodically in both space and time. Several different groups have demonstrated matter with stable periodic evolution in systems that are periodically driven.

In condensed matter physics (the field of physics that deals with the macroscopic and microscopic physical properties of matter, especially the solid and liquid phases which arise from electromagnetic forces between atoms), a time crystal is a quantum system of particles whos e lowest-energy state is one in which the particles are in repetitive motion. The system cannot lose energy to the environment and come to rest because it is already in its quantum ground state. Because of this, the motion of the particles does not really represent kinetic energy like other motion; it has "motion without energy."

Theoretically, time crystals tick at their lowest possible energy state, known as the ground state, and are therefore stable and coherent over long periods of time. So, where the structure of regular crystals repeats in space, in time crystals it repeats in space and time, thus exhibiting perpetual ground state motion.

In quantum physics, objects that can have more than one state exist in a mix of those states before they have been pinned down by a clear measurement. So having a time crystal operating in a two-state system provides rich new pickings as a basis for quantum-based technologies. Time crystals are a fair way from being deployed as qubits, as there are a significant number of hurdles to solve first.

However, the pieces are starting to fall into place. *Sciencesprings* reported in June 2022 that a team from Lancaster University in England had successfully created room temperature time crystals that do not need to be isolated from their ambient surroundings.

More sophisticated interactions between time crystals and methods to exercise fine control over them will need to be developed further, as will observing interacting time crystals without the need for cooled superfluids.

Quasicrystals
The Gaia hypothesis, also known as Gaia theory, proposes that all organisms and their inorganic surroundings on Earth are closely integrated to form a single and self-regulating complex system, maintaining the conditions for life on the planet. The hypothesis was formulated by the chemist James Lovelock (1919-2022) and co-developed by the microbiologist Lynn Margulis in the 1970s.

Initially received with hostility by the scientific community, it is now studied in the disciplines of geophysiology and Earth system science, and some of its principles have been adopted in fields like biogeochemistry and systems ecology.

In the 1990s the Gaia hypothesis theory was revived as an explanation for the increase of crop circles, both in numbers and complexity, and was thus interpreted as an SOS call by our planet. Native Americans believe that crop circles are delivering messages that Mother Nature is in serious difficulties, a view that corresponds with Lovelock's Gaia hypothesis in which human activity has created a tumour that is affecting the Earth's ability to make the self-preserving, self-regulating adjustments necessary to maintain optimal conditions for life. It is believed that the complex maths and geometry inherent in crop circles has been deliberately seeded by their makers so that humanity may discover how to read them and, most importantly, act on them.

Present day emergence theory describes the phenomenon of "quasicrystals," irregular but not random patterns, which are created by projecting a crystal from a higher dimension to a lower one. "Imagine" projecting a 3-dimensional image onto a 2-dimensional plane at a certain angle. By analysing the 2-D projection, it is possible with the correct mathematical toolkit to recover the "mother" object in 3-D. Emergence theory then goes further, positing that the 3-D mother object is, in turn, a projection from a higher dimension of a 4-D quasicrystal, which is itself a projection from an 8-D crystal!

This mind-boggling and inconceivable eight-dimensional state is akin David Bohn's concept of the plenum. Space, he maintained, is not empty. It is full, a plenum as opposed to a vacuum, and is the ground for the existence of everything, including ourselves. The universe is not separate from this cosmic sea of energy and, it appears, the unique properties of cryst al at quantum level play no small part in its unimaginably complex workings.

Nuclear Fusion

In December 2022, s cientists at the National Ignition Facility (NIF) in California, part of the Lawrence Livermore National Laboratory (LLNL), succeeded in aiming their 192-beam laser at a cylinder containing a tiny diamond fuel capsule a breakthrough that could unlock the Holy Grail of clean power —nuclear fusion. That powerful burst of laser light created immense temperatures and press ures and sparked a fusion reaction, the reaction which powers the sun. The NIF had done such experiments before but this time the energy that came out of the reaction, was more than the laser power used to trigger it.

Scientists have been trying for decades to meet that threshold and the hope is, one day, to build power stations that employ a fusion reaction to generate abundant, carbon-free electricity. That is still some way off and much work needs to be done in developing the technology.

One of the key components at NIF is a peppercorn -sized synthetic diamond capsule, which holds the fuel. The properties of that spherical capsule are crucial to creating a successful fusion experiment.The sphere has to be perfectly smooth and contaminant -free; any anomalies could ruin the reaction.

Those precisely engineered spheres are not made in California though. They are the result of years of work by Diamond Materials, a company based in Freiburg, Germany, which manufactures synthetic diamond through a process called chemical vapour deposition. It takes around two months to create each batch of 20-40 capsules, which are made by painstakingly layering tiny diamond crystals around a silicon carbide core and polishing repeatedly.

During the development process they discovered that even the most meticulous polishing was not enough as at the microscopic level the surface was still pitted and uneven. Working with teams at LLNL, they eventually discovered they could glaze a polished capsule with a fresh layer of diamond crystals to achieve the clean mirror-like finish they needed.

When the diamond capsules arrive at LLNL, the silicon core is removed and a tiny glass tube is used to fill the hollow sphere with deuterium and tritium, both heavy kinds of hydrogen that fuel the fusion reaction. Around that fuel pellet is a gold and depleted uranium cylinder that is used to cool down the contents of the capsule before the reaction.

Following the successful experiment, the next challenge for NIF and its partners will be to further advance the technology in order to replicate and improve the reaction. The team is pleased that the experiment has changed scientific opinion. Ignition was always thought of as almost unattainable or, at least, that it might only happen 40 years in the future.

Teams around the world are scrambling to build a working fusion power plant, using all sorts of approaches but it will take many years and billions of dollars of investment. The landmark achievement at NIF, made possible by a humble and tiny diamond crystal, is likely to give the sector a boost. It is hopeful that governmental and corporate funding may be easier to come by now that ignition has been proven possible.

Diamond sphere and its nuclear fusion infrastructure at NIF, California

A pair of crystal balls carved and polished by
Frank Dorland, gifted to the author in 1977.

CRYSTAL
TREASURES

A stunning clear quartz crystal on green tourmeline matrix, Afghanistan (author's collection)

Apophyllite

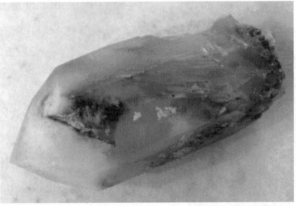

Amphibole quartz, Pakistan

Azeztulite quartz

Aurelia-23 quartz

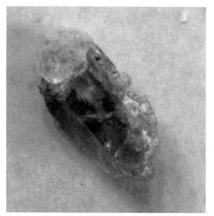

Brookite Chocolate
Phantom inclusion quartz

Cathedral quartz

Elestial quartz

Celestite

Satya Mani Quartz

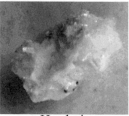

Herderite

Black Tourmeline (Schorl)

Chlorite quartz

Thomsonite Ball on
Stilbite-Heulandite

Tibetan Tektite

Turquoise

Tanzanite

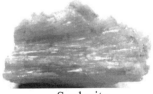

Scolecite

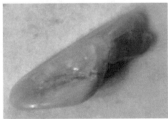

Healerite

Kulli Mundi Himalaya Nirvana quartz

Kyanite with Mica

Green Phantom quartz

Faden quartz

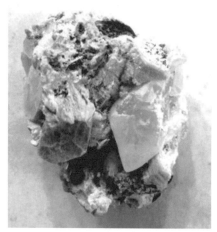

Green Tourmeline

Hematite quartz

Laser quartz

Lemurian Blue Seed
Angel Feathers quartz

Larimar Pear Cabochon

Lithium quartz

Phantom Black quartz

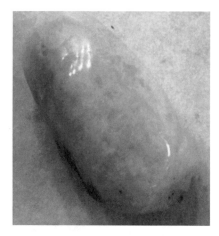

Petalite

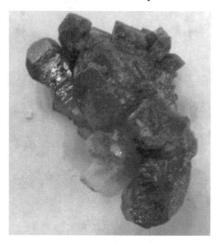

Brown Sceptre quartz

Petroleum Diamond quartz

Agnitite Palm Cabochon

Shangaan Amethyst

Amethyst

Corundum

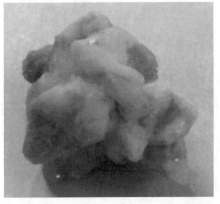

Green and White Heulandite Cluster

Petroleum Diamond quartz

Spirit Cactus quartz

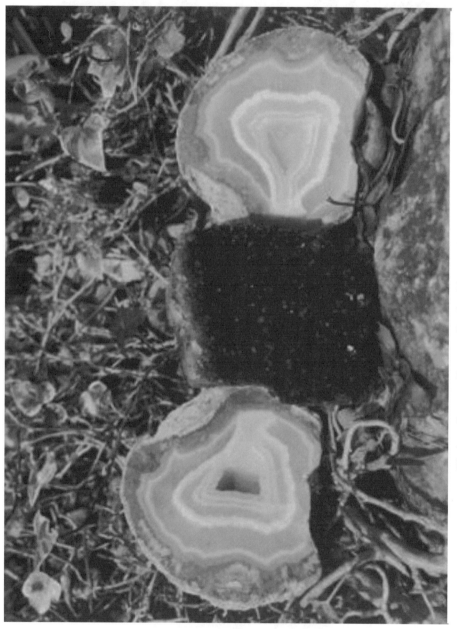

Citrine Quartz Druse flanked by polished Agates

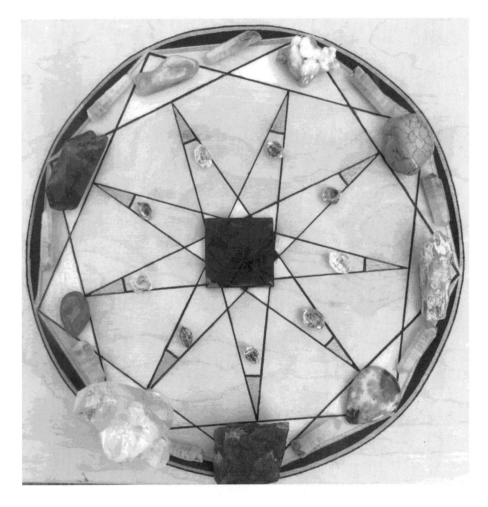

Enneagon Crystal Grid (author's collection)

Venus/Ishtar/Isis

PART 3
LIVING CRYSTAL

Pandorah, Goddess of the Garden,
in the shade of the olive tree

Ode to Psyche

O Goddess! hear these tuneless numbers, wrung
By sweet enforcement and remembrance dear,
And pardon that thy secrets should be sung
Even into thine own soft-conched ear:
Surely I dreamt to-day, or did I see
The winged Psyche with awaken'd eyes?
I wander'd in a forest thoughtlessly,
And, on the sudden, fainting with surprise,
Saw two fair creatures, couched side by side
In deepest grass, beneath the whisp'ring roof
Of leaves and trembled blossoms, where there ran
A brooklet, scarce espied:

Mid hush'd, cool-rooted flowers, fragrant-eyed,
Blue, silver-white, and budded Tyrian,
They lay calm-breathing, on the bedded grass;
Their arms embraced, and their pinions too;
Their lips touch'd not, but had not bade adieu,
As if disjoined by soft-handed slumber,
And ready still past kisses to outnumber
At tender eye-dawn of aurorean love:
The winged boy I knew;
But who wast thou, O happy, happy dove?
His Psyche true!

O latest born and loveliest vision far
Of all Olympus' faded hierarchy!
Fairer than Phoebe's sapphire-region'd star,
Or Vesper, amorous glow-worm of the sky;
Fairer than these, though temple thou hast none,
Nor altar heap'd with flowers;
Nor virgin-choir to make delicious moan
Upon the midnight hours;
No voice, no lute, no pipe, no incense sweet
From chain-swung censer teeming;
No shrine, no grove, no oracle, no heat
Of pale-mouth'd prophet dreaming.

O brightest! though too late for antique vows,
Too, too late for the fond believing lyre,
When holy were the haunted forest boughs,
Holy the air, the water, and the fire;
Yet even in these days so far retir'd
From happy pieties, thy lucent fans,
Fluttering among the faint Olympians,
I see, and sing, by my own eyes inspir'd.
So let me be thy choir, and make a moan
Upon the midnight hours;
Thy voice, thy lute, thy pipe, thy incense sweet
From swinged censer teeming;
Thy shrine, thy grove, thy oracle, thy heat
Of pale-mouth'd prophet dreaming.

Yes, I will be thy priest, and build a fane
In some untrodden region of my mind,
Where branched thoughts, new grown with pleasant pain,
Instead of pines shall murmur in the wind:
Far, far around shall those dark-cluster'd trees
Fledge the wild-ridged mountains steep by steep;
And there by zephyrs, streams, and birds, and bees,
The moss-lain Dryads shall be lull'd to sleep;
And in the midst of this wide quietness
A rosy sanctuary will I dress
With the wreath'd trellis of a working brain,
With buds, and bells, and stars without a name,
With all the gardener Fancy e'er could feign,
Who breeding flowers, will never breed the same:
And there shall be for thee all soft delight
That shadowy thought can win,
A bright torch, and a casement ope at night,
To let the warm Love in!

                              — John Keats

Chapter 13

Mother Earth and the Forces of Living Nature

Every part of this earth is sacred to my people. Every shining pine needle, every sandy shore, every mist in the dark woods, every meadow, every humming insect. All are holy in the memory and experience of my people. We know the sap which courses through the trees as we know the blood that courses through our veins. We are part of the earth, and it is part of us. The perfumed flowers are our sisters. The bear, the deer, the great eagle, these are our brothers. The rocky crests, the juices in the meadow, the body heat of the pony, and man, all belong to the same family. The shining water thatmoves in the streams and rivers is not just water, but the blood of our ancestors. Each ghostly reflection in the clear water of the lakes tells of events and memories in the life of my people. The water's murmur is the voice of my father's father. The riv ers are our brothers. They quench our thirst. They carry our canoes and feed our children.   So, you must give to the rivers the kindness you would give your brother... Remember that the air is precious to us, that the air shares its spirit with all the lif e it supports. The wind that gave our grandfather his first breath also receives his last sigh. The wind also gives our children the spirit of life... Will you teach your children what we have taught our children? That the earth is our mother? … the earth does not belong to man; man belongs to the earth. All things are connected like the blood which unites us all. Man did not weave the web of life; he is merely a strand in it. Whatever he does to the web, he does to himself.

—Chief Seattle, 1855

Mother Earth

It is evident from observation and media reporting that humanity's actions towards nature are far more combative than loving and respectful. What is also painfully evident is that governments cannot be relied upon to take the lead in redressing the assaults upon Mother Earth; they seem to have abandoned all efforts to exercise environmental altruism and

155

rather put their energies into appeasing the dark gods of big business and powerful vested interests. For example, the British Government is walking back on penalising water companies that regularly release huge amounts of sewage into our rivers and seas because, they say, they don't want to dent investor confidence. For as long as such pusillanimous attitudes prevail, the onus to protect nature must fall upon the citizen, just as it did in days of old.

Up to approximately 4,000 years ago the feminine principle, represented in mythological life as "the goddess" and in culture as the qualities of spontaneity, feeling, instinct and intuition, was a vital expression of the sanctity of life. Today, there are few indications of the feminine dimension of the divine, even in our "New Age" times. This woeful omission is a product of humanity's choice to structure global cultures in the image of a masculine god who is beyond creation, not *within* creation, as were the mother goddesses before him. This has resulted in an imbalance of the masculine and feminine principles, which has fundamental implications for how we create and maintain a positive perspective upon our world and how we live in it.

The religious images in the present day are those of the father god who created heaven and earth through his word, so that he is *beyond* his creation, not within it. As a reflection of this imbalance, we have become increasingly used to a mythological tradition in which nature—the earth, the animals, seas, rivers, birds and mountains—is not sacred.

However, an underlying belief in the unity and sacredness of life has lived in the roots of the human psyche for far longer than the negative mutations of religious thought.

Formal religions tend to dismiss as animism the feeling of people for whom nature is truly alive. They also largely ignore contemporary psychological discoveries, especially those of Jung which show that the knowledge of all the human race is stored within the psyche and so is potentially available to every one of us.

The story of the Goddess is very powerful. She reigned supreme long before Christianity. Approximate to the time of the final Atlantean cataclysm, circa 10,000 BC, the last Cro-Magnon wave of settlers in the form of the Magdalenian culture arrived in Britain across the relatively recently formed channel that had flooded the land bridge to the European Continent. These culturally developed incomers were skilled in hunting and in the making of prehistoric art. They included the Nemeans and Melasians from Greece, the Formorians from Iberia (Spain), and, later, beginning around 2,800 BC, the Beaker people, a complex culture rich in shared ideological, cultural and religious ideas with skills in precious metalwork, archery and ornamental work. Next came the Phœnicians, the greatest traders in their day who arrived in long-oared galleys to procure tin from Britons.

Arguably, one of the biggest upheavals came with the arrival of the Celts, whose beginnings can be traced back approximately 3,300 years to the Urnfield culture of central Europe. Nevertheless, it was not until around 800 BC that the first people to adopt distinctly cultural characteristics that are regarded as Celt appeared in central Europe, particularly in Austria, an area often called the "Celtic homeland."

In their early history the Celts first occupied an area between the upper reaches of the rivers Elbe, Danube and Rhine, spreading into northern Italy around 2,500 years ago. Subsequently, over a 300 -year period beginning around 450 BC the Celts (or Kelts) spread rapidly over the European continent; the Romans called them Gauls.

During this latter period the Celts sacked Rome (387 BC), plundered the treasures of Delphi (the "Underworld") in Greece, and populated Spain, Britain and Ireland. Written evidence that could throw light on the development of the Celtic language, spoken today mainly in Brittany in France, Ireland, Scotland, Wales, Cornwall and the Isle of Man, is scarce as the early Celts preferred word-of-mouth communications.

The Celts' primal deity was the earth goddess, the Mother who was known by many names according to different sites with which she was associated. One such was Minerva, known in Britain as Brighd or Brigit and who represented the virgin aspect of the Great Goddess. In Aqua Sulis (modern day English city of Bath) a perpetual fire was maintained in honour of Minerva. Brighd, a goddess of poetry and divine inspiration, was the patroness of the celebrated Druid bard, Taliesin.

Nigel Pennick[22] wrote of the Celtic bards, who saw no distinction between history and mythology and held a poetic vision of the landscape, a realm ensouled with spirits. Mother Earth was the goddess of the landscape, both the genius loci, the spirit of the place, and the anima loci, the soul-place, the essential personality of a location where the unseen may be brought into physical presence if one has a loving, neutral, non-judgmental relationship with nature.

The forces of living nature may be sensed as a presence or being that exists beyond the everyday realms of human cognizance, possessing its own consciousness and personality. The philosophers of old recognised this very clearly. Aristotle, for example, expressed it beautifully:

We say that the Sensible World is an image of another; therefore

---

[22] Pennick, N., *Celtic Sacred Landscapes*, Thames & Hudson, 1996.

since this world is vivid or alive, how much more, then, that other must live... Yonder, therefore, above the stellar virtues, stand other heavens to be attained, like the heavens of this world; beyond them, because they are of a higher kind, brighter and vaster; nor are they distant from each other like this one, for they are incorporeal. Yonder, too, exists an earth, not of inanimate matter, but vivid with animal life and all natural terrestrial phenomena like this one, but of other kinds and perfections. There are plants, also, and gardens, and flowing water; there are aquatic animals but of nobler species. Yonder is air and life appropriate to it, all immortal. And although the life there is analogous to ours, yet it is nobler, seeing that it is intellectual, perpetual and unalterable.

Pennick described the Celtic world-system, symbolised as three circles or worlds and viewed as concentric circles or ascending planes upon the column of the world tree. The idea of a world tree or cosmic axis tells of a vertical axis that runs through this physical plane, linking us to other planes of existence, their vibratory rates increasing as one ascends the axis, or decreasing as one descends to the lower interconnecting planes. Cylch y Abred, the middle earth on which we walk, the realm of the ego, stands above the underworld, the Celtic "Annwn," realm of the unconscious and the incorporeal abode of unformed matter, wraiths and demonic spirits. Above is Cylch y Gwynvyd, the heavenly upperworld abode of enlightened divine beings and those humans who have transcended the cycles of their earthly lives; and, highest, Cylch y Ceugant, the ineffable place of Hen Ddihenydd, the "Ancient and Unoriginated One," the unattainable sole abode of God of the monotheistic system. Goethe wrote that, 'In the symbol, the particular represents the general, not as in a dream, nor as in a shadow, but as a living and instantaneous revelation of the inscrutable.'

Ancient teachings inform us that the earth is not a dead body but is infused by a spirit that is its life and soul. Natural places such as stones, springs, mountains, islands and trees are ensouled locations where the anima loci may be best experienced in elevated consciousness, where we can receive religious or mystical inspiration and be most receptive to healing body and mind. They become powerful indicators of metaphysical realities in which the reward is to experience revelations of the archetypal qualities of an eternal otherworld—paradise. Enhancing the anima loci is akin to spiritual gardening in which participating consciously in Nature induces an ennobling presence in the observer.

Goddess figures of antiquity

Traditional cultures held that all existence is pervaded by a subtle cosmic breath which animates all things and empowers their continued existence. In the West this magical breath is the pneuma or the fifth Platonic element, the Quintessence. The Welsh bards called it anal or anadyl.

In the Celtic belief system, the realms of animals, humans, gods and goddesses, Nature Spirits, life and death are not separate. Together, they are simply the one magnificent world of natural existence, a great integrated continuum in which everything is an harmonious element of the whole.

Classical Pagan belief held that man is made in the image of God and in the image of the Universe. Gregory Nazianzene, 4th-century Archbishop of Constantinople, said that 'Every creature, both of heaven and earth, is in man,' illustrating that the workings of the human body and soul are reflections of the universe.

This vital connection between nature and the nature of human beings is represented by The Book of Llanrwst, attributed to the Bard Taliesin:

There are eight parts in man. The first is the earth, which is inert and heavy, and from it proceeds the flesh; the second are the stones, which are hard, and the substance of the bones; the third is water, which is moist and cold, and is the substance of the blood; the fourth is the salt, which is briny and sharp, and from it are the nerves, and the temperament of feeling, as regards bodily sense and faculty; the fifth is the firmament or wind, out of which proceeds the breathing; the sixth is the sun, which is clear and fair, and from it proceed the fire, or bodily heat, the light and colour; the seventh is the Holy Ghost, from whom issues the soul and life; and the eighth is Christ, that is, the intellect, wisdom and the light of soul and life.

According to pagan belief, when we die our physical bodies return to Mother Earth. In northern Europe, tradition had it that the souls of the dead go into the hills and spirit-mountains, where they dwell with other otherworldly beings.

The custom of interring the dead and their goods in earth mounds was common among the Celts who believed that in burying in this manner those that had passed created a model of the otherworld. They regarded the otherworld as a symbolic realm in which everything must be carried out correctly, according to universal principles that reflect the underlying orderly structure of existence. Those whose remains go into the earth leave the world of the living and re-enter the womb of Mother Earth from whom they emerged at the time of birth. At death, part of the human spirit goes into the otherworld to be regenerated and reborn; the ir goods are taken into the fairy kingdom; and the burial mound serves as a memorial to the life and deeds of the departed.

As Baring and Cashford[23] astutely point out, whereas history as a true record of the past has been told almost entirely in terms of its outer eventfulness, its rol e as a reflector of the nurturing of the human spirit and societies' inner qualities has been radically downplayed. The most neglectful aspect of this phenomenon is the way the feminine half of the human spirit has been wholly downgraded by masculine-dominated societies. As a consequence, we see today an increasing decay of the caring values of life at the same time as global society wilfully pursues choices and policies driven by male dominance. This loss of feminine eventfulness has led inexorably to the exploitation and rejection of our Mother Earth, in olden days symbolised by the Mother Goddess.

The Mother Goddess, as a symbolic icon of worship and veneration, is an image that focuses and inspires a perception of the universe as an organic, sacred and sentient whole in which humanity, the Earth and all life on it participate as "her children." Everything is woven together in one cosmic web, where all orders of physical and spiritual life (the manifest and the unmanifest) are related, because all share in the sanctity of the original source.

Ours i s the age above all others that has removed the essence of sacredness from nature. It seems from the evidence of inc reasing pollution (itself a term that originally meant the profaning of what was sacred) that humanity no longer enjoys instinctively the profound feeling that the Earth is a living being. As a consequence, the whole body of the Earth is threatened in a way unique to the history of the planet.

The Neolithic period (10,000 BC to 5,500 BC) was the great age of discovery, which saw mankind enjoying a new relation ship to the universe. This was the time when humanity truly learned to participate in the mysterious processes of growing. With the realisation that certain seeds changed into wheat and corn, which could be transformed into bread, and that certain animals would live close to the home and provide milk, eggs and meat, a new spirit of conscious co -operation between human beings and their world took shape. Nigel Pennick described beautifully early man's symbiotic relationship with Mother Earth:[24]

[23] Baring, A; Cashford, J., *The Myth of the Goddess: Evolution of an Image*, Penguin Books Ltd., 1991
[24] Pennick, N., *The Ancient Science of Geomancy*, Thames and Hudson, 1979

Like the animal kingdom, early man was integrated with the environment, occupying his niche in a completetely natural and unconscious manner. His life was controlled by the passage of the seasons, his nomadic wanderings directed by necessity. The faculty of intuition was his guiding principle. It led him to find water, nourishment and shelter... His symbiotic relationship with the "ecosystem" was not yet broken. Possessing intelligence, he recognized his dependence upon Mother Earth, who had brought him into being and sustained him. She was the universal deity. Each part of her was therefore sacred, suffused with her spirit and manifest in different forms according to the place. The various powers present in rocks were operative and available at the appropriate times. To such people, any alteration of the earth was an unthinkable sacrilege... Ancient peoples were able directly to experience the energies in the earth and attributed them to the activity of the earth spirit. The places where they occurred became sites of special reverence, later to be incorporated as the active sites in sacred buildings... A natural reverence, alien to the modern spirit, guarded and nurtured these sites where anyone could experience his or her own direct magical relationship with the essential nature of the earth.

This expression of consciousness in the Neolithic was explored through the medium of the goddess. The Mother Goddess in this era is an image that more than ever before inspired a perception of an holistic universe as organic, alive and sacred in which humanity, the earth and all life on it participate as "her children." As the Great Mother, she presided over the whole of creation as goddess of life, death and regeneration, containing within herself the life of plants as well as the life of animals and human beings. Equally, there was the same recognition of a dynamic relationship between an invisible cosmic order that governed the revolving phases of the moon, and a visible earthly order in the cycles of human and animal life, and the seasons and the agricultural year.

As the great light shining in the darkness of the night, the moon, in all mythologies up to the Iron Age (*c.* 1,250 BC), was regarded as one of the supreme images of the Goddess, who was the measure of the cycles of time and of cosmic and earthly connection. Duality, symbolised as the waxing and waning moon, was contained and transcended in her. Analogously, life and death did not have to be perceived as opposites but could be seen as phases succeeding each other in eternal rhythm. Similarly, she governed the fertility of women, the waters of the seas and the phases of increase and decrease. The seasons followed each other in sequence as the phases of the moon followed each other. The Goddess was an enduring image of the renewal of time because what appeared to be lost with the waning moon was restored with the waxing moon.

Neolithic pottery depicts the mystery of birth through the body of the goddess. Images show her as the portal th rough which lives enter and leave this world. Figures often show her adorned on her front and back with a labyrinth or similar meander design, symbolizing the goddess as the vessel that is the gateway to the dimension beyond human life.

> The Goddess in all her manifestations was the symbol of the
> unity of all life in Nature. Her power was in the water and stone,
> in tomb and cave, in animals and birds, snakes and fish, trees and
> flowers. Hence the holistic and mythopoeic perception of the
> sacredness and mystery of all there is on Earth.'

> —Marija Gimbutas, *The Language of the Goddess*

The concept of a "standalone" male god in the Neolithic era was largely unknown. The male influence existed only within the Goddess. In Crete, for example, the male aspect of the goddess, an androgynous all-powerful deity uniting both male and female roles, was symbolized by the crescent horns of the bull or by a male animal: bull, ram or stag.

Later, in the Bronze Age (*c.*3,300 BC - 1,200 BC) the male in the Minoan belief system had to some extent separated from the Goddess but was not yet independent of her . This is evidenced by archaeological examination of seals and carvings in which the representation of the masculine and feminine principles is seen as an image of the great goddess and a young god , which is never shown as a male that has advanced beyond childhood. Instead, when the young god and the mother goddess are depicted together, the relation is not one of equal power - sharing between an adult god and an adult goddess, but one of service by a young god paying homage to the Mother Goddess.

In Neolithic doxology, the god was the "son" of the goddess, a relationship that personified the forces of growth, which, like flowers and trees, die an annual death into the body of the goddess in order to be reborn from her the following spring. In this way, the young god symbolises the form of life that has to change, while the goddess remains as the principle of life that never dies and continually renews itself through its myriad changing forms.

In Minoan culture the all -supreme Goddess was not known by a particular name but was simply regarded as the eternal power of life, death and regeneration. Elsewhere in the Bronze Age era, the great goddesses of the day were given names, as in Sumeria, Egypt and Anatolia, for example. Their three great goddesses were Innana (or Ishtar as she was called in northern Sumeria), Isis and Cybele respectively. All three reflect the image of the Great Mother who presided over the earliest civilisations that arose between Europe and the Indian subcontinent.

This was a period when nature was still experienced as numinous: a divine force that is both sacred and alive. It was seen in the sun's rays, in the river's rise and fall, in the twinkling stars of heaven, in the violence of floodwaters, in the green shoots of cereals crops, and in the grapes of the vine. Similarly, its mysterious energies were perceived in the attraction of male and female, in health and disease, and in life and death. These phenomena revealed to humanity not so much that the divine is every*where* but that the divine is every*thing*.

In Sumerian cosmology the Mother Goddess, Ki-Ninhursag, was the mother of all living, of the gods and of humanity, mother of the earth itself, the soil and the rocky ground, and all the plants and crops it brought forth. She was the Holy Shepherdess, Queen of Stall and Fold.

Later she was personified by Inanna, Great Mother, Virgin Queen of Heaven and Earth, Holy Shepherdess, Light of the World, Moon Goddess and Morning and Evening Star. She said, 'I step onto the heavens, and the rain rains down; I step onto the earth, and grass and herbs sprout up.' Inanna was clothed with the heavens and crowned with the stars, her lapis crystal jewels reflecting the blue of the sky and the blue of the waters of space that the Sumerians named "The Deep." She wore the rainbow as her necklace and the zodiac as her girdle. Innana was truly Mother Nature in all her power and glory. She is also known as "The Green One, she of the springing verdure," after the green corn that the earth wears as her mantle in spring. Inanna carries on her head the lunar horns, which proclaim her to be the descendant of the ancient goddess who originally was the sky, earth and underworld. Her cult endured 4000 years.

The myth of Ishtar and Tammuz, esoteric god of the sun and one of the guardians of the gates of the underworld, is one of the earliest examples of the dying-God allegory. According to the myth, Tammuz was killed every year by a wild boar but was rescued from the nether world by Ishtar, who descended into the underworld in search for the sacred elixir which alone could restore Tammuz to life.

Acclaimed mystical-metaphysical philosopher Manly P. Hall (1901-1990) relates the story of Ishtar's mission to rescue her lover.[25] With outspread wings, Ishtar, the daughter of Sin (the Moon), sweeps

---

[25] Hall, M., *The Secret Teachings of all Ages*, Philosophical Research Society, 1928

downward to the gates of death. The house of darkness—the dwelling of the god Irkalla —is described as "the place of no return ." It is without light; the nourishment of those who dwell the rein is dust, and their food is mud. Over the bolts on the door of the house of Irkalla is scattered dust, and the keepers of the house are covered with feathers like birds. Ishtar demands that the keepers open the gates, otherwise she will shatter the doorposts and strike the hinges and raise up dead devourers of the living. The guardians of the gates beg her to be patient while they go to the queen of Hades from whom they secure permission to admit Ishtar, but only in the same manner as all others came to this dreary house.

Ishtar thereupon descends through the seven gates which lead downward into the depths of the underworld. At the first gate the great crown is removed from her head, at the second gate the earrings from her ears, at the third the necklace from her neck, at the fourth the ornaments from her breast, at the fifth the girdle from her waist, at the sixth the bracelets from her hands and feet, and at the seventh gate the covering cloak of her body. Ishtar remonstrates as each successive artide of apparel is taken from her, but the guardian tells her that this is the experience of all who enter the somb re domain of death. Enraged upon beholding Ishtar, the Mistress of Hades inflicts upon her all manner of disease and imprisons her in the under world. As Ishtar represents the spirit of fertility, her loss prevents the ripening of the crops and the maturing of all life upon the earth. In this respect the story parallels the Greek legend of Persephone.

The gods, realizing that the loss of Ishtar is disorganizing all Nature, send a messenger to the underworld and demand her release. The Mistress of Hades is forced to comply, and the water of life is poured over Ishtar. Thus, cured of the infirmities inflicted on her, Ishtar retraces her way upward through the seven gates, at each of which she is reinvested with the article of apparel which the guardians had removed.

The myth of Ishtar symbolizes the descent of the human spirit through the seven worlds, or spheres , of the sacred planets until, finally deprived of its spiritual adornments, it incarnates in the physical body—Hades—where the mistress of that body heaps every form of sorrow and misery upon the imprisoned consciousness. The waters of life—the secret doctrine of the Ancient Wisdoms—cure the diseases of ignorance; and the spirit, re-ascending to its divine source, regains its God -given adornments as it passes upward through the rings of the planets.

It is generally agreed that the Greek cult of Athena, goddess of war and handicraft, was influenced by th ose of Inanna and Ishtar, all three being associated with creation. Athena particularly resembles Inanna in her role as a terrifying warrior goddess. It is believed that Athena's birth from the head of Zeus may derive from the earlier Sumerian myth of Inanna's descent into and return from the Underworld. Egypt's foremost female deity was Isis, Queen of Heaven, Earth and the Underworld, who was worshiped from before 3,000 BC to the second century AD, after which Isis was metamorphosed into the Virgin Mary because, although she gave birth to all living things, she remained a virgin.

> Isis is, in fact, the female principle of Nature, and is receptive of every form of generation, in accord with which she is called by Plato the gentle nurse and the all-receptive, and by most people has been called by countless names, since, because of the force of Reason, she turns herself to this thing or that and is receptive of all manner of shapes and forms. She has an innate love for the first and most dominant of all things, which is identical with the good, and this she yearns for and pursues; but the portion which comes from evil she tries to avoid and to reject, for she serves them both as a place and means of growth, but inclines always towards the better and offers to it opportunity to create from her and to impregnate her with effluxes and likenesses in which she rejoices and is glad that she is made pregnant and teeming with these creations. For creation is the image of being in matter, and the thing created is a picture of reality.

> —Plutarch, *Isis and Osiris*

Apuleius in *The Golden Ass* ascribes to Isis, she of the ten thousand appellations, her self-declared statement concerning her powers, which clearly identify her as Mother Earth, Goddess without equal:

> Behold, I, moved by thy prayers, am present with thee; I, who am Nature, the parent of things, the queen of all the elements, the primordial progeny of ages, the supreme of Divinities, the sovereign of the spirits of the dead, the first of the celestials, and the uni-form resemblance of Gods and Goddesses. I, who rule by my nod the luminous summits of the heavens, the salubrious breezes of the sea, and the deplorable silences of the realms beneath and whose one divinity the whole orb of the earth venerates under a manifold form, by different rites and a variety of appellations... Minerva, Venus, Diana, Proserpine, Ceres, Junio, Hecate... And those who are illuminated by the incipient rays of that divinity the Sun, when he rises, call me by my true name, Queen Isis.

Ishtar

"When disaster batters down the door, fresh air also enters."

—from the ancient Vestal Virgins initiation ceremony

Isis

Augustus Le Plongeon (1825-1908), a British-American archeologist and photographer who studied the pre-Columbian ruins of America, believed that the Egyptian myth of Isis had a historical basis among the Mayans, to whom she was known as Queen Moo. He based this belief on the theory that Mayan civilisation was far older than that of Egypt. After the death of her husband, Prince Coh, Moo took refuge among the Mayan colonies in Egypt where she was accepted as their Queen and named Isis.

Isis is represented in the Song of Solomon by the dark maid of Jerusalem, symbolic of receptive Nature. In the story of Solomon and his wives, one reads an allegory in which Solomon is the sun and his wives are the planets, moons, asteroids and other heavenly bodies in his house, the solar mansion.

In statues of Isis can be seen a deep box filled with flaming coals and incense descending down a thread from a golden ring on her left arm. Isis, Nature personified, carries with her the sacred fire, religiously preserved and kept burning in a special temple by the Vestal Virgins. This fire is the genuine, immortal flame of Nature—ethereal, essential, the author of life. From the figure's right arm also descends a thread, to the end of which is fastened a pair of scales, signifying the preciseness of Nature in her weights and measures.

The Druids of Britain greatly venerated Isis under her symbol of the moon. In Druid cosmology the sun was the father, and the moon, Isis, the mother of all things. By means of these powers, the Druids worshiped Universal Nature. Recognising the sun as the proxy of the Supreme Deity, the Druidic priests of Britain used a ray of solar light to spark their altar fires. They did this by concentrating the ray upon a specially cut crystal or aquamarine, set in the form of a magical brooch on the belt of the Arch-Druid. This brooch was called the 'Liath Meisieith' and was reputed to possess the power of drawing the divine fire of the gods down from heaven and concentrating its energies for the service of men.

Crystal also featured in the Druids' magical quest to travel to the blessed realm of Gwynedd, the world of the Twice-born. To achieve success, they first had to pass through three Veils, one of which, the Veil of Cythraul, was symbolised by Cwrwg Gwydrin, a glass (crystal) boat for travel to the in-between realms of the Otherworld.

Inanna and Isis were only two among a whole plethora of goddesses that reigned over human society in ancient times. Among them were Tiamat of Babylon; Cybele of Anatolia and Rome; and Gaia, Hera, Artemis, Athena, Aphrodite, Demeter, Persephone and Asteria of Greece. Asteria, the Starry One, the Queen of Heaven and the 'shining light,' was the benevolent goddess of crystal workers. She loved working with crystals because all the stars in her glittering heavens were considered crystals. Her colours are green and silver with the blue of the heavens. The story goes that at one time the earth was perfectly flat and considered very precious. To protect it, Asteria magically fashioned a huge, hollow crystal dome to cover it. She cut holes in the dome to allow the clouds, wind and rain to pass through. She then created hollow crystal globes in which to carry the moon and the planets. She p laced each one inside its own crystal sphere for safekeeping and suspended them by silver threads among all her stars.

Later, Asteria discovered that when the winds blew across the hollow crystal globes carrying the moon and planets, she would hear celes   tial harmonies like a great pipe organ in the sky. Asteria called this   "the music of the spheres " and the tones delighted her, for this was her own heavenly orchestration. In time, the silver threads became black with oxidation and could no longer be seen.Today, the stars and the moon and the planets seem to be magically suspended in dark space above the world as Asteria manipulates their nightly travels across her heavenly domain.

In Israel, even though t here is no word for Goddess in Hebrew , in Judaean cosmology Yahweh did not reign supreme. There   is a hidden goddess in the Old Testament, seen in the Cherubim that adorn the Ark of the Covenant, and which represent the sister goddesses of Egypt, Isis and Nephthys, the winged beings protecting the Assyrian Tree of Life in Mesopotamia. The veil that protected Solomon's Temple's Holy of Holies was also woven with the same image.

The hidden Hebrew Goddess is also represented by the Canaanite Asherah (the Mother of the Gods), by Anath (sister -wife of god Baal), Lady of Heaven and Mistress of all the Gods, by Astarte (Ashtoreth in Hebrew), and Hokhmah (in Greek, Sophia), the invisible unnamed consort of Yahweh, the master transcendent craftswoman of creation, the "Wisdom." Later came Mary, in Church dogma Mothe r of God, Perpetually Virgin, Immaculately Conceived, and Assumed into Heaven, Body and Soul, where she reigns as Queen.

As the Bronze Age reaches its final millenium, its culture changes. The Mother Godddess starts to recede into the background as father   gods begin to move centre-stage. Gradually, she loses her capacity to inspire, and the male force assumes an increasingly dynamic role in which the Father God occupies front and centre.

The once powerful myth of the separation between Heaven and Earth is to become the foundation of Iron Age theologies in which humanity is set apart from nature. Increasingly, humans act reflectively rather than instinctively, which commences a dissociation from the instinctive life of nature and instils the temptation in man to call the goddess (nature) "lower" and the god (spirit) "higher."

One can only speculate on how the goddess cultures of the Bronze Age would have maintained precedence had they not been disrupted by the arrival of warrior tribesmen (principally the Semites from the Syro-Arabian deserts, and what would evolve into the Hellenic-Aryan races from the plains of Europe and south Russia), who imposed their mythology and their patriarchal customs on those they invaded. The impact on the Bronze Age goddess cultures from Europe to India was profound.

After a long struggle, in 1,750 BC cities to the north of Sumeria—Nippur, Akkad, Sippar, Kush and Babylon—gained supremacy over their southern neighbours. Consequently, Inanna's Babylonian counterpart, Ishtar, inherited her imagery and ritual drama.

> Towards the close of the Age of Bronze and... with the dawn of the Iron Age..., the old cosmology and mythologies of the goddess mother were radically transformed, reinterpreted, and in large measure even suppressed, by these suddenly intrusive patriarchal warrior tribesmen whose traditions have come down to us chiefly in the Old and New Testaments and in the myths of Greece. Two extensive geographical matrices were the source lands of these insurgent warrior waves: for the Semites, the Syro-Arabia deserst, where, as ranging nomads, they herded sheep and goats and later mastered the camel, and, for the Hellenic-Aryan stems, the broad plains of Europe and south Russia, where they had grazed their herds of cattle and early mastered the horse.

> —Joseph Campbell, *Occidental Mythology*

Both invading forces introducd the idea of an opposition between the powers of light and darkness, in contrast to the former prevailing belief in which the whole contains both light and darkness in an ever-changing relationship.

Increasingly, there arose a desacralization of nature and human life, very much at odds with the instinctive attitude of the Neolithic farmer who lived close to the soil and perceived the rhythmic laws of the goddess as inherent in all life. Eventually, the feminine-centric cosmology of the settled agriculturalists was undermined, and a pattern of war and conflict was established in the Near East that endures to the present day.

Additionally, in another crucial change in consciousness a new attitude to death appeared around 2,500 BC, in which physical decease came to be regarded as the absolute end and opposite of life. The lunar (goddess), cyclical concept of death and rebirth no longer prevaile d; darkness was now associated with what was *not* light or life . Death became something final, and terrifying, without the promise of rebirth. The profound implications of this new and brutal cosmology were reflected in the remarkable increases in bloodshed and war, in which it seemed that the constant *celebration* of the killing of the enemy can be explained psychologically only through the concept of ritual sacrifice.

The tribes that conquered Sumeria brought with them their sky gods. Subsequently, the resultant trinity became the gods An, Enlil, and Enki, out of which Enlil, the god of air, whose city was Nippur, gradually rose to prominence. A major consequence was that Ki, Mother Earth, could no longer be worshiped and adored as the mother of Enlil; instead , she was conceived by Sumeria's theologian s as Enlil's big sister, suggesting that her role as Mother Earth was usurped by Enlil and , thus, it came about that the god as son evolved into God as father.

The Iron Age saw the culmination of the process b y which the numinous forces of living nature—the Mother Goddess—were transferred to the Father God, who gradually evolved in human perception into the consortless God of the three patriarchal religions known to us today: Judaism, Christianity and Islam. From this time forward, the male god is the sole primal creator, completely usurping the goddess as the only source of life.

However, this process generated a god who is weaker in power and numinosity than the Goddess because he has only become the *maker* of heaven and earth, whereas the goddess *was* heaven and earth, the creations emerging from her being *part* of her, and she of them. Henceforth, the essential identity between creator and creation was broken, and a profound sense of dualism—spirit and nature—prevailed, a totally alien concept in Goddess mythology, which recognised no separation between them. From then on, the mythic model of the new culture, ruled by a zealous, male Father God , is one of mastery and control, expressing the desire to shape and order what had been created.

Despite the birth of religion movements that worshiped only the patriarchal principle, humanity understood deep within its collective psyche that the emergence of the Father God had brought forward a deity that was intrinsically less appealing and far less cosmica lly and spiritually substantial than the Mother Goddess.

Humanity never abandoned her completely, particularly in the west.

As late as the fourth century it seemed probable to an observer that if the Roman Empire survived, a religious consensus would prevail based on the worship of the universal Great Mother. Lyons was already the city of Cybele by the third century. In Paris, the rule of Isis was especially strong. She reigned in the city until Saint Genevieve took over as patroness in the sixth century. A writer called Jacques leGrand, writing in about the 1400s, recorded this Isis-Paris connection:

> In the days of Charlemagne... there was a city named Iseos, so named because of the goddess Isis who was venerated there. Now it is called Melun [about an hour south of Paris.] Paris owes its name to the same circumstances. Parisius is said to be similar to Iseos because it is located on the river Seine in the same manner as Melun.

Nevertheless, the Christian Church that Constantine established became strongly patriarchal with the growing emphasis on the martyr qualities of defiant steadfastness and simple faith of Christian soldiers, rather than subtler, gentler qualities. Judaeo-Christian religion or mythology (depending on one's point of vew) had inherited the paradigm images of Babylonian mythology, particularly the opposition between Creative Spirit and Chaotic Nature, and also the habit of thinking in oppositions, especially in a common assumption that the spiritual and the physical worlds are different in kind, an opinion that separates mind from matter, soul from body, thinking from feeling, intellect from intuition, and reason from instinct.

Despite humanity's psychic recognition that the Goddess is a vital part of mankind's evolutionary journey through the classrooms of the physical experience, Christian patriarchy spared no efforts in seeking to bury any re-emergence of the mysticism and magic of the Goddess and her priestess representative, the Sacred Prostitute. In the twelfth century the Church carried out its most brutal stage of its feminine-principal extermination programme with the advent of the Albigensian Crusade. The courts of the Inquisition replaced the courts of the Minne—courtly love—with mass torture. Millions were killed, the vast majority being women. But the Church's goal of total extinction of the Goddess was always doomed to fail because the "Mother" is a holy and eternal force that is resident in all of nature, including in the hearts and minds of those that would have her killed, rather than have to give up the illusory and temporal trappings of masculine "superiority."

The Goddess as an archetypal constant cannot be killed. If that were possible then the entire human race would become tremendously imbalanced because we are a dualist creation. Women have an outer female self centred round the spiritual qualities of conceptio n, incubation, birth and nurturing, which is balanced by the projective and guardian qualities of an inner male self. The converse is true in males. All Ancient Wisdoms and master philosophers taught this truth.

A fundamental part of men and women's refreshment of the immortal goddess energies that exist within oneself is to constantly re-charge and re-generate them through maintaining a loving relationship with Mother Nature, a practice that is an individual action and responsibility. Russell described in *The Candle of Vision* his experiences in communing with Mother Earth:

> I must in some fashion indicate the nature of the visions which led me to believe with Plato that the earth is not at all what the geographers suppose it to be, and that we live like f rogs at the bottom of a marsh knowing nothing of that Many-Coloured Earth which is superior to this we know, yet related to it as soul to body. On that Many-Coloured Earth, he tells us, live a divine folk, and there are temples wherein the gods [and goddesses] do truly dwell, and I wish to convey, so far as words may, how some apparitions of that ancient beauty came to me in wood or on hillside or by the shores of the western sea. Sometimes lying on the hillside with the eyes of the body shut as in sleep I could see valleys and hills, lustrous as a jewel, where all was self-shining, the colours brighter and purer, yet making a softer harmony together than the colours of the world I know. The winds sparkled as they blew hither and thither, yet far distances w ere clear through that glowing air. What was far off was precise as what was near, and the will to see hurried me to what I desired. There, too, in that land I saw fountains as of luminous mist jetting from some hidden heart of power, and shining folk who passed into those fountains inhaled them and drew life from the magical air... Once I lay on the sand dunes by the western sea. The air seemed filled with melody. The motion of the wind made a continuous musical vibration. Now and then the silvery sound of bells broke on my ear. I saw nothing for a time. Then there was an intensity of light before my eyes like the flashing of sunlight through a crystal. It widened like the opening of a gate, and I saw the light was streaming from the heart of a glowing figure. Its body was pervaded with light as if sunfire rather than blood ran through its limbs. Light streams flowed from it. It

moved over me along the winds, carrying a harp, and there was a circling of golden hair that swept across the strings. Birds flew about it, and over the brows was a fiery plumage as of wings of outspread flame. On the face was an ecstasy of beauty and immortal youth... and I knew the Golden Age was all about me, and it was we who had been blind to it but that it had never passed away from the world.

The forces of living nature—the Goddess at work in the visible and invisible worlds of earthly creation—reside within oneself. If we want to find it on the outside, then where may we look for the goddess myth? Remarkably, one must turn to the "new" sciences in which innovative ideas are expressing an ideal in which the old goddess myth is emerging in a new form. This form is not symbolised as a personalised image of a female deity but as what it represents: a vision of life as a sacred whole in which all participate in mutual relationship, and where all participants are very much "alive".

Beginning with Heisenberg and Einstein, physicists are claiming that in subatomic physics the universe can be understood only as unity, that this unity is expressed in patterns of relationship, and that the observer is necessarily included in the act of observation. But have a care; Einstein as prophet remarked, 'With the splitting of the atom everything has changed save our mode of thinking, and thus we drift towards unparalleled disaster.'

The goddess myth can also be seen in the attempts of many humans at the individual level to live in a new way, allowing their feeling of participation with the Earth to shape and influence how they think about it and act towards it.

The Rose Queen of Languedoc

May it be the case that the Goddess is not just an abstract mythological concept formulated to inspire one to nurture life's inner qualities? May she in certain circumstances actually appear in the flesh to perform a service for a worthy soul? Consider this account passed down the generations in Templar circles concerning a Knight, Rossal, who was returning home from the Crusades to France. Welcome to the legend of the Rose Queen of Languedoc.

The exhausted Knight was on board a galleon. It was just before dawn. He had no sea legs and the rough passage of the boat over choppy waters was making him very ill. The galleon lurched violently and Rossal swallowed salt water. He wretched and vomited. 'Hell is not heat and fire,' he shouted into the wind. 'Hell is a cold and stormy sea!'

For the past three yearsRossal had fought side by side with Raymond of Toulouse. Together, they had stormed the ramparts of Nicaea, Antioch and Jerusalem. His body had been cut, stabbed, sliced and beaten by every weapon known to man but never had he felt so weak, tired an   d emaciated as in these moments.

Soon the sun rose, and its warm healing rays settled his spirit. He gazed toward the horizon. In the distance he thought he could make out a human figure. Startled, the Knight opened his eys wide, looked again and saw nothing except the waves.

He took a sip of mulled wine that had been prepared by an accommodating captain and closed his eyes. To his surprise, he was once more observing the figure, arms outstretched, walking across the sea towards the boat. He felt a shiver of energy coursing through his body as he beheld a beautiful radiant woman. Her blonde hair with a long braid hanging lightly over her left shoulder was accented by a smile that eclipsed the newly risen sun.

'Welcome, Sir Knight,' she said reassuringly. He felt her arms close around him and, instantly, their surroundings changed into an enormous castle hall. The hall was pure white, oblong in shape with a golden throne positioned centrally againt one wall.

'You have been washed and cleansed by the sea,' she began. 'Your vomiting is the symbol of release of all physical, emotional and mental encumbrances. At this moment, all of your past wounds are being mended by the morning sun. You are being *prepared*.'

Ethereally, the Knight knew that his body was sitting in a chair in the bow of an Italian merchant ship , while at the same time his spirit was sitting in a massive hall far away. 'In preparation for what and how?' he asked.

'Sir Knight, how do you prepare yourself for battle?'

'With armour, sword, battle-axe and horse,' he replied.

'Is it the armour, swor d, battle-axe and horse who fight that battle?' she asked.

'Of course not, it is I who uses these things to fight the battle.'

'Well, then, how does the 'I" prepare for battle?' said the lyrical voice.

Rossal felt his spirit fluctuating, beginning to mo ve away from the mystical hall. The feeling of slipping away quickened but a sudden whiff of cinnamon suddenly caressed his nostrils, allowing new energy to flow through his body and stop his withdrawal.

He answered the question. 'First, I prepare by sev ering myself from all that is past. Literally, I see a sword cutting any lin k that holds me to the past, whether it is something that I own, love, long for, or whether it be failures, mistakes and temptations. If I feel that my land in Languedoc or any other possession concerns me, I release it. If the woman I love or my family confine me within their expectations, I release them. If I dream of spring days and warm meals, I release them. If my wounds from a past battle fill me with pain and fear, I release them. If my unwise choice of friends concerns me, I release them. If anything connects me to the past before I enter battle, I will either die or be wounded. To survive my battles, I must be an island unto myself for a true opponent will exploit all weaknesses, especially those of the mind and heart.'

'Sir Knight, what instrument of your mind do you use to release or sever your past?' asked the myserious lady.

'First, I bathe in cold water, then I drink mulled wine. Next, I draw a circle or stand on a drying cloth without clothes and visualise myself on an island, a very small one where I can see the sea on all sides. Nothing connects me with the land; I am alone, free and in control. Standing nude eliminates any connection to objects given to me. Then I dress, seeing each piece of clothing or amour as a protecting or illuminating force. I repeat to myself constantly, "I am as brillaint and powerful as the sun, as agile and mysterious as the wind, and as fresh as the rain, I am a mirror to all I meet and the magic is always within me." I do this every morning.'

'What else do you do to prepare for battle?'

'Second, I light a candle, relax and close my eyes. I know that the destiny of every candle is to be consumed by fire, that the wax or tallow of a candle is the representation of man's body, and that the flame represents the spirit. Then, slowly, I re-open my eyes until I can just see the halo around the candle flame. I bring the halo and flame to me in my mind. Next, I become the flame and go beyond it to a light that begins to burn within me. It is at this time that all fear vanishes.'

'Excellent, Sir Knight,' replied the woman. 'By becoming one with the light, one releases all obligation, all responsibility and all karma. Obligation is something that you assume in regard to a physical or material situation. Responsibility is something you assume in regard to law and people. Karma is something chosen before birth and increased or decreased in direct proportion to your daily experiences. Sir Knight, is there anything else you do in preparation for battle?'

'Yes, I look through or beyond my goal. My goal becomes a threshold to new adventure and opportunity. My goal as a Crusader was to take Jerusalem and hold it for Christendom. As a Knight, my goals were fidelity, zeal and valour, not to take Jerusalem; I had strict faithfulness to promises, duties and requests. My zeal is an essence that comes from deep within in the form of earnest and diligent enthusiasm for any adventure or journey I undertake. Valour is the courage to be free in any undertaking without fear or failure. It is though these qualities that I naturally fulfill all physical or material goals...and go beyond them.'

'Excellent, Sir Knight, you have embraced the essence of preparation. Your adventure has just begun!'

He felt as if he were sand draining from an hourglass. The hall disappeared and he left the arms of the mysterious woman. His eyes flickered open, and he gazed out to sea once more. 'Sever my past, enter the light and go beyond my goals,' he said aloud as he walked to his cabin.

'Genoa! We dock in one hour,' announced the captain.

Head bent against driving rain and buffeting wind, Rossal led his battle-worn horse, Victor, through the streets of Genoa. Once away from the city centre, the Knight found a sma ll stone wall and used it as a stepping support to mount his white stallion. His armour, rusted and damaged from many battles, squeaked and strained as he made the difficult manouevre of mounting. His still-tender wounds made him moan and wince.

Slowly, the pair travelled northwest, into Burgundy and eventually, home to Languedoc. The winter winds now blew frozen rain hard against the armoured Knight. Carefully, the tired stallion made his way over roads and tracks pocked with holes and ankle deep in mud. Sleet and snow made the armour frosty, causing the Knight's skin to stick to it painfully. His nights were long and cold because he could not afford the price of a room, so he slep t in the forests, drafty stables or deserted peasant huts.

It was a week before they crossed the border into Languedoc . 'Ah, home!' the Knight whispered to his stallion. 'At last, I can die in peace, never before have I felt so tired.'

Suddenly, Victor stumbled over a concealed obstacle and threw his rider violently into the snow at the base of a huge oak. Rossal distinctly heard an ominous 'snap.' Feebly, he strained to get up, but his right leg was bent outwards at an impossible angle . B lood was seep ing through the louvres of his armour at the knee. 'Broken,' he said aloud. 'Well, Victor, this is where I die and with no regrets.'

Gingerly, Rossal pulled himself up to rest against the trunk of the oak. Eyes closed, the seasoned warrior felt every wound a nd battle scar as if they had just been inflicted. Victor stomped the ground and nuzzled his warm nose against his master's cheek. The Knight responded by reaching up and stroking the stallion's chin.

He intoned, 'I sever the past, I go to the light, I go...' He stopped and blinked his eyes. Through the trees, he could actually see a light. He reached up and grabbed Victor's halter and, with his remaining reserves, pulled himself up and erect, 'Go to the light, old friend.'

The Knight held tight to his horse's mane, the faithful companion walking slowly beside his master as they hobbled through the snow to the inviting light. Tears of pain ran down the Knight's bearded features as he felt his grip slipping. Unexpectedly, the horse stopped and gave a soft whinny. The Knight glanced up and was astonished to see before him a large castle seated in the centre of a small valley. Its multitude of bright lights seemed to be inviting every stranger to come and enter. Rossal needed no further invitation.

Victor swished his tail confidently then moved assuredly down the small slope to the edge of the castle moat. From somewhere inside came the sound of a harp playing the haunting melody of an old Yuletide carol. Rossal smiled and felt a glimmer of hope. 'But how am I going to muster the strength to yell for the drawbridge to be lowered?' he asked in frustration.

No sooner had he voiced the question when the drawbridge fell with a thump only a few feet in front of them. After making what seemed like an endless crossing, they entered an inner courtyard that was free from snow. He turned slightly and briefly saw in the forest that it was snowing heavily, and then the gate swung into place. Then he looked above him. 'Stars,' he said incredulously. Unwittingly, he let go of Victor's mane and began to fall. Immediately, two young pages caught both arms, while another two helpers started to lead the horse away.

Diligently, the first two pages guided the Knight across the courtyard to the castle entrance. Hobbling forward with his two human crutches, the Knight descended many winding stairs, the music of the harp and the smell of evergreen becoming ever stronger. Finally, at the bottom of the stairs they entered a great hall...the same one that he had seen and visited in his mind while on the boat!

The two pages gently steered him across the hall to a chair in the middle of the floor, about twenty feet from a golden throne. With great effort, Rossal pulled his helmet from his head and placed it in his lap. To his right was a colossal fireplace heaped with blazing evergreen logs. On his left sat a harpist who was playing the same mesmerising melody he had heard in the forest. There was also a long half-crescent table positioned just below the throne with nine stools spread evenly from one end to the other. From somewhere within the castle came the sound of a single resonating bell, causing the harpist to cease playing.

A curtain behind the throne began to move and nine hooded figures entered the hall . To the Knight, they did not feel like monks, nuns or priests but he could not see their faces.   They crossed directly to the crescent table and sat on the stools.

Once more, the bell rang. This time a blonde woman stepped from behind the curtain, 'The woman from the boat,' gasped the Knight and, to himself, added silently, ' but even more beautiful.' She was wearing a long, flowing red garment, an exquisite combination coat, cape and gown that was trimmed with white fur. She hesitated for a moment, looked over at the Knight, then gracefully sat on the throne.

'Welcome, once again, Sir Knight.' The next instant she clapped her hands, and a serving girl brought a large cup of mulled wine to the Knight. Another serving girl entered with nine cups, one each for the hooded figures. Finally, a third girl entered bringing a golden goblet to the woman on the throne.

The mysterious woman lifted her goblet high in the air and said, 'To a Knight of the Holy Sepulchre, who has severed all past experiences, moved on to the light, and gone beyond his goal.The nine hooded figures raised their cups in toast and joined the Knight in a long deep drink. For the first time in weeks, Rossal felt completely warm.

One of the hooded men rose and walked over to the Knight. In kneeling position, he reached out his soft hands and touched the bleeding, broken leg. Immediately, the Knight's leg felt first very cold and then warm. The hooded healer stood, bowed,   and moved back to his stool. Rossal was about to remark on it when the woman spoke.

'Sir Knight, I am Queen Ros Niveus, and this is the Castle and Kingdom of the Way of the White Rose. On this, the second day of the Solstice, having made your Preparation, are you willing to meet the Challenge?'

'The Challenge?' said the Knight, 'Does this mean I am still alive?'

The Queen smiled, 'Yes, brave Knight, but you are about to leave one kind of life behind and enter into another.'

The wine had given Rossal the courage to speak more . 'You said I was here once before. I know my body was   never here, but maybe my mind or spirit?'

'If your spirit was here, then all of you was here   ,' said the Queen. 'Your body is a reflection of your spirit, not your spirit a reflection of your body. Listen to my companions who sit before you as they present you with the challenge. Relax, close your eyes and quaff one more drink from your cup. Now hear the words of these companion energies. Together, these energies comprise the learning experiences we must undertake in the University of the Physical. By worki ng on them fully, consistently and joyfully we open that hidden door to unlimited adventures. Which of their symbols do you feel can be a tool to enhance your greatest strength, and which of them could be your greatest vulnerability? Try to feel these symbols of power in your life, for you will use them for the next nine years.'

To the Knight's left, the first companion placed an Eye-Shaped Diamond on the table, and spoke:

'I am the Energy of clear sight and unlimitedness. With me, you can be unlimited in any aspect of your life. Within me, there are always beginnings...never status quo. The all-seeing eye symbolises divine consciousness. Only through clear inner-sight will you gain balance. I am Infinity!'

The second hooded figure rose and placed a Red Amber Pyramid on the crescent table.

'I am the Energy of perfect creation, and my greatest power comes through companionship. Within me, you will balance your masculine self with your electro-negative feminine self. This bonding allows you to reach your ultimate physical and spiritual creativity within your lifetime. I am Man!'

The third figure rose and placed a Rosewood Maul on the table with the other symbols.

'I am the Energy of controlled force. Within me, you will find happiness and joy in being a creator. Through the concept of mystical-metaphysical conception, incubation, birth and nurturing, you become the ultimate creator who is able to channel any power or energy into one place. All creation: art, music and the spirit, must exerience conception, incubation, birth and nurturing. I am Woman!'

The fourth figure remained seated and placed an Amethyst Beehive on the table.

'I am the Energy of hard labour. Within me, one will find richness and sweetness in daily living through unselfish motives. I am a miniature world manifested in the circle of power, and the training ground which is responsible for the seeds and roots of integrity, honesty, spiritual insight and personal freedom. I am Family!'

The fifth and middle figure of the nine companions rose and placed a Bouquet of Wildflowers on the table.

'I am the Energy of the Soul. Through me, there is blossoming of the mind and a flowering of the body. Like this bouquet, each flower must be healthy for the whole to survive. As an extension of nature, I can not maintain my beauty and health in the midst of doubt and fear. I am Healing!'

180

The sixth figure rem ained seated and carefully placed a bea utiful clear crystal Winged Hourglass with the other symbols on the table.

'I am the Energy of opportunity through timelessness. By a benevolent attitude in all aspects of life: personal, home, business and recreation, I allow new doors to always open. I am expectation, aspiration, hope and belief wrapped into one. I am Treasure!'

Slowly, the seventh figure rose and brought forward a Golden Pot of Incense. Magically, from out of nowhere came a flame, and a fragrant scent filled the air.

'I am the symbol of the five senses. My incense is prepared from ancient alchemic laws. Proper inhalation takes one from a physical, emotional and mental state into an intuitive power. I am always patient as my aroma opens the senses to clairaudience, clairvoyance and clairsentience. I am Senses!'

The eighth figure stood and carefully p laced a Silver Bladed Scythe on the table.

'I am the Energy of transition and regeneration. That which is created within me is transitory, always changing and becoming something else. I am a progression from the Godforce withinNature to nature within me. My consistency is an inconsistency because I am always neutral. I am Nature!'

The ninth figure rose and placed a Blue Lapis Nine -Pointed Star on the table.

'This is the symbol of symbol and energy of love, joy, temperance, and all things positive. Nine alludes to ultimate completion and the finest perfection of any undertaking. I am the whole, for what comes into me, must leave me. I am not death but eternal life. I am Evolution!'

The ninth figure bowed, and Queen Ros Niveus approached the Knight.

'Sir Knight, it is time for you to relax and sleep. As you drift off to sleep, go through each of these energies in your mind: Infinity, Man, Woman, Family, Healing, Treasure, Senses, Nature and Evolution. This is your challenge. Choose one energy as your personal symbol for the coming nine years.'

Rossal slept soundly, having gone through the repetitions before dropping off. In the morning a squire accompanied the Knight to the Great Hall. As he en tered, the Queen stood up from her thr one, along with her nine companions.

'Welcome, Sir Knight, you look strong, refreshed and healthy this morning. Please, sit and place your helmet on the floor by your chair for you will need your hands.'

She clapped loudly and two pages brought into the hall a small wooden table, which they placed directly in front of the Knight's chair.

The Queen resumed speaking, 'Your world is made up of many powerful and diverse energies. Some call themselves religions, philosophical societies, political movements, while others call themselves ancient mystical teachings. However, you are now in the castle of The Way of the White Rose. We, here, are your bonders! We interconnect between all beliefs but always quietly, silently and secretly. Those, like yourself, will seem as if they are one thing. However, in reality, you will be another.

'Within you is a divine seed. That seed is called God, while others call it Allah and Jehovah. No matter how hard you try, you can never explain what that seed is. If you don't feel this seed, and doubt that it can be within you, you may go to a church, mosque or temple to find it. Within these "Holy" places, in silence, you may feel that you hear or connect with God. In reality, you are just listening to yourself. God is a seed within everyone, but that seed does not grow in everyone. Nurture that seed silently with love and patient devotion while seeking beauty in all things, and that seed of the Godforce within will sprout and grow.

'A caution—when the seed sprouts, most individuals tell everyone that he or she has found God. At that point, that sprout is in danger. If one declares their wealth, others will take it. If a person expounds upon their own beauty, there will always be someone who is more beautiful. In truth, if you want that seed to sprout, grow and blossom you will maintain a silence. Your strength, beauty and wealth will come from knowing and believing what is within you.

'Sir Knight, place your hands flat upon the table. Now, spread them apart so that the tips of your extended thumbs are touching. You will see that you have an open-ended square.'

The Queen stepped down from her throne and placed a small rose-scented candle between Rossal's hands. A flautist began to play and the cande flame magically came to life, flickering in time with the music.

The Queen asked, 'Sir Knight, look into the flame and tell us which Energy you have chosen.'

'I have chosen unlimited Infinity!'

No sooner had Rossal spoken these words than the candle flame brilliance consumed the entire hall and fused the Knight into the light. A commanding vibrant voice filled and refreshed every part of his body.

'You are now Man, the Guardian. First and foremost, you will realise that you are one with the Godforce. All power lies within you and comes from within. Your physical symbology is the Eye-Shaped Diamond. You are the Energy of clear sight, which leads to realisation. You can be unlimited in any aspect of your life. Within you, there are always beginnings...never status quo. The all-seeing eye symbolises divine consciousness. Through patient, clear inner-sight will you gain balance.'

The light subsided and again the Knight was in his chair. Before him was the Queen who was holding a sword. 'Sir Knight, bow your head.'

'Sir Knight,' said the Queen, ' I christen you with this double -edged sword. One edge stands for justice, the other for chivalry. You have been initiated by the Nine, and you are now a Knight of the Way of the White Rose. What you have the ability to be and what you have become is the reason you are here today. As you step forward on your journey, the inner power of this Path will be revealed to you, step by step.

'Unknowingly, your actions will automatically make you a bonder of positive energies. What you seem to be on your journey will not what you will be. The experiences, the perceptions and the changes that you have undergone here will open doors for years to c ome. This castle is your sanctuary. It will be available to you, upon request, no matter where you are.'

The Queen ended the ceremony by dubbing the Knight on both shoulders and asked him to stand. He reached out to receive the sword now being offered. The Queen clapped her hands and the Squire returned. 'Squire, please take our esteemed guest to his horse.' The Knight bowed, turned and departed the Great Hall.

As they entered the courtyard, the Knight saw Victor happily pawing the cobblestones. His white coat glistened in the morning sun.

'Victor, your scars and wounds are gone, just like mine. You look years younger, yet much more powerful. You must have experienced an initiation of your own!'

Victor whinnied loudly. With the help of two stable boys   Rossal swung up into the saddle and grabbed Victor's reins. The stallion lunged forward in anticipation but the Kni ght held him in ch eck until the gate could rise, and the bridge lowered.

'Sir Knight...Rossal!' This startled the Knight who turned in his saddle to see the Queen standing by the great doors of the Castle. She had called him by his name for the first time. 'May your journey within give you the strength and the power you will need for your Journey without.'

He waved and crossed the bridge. It   was still snowing but now it seemed a lot more inviting. Victor pranced up the small hill, and Rossal turned to take a last look at the Castle.

'It's gone, Victor, it's gone!'

The horse whinnied slightly, as if to say, 'I know!'

The Knight loosened his hold on the reins and said, thoughtfully, 'Well, old friend, we begin a new Journey.'

Rossal's adventure in the company of the Rose Queen in 12th century Languedoc is a rare example of an initiatory encounter with a Goddess, not of the east but of the Occident. This coming together of the human and the divine was made all the more extraordinary because it took place six hundred years after the demise of the Goddess cults in the west, marked by Saint Genevieve's supplanting of Isis in Paris. Nevertheless, it illustrates that provided one is prepared to believe that such encounters are possible, an act of faith perhaps on a par with a belief in fairy folk and the Elementals, then Rossal's experience indicates that teachers in the invisible worlds are always available to those that seek another way.

The fact that a few years afterwards Rossal would be invited by Hugues de Payens to be one of the founding fathers of the Knights Templar, might explain why Queen Ros Niveus believed it necessary to initiate this particular Knight into the Ancient Mysteries, especially when Rossal was destined to turn down the offer and assume a more important role in the safeguarding of an esoteric tradition that dated back to Mary Magdalene's arrival in Gaul. Moreover, Rossal's adventure was all the more remarkable because the Rose Queen's teachings appear to indicate a metaphysical alignment with the ancient Ennead energies that underpinned the Crystal Skulls community that survived the destruction of Atlantis and settled in what is now southern Chile, a linkage that demonstrates the universality of symbols of power and spiritual endeavour. Transcendental teachings are not limited by geography; they recognise no limits of any kind.

'Arise, Sir Knight!'

The Forces of Living Nature

It is wrong for science to consider that the study of the Earth can be divided into physical disciplines such as geology, biology, meteorology, astronomy, and all the rest. The Earth is one whole, living system   that resonates. All these forces and reactions play back and forth, creating responses, changes and echoes in all terrestrial structures and processes, from the densest to the most subtle. There are countless examples of the forces of living nature. Among them are phenomena such as tornadoes, hurricanes, snowstorms, landslides, tsunamis, earthquakes, volcanic explosions and lightning strikes.

The ancients regarded l ightning as the grace of God. Grace is a balance between the positive and the negative in the world and lightning clears the air from both and leaves a neutrality. One on one, Nature has a thousand times the power of man. A forest of trees is pure, healing and replenishing. A forest of humans is largely demanding, diseased and self centred.

This section does not examine meteorological events, which, in my mind, are largly influenced by Nature's regulators, the Elementals, which merit their own chapter in later pages . Rather, it is concerned with two very striking phenomena of our time—crop circles and UFOs—that indicate that the Earth is very much alive and enriched with a consciousness that is unimaginably complex and powerful. The formations in the fields and the strange things seen in the skies, although both dating back centuries, but which have seen exponential increases in recent decades, are very striking occurrences, which, evidence suggests, are exotic extrusions from Mother Earth (crystal phenomena playing n o small part), and neither hoaxes nor extraterrestial.

We have seen that the electro-magnetic polarity of Earth's transcendental super-consciousness is feminine. In Greek mythology, this spirit energy was known as Gaia, meaning land or earth. She was the personification of the Earth . In the Greek pantheon , Gaia, a primordial deity, is the ancestral mother of all life. She is the mother of Uranus (the sky), from whose sexual union she bore the Titans (themselves parents of many of the Olympian gods), the Cyclopes and the Giants; as well as of Pontus (the sea), from whose union she bore the primordial sea gods.

We saw in Chapter 12 that t he Gaia hypothesis, also known as Gaia theory, proposes that all organisms and their inorganic surroundings on Earth are closely integrated to form a single   , s elf-regulating complex system, which is powered and maintained by the forces of living nature. Although the Gaia forces largely go about their work unseen they occasionally are observed through the emergence of visible phenomena.

The ancients taught that the neutral lifeforce within animals, plants and minerals keeps the earth in an "existence charge" of perfect balance. For billions of years the planet existed in this happy equilibrium until the

Universal Law judged it was time to raise life on earth to the next level of creative expression with the introduction of humans equipped with a new unit called the mind. The mind's constant conflict with good and evil and one's relentless struggle to forge a path of balance between them generates a tremendous amount of power that feeds back into the Universal Law, thus increasing it.

In line with David Bohm's thinking, humanity may be a necessary contributor to beneficial increase in the universal scheme of things, but we should not delude ourselves that our planet cannot do without our presence when circumstances demand. Surely, this is a fundamental aspect of the messages being transmitted with increasing regularity by Mother Nature and her invisible cohorts.

Some of the most dramatic signs are those conveyed in crop circles, UFOs and rare appearances of extra-biological energy forms. I discussed these phenomena in detail in previous works for AUP[26] but a recap of the essentials and a reproduction of key texts in the context of the forces of living nature will be useful.

Crop Circles

Crop circles appear regularly worldwide. Remarkably, most of them appear in Britain, with most of these located in the county of Wiltshire (home to Stonehenge and the Avebury complex). Here is not the place to debate the "why," except to note that a key contributory factor in this embarrassment of circle delights is the presence of the "Michael and Mary" ley line that stretches from Cornwall to Norfolk. Michael and Mary are the intertwining male and female, solar and lunar serpent energies that snake through the English countryside, and which appear to grow in power as they weave through the Avebury complex.

However, the crop circle makers in Wiltshire show a clear feminine bias when it comes to making choices for locating their beautiful designs. Dowsing investigators Miller and Broadhurst[27] found that all 51 crop circles recorded at Avebury and Silbury Hill up to and during their investigations, were positioned 'exactly on the course of the "female" [Mary] energy flow.'

John Michell's investigations[28] indicated that the earliest record of crop circles came from UFO investigators in the 1960s. Areas of crushed grass or corn associated with UFO appearances were observed in

---

[26] *The Landing Lights of Magonia* (2018), and *The Gods in the Fields* (2020)
[27] Miller, H; Broadhurst, P., *The Sun and the Serpent*, Pendragon Press, Launceston, Cornwall, 1989.
[28] *Crop Circles: Harbingers of World Change*, ed. Bartholomew A., Gateway, 1991

Australia, Britain and elsewhere, dubbed at the time "UFO nests."

Michell[29] supported alchemist Patrick Harpur's opinion that the "god" behind the circles is Hermes, the messenger of the gods, the Soul of the World, the guardian of mysteries, and the inventor of the first symbols in the birth of writing. He is the notorious tricks ter associated with the wandering nocturnal spirit of the earth whose m ysterious flickering lights were known in old England as"Hermes lights." Looking at the messages and symbology in the fields has be en described as like seeing something once known but now quite forgotten. Michell and Harpur believed that Hermes seems to be once more speaking to us in person, an act that they descri be as uniquely and immensely important for humankind, which is providing a new revelation that we must take pains to recognize, interpret and act upon.

In the 1990s, the Gaia theory was revived as an explanation for the increase of crop circles, both in numbers and complexity, and was thus interpreted as an SOS call by our planet.The Cambridge physicist Rupert Sheldrake supports the "SOS" theory, suggesting that the Earth's organic systems are regulated not only by physical laws but also by "morphogenetic fields," an invisible "form-producing" consciousness that is inherent in nature. In this model, the Earth appropriates the symbols in the crop circles from human thoughtforms that derive from our collective unconscious or "egregore." This being the case, the crop designs are necessarily formulated from an invisible dimension of living nature within the earth itself. Sheldrake developed his idea in his visualisation of an interacting universe whose tiniest element—he gives the example of a hologram, but a crop circle will equally suffice—contains the information of the entire universe. In this model there is no process of "chance," only a blueprint of evolution, which is transmitted throughout the universe. Progressing these scientific opinions, there are those who believe that the two -dimensional designs we see in the fields are an unfoldment from their true multi-dimensional forms.

One imaginative way to reflect on these incredible theories is to liken a crop circle to a UFO parked in a field. That the formation appears to be a flat, inert imprint on solid ground is a trick of perception whereas, in reality, there is no "ground," only a living, spinning "alien" extrusion from dimensions beyond conscious human comprehension.

In terms of symbological interpretation, Carl Jung suggested that phenomena associated with Mother Earth's forces of living nature, such as crop circles and UFOs, may be regarded as examples of what he

---

[29]Michell, J., *The Face and the Message*, Gothic Image Publications, 2002

termed a visionary rumour, typified by the visions seen during WWI by soldiers at Mons and the Catholic faithful at Fátima.

The first requisite for a visionary rumour is the experiencing by the many of an unusual emotion, experienced as an intense delusion of the senses that springs from a stronger excitation and, therefore, arises from a deeper source. Jung argued that psychological projections such as these must have a psychic cause because striking phenomena which indicate the presence of the forces of living nature cannot possibly have no importance in the grand scheme of human consciousness and, therefore, represent a psychological situation common to all mankind that must be considered, weighed and interpreted with all due urgency.

Jung's opinions on the nature of "alien" energy forms continued to resonate with circle investigators through the years. Experts Colin Andrews and Pat Delgado considered that the circles were created by "an unknown intelligence using an unknown force-field."

Fellow investigator George Wingfield, graduate in natural sciences from Trinity College Dublin, did his practical work experience at the Royal Observatory in Greenwich in stellar spectra and the Earth's magnetism. In the 1980s the Wingfield family was living in Wiltshire and became eager circle watchers. Wanting to get to the bottom of the puzzling phenomenon, George Wingfield concluded after much study that the circles were "the product of a non-human intelligence whose nature we still have to investigate as far as we can do that." He set out twenty fundamental characteristics of crop circles, mostly concerning placement and form but the last in the list reads:

Intelligent reaction to the circle researchers' discussions and theories, apparently in an attempt to communicate and to lead us in a certain intended direction.

I concur. The circles are made to be read and interpreted psychically or scientifically. Those observers that have some "shine" about them may come away from their experience with thoughts and feelings about what improvements they can make in their lives to help heal a planet in pain.

Scientists, who, by and large, comprise a community whose members are more intellectually than intuitively gifted, are invited to interpret a design's math and geometry and take collective action to achieve the same objective. Rarely, a great thinker who also believes in the unseen such as scientists Isaac Newton, Albert Einstein, David Bohm and logician Charles Dodgson, comes along and by virtue of their combined left-brain/right-brain flare brings new levels of understanding to complex metaphysical phenomena.

Pure unadulterated circles, genuine extrusions from the etheric world of higher Nature, rang e from rudimentary geometrical forms to designs of extraordinary complexity . Some have wondered if crop circles are intended to provide mathematical insight, which, once understood, will help mankind to restore its reverence for the Earth. Reflecting on th is, researcher Linda Moulton Howe asks: 'Could something out there be trying to reinforce the idea that our universe and all its energy and mass are defined by a repeating feedback loop that is mathematical in evolution and powered by consciousness?'[30]

John Michell decried the modern-day tendency to confuse the medium with the message, which in the context of crop circle phenomena he regarded as essentially apocalyptic:

> ...There are no known precedents that messages from the gods
> of Heaven or Earth ever cons isted of good news or of
> congratulations on the happy course of things. Almost always
> they appear as warnings and omens of approaching difficulties.
> As a consequence, it is hardly surprising that many people
> associate crop circles with ecological crisis and comprehend
> them as a spontaneous expression of protest on the part of our
> mishandled Earth.

There is no shortage of support from earth watchers for Michell's sobering words. Native Americans believe that crop circles are delivering messages that the Earth is in serious difficulties. Hopi Indians told Colin Andrews that Mother Earth is speaking to us in symbols directly to man's consciousness through the circles. She is reaching the limits of her endurance to sustain further assaults and is reaching out in an attempt to convince her children to change their behaviour.

And so, yes, we are good for   contributing cosmologically to the beneficial increase in the universal scheme of things but let us not kid ourselves that our planet cannot do without our presence when circumstances demand. Surely, this is a fundamental aspect of the messages in the fiel ds, whose authorship is increasingly suspected of having a strong feminine, Mother Nature aspect.

Evidence suggests that crop circles incorporate goddess symbology. Carol Cochrane, member of the London -based Centre for Crop Circle Studies, has carried out studies in many formations. Her work indicates that "Isis" is encoded in 90% of the circles, and "Osiris" in 60%.

---

[30] Howe, L., *Glimpses of Other Realities, Volume II: High Strangeness*, New Orleans. Paper Chase Press, 1998

Recurring phrases in the goddess context include, "the answers are in the letters," and "the letters are at all the sites."

Isabelle Kingston, a British trance medium who earns considerable respect among circle researchers, offers a psychic solution to the meaning of the "letters." The gifted daughter of a doctor, Isabelle had a successful career in banking and finance before developing her channeling skills. She is a modest person who readily admits she is the unlikeliest person to have any kind of dealings with the Circlemakers. Researcher Michael Hesemann is convinced that Kingston warrants attention because she has a convincing record of accurately predicting where and when formations will appear. She correctly predicted the mysterious quintuplet design at Sibury Hill in June 1988, before going on to say that the number of circles would grow enormously. In the following twelve months there were approximately 300 circles compared with 120 in the previous year.

Kingston said that the "old ones" built Silbury Hill, the largest, and most mysterious artificial mound, in Europe, as an insurance policy for a time when humanity would expand its energy from the opening up of these centres, hence Hesemann's obervation that Silbury Hill in Wiltshire is the "Archimedean point" of the circle phenomenon.

Kingston said that the triangle in the Barbury Castle pictogram is an 'indication of different dimensions, and the gates to these dimensions are given to us, which are contained in the power of the pyramid. I feel we can learn of a new form of energy through studying the pictograms, which possibly can be used in humankind's future.'

In his masterwork, Manly P. Hall[31] included a number of illustrations regarding the Rosicrucian mysteries. One illustration's upper part closely resembles the Barbury design. The resemblance between Hall's diagram and the Barbury Castle imagery that appeared in a Wiltshire field 63 years later is so striking that one wonders if the circle maker desired to make a deliberate reproduction. May this provide a clue as to the identity of the circle's creators? Hall described the diagram's upper part as a representation of the realm of the gods, the first divine manifestation symbolized by the equilateral triangle. The 7 outer circles are the angelic world. The diagram's bottom part is the "Ungrund," the Abyss. Kingston's told Hesemann that the circle makers are "The Watchers," about which trance communications have remarked:

> ...a term for a cosmic universal consciousness, for beings which
> are concerned about the planet and what is happening on Earth
> at present. It is a collective intelligence which guides you mortal

---

[31]Ibid

humans... linked to angelic beings, part of cosmic consciousness... Britain lies in the centre of the great pyramid of light which encircles your world... You are the immune system of your planet, the healing system which will create the changes...

This country is a testing ground, it has to be right before the whole can be l ined up with other dimensions... Circles have appeared as a blueprint for humankind to mark that place as a place of power... There are ley lines running through the Earth and at various points lines of power are energised... This ancient land [Britain] holds the balance, it is the key to the world. Many of these sacred sites are being cleansed... so that they are channels of new energy.

Spiritual energy from other dimensions is drawn down to the Hill of Silbury, the hill of the Shining Beings... The energy has been put through thought-processes with light beams, so we input power into the Earth's grid. This is to stabilise the energies in the Earth, to stop the Earth destroying you. This has been going on for some time. You have been told of the purpose of Silbury Hill: if we placed the circles elsewhere you would not have recognized it.

Crop circles have multi -layered meanings, many components, many types of energies coming together, energies of the Earth and of the Universe. They are created by an energy form, a fo rm of consciousness, possibly out of one's own self, possibly from other dimensions.

The nature realms and spiritual systems are creating formations, which have a profound effect on people who see and experience them. The crop circles are like a score of music between the Earth and the cosmos.

You do not at this time need to learn to read the score. The best is to feel it... the energies being transmitted at this time are a combination of all elements and all elemental beings, as well as interplanetary info rmation... Go to the hills and call for the Brethren. Link yourselves wth the Cosmos and draw the energies in to help. Become lightning conductors. Channel the light into the very soil. Transfer it into pure love and wait for the explosion.

The goddess forces in the fields are urging us to wake up and smell the coffee while there is still time. There are indications that they are very much on our side; they want us to succeed in turning things around and reconnecting humankind with the natural world.

There is a remarkable theory that crop circles are a method of "earth acupuncture," a healing process administered by unseen physicians to activate southern England's energy lines in accordance with prophecies concerning the emergence of a New Jerusalem. Mary and Michael's wild dance across England's sacred landscape generates enormous power, power that the dragon-fixing characteristic of crop circles absorbs and magnifies so that messages achieve maximum potency, readability and comprehensibility. Something is building. The feeling is palpable.

Simeon Hein[32] has examined the association between crop circles and anomalous electromagnetic phenomena, such as battery failure, camera malfunctions, and strange balls of light which are sometimes experienced in and around the formations. Accepting that there has not yet been a satisfactory explanation for these observations, he proposes a theory based on the similarities between crop formations and crystals.

Specifically, Hein believes that at least three properties of crystals are at work in crop formations and these may explain some of their anomalous effects; i) pushing down on the crop may activate the piezo-electric effect; ii) the shape of a crop formation may affect the crystalline properties of wheat and other grain crops by interacting with the chlorophyll in their cells; iii) the periodic and symmetrical alignment of the individual stalks may create resonance.

Crystal radios, which use no batteries, are an example of the piezo-electric effect. In a crystal radio, the crystal acts to transform the energy of the radio signal into an audible sound that is perceivable through an earpiece. The piezo-electro effect allows the crystal to convert radio signals into electricity. Similarly, in Hein's thinking, pushing down on the grain crop "activates" its latent crystal properties. The energy intrinsic to the plants may be converted into another type of energy that resonates with people and objects. Thus, the way in which the crop formation is created could directly affect its subsequent energetic properties. One of the main characteristics of crop formations is that the positions of the individual crop stems are changed from a vertical position to a flattened, horizontal one. In making crop patterns, pressure is put on the plants to create a particular shape.

Crop patterns can often affect areas several acres in size or larger. If the piezo-electric effect due to the circle makers' "pushing down" actions

---

[32] *Electromagnetic and Crystalline Properties of Crop Formations*, January 2002

were to be activated at this large scale , this might result in a significant change in the electromagnetic a nd other properties of the crop . In their recent research, Hein and Russell of Midwest Research and Colin Andrews of CPRI (Circles Phenomenon Research International) have found large changes in the electrostatic and magnetic fields in many crop formations.

The overall shape of crop formations must also be considered. Generally, formations are periodic (internally repetitive) and symmetrical, an important quality of crystals. The fields are planted by a seed-drill machine that plants the seeds at regular in tervals, about every inch or so. In doing so, the net result is acres of plants planted at evenly spaced intervals.

In effect, this agricultural lattice -array is created with periodicity similar to a natural crystal. One of the effects of a lattice array in a natural crystal is a highly periodic, repetitive arrangement of atoms across large distances, atomically speaking. In a desire to maximize crop yields, the farmer has unintentionally created the same arrangement. The crop circle functions as another periodic pattern overlaid on a pre-existing one. These coherent patterns may be responsible for creating some of the subtle energy effects that are sometimes reported in the vicinity of these formations.

Often defying a conventional, physical explanation, the effect of all these crystalline components is to create a self-sustaining resonance field capable of conducting various frequencies and subtle energies. Hein believes that this transduction effect is responsible for creating many of the anomalies experienced in and around crop formations.

Liquid crystals and crop formations share many of the same properties in terms of the orientation of the individual crystals or stalks. Liquid crystals exhibit various types of phases which describe the orientation of the individual crystals. Two phases, the smectic and nematic phases, describe conditions in which the individual crystals have large-scale order with respect to their orientation. In these phases, the crystals begin to point in the same directions , creating long-range orientational order. This order is characterized by parallel but not lateral (end-to-end) order. This parallel, orientational coherency as opposed to random orientation, gives the crystal its properties.

Similarly, in a crop formation, the process of patterning the crop gives the stalks an overall orientational coherency. Crop formations act as a perturbation or disturbance from equilibrium conditions of the grain field. In a liquid crystal, all of the crystals can align in one direction or another to form layers that can superimpose on each other, a property very similar to the effect often found in the lay of crop formations. As the individual plant stalks are arranged as a whole in crystal-like patterns, the whole formation may resonate like a crystal.

In a liquid crystal lattice-array, such as in a computer display, the crystals are in a semi-liquid state that allows them to move in response to electrical fields that are turned on and off very quickly. The crystals are evenly space across the lattice. As electrical current is precisely applied to the array, the crystals twist and untwist very rapidly allowing precise points in the light screen behind the crystal lattice to show through. This is called a "chiral nematic" phase whereby the liquid crystals all point in a coherent direction and certain crystals twist as groups. The direction in which a group of crystals points is called the "director."

However, while the same principle is in operation in both liquid crystals and crop formations, in the latter it is reversed. In a liquid crystal, an electric current is applied to change the orientation of the crystals. In a crop formation, the circle-makers change the orientation of groups of individual stalks. If each stalk is seen as an individual crystal, then it follows that modifying the orientation of the stalks generates or changes the flow of energy in the field.

Hein concludes that the similarity between crystals—particularly liquid crystals— and crop formations provides an intriguing model with which to understand some of the anomalous objects and phenomena present near crop formations.

As crystals act to transduce energy through the piezo-electric effect, this may explain how crop formations act to disrupt electronic equipment and interact with the consciousness of human researchers and other visitors. In effect, crop circles may simultaneously serve as a form of natural magic and as an elemental resonant technology.

UFOs

A review of current scientific and esoteric opinion suggests that UFOs and their occupants are not only a psychic manifestation but are extrusions from dimensions that interwine with our Earth. Psychoanalytical interpretation of UFO activity provides an invaluable opportunity to consider the vexing question as to the phenomenon's origins. Even in the very early days of UFO research astute minds were ascribing a psychic component to the phenomenon.

The British science writer Gerald Heard in *Is Another World Watching* (1950) proposed his "bee" theory, in which UFOs represent a mindless order organised and controlled by a larger intelligence. Arthur

C. Clarke said much the same thing, arriving at the conclusion that UFOs were paraphysical and not from other planets.

In his response to a let ter from authors Randall Pugh and Frederick Holiday, John Keel also said that UFOs are related to psychic phenomena.[33] Keel believed that history, psychiatry, religion and the occult are far more important for an understanding of the flying saucer mystery than the publication of books that simply recount sightings.

Researcher Michael Gosso also advanced the idea that despite their encroachment into the world of matter UFOs are more akin to a psychic projection than non-human intelligence. He said, 'UFOs and other extraordinary phenomena are manifestations of a disturbance in the collective unconscious of the human species.'[34]

To many analysts, the observed behaviour of UFOs indicates that they are evidently not constructed of solid matter and, hence, are paraphysical in nature. They move at incredible speeds but create no sonic booms. They perform impossible manoeuvres that defy the laws of inertia and appear and disappear instantly like phantoms.

In 1955, eight years after seeing a string of nine, shiny un identified flying objects flying past Mount Rainier at speeds of 1,200 miles per hour, private pilot Kenneth Arnold expressed his view that spaceships were a form of living energy. Also in 1955, Air Marshall Lord Dowding (the man who directed the Battle ofBritain in 1940) made the astonishing statement in a public lecture that the phenomenon was paraphysical, declaring that not only were UFO visitors immortal but also could make themselves invisible to human sight, take on human form, and walk and work among us unnoticed.

In 1957 Ray Palmer, founder of *Flying Saucers* magazine, said that in his opinion UFOs hailed from civilisations with paraphysical ties to the human race. Earlier, in 1949, Palmer had already said that he believed UFOs to be extra-dimensional, not extra-terrestrial.

Engineer Bryant Reeve in his 1965 book *The Advent of the Cosmic Viewpoint* concluded that UFO sightings in themselves are irrelevant, subordinate in importance to the far more fundamental recognition that they are actually a part of a larger paraphysical phenomenon.

What is the paraphysical hypothesis? It is stated succinctly by RAF Air-Marshal Sir Victor Goddard, KCB, CBE, MA. On 3 May 1969 he delivered a public lecture in which he said:

---

[33] Keel, J. *Operation Trojan Horse*, Anomalist Books, San Antonio, 1970
[34] Grosso, M., *"UFOs and the Myth of the New Age,"* in *Cyberbiological Studies of the Imaginal Component in the UFO Contact Experience*, ed. Dennis Stillings [St. Paul, Minnesota Archaeus Project, 1989], P. 81

That while it may be that some operators of UFO are normally the paraphysical denizens of a planet other than Earth, there is no logical need for this to be so. For, if the materiality of UFO is paraphysical (and consequently normally invisible), UFO could more plausibly be creations of an invisible world coincident with the space of our physical Earth planet than creations in the paraphysical realms of any other planet in the solar system... Given that real UFO are paraphysical, capable of reflecting light like ghosts; and given also that, according to many observers, they remain visible as they change position at ultrahigh speeds from one point to another, it follows that those that remain visible in transition do not dematerialize for that swift transition and therefore, their mass must be of a diaphanous, very diffuse nature, and their substance relatively etheric... The observed validity of this supports the paraphysical assertion and makes the likelihood of UFO being Earth-created greater than the likelihood of their creation on another planet... The astral world of illusion, which (on psychical evidence) is greatly inhabited by illusion-prone spirits, is well known for its multifarious imaginative activities and exhortations. Seemingly, some of its denizens are eager to exemplify principalities and powers. Others pronounce upon morality, spirituality, Deity, et cetera. All of these astral components who invoke human consciousness may be sincere but many of their theses may be framed to propagate some special phantasm, perhaps of an earlier incarnation, or to indulge an inveterate and continuing technological urge toward materialistic progress, or simply to astonish and disturb the gullible for the devil of it.

The late John Napier, anthropologist and one time Visiting Professor of Primate Biology at London University and Director of the Primate Biology Programme at the Smithsonian Institute, said that as a result of the natural inclination of human reason to deny the existence of UFO humanoid types, the only alternative explanation, if the establishment is intent on preserving the illusion of non-existence, is the "Great Conspiracy" theory. For Napier, this option was unacceptable as it ignored the testimony of countless eyewitnesses or, absurdly, made them party to the Great Conspiracy. Napier said that this must open the door to a third hypothesis, which is neither a matter of reason nor fakery, namely one that is unreasonable in human terms but entirely rational from the perspective of what Napier termed the "Goblin Universe." In this context, Napier observed, the third explanation must concern the minds of men (and, by extension humanity's u nconscious and complex relationship with the forces of living nature).

In *Operation Trojan Horse* John Keel advanced the idea that somewhere in the vast electromagnetic spectrum there is an omnipotent intelligence able to manipulate energy, one that litera lly can bring phenomena into existence in this plane. In contemplating the same topic, Paul Devereux suggested[35] that this manipulative energy is here on our doorstep. He believes that the Gaia energy of Earth is the source of input for the UFO form, wherein the entire planet is a single self -monitoring organism that enables the planet to dream forms into existence.

Keel went on toquestion ifthere really UFOs at all UFOs were being variously described as triangles, spheres, hexagons, flying cubes, cigar shapes and doughnuts dressed in dazzling arrays of colours and light formations. Keel reflected on this and dec ided that hard objects such as the disc and cigar shapes, for example, existed merely as "temporary transmogrifications." They would land, could be seen and touched and leave markings where they set down. Keel became convinced that these illusory forms are intended as decoys for the soft objects such as the dirigibles seen in the 1897 flap and the mysterious "Ghost Planes" observed over Scandinavia in the 1940s. The "soft" crafts' abilities to exhibit bizarre forms of behaviour, make impossible turns and re ach unheard ofspeeds, led some investigators to believe they that are in some sense sentient, maybe even alive. Keel concluded that the immense breadth of the phenomenon and the sheer number of sightings serves only to give the lie to its validity, and makes it far more likely that UFOs are temporary extrusions from exotic energies originating in the higher bands of the electromagnetic spectrum.

Devereux believes that UFO entities are not travellers within a separate aeroform structure but that they are formed in the same way as the UFO shape itself and that they share the same substance, the one being merely a different aspect of one common phenomenon.

In a similar vein, Jacques Vallée proposed [36] that UFOs are neither extraterrestrial nor the result of hoaxes or delusions but rather are a control system, which is intended to stabilise the relationship between man's conscious needs and the rapidly evolving complexities of living in the physical world. He believes that UFOs have both a visible reality (with mass, volume, inertia and so on) and a window to other planes of

---

[35] Devereaux, P., *Spirit Roads*, Collins & Brown, London, 2003
[36] Vallée, J., *UFOs: The Psychic Solution,* Panther Books Ltd, St. Albans, 1977

reality. Its occupants, he suggests, are creations from the dreamscape, a reality ("Magonia") that intersects ours at right angles where we encounter and witness UFOs in the psychic planes of perception.

In Vallée's opinion UFOs neither fly nor are they objects; they materialise and dematerialise, violating in the process all known laws of motion. Vallée maintains that they are not necessarily an aspect of some form of an unknowable higher order of life but are products of a well defined and regulated technology, seemingly utterly bizarre by human standards. He suggests that the same power imputed to saucer people of influencing human events was once the exclusive property of fairies. He believes that the UFO phenomenon could be an "instance of a still undiscovered natural occurrence."

Vallée pondered on the oft-asked question as to whether it is necessarily true that we would detect meaningful patterns (by our objective standards) in the behaviour of a superior race. In his opinion, the inferior race would by necessity translate the seemingly absurd actions of the other as random impressions. For humankind's collective conscious to be able to see the underlying patterns in the superior race's actions would require a quantum leap in our evolutionary journey as a smart species. Understanding this, the superior race compensates for our lack of perceptive ability by limiting its communications to the level of signs and symbols and in the case of crop circles, for example, to pictographic and mathematical symmetry.

Keel believed that, innately, humankind has always been aware of these special energies, largely by virtue of the ufonauts' practice to tailor their appearances in accordance with witnesses' personal beliefs and subconscious mores. This sleight of hand practice suggests that the objective of the UFO entities is to sew confusion. This "now you see it, now you don't" trickery ensures that observers never identify what cup is covering the ball. In the face of such powerful psychological control, it is little wonder that man has always worshipped visiting gods.

It has long been observed that UFOs form on or close to the ground, the period of visibility rarely lasting longer than fifteen minutes or so. They can build up an inner shape and rise up into the atmosphere. During the Egryn Lights wave of 1904-1905 in North Wales oval UFOs grew out of balls of fire with two brilliant arms protruding towards the earth. Between the arms were more lights, resembling a quivering star cluster.

The ability of UFOs to harden into the finally recognised form— spaceship and its ufonauts—demonstrates that the craft and their occupants can shapeshift, a phenomenon parallel to Jung's thinking that "there exists a yet unknown substrate possessing material and at the same

198

time psychic qualities. " In WWII observers reported that German foo fighters responded to their thoughts, suggesting that U FOs are sentient energies able to respond to percipients' mental processes.

Vallée made the observation[37] that many, if not all, materialisations of UFOs and their occupants are three-dimensional holograms projected through space, time and other dimensions, the same hypothesis applying to fairy-folk appearances. Moreover, he believes that materialisations are deliberately exposed to observers so that they will record their details and transmit them to others. This line of thinking suggests that the mechanisms underlying the phenomena and our belief in them derive from a single source.

John Michell, too, reflected on this topic. He remarked [38] that ufonauts' appearances as humanoids complete withspacesuits, breathing apparatus, radios, aerials and the like i s a relatively new phenomenon. He pointed out that fairy witnesses see no such thing and that it is presumably something passed off by UFOlk convincingly for show. Michell noted the success of this trickery, which has been instrumental in spawning cultist beliefs about how we are visited by godlike men and angels from space.

Because fairies inhabit a different dimension contact has been likened to the operation of a short-wave radio that may crackle and then suddenly become clear for a few moments. It is be lieved that there are doorways to such realms located at special points throughout nature, such as exemplified in the Narnia stories. In *The Coming of the Fairies*[39] Arthur Conan Doyle reflected upon the humanoid appearance of elemental spirits. He said that it was not clear what determines the shape observed by humans and how the transformation from their usual working body (small, hazy, luminous clouds of colour with a brighter spark-like nucleus) is affected. However, he suggested that human thought, either individually or in the mass, plays a key part in determining what percipients see.

Michael Talbot suggests [40] that UFO and fairy sightings are neither objective nor subjective but "omnijective," a concept mindful of the Hindu Tantric tradition, for example, that recognises no distinction between the mind and reality and between the observer and the observed.

Vallée spoke of the medium in which human dreams can be

[37] Vallée, J., *Passport to Magonia*, Daily Grail Publishing, Brisbane, 2014.

[38] Michell, J., *The New View Over Atlantis*, Thames and Hudson, London, 1983

[39] Conan Doyle, A., *The Coming of the Fairies*, Hodder & Stoughton Ltd., London, 1922

[40] Talbot, M., *Mysticism and the New Physics*, Arkana, London, 1993

implemented and which serves as the mechanism that generates UFO events. He posited the existence of a natural phenomenon/field of consciousness, whose manifestations border on both the physical and the mental, "which serves as the mechanism that generates UFO events, obviating the requirement for a superior intelligence to trigger them."

It follows from these striking lines of thought that the task before one is not so much to seek to understand what UFOs are made of but rather to comprehend the phenomenon's effect on one's psychological and metaphysical states of being. One logical conclusion that can be drawn from these insights is that there may be no such thing as an objective UFO phenomenon. In this context the entire matter is a purely subjective process in which UFO forms and entities are drawn forth from Bohm's Implicate Order into the Explicate Order (the reality that humans normally perceive) by the power of the mind.

Devereux proposes something slightly different, suggesting, like Vallée, that there *is* an objective component but one that derives from a form of natural phenomenon not yet identified as such by present-day science.

By 1950, Dr. Meade Layne, a proponent of an interdimensional hypothesis to explain UFO sightings, was directing his research efforts on the paraphysicality of UFOs and the parapsychological elements of the contactee syndrome.[41] Before founding Borderland Sciences Research Associates (BSRA) in San Diego, Layne was professor at the University of Southern California, and English department head at Illinois Wesleyan University and Florida Southern College.

Layne's research bears a distinctly esoteric flavour. He believed that the separation of science from metaphysics and occultism is arbitrary and must be understood if one is to arrive at a totality of understanding on UFO matters and associated phenomena. In Layne's thinking the concepts of "here" and "there" are solely determined by frequencies, densities and wavelengths and not by spatial, three-dimensional considerations. He proposed that there are an infinite number of etheric planes or fields whose vibratory rates respond to finer forces such as those of mind and thought. He said that any thoughtform can be materialised in etheric matter and can be seen and touched at the appropriate rate of vibration. The discs are one such thoughtform, he maintained.

Much like Bohm, Layne believed that spacetime is manufactured by

---

[41] Layne, M., *MAT and DEMAT: Etheric Aspects of the UFO*, Flying Saucer Review, Vol. 1, No. 4, 1955

the self (by consciousness) and projected from it in extremely minute pulses. On the earth plane these impulses are chemical particles. Dee p within the gross matter field (Bohm's *Explicate Order*) there exists a subtler field, the etheric plane (Bohm's *Implicate Order*.) It is from this latter order, Layne held, that solidified matter draws its maintenance energy in the physical world.

BSRA sought information from diverse sources, including trance mediums. From these came the disclosure that the release of atomic forces has greatly disturbed the etheric planes from which UFOs originate (as components of Mother Earth's forces of living nature) hence, the purpose of their visits is to force our attention upon our infringing actions. The entities populating these planes (the "Ethereans" as Layne called them) belong to an invisible Earth-derived order of evolution but are vastly our superiors in science and intelligence. They are appearing in ever -larger numbers because our civilisation is on the point of collapse. They come also to make an examination and a final record in an anthropological sense.

Layne believed that the etheric regions (home t o devas, elementals, fairies and the like) are the regions of life ; they have knowledge of our world and can and do penetrate it.

UFOs and other strange phenomena, Layne said, are the result of one form of matter merging with another with which it shares an affinity, the process sometimes taking place at such a high speed that an explosion occurs. A sudden explosion is but one way in which a dimension may merge with another, instantly regrouping to form new substance.

Layne used the term a eroforms to descr ibe UFOs as actually the living bodies of etheric entities , proposing that UFO entities and their UFO aeroform structure are one and the same substance. Light phenomena can partially form into anthropomorphic, zoomorphic and indeterminate figures in which case they will be interpreted as a craft containing occupants and can also wholly transform into transient figures that are mobile in their own terms.

Layne held that the "vehicle" of an intra-dimensional entity, whether this be its body or its "ship," is a thoughtform and a thoughtform can be positioned anywhere. All the aeroforms can pass through each other and through our dwellings at will and are (and always have been) invisibly present in great numbers.

Layne explained that the problems of space tr avel as we conceive them do not exist for the Etherian. By altering his vibratory rates, the Etherian penetrates our seas and the substance of our globe as easily as he does our atmosphere. The ship and its occupants become light waves or frequencies from the ether, all the while consciousness continuing to abide in the entities.

They are extradimensional "emergents"; that is, they extrude into our plane of perception from a spacetime frame of reference, which is different from ours. This process is marked by a conversion of energy and a change of vibratory rates. When the energy conversion takes place, the aeroform becomes visible and tangible. It appears as solid substance and remains so until the vibratory rate is again converted.

The "steel" of a landed disc is etheric steel, and its "copper" is etheric copper, since the prototypes of all our metals exist equally in etheric matter. The conversion process is one of materialisation and dematerialisation (truncated by Layne to "mat" and "demat"). Layne emphasised that in the mat and demat processes there is *no* "crossing of space" involved at any time. There is simply a change of location, equivalent to a change of frequency or conversion of vibratory rates.

From Layne's channelling sessions came the message that there will come an "ether-quake," which shall be characterised by great disruption of magnetic and etheric fields. The sky will seem filled with fire. Landmasses will be displaced, and great inundations will occur. After cataclysm the Ethereans will, as on many previous occasions, begin to hand down to Earth people the knowledge from before to assist in the gradual rebuilding of civilisation.

Remarkably, among the most profound insights on the UFO phenomenon are those that came from the founder of analytical psychology, Carl Gustav Jung.[42] He concluded that myths, dreams, hallucinations and visions emanate from the same source. The reason why we are not all walking encyclopaedias is that we can only tap into the implicate order for information that is of direct relevance to our personal memories, and which conforms to a system of personal resonance. Jung was greatly concerned that UFOs are powerful portents of rapidly approaching great changes and turned his attention to the phenomena to warn humanity of them. He was struck by the weightlessness and the psychic nature of UFOs. He concluded that the disc is a symbol of order, a mandala or magic circle that organizes and encloses the psychic totality, thus expressing the archetype of the self, the totality of the conscious and unconscious, not just the ego. He described those things seen in the sky as "long-lasting transformations of the collective psyche."

---

[42] Jung, C.G., *Flying Saucers-A Modern Myth of Things Seen in the Skies*, Ark Paperbacks edition, London, 1987

John Michell enlarged on the remarkable aspects of Jung's thinking. In *The Flying Saucer Vision*[43] Michell suggested that it is probable that UFOs, having a nature and meaning outside our experience belong, like ghosts, to another order of matter and that their coming is a part of some approaching vision with which we shall soon be confronted.Michell also observed how often UFOs appear to percipients as if they are moving in their natural element like fish or fireflies rather than as mechanical craft.

This supports the notion that   we are visited by energies of other elements or dimensions, appearing in a way that conforms to what we expect of them and related to the psychological condition of percipients.

Jung associated UFOs with changes in the constellation of psychic dominants, of the archetypes or gods, which bring about or accompany long lasting transformations of the collective psyche. These changes take place in the mind as the sun comes under a new sign of the zodiac every 2,160 years (one Platonic Month) and portend great seasonal changes in mental attitudes and perceptions. Our entrance into the Age of Aquarius is, Jung said, provoking such psychic changes. Michell agreed,   saying: 'Maybe our hope of development and survival seems to lie in the achievement of a new, higher vision... It may be that flying saucers are a portent of a future evolutionary step to be brought about through the working of some influence from outside the earth.'[44]

Continuing to puzzle over the phenomenon, Jung said that UFOs are an involuntary archetype or mythological conception of an unconscious content, a "rotundem" as the Renaissance alchemists called it, which expresses the totality of an individual. He was struck by the UFO discs' resemblance to the mandala, a magic circle that organises and en closes the psychic totality. In this symbology it is expressive of the archetype of the self, which comprises both the conscious and unconscious minds (the soul) and not merely the ego. He compared this notion to the Platonic belief that the soul is spheri cal, symbolic of the heavenly spheres. Plato spoke of the "supra-celestial place" where the "Ideas" of all things are stored up. Esoteric philosophy describes this spirit storehouse or library as the Akashic Record.

Jung concluded that a UFO is an 'an involuntary archetype or mythological conception of an unconscious content, the alchemist's rotundem that expresses the totality of the individual ,' the phenomenon generated, he suggested, by mass fear of nuclear war post-WWII.

Regarding the question of the objective origins of UFOs, Jung

---

[43] Michell, J., *The Flying Saucer Vision*, Abacus, London, 1974
[44] ibid

suggested that an unknown natural phenomenon [the forces of living nature] occurs onto which the mandalic imagery so needed by the witness's psyche at that moment becomes projected. In effect, Jung provided a description of the invisible realm of the forces of living nature when he referred to an "as yet unknown substrate possessing material and at the same time psychic qualities."

If it were the case that UFOs are a psychological projection, Jung posited, there must be a powerful psychic cause for it because it is obviously an issue of great importance due to the thousands of sightings. He felt that the projection and cause must have a basis in an "emotional tension," having its cause in a situation of collective distress or danger, one that was very obvious at the time that Jung was writing in the Cold War era.

Ultimately, Jung arrived at what for him personally was an uncomfortable possibility. He speculated that UFOs might actually be living creatures of an unfathomable kind, one that is both a psychic projection and also an exteriorisation that assumes material attributes: a "materialised psychism." This exteriorisation comes not from physical space but rather from a mechanism in which an internal projection from the unconscious emerges onto conscious awareness.

Devereux[45] offers a theory that the objective component of the total UFO event is a form of natural phenomenon currently not identified as such by establishment science. He believes that ancient peoples may have had an understanding of the nature of UFOs, of their origin and application to human concsiousness. Devereux believes that UFO entities are formed in the same way as the UFO shape itself and that they partake of the same substance, representing merely a different development of the same phenomenon. It follows that they are not occupants of a craft but are further formations from the same material.

That the things observed in UFO phenomena are directly connected to the mind and distinct personality of the witness observing them is evidenced, Devereux suggests, in the case of devout Catholic Mary McLoughlin seeing a tableau of the Virgin Mary, St Joseph and St John the Evangelist in a field by the village church at Knock in the west of Ireland in 1897. In these moments the witness's consciousness and the forces of living nature converge to create a phenomenon that is of manifestly important meaning to the observer, albeit an event taking place at an unconscious level of experience and interpretation whose significance may never be understood wholly or even partially.

---

[45] Devereux, P., *Earthlights*, Turnstone Press Limited, Wellingborough, 1982.

Sightings such as these do not meet John Keel's criteria for proof [46] of a genuine "hard" UFO , in that the object must appear at all times as the same solid form; being seen first in the sky and then being seen to land conventionally; any occupants must appear as solid, biological creatures, no matter how bizarre; and witnesses must be demonstrably free of any pathological or mental aberrations. Keel believed that the UFO enigma is one that always been present onEarth and is most evident where geological conditions cause electro-magnetic conditions to prevail that precipitate the phenomenon to mani fest. That is, it is entirely a process of natural forces at work in a way that is beyond current human understanding. He coined the term "ultra -terrestrial" to describe UFO entities that are otherwise known in folklore as Paracelscian "Elementals," which share the earth with us but whose home is the interlacing Gaia dimension of the forces of living nature.

Keel believed that these forces, part of our immediate environment in some unfathomable fashion, interact with humanity through various geophysical g ateways, appearing not only as UFO entities but also as parahuman elementals (such as M en-in-Black), called in former times angels, demons and fairy folk. These forces of living nature, posessed of omnipotent intelligence, are able to manipulate energy and   can quite literally bring any kind of object into existence in our visible world.

Vallee in *Passport to Magonia* said, 'there exists a natural phenomenon whose manifestations border on both the physical and the mental.' I would add to this sentence, 'and the spiritual,' thus providing a neat description of the forces of living nature.

A vital clue as to a UFO's origin is its ability to shapeshift. Even apparently solid metallic structures frequently during their cycle of movement pass through a stage tha t indicates a nature that is basically less dense, stable and substantial. Witnesses' descriptions of electro-magnetic disturbances that affect people and machines reveal something about the process that produces a UFO manifestation.

Devereux suggests that these energy processes may produce occasionally transient phases of coherence that create tenuous solid material. He also suggests that mental processes are involved with this objective phenomenon in some way, pointing out that UFOs' intelligence, inquisitiveness and apparent evasive behaviour may be the result of energy interactions between the phenomenon and the invisible fields surrounding the bodies of the witness. Place is also important.

Devereux posits that t here is no separation between our phys   ical

[46] Keel, J., *Operation Trojan Horse*, Anomalist Books, San Antonio, 1970.

earth and the invisible dimension of the forces of living nature, that it is one continuum. He says, 'patterns that move the stars also move in different ratios within human consciousness... Geometry, symbolism, music and visual form are the only means of comprehending this ultimately transcendental process, for their truths operate at all levels in different ratios.'[47] Devereux refers to the ideas of author and geomancy researcher Anthony Roberts who believes that UFOs are planetary ectoplasm. Devereux believes that the remarkable genius Nikola Tesla (1856-1943) may have succeeded in replicating an energy form similar to this ectoplasmic nature of UFOs:

> I was confident... that with properly designed machinery, signals could be transmitted to any parts of the globe, no matter what the distance, without the necessity of using such intermediate stations. I gained this conviction through the discovery of a singular electrical phenomenon... which I have called a "rotating brush." This is a bundle of light which is formed, under certain conditions, in a vacuum-bulb, and which is of a sensitiveness to magnetic and electric influences bordering... on the supernatural. This light bundle is rapidly rotated by the earth's magnetism as many as twenty-thousand times per second, the rotation in these parts being opposite to what it would be in the southern hemisphere, while in the region of the magnetic equator it should not rotate at all. In its most sensitive state, which is difficult to attain, it is responsive to electric or magnetic influences to an incredible degree. The stiffening of the muscles of an arm and consequent slight electrical charge in an observer standing some distance from it, will perceptibly affect it. When in this highly sensitive state it is capable of indicating the slightest magnetic and electric changes taking place in the earth. The observation of this wonderful phenomenon impressed me strongly...[48]

The scientific work of Canadians Michael Persinger and Gyslaine Lafreniere[49] gives an insight into how the forces of living nature may materialise UFO-related phenomena via the medium of crystal. Their research shows that during periods of seismic unrest, pressure on rock crystals produce electric fields through a modification of the piezo-electrical effect. These pre-fracture fields can reach values of several

---

[47] ibid

[48] quoted by Andre Puharich in a lecture at University of Toronto, 13 October 1976

[49] Persinger, M; Lafrenière, G., *Space-Time Transients and Unusual Events*, Burnham Inc. Publishing, 1977

thousand volts per metre, intensities capable o f ionizing the local area into visible luminosities. It is also possible that sonic energy could be produced during periods of seismic stress, producing audible as well as infrasonic and ultrasonic effects. Their investigations also indicate that the build-up of electrical columns produced by accumulating tectonic stress can act on the human brain to induce dreamlike states, even creating vivid imagery experienced in waking consciousness. Similarly, magnetic anomalies can be produced at the Earth's surface above certain mineral deposits, which include rock crystal with its piezoelectrical properties, during times of geomagnetic storms.

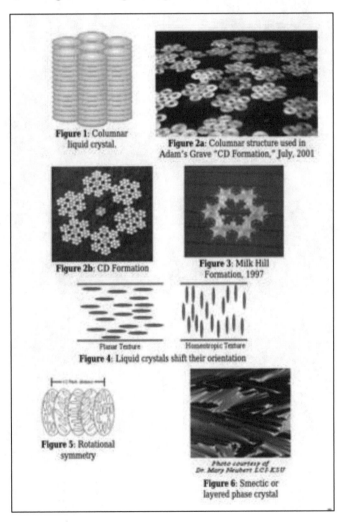

Figure 1: Columnar liquid crystal.

Figure 2a: Columnar structure used in Adam's Grave "CD Formation," July, 2001

Figure 2b: CD Formation

Figure 3: Milk Hill Formation, 1997

Planar Texture
Homeotropic Texture
Figure 4: Liquid crystals shift their orientation

Figure 5: Rotational symmetry

Photo courtesy of
Dr. Mary Newbert LCI KSU
Figure 6: Smectic or layered phase crystal

The liquid crystal properties of crop formations,
Institute of Resonance, 2002.

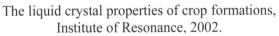

207

Don Quixote, the peerless Knight of la Mancha who quested for his
Holy Grail, the Goddess within, through his beloved Dulcinea.

Isis/Ishtar/Venus in repose

Mexico provides sensational "evidence" of the forces of living Nature. Top: a mummified figure described as a goblin or nagual foetus, found in a disused warehouse in April 2023. Bottom: February 2023, President Andrés Obrador affirms his personal belief in fairy-folk by publishing a photo of a creature in a tree and states that it depicts an alux, an elf from Yucatán folklore.

Chapter 14

Man, Nature and Ancient Wisdom

"Vincit qui se vincit"

(He conquers who conquers himself)

The Ancient Wisdoms taught that the illusory concepts of "Time" and "Space" were created long ago by man in order that he can feel he controls his environment. However, the teachings explain that the only true time is experienced in the movements of the sun, moon, stars and in the changing seasons. Within these movements, from time to time a synchronicity of Nature allows for doorways to open. Throug h these doorways one finds companion worlds and experiences that can only expand life. Those who are open to nature and its inner worlds can have experiences in these doorways, called by some "Phantom Thresholds."

There is always a larger part of us. What we are now is only a small part of what we really are. The five senses are the door to that higher part of oneself, attainable when one understands that there is only life, not death. Our true mother and creator is Mother Earth.

We should consider that our human form began its evolutionary journey to physical creation one or two billion years ago when living creatures first appeared on the planet . Consequently, when life -forms recognisable as humans did finally appear their physical birth process was not just nine months; it was way beyond nine million years ago.

Through the immensely long period that humans have walked this earth, long after other life was nourishing it, it has created a "humanity world" that sees only its own creations. The teachers of old called this humanity world the "Human Cocoon" or the "Human Condition."

In Mother Earth's world one in five hundred caterpillars survive s their cocoon to become butterflies or moths. Humanity's "Cocoon" indicates that in the world today very few humans ever become free from their self-imposed cocoon. We can consider that the "human condition" is our soul, a combination of our conscious and subconscious minds. Everything that we are in our present lifetime is our soul: our conscious, subconscious, sadness, happiness, hopes, beliefs and a whole plethora of other emotions and thoughtforms.

A doorway to a secret garden

The Life-force, the spirit, within all living creatures, including humans, is neutral, as are the forces of living Nature. Within our spirit and Mother Earth, there is no good or bad, heaven or hell, truth or lies, gods or devils, positive or negative, or preference to male or female. All is neutral and all in natural balance. As soon as we are born, we begin building the walls of the "human condition" that deny us the visibility and awareness of our infinite connections with the forces of living Nature, and of our ultimate potentials while living on this beautiful planet. It is in the depths of true silence that we are able to listen to the energies of Mother Earth while releasing any human sounds of interference. Our spirit can then begin to offer the soul the power of neutrality.

Each living creature is evolutionary from the beginnings of this planet over a billion years ago. The "creation energy" gives each living creature life and connects it to the multitude of wonders that is Mother Earth. Humanity, with a mental awareness higher than most creatures, has developed a soul that tends to create its own world, a cocoon bound by walls of our own creation, which has good and bad, heaven and hell, truth and lies, sadness and happiness , and the need to have gods that accentuate and verify our self-created belief systems.

What the human condition has c reated has been solely out of fear: fear of tomorrow, next week, next year , and so on, ad infinitum . Those who live within the moment know that what they are is what they have allowed themselves to become. Once we enjoy what we have become we are becoming neutral and no longer need the gods that others have created.

The forces of living Nature are neutral and, in that neutrality, there is no sympathy for what humans call victims, the poor, the disabled. This is not callousness but the neutral processes of Mother Earth maintaining a balance on this planet for billions of years.

Flowers drop their seeds and grow...but some do not grow. Some die and return to earth quickly. Some are malformed and do not have the stamina of other flowers...they return to the earth. This phenomenon is true of amoeba, insects, plants, flowers , trees, fish, birds, reptiles and animals. There are no poor in the neutrality of the earth, no handicapped or malformed in neutrality.

For millions and millions of years there was neutr ality among all living things, including humans. While all this time eternal life was going on, humanity's self-constructed "cocoon" isolated it from the truly vibrant energy of living Nature. Some powerful civilisations could feel the connection of eternal life with the Earth and cremated their dead. The ashes returned to earth to fertilise and stimulate growth in a new form. Others buried their dead without coffins and planted trees, flowers and plants above them to assure their immortality. Like all livi ng creatures, humans are here to return and energise the Earth, not to destroy her.

Humans feel they are different and more advanced than all other living things on earth. We are not! We have created "gods" so we can blame something or someone else for the actions we should be responsible for. 'That was God's will,' or 'In my prayer God told me ,' or

'My God is the only God and if you don't believe in him, you will be punished and not have eternal life,' one will hear. Most humans create gods to justify ignorant action or to eliminate fear of death.

Humans believe in good and bad because "either/or" allows us an excuse for not adopting a neutral attitude. The human mind is either like a thousand flames which bring brightness and light into one's life, or it can be total darkness which instils fear and frustration.

Immortality is beyond the mind and brings comfort and control in spite of the mind's power. Once we conceive of and accept that we are "immortal" only when we return to Mother Earth, it is only then that we understand that we are a part of an evolutionary process that keeps this planet alive.

The Ancient Wisdoms taught that Man is the imbalance, the acid, the negativity on this planet. Man is an energy in himself. Each person is atom and molecule in the utmost finite part of the infinite part of his structure. Take a flower, a particular animal, or a crystal worn on the person: each has a molecular structure. This molecular structure can be seen or constructed by a scientist, who says, 'This is a neutron, this is an atom, this is a molecule.' Man's structure would fill a large room if they reproduced it but according to the metaphysical teachings of the Ancients, within man is every structure that is within the world. If you look within a flower, you could fit it in somewhere within the atomic structure of man.

Man has within him everything of this physical planet but man is the imbalance. It is man that causes the chaos. It is man who says that we have got to stop raging rivers, destructive earthquakes and damaging typhoons and hurricanes. It is man who says we have to fight Nature even when it is evident that she is just doing her own thing. It is man who cuts down trees, eliminates mountains and causes erosion.

And then he wonders and says, 'Isn't it sad, my home has washed away. Isn't it sad that the rain blew this away or the wind did that.' It is not sad. It's Nature, the natural force. But man feels, 'I have to command, I have to be in charge. I am in charge of the animal, mineral and plant kingdoms and nothing can challenge me,' and so he challenges nature at its highest power and is constantly beaten down to his knees.

Disease is not a part of the animal or plant kingdoms. If a plant fades and dies, they do not consider it to be disease; they consider it to be evolution. Plants have no poverty. Animals have no famine. They may go without food. They may die but they return to the earth for there is no death, only continuation.

Man is an enigma. He can go along for years dissatisfied with life, walking the precipice of a boring existence. Then "snap," something within him is triggered and a passion is released. From that day forward the days are not long enough, his energy increases and he becomes an inspiration to those around him. It's as if he sees the magnificence of life for the very first time. This individual has come to understand that in this world things are never what they seem. What is perceived by the physical senses is but a façade to the powers that work silently and mystically while keeping the human experience moving forward.

The ancients taught that before we enter the human experience, our spirit is everything we could have ever been with a perception of what we can be. This condition is best described as "God," the Universal Mind. It follows that each person had the essence of what the human condition calls "God" before reincarnating into the great university of the human experience. This is the main reason people are always searching for "God," which is really the whole part of one's self. However, in the wisdom of the universe, the human experience has to be an adventure where one was less than God.

God is a realization, not an individual force. When we take control of our life and realise that our destiny is solely the product of what we think and do today then we are "God." This Godliness has no control over anyone other than oneself. Infringement on anyone else catapults us immediately back into mass consciousness.

Time and time again we all wonder and say: 'Why am I here?' We are here to learn to live in balance with our plane. Not to challenge, not to yell and scream but to learn self-discipline and one's limitations and how they affect our life. Man is here to work with balance and imbalance, the electro-magnetic polarities of positive and negative. These are part of the challenges of one's infinite evolution.

The world is filled with limitations. We limit ourselves daily. People make excuses, make things up in their minds, 'I cannot do it, it's impossible, there's no way...' The individual that says, 'I can't do it, it's impossible, it costs too much, it's not the way,' is not facing up to their highest potential. If one says their body is weak, then that thoughtform is controlling the subconscious. In the depths of the subconscious, one can do anything. A physician can hypnotize an individual that has acrophobia and can get them to walk along a tightrope and they do it without falling. Under hypnosis, a person who has never played the violin or piano can play within fifteen minutes, just by listening.

The Mysteries taught that every colour, every piece of cloth, every animal, everything, is either electro-magnetically positive or negative. If man pulls around him too much negativity, then he will have negativity.

Red, orange, yellow and black are negative colours. Indigo, blue, violet and white are positive colours. Green is neutral. Music is positive and negative. Even the languages we speak—the Romance languages are negative. Heat is negative, cold is positive. The clothes you wear—silk, wool and cotton—are positive, but synthetics are negative. Even the coarseness of a cloth can be a positive or negative force.

One begins to understand that even though we may be diligently achieving the correct acid-alkaline nutritional requirements for our body, but we continue to gather around us too much of the negative in other areas our lives will be equally unbalanced. So, we begin to understand that by an individual changing his life, he must first change those things around him that are causing the imbalance, then he will have more positive response coming to him.

Now, mankind is the acid, and the plant and animal kingdoms are alkaline, the positive: this is an 80%-20% balance. But within each kingdom there is a balance of the same proportion. The spiritual essence of a woman is positive and that of of a man is negative (one is not speaking here of positive equating with "good" and negative with "bad," but of natural, neutral electro-magnetic polarity), so there is a balance if worked correctly. This is the natural energy of pulling in (negative) and projecting (positive).

In the animal kingdom there are animals within the kingdom that are negative, that balance the positive. This means that 80% of each of those kingdoms will be positive elements. Cats are a negative energy; dogs are a positive one. Have you ever seen a cat that will run and greet you; that will jump up and lick your hand and be glad that you are home? A cat looks at you and says, 'It's about time you got here, when are you going to feed me?' A dog runs out and jumps all over you and says, 'Where have you been all of my life? It's about time you got home, but I'm glad to see you.' The outgoing, the ingoing, very simple.

So, within the positivity of the animal, plant and mineral kingdoms there are the negative forces. These negative forces within these kingdoms are the scavengers, the equalizers: big cats, birds of prey, sharks, and so on. And they have been placed there to allow the acidity, to allow the growth and the evolution of the kingdom itself.

With the positivity of these kingdoms, they could exist for eternity upon the earth, for they are the alkaline, and they have within them the predator, the balancing acid force. The earth is negative, all things that grow from it are positive. It pulls, and the minerals, the plants and the animals project, stand above it. The sun (projecting) is positive, the moon (pulling) negative.

Man must try to have a balance of 80% alkaline and 20% acid, not only in the food he eats and the plants with which he surrounds himself, but in the animals, minerals and the clothes. This necessity is especially powerful and important in our thinking processes. The acid or the negative thought is powerful. By saying,'I hate that individual,' it returns to you.

One says to oneself, 'My life is complicated. There are things around me that I don't know anything about.' If one thinks that they are beginning to perceive something, understand that what one knows about it is only the beginning. For everything has an infinity of knowledge connected to it and one is only able to deal with a finite perception. That is the limitation of one's subconscious mind. We are a part of all things, but we are not all things.

The place where we live is made from rock, wood and metal. The mortar binding the brickwork that supports our home is made from sand and cement. Our kitchen work surfaces are made from marble and granite. Each of the substances that went into the construction of that building has Life-force energy within it.

A blacksmith may reach down and pick up a piece of discarded metal and hold it in front of you. 'This may look lifeless, but it is not,' he will say. He will walk back to the fire and places one end of the metal in the flames. Soon, it as red hot. He will turn and hold it to your face. The extreme heat makes you flinch and move backward. 'Look closely at the red, what do you se e?' the smith will ask. You will peer carefully at the red-hot metal and see a throbbing motion in the midst of the red. Suddenly, this lifeless form is alive. The smith will then immerse the metal into nearby water and once again put it close to your eyes . Now see it shrink; it is most definitely alive!

The Life-force and the Universal Law

Sameness in groups creates the "spiritual herd." The major experience or adventure within the world is individual. No matter how much we talk, share, procreate and participate, what we really think and feel will be known only to oneself. A part of every human experience denies this reality. We seek the comfort of temples, cities, groups, armies and social gatherings. In essence, all this effort is a search for the inner self and its immortal Life-force. The Masters taught that the same Life-force that is within us now exists from one period of time to another ; it just chooses different structures and living situations to let it experience th e many different adventures within this world.

The Life-force experiences through our body. Our body is like the materials in our house. There are unseen living organisms within it that make it what it is. This Life-force, which has been in existence forever, is now within us. The Life-force experiences the world through our body outwardly but not through the five senses—sight, sound, taste, touch and smell. These five senses are the impulses that our body absorbs and becomes. The Life-force within one's body only experiences the physical, emotional and mental in the form of transformed energy. These experiences create a vibrational energy that feeds the Life-force. This, in turn, is connected to our unique spirit library (Akashic record). The Ancient Wisdoms taught that all living things—animals, trees, flowers, water and everything that we can see—are a natural expression of the Life-force. The bodies of man and woman are a type of universal filter in which the Life-force refines and regenerates itself. All other living things keep the Life-force. Nature and its animals are a producer of neutralised energy, which produces an "existence" charge for what the ancient teachings described as the Universal Law—some call it God—but man has within him a unit which is called the mind. Its constant conflict with good and evil or positive and negative generates a tremendous amount of power. Man is able to transfer the energy with which he is involved in his daily life by becoming neutral. Positive is weak, and negative is weak; they must work together. When these energies work together in perfect balance, man progresses to the inner realisation that he can project this power to his spirit library. Many human beings do this unknowingly through various forms of prayer, meditation, devotion or work.

The individual who has become the neutral observer or participant within this world becomes a condenser. The universal laws of our world are few. Each of them can be seen or felt within Nature. "Coming together" with Nature assures an inner peace. Nature is the true communion place of all the powers that work within our world.

The Universal Law is neutral and therefore all powerful. There is an energy and a pattern beyond what we sense each day. These are the constituents of the Universal Law. All living things are but building blocks to

A Bluebell Wood

218

this energy and pattern. No one Life-force is a building unto itself. Each of us is but a building block in a special pattern that allows energy to keep all living things in motion. Some building blocks build only small abodes, while others build palaces or circuses but each is a distinctive part of a larger whole. The manner in which one dies or by which another lives is but a vital piece in the larger structure.

One's main role in a life may be one of support, while some are born to be a foundation of some kind, others to be the inner walls, others the outer façade, others the gaudy trim. The Universal Law does not plot, plan, organise, direct or discipline. In its neutrality, it does not need devotion, worship or adoration. The Universal Law must have energy input in order to continue to exist. A sword needs the energy of the swordsman's arm to be effective. However, the energy that the Universal Law uses must be a perfect balance of attraction and repulsion, offensive and defensive, sweet and sour, strong and weak, positive and negative.

Man and woman are the only instruments in the world which transform the Life-force into a more powerful unit. Every thought, word or action while we live in the world is an act of either attraction of repulsion—positive or negative.

Worship of gods does not protect us from death, nourish our crops or makes us fertile. Any changes to our lives come from using the Life-force energy within us. This energy is limitless and is one's direct connection to the Universal Law. There are no gods in any form, just un limited power through use of energy—positive and negative, attracting and repulsing. Mother Earth and her forces of living Nature are a perfect illustration of the Universal Law's unlimited powers at work.

Nature has been defined as the sum total of the forces at work throughout the Universe. The power of Nature resides in its neutrality. The act of being neutral or non-active is a very difficult action for almost every individual. We hear of earthquakes, hurricanes, tornadoes and the like and, in most cas es, we think of destruction and human sadness. However, it is vital to understand that these reactions are our interpretations of a natural, neutral, unintentionally harmful act. A hurricane can bring death and destruction to one city and at the same time its distant rains bring much needed relief to parched crops elsewhere.

Nature is the ultimate of continuance, only becoming a problem to those who get caught up in the challenges posed by the illusory nature of time and space. Nature is the only energy t hat we cannot control or harness with our scientific knowledge and laws. Because of this, Nature plays a vital role in our lives; it reminds us of our vulnerability. This tends to make life more exciting to live...Nature is never stagnant.

Learning the lessons of the neutrality of the forces of living Nature comes from being very closely connected to all aspects of Nature. Nature brings excitement into our lives and can be the condiment in an otherwise bland and boring existence. The observer becomes more centred and balanced than the activist or doer. In general, if we observe, we are left alone. However, if we participate in a situation or cause, we are drawn into its action by one or more individuals. To be neutral and an observer allows us to see that there is always more than one way of doing things. Rest and relaxation in Nature have been among the greatest healers of all time. It will take place faster and with more positive accuracy and successful outcome when we use Nature as our prime healing source. Walking along a beach with the waves breaking rhythmically around our ankles is the prime healer. There seems to be a cohesive bond between the natural forces in the body, the rhythm of the waves, tidal movement and sand and fresh sea air. All of these tend to reach into the most imbalanced parts of our body and to refurbish the old with the new.

A walk in a forest or wooded area begins to unlock the mental, emotional and emotional shackles that take their toll by creating dis-eases of all kinds. Trees, shrubs, birds, insects and animals in their Nature settings will purify the most polluted aspects of the human body. Snow symbolises freshness and purity. Living and healing in a winter mountain recreational area will also revitalise the body. The snow and clean air of the mountain seems to work on mental irrationalities better than any other Nature setting. Desert and its sun attract those who are reaching their last years. Its warmth and dryness help to keep bodies with the thinnest blood comfortable. Arthritis, bursitis and respiratory diseases seem to subside in these areas. The ancient Essenes chose the desert because of the power of the sun and the stability that was attainable with nature. Nature is the perfect healer. A daily relationship with Nature will help bring physical balance, emotional calm, mental insight and a very stable bridge to philosophical and spiritual insights.

Nature is the only energy that is legally known as God. Insurance companies will insure our home, personal belongings and even our person from damage and injury caused by "acts of God." These "acts of God" are all the neutral acts of Nature: hurricane, flood, wind, tornado, tidal wave, earthquake and fire. This means that basically, most of us accept Nature as the physical manifestation of God!

Interestingly, we usually want to build and live where Nature does not want us: the prime property along beaches, farms in riverbeds where the soil is rich, on earthquake faults, in tornado alleys, alongside streams, rivers and lakes, perched high on hillsides, or in any one of many precarious places.Nature is the key to one's ultimate spiritual experience. The teachers of old taught that within each human being is a Nature-self. The mind is always in conflict with its surroundings and the key to a balanced mind is the magnification of the Nature -self. This part of us is a communicator, healer and seer , for its communication system is the very essence of Nature.

Within Nature is an overriding element of chaos. Within this , there is an ultimate order. It is the eye of the storm, so to speak. Once we find the order within the chaos, we attain freedom. It is within chaos that we reach our highest physical evolution. Once we accept the chaotic times and are not frightened of them, we are open to the ultimate order which lies deep within all chaos. The great agonies of the world are a resu lt of the mind, combined with a deluded sense of superiority over all other parts of Nature.

The Hermetic Mysteries

The ancient teachings were born from the Wisdom of the Hermetic Mysteries. This developed when very wise teachers, symbolised in legend as Hermes , Cadmus or Thoth, gathered all the intimacies and subtleties of the evolutionary process within Mother Earth. This was long before the development of the written word in an era in which there was a "word by mouth" insight into living on this planet and being a vital part of the earth. In time this word -by-mouth knowledge was put in writing and placed in the great library at Alexandria. The Hermetics taught that the mind is always in conflict with its surro undings and the key to a balanced mind is the ability to magnify, without words, the living energy of the Earth. This life force is the *archœus*, the vital substance in Nature upon which all things subsist. To magnify the living energy of the Earth is to ta ke time to let the senses relax and listen to what is beyond the façade of the obvious and be open to the unobvious.

Not long after meeting the gatekeeper in the Fl ying A gas sation, Brad Pulaski, enjoying a brief vacation in Paris, had a vivid dream. I n it, he had been washed onto a beach after his small boat had been dashed on the rocks by a storm. It was chilly and so he built a fire. He caught fish and cooked them. While he was resting after his meal, he was astonished to see a man standing in the ce ntre of the fire, its flames leaping higher and higher. The man extended his right hand and said, 'Come with me! Do not be afraid, just come with me...' Brad took a deep breath and stepped into the flames to join the old man. Instantly, he found h imself in a tremendous room that was literally on fire. Leading away from the room was a corridor lined with fire.

The old man began to retreat down the corridor, followed by Brad. Eventually, he came to a giant marble temple. Sitting on a high throne at one end of the temple was the old man. Around him stood forty-two white-robed men and women. He walked cautiously to the centre of the temple. A deep baritone chant broke forth. One by one the forty-two turned toward the man on the throne and said, 'May your wisdom and light shine on all of us this day, Great Hermes Mercurius Trismegistus, Master of all Knowledge, Initiator of all Craftsmanship, Master of Three Worlds, Scribe of the Gods, Librarian of the Books of Life, Scribe of the Book of Truth, and Master of Mysteries.'

Brad gasped. The man who had appeared in the fire was Hermes whose symbol was Mercury, the planet nearest to the Sun! He was closest to the Universal Life which made the world grow and move. Brad fell to his knees, half out of respect and half from an overwhelming emotional sense of awe.

Hermes descended from his throne, faced the young man and said, pointing to the robed oracles who attended him, 'These are the physical manifestations of the books I created which were burned in the library of Alexandria. Two books are related to hymns and the music of the Gods. Four are concerned with astrology, the fixed stars and their conjunctions and risings. Ten are under the responsibility of the Scribe and relate to hieroglyphics, cosmography, geography, the sun, moon and planets and the disciplines of the priesthood, and of the Stole-keeper who bears a cubit of justice and the cup of libations. Ten concern the honour paid to the gods and matters of worship as that relating to sacrifices, processions, festivals and the like. Ten more concern the Hieratic and relate to the laws, the gods and the training of priests. The final six books concern healing and medicines. You, Brad, want to work with herbs and plants and be a healer. You will be taught by these six.'

Hermes moved quickly to his throne and nodded his head. The six formed a corridor, three on each side, and began chanting once again. Brad found himself walking forward along the corridor. Soon it became sponge-like, absorbing every part of him into this magical teaching experience. It was as if he was a giant pen beginning to write indelibly on his innermost being.

The great temple literally vibrated as the energy of the initiation grew. Finally, the energy peaked, and the temple was suddenly empty. Brad was instantly in other realms, becoming the unique power of the Hermetic Mysteries. He heard a spoken voice: 'To heal is to be without any personal reference and be pure of thought and action.' He puzzled over this but was made aware of everything he needed to know.   He understood that if he was totally disconnected from himself when he was using his healing powers, he would be pure in thought and action. The first healing book of Hermes was "THE SELF.   " Brad found himself becoming a part of its pages. In fact, he soon felt that he was the actual book itself. Learning how not to be himself, but to be in spite of himself would be a major change in consciousness.

The second book was "THE MIND." Whereas the first book of healing was centred on his relationship to all living things and his separation, this book presented the fact that the mind is always in conflict with its surroundings, and that the key to a balanced mind is the magnification of the Nature Self. Brad perceived that the great agonies of the world were a result of the mind, non -acceptance and a sense of superiority. Herein, lay the "GREAT DELUSION." Humanity thought that it was the superior living creature when, in fact, any acceptan ce of that thought made it inferior. He must learn to step beyond this delusion.

The third book healing was a "NATURAL SOURCE." Brad learned of the power of the natural healing sources as a living energy.He learned how to communicate with the natural res ources which he would use in order that, when used in healing, the "Nature Consciousness" would be passed on to the essence of the individual. Flowers, leaves, roots and buds have great strength on their own but an intimate connection between their consciousness and the Nature Self provided the ultimate in healing.

The fourth and fifth healing books of   Hermes were "ALCHEMY: SIGNS AND SYMBOLS" and "ALCHEMY: MIXTURES AND INCANTATIONS." In Brad's adventures with the teachers of these two books, he learned how important it is to work at certain times of the day, week and year for the maximum results.Through his inner consciousness were threaded the teachings of the many symbols that a healer could use in creating a harmonious atmosphere in the place where hewas working. He was shown the days on which certain illnesses were more receptive to healing, as well as certain hours of the day when the potions would be the most efficacious. The fifth book also blended the knowledge of the use of the consciousness of n ature with one's Nature Self. It taught how to dry and grind flowers, roots, buds and leaves and to put their spiritual essence in a state of suspension, enabling it to bring the poultice, salve or mixture back to life. Brad began to perceive the power of sound and words in relationship to healing.

The sixth book of healing was "IMMORTALITY." This teacher opened worlds to   Brad that he had barely imagined. He related that immortality is a state of mind and that a sense of mortality is a lack of belief in the power of the mind in relationship to all living things. Mentally, Brad understood the concept of mortality. However, to be able to experience it in order that mortality would be eliminated was still out of his reach. The teacher who was opening this book to him understood this inability. Instantly, before Brad was a powerful light that was so bright and strong that it momentarily blinded him. The brightness faded and he felt himself in a large room filled with hundreds of flaming lamps. The teacher was pointing his finger to his eye as an indication for him to observe. In one flowing movement all of the lamps were blown out and he stood alone in the darkness. The first few moments were no problem but soon he found that the room was so dark that his eyes would not become accustomed. There was not a sound, smell or sense of any kind. He began to feel mentally disoriented, completely out of control of his thoughts. He was afraid to move for there were no reference points for him to fix on.

In the distance one small flame began to burn and Brad started to feel in control and to relax. His teacher said, 'Your mind is either like a thousand flames which bring brightness and light into your life, or it can be total darkness which instils fear and frustration. Immortality is that beyond the mind which brings comfort and control in spite of the mind's power.' He let these words sink into his pupil's thoughts for a moment and then continued. 'Identification with your current body is the darkness. The eternal light is beyond the darkness, just like that single flame. Once you conceive of and accept this truth, you are immortal and will never live a mortal life again.' As Brad began to walk toward the single light, it became bigger and bigger until it was as brilliant as the sun. Becoming like an eternal flame, the setting changed and once again he was all alone. Hermes walked up beside Brad and smiled broadly. 'You have learned of the Wisdom of the Hermetic Mysteries; you are now part of that tradition. It is time you returned and woke to a new and sunny day in Paris. An opportunity for you to become a powerful healer will present itself very soon!'

The Three Graces

Chapter 15

The Elementals

The pulse of the Universal Law, the Universal Mind, the God   -Force, Jehovah—no matter what we call it   —are the Elementals , the Nature Spirits. These are an integral and vital part of the higher consciousness of Mother Earth. They flow through her unseen veins.

Ancient Wisdom taught that the Elementals are the caretakers of nature, its living essence through whose portals men and women find their spirit and a corresponding sense of immortality and universality. They are always close by, but one must have a daily, reverential immersion in nature to begin to feel and perceive their magical presence. Throughout history men have mistaken nature spirits for angels, demons and other supernatural forms. From to time, a person may experience the privilege of meeting an Elemental.

A Languedoc Minstrel's Adventure, Winter, 999 AD

A Minstrel was travelling to Languedoc to stay for a few days at the home of his friend Rossal before the Knight travelled to the Holy Lands to fight in the Crusades.

When he was less than a day's ride to Rossal's home, the minstrel stopped by a waterfall to rest. It was a warm winter's day and he lay on the ground under a large oak. He crossed his right ankle over the left and spread his arms outwards in the shape of a   cross. With eyes closed, he relaxed and listened to the   hypnotic sounds of the fall as its frothing waters poured into a deep indigo pool.

At length, after a few moments that had seemed   like hours, he felt something on his right hand. He opened   his eyes but saw nothing. He closed his eyes once more and adopted his relaxation posture. Presently, he felt something soft upon his left hand. This time he barely opened his eyes and squinted through his eyelashes. He was amazed to see small balls of lig ht moving up his left arm. Moments later he saw the same wispy movement on his right arm and then up both of his legs. Just as he about to open his eyes wide the movement stopped. He thought to himself, 'who or what are these things?'

'We are Elementals, Minstrel,' came the immediate mental reply.

'Oh, my God, they can read my thoughts,' the Minstrel said to himself. 'How do I censor them?'

'We do not read your thoughts, Minstrel! Thoughts are energy. Thoughts create words. You may think that your thoughts are private, known only to you. To us, the Elementals, and those that are bonded to the inner powers of nature, thoughts have sound and are like the spoken word.'

'That means I have no privacy; I am not an individ…'

The Elementals cut in. 'If you are in physical balance, then you will have contact with the Elementals. Your thoughts will be pure and filled with the truths of the universe. What you think will not be harmful, infringing, spiteful or judging. Only then will you be able to see us and to communicate with us.'

'Frankly, that would be a very boring world,' countered the Minstrel. 'What would I find to sing about?'

'The observer sees, hears, smells, tastes and touches but does not allow themselves to have a negative reaction to their senses. You can sing of what you see and hear but you do not have to judge it.'

'This is getting scary. I'm having a conversation with a bunch of lights without using my voice. I must be losing my mind!'

'We are the pulse of your God, whoever or whatever you feel your God is,' said the Elementals. 'As blood flows through veins, so we flow through the unseen veins of nature. The beauty you see in a woman is enhanced a thousandfold when you see her through the subtle power of nature.'

The Minstrel opened his eyes. There, standing on his chest, was a small elf-like man. Flashing a broad smile and twinkling eyes, he stood there completely naked. 'Who are you, where did all the lights go and why are you naked?' the Minstrel asked in alarm.

'I am those lights,' explained the elf-man, 'and I am the composite of what your mind wants me to be in order that it can begin to comprehend a reality behind the physical and the five senses. I am the wind, rain, earth and fire all in one. Although I am an Elemental, my energy or my essence is in the form that you want it to be. You sing of the little people of the Celts who live in the forest and dance and sing. You have heard of the sprites of the water and the sylphs of the air…I am a composite of those. It is because you mind doesn't know how to clothe me that I am naked!'

The Minstrel felt a slight shift in movement. Opening his eyes once more he saw sitting cross-legged on his chest the most beautiful maiden he had ever seen. She, too, was naked.'Oh no, I'm in trouble now. I can't concentrate with someone so beautiful and nude sitting on my chest. I want the little man back!'

'Pure powerful energy has no form, ' said the Elemental. 'It is only when your mind tries to put form to it that energy loses its power. When you play your lute, the music is energy…there is no form. When you walk or move you create energy…there is no form. Minstrel, pure, powerful energy is God. It is through the pulse of God—the Elementals—that you reach the heights within yourself.

'We are the spirit that pulsates through nature. Your spirit pulsat es through the body that you have chosen for this lifetime. Our elemental spirit and your spirit are related, something like brother and sister. You have come to this earth to feel, express and project your spirit. When you do that, you will discover that your God is actually you. We are neutral and, as a human, your neutrality will lead to personal control. It will free you from the spectacle of seeing yourself the way you feel others want you to be.'

The Elemental withdrew. After taking a few minutes to compose himself after his extraordinary experience, the minstrel resumed his journey. 'Rossal is never going to be believe my adventure, maybe I shouldn't mention it...'

The story of the Minstrel's adventure has been handed down to storytellers through the generations. Whether it is a parable, or a true tale is immaterial, although I like to think that it is not beyond the bounds of possibility for one to communicate directly with the nature spirits. There have been accounts from people drowning who have been saved by the intervention of brightly coloured balls of light that have literally pulled them out of the waves and propelled them to safety.

The elf man and his analog, the beautiful maiden, taught the Minstrel of the unlimited power of the mind, of the strength of being an observer, rather than remaining a slave to the senses.

Swiss physician, alchemist, and philosopher "Paracelsus" (Philippus Aureolus Theophrastus Bombastus von Hohenheim , 1493 -1541), said that the Earth is not just our visible spinning ball. It comprises other, more subtle dimensions that are home to the higher powers of Nature. It is these invisible "mansions" in the "house" of the Earth that accommodate, in the words of the Minstrel's elf man, 'the Elementals and those that are bonded to the inner powers of nature.'

Paracelsus explained that we are unable to see these higher dimensions because our undeveloped senses are incapable of functioning beyond the limitations of the grosser parts of the elements.

He believed that each of the four primary elements known to the ancients (earth, fire, air, and water) consisted of a subtle, vaporous principle and a gross corporeal substance. Air is, therefore, twofold in nature: a tangible atmosphere and an intangible, volatile substratum, which may be termed spiritual air. Fire is visible and invisible, discernible and indiscernible—a spiritual, ethereal flame manifesting through a material, substantial flame. Carrying the analogy further, water consists of a dense fluid and a potential essence of a fluidic nature. Earth has likewise two essential parts—the lower being fixed, terreous, immobile; the higher, rarefied, mobile, and virtual.

Minerals, plants, animals and men live in a world composed of the gross side of these four elements. Just as visible Nature is populated by an infinite number of living creatures, so, according to Paracelsus, the invisible, spiritual counterpart of visible Nature, composed of the tenuous principles of the visible elements, is inhabited by a host of beings to whom he gave the name elementals, and which have later been termed the Nature spirits.

Paracelsus divided these beings into four distinct groups, which he called gnomes, undines, sylphs and salamanders. He taught that they were really living entities, many resembling human beings in shape, which inhabit worlds unknown to man because his undeveloped senses are incapable of functioning beyond the limitations of the grosser elements.

The civilizations of Greece, Rome, Egypt, China, and India believed implicitly in satyrs, sprites, and goblins. They peopled the sea with mermaids, the rivers and fountains with nymphs, the air with fairies, the fire with Lares and Penates, and the earth with fauns, dryads, and hamadryads. These Nature spirits were held in the highest esteem, and propitiatory offerings were made to them.

Occasionally, as the result of atmospheric conditions or the peculiar sensitiveness of the devotee, they became visible. Many authors wrote concerning them in terms which signify that they had actually beheld these inhabitants of Nature's finer realms. A number of authorities are of the opinion that many of the gods worshiped by the pagans were elementals, for some of these invisibles were believed to be of commanding stature and magnificent deportment.

The idea that the invisible elements surrounding and interpenetrating the earth were peopled with living, intelligent beings may seem ridiculous to the prosaic mind of today . This doctrine, however, has found favour with some of the greatest intellects of the world. The sylphs of Facius Card an, the philosopher of Milan , the salamander seen by Benvenuto Cellini, the pan of St. Anthony, "Le Petit Homme Rouge" (the little red man, or gnome) of Napoleon Bonaparte, and Carroll's live flowers of Wonderland have found their places in the pages of history.

Literature has also perpetuated the concept of Nature spirits. The mischievous Puck of Shakespeare's *Midsummer Night's Dream* and James Barrie's immortal Tinker Bell are well -known characters to students of literature. The folklore and mythology of all peoples abound in legends concerning these mysterious little figures that haunt old castles, guard treasures in the depths of the earth, and build their homes under the spreading protection of toadstools.

Paracelsus, when describing the substances which constitute the bodies of the elementals, divided flesh into two kinds, the first being that which we have all inherited through Adam. This is the visible, corporeal flesh. The second was that flesh which had not descended from the Adam line and being more attenuated, was not subject to the limitations of the former. The bodies of the elementals were composed of this transubstantial flesh.

Paracelsus stated that there is as much difference between the bodies of men and the bodies of the Nature spirits as there is between matter and spirit. 'Yet,' he adds, 'the Elementals are not spirits, because they have flesh, blood and bones; they live and propagate offspring; they eat and talk, act and sleep, and consequently they cannot be properly called "spirits." They are beings occupying a place between men and spirits, resembling men and spirits, resembling men and women in their organization and form, and resembling spirits in the rapidity of their locomotion.' Paracelsus called these creatures "composita," inasmuch the substance out of which they are composed seems to be a composite of spirit and matter. He uses colour to explain the idea. Thus, the mixture of blue and red gives purple, a new colour, resembling neither of the others yet composed of both. Such is the case with the Nature spirits; they resemble neither spiritual creatures nor material beings yet are composed of the substance which we may call spiritual matter, or ether. Paracelsus added that whereas man is composed of several natures (spirit, soul,

Paracelsus

229

mind, and body) combined in one unit, the elemental has but one principle, the ether out of which it is composed and in which it lives. By ether is meant the spiritual essence of one of the four elements. There are as many ethers as there are elements and as many distinct families of Nature spirits as there are ethers.

The Nature spirits cannot be destroyed by the grosser elements, such as material fire, earth, air, or water, for they function in a rate of vibration higher than that of earthy substances. Being composed of only one element or principle (the ether in which they function), they have no immortal spirit and at death merely disintegrate back into the element from which they were originally individualized.

No individual consciousness is preserved after death, for there is no superior vehicle present to contain it. They can live to a great age, the average lifespan being between three hundred and a thousand years. Those composed of earth ether are the shortest lived; those composed of air ether, the longest.

Paracelsus believed that they live in conditions similar to our earth environments and are somewhat subject to disease. These creatures, he said, are thought to be incapable of spiritual development but most of them are of a high moral character.

Concerning the elemental ethers in which the Nature spirits exist, Paracelsus wrote: 'They dwell at the four corners of the Earth: the gnomes of the Earth in the North, the nymphae and undines of the Water in the West, the salamanders of Fire in the South, and the sylphs of the Air in the East. None of them can go out of its appropriate element, which is to them as the air is to us, or the water to fishes; and none of them can live in the element belonging to another class. To each elemental being the element in which it lives is transparent, invisible and respirable, as the atmosphere is to us.'

Manly P. Hall[50] explained that the ancients symbolised these four elemental principles or vehicles as the arms of the cross representing the major crossing points of the vital forces in the human body. These intersecting points of the etheric world have their seat in the solar plexus and spleen. The etheric world is often referred to as the molten sea for in its depths the soul must ultimately be washed and purified. As each kingdom of nature in the outer world of earth life has diverse lives evolving through it, so the four divisions of ether inhabited by intelligent

---

[50] Hall, M., *Unseen Forces: Nature Spirits, Thought Forms, Ghosts and Specters, The Dweller on the Threshold*, Philosophical Research Society, 1978

life forms a re evolving through the four elemental essences. He stated that the four Elements are under the rulership of the great body-building Devas, the Lords of Form, also known as the four-headed Cherubim that stood at the gates of the Garden of Eden and which al so knelt upon the mercy seat of the Ark of the Covenant.

Theosophist Edward L. Gardner[51] described the life, work and appearance of the Nature Spirits:

> The life of the nature spirit, nearly the lowest or outermost of all, is active in woodland, meadow an d garden, in fact with vegetation everywhere, for its function is to furnish the vital connecting link between the stimulating energy of the sun and the raw material of the form -to-be. The growth of a plant from seed, which we regard as the "natural" result of its being placed in a warm and moist soil, could not happen unless nature's builders played their part. Just as music from an organ is not produced by merely bringing wind -pressure and a composer's score together but needs also the vital link supplied by the organist, so must nature's craftsmen be present to weave and convert the constituents of the soil into the structure of a plant. The normal working body of the sprites, used when they are engaged in assisting growth processes, is not of human nor o f any other definite fom... They have no clear-cut shape, and their working bodies can be described only as clouds of colour, rather hazy, somewhat luminous, with a bright spark -like nucleus ... Although the nature spirit must be regarded as irresponsible, living seemingly a gladsome, joyous and untroubled life, with an eager enjoyment of its work, it occasionally leaves that work and steps out of the plant, as it were and instantly changes shape into that of a dimunitive human being, not necessarily then visible to ordinary sight but quite near to the range of visibility. Assumed in a flash, it may disappear as quickly.

According to Paracelsus, the gnomes (female gnomes are gnomides) live in a world the Norse people call Elfheim. Their king is Gob. They are able to penetrate into the very core of the earth. They have charge over the solids, bones and other tissues of the human body. No bone could set without them . Some work with the stones, gems, and metals and are supposed to be the guardians of hidden tre asures. Gnomes build houses of substances resembling alabaster, marble and cement but only

---

[51] Gardner, E., *A Book of Real Fairies*, Theosophical Publishing House, 1972

the gnomes know the true nature of these materials, which have no counterpart in physical nature. They live in caves, far down in what the Scandinavians called the Land of the Nibelungen. In Wagner's opera cycle, *The Ring of the Nibelungen*, Alberich makes himself King of the Pygmies and forces these little creatures to gather for him the treasures concealed beneath the surface of the earth. Tree and forest sprites also belong to the grand company of the gnomes. Here one finds the sylvestres, satyrs, pans, dryads, hamadryads, durdalis, elves, brownies and little old men of the woods. Some families of gnomes gather in communities, while others are indigenous to the substances with which they work. For example, the hamadryads live and die with the plants or trees of which they are a part. Every shrub and flower are said to have its own Nature spirit, which often uses the physical body of the plant as its home. The archetypal form of gnome most frequently seen is the brownie, or elf, a mischievous little creature from twelve to eighteen inches high, usually dressed in green or russet brown. Most of them appear as very aged, often with long white beards, their figures inclined to rotundity. They can be seen scampering out of holes in the stumps of trees and sometimes they vanish by actually dissolving into the tree itself. Most of them are of a miserly temperament, fond of storing things away in secret places.

The undines comprise the limoniades, nymphs, niaids, mermaids, oreades, sirens, oceanids, potamides, harpies, sea-daughters and sea-goddesses of ancient lore. Their ruler is Necksa. Beauty is the

cornerstone and key feature of their power. They govern the liquids and vital forces in plants, animals and human beings. There are many groups of undines such as the Naga-Maidens of the Hindus that dwell in pools and streams. The water spirits do not establish homes in the same way that the gnomes do but live in coral caves under the ocean or among the reeds growing on the banks of rivers. Some inhabit waterfalls where they can be seen in the spray; others are indigenous to swiftly moving rivers;

Gnome (top) and Undine

some have their habitat in dripping, oozing fens or marshes, while other groups dwell in clear mountain lakes. Diminutive undines live under lily pads and in little houses of moss sprayed by waterfalls. According to the philosophers of antiquity, every fountain had its nymph; every oceanwave its oceanid. Often the water nymphs derived their names from the streams, lakes or seas in which they dwelt. In describing the undines, the ancients agreed on certain common features. In general, nearly all the undines closely resemble human beings in app earance and size, though the ones inhabiting small streams and fountains are of correspondingly lesser proportions.

It was believed that these water spirits are occasionally capable of assuming the appearance of normal human beings and actually associating with men and women. When seen, the undines generally resemble the goddesses of Greek statuary. There are many legends about these spirits and their adoption by the families of fishermen but in nearly every case the undines heard the call of the waters a nd returned to the realm of Neptune, the King of the Sea. Among the Celts there is a legend that Ireland was once peopled by a strange race of semi-divine creatures. With the coming of the modem Celts, they retired into the marshes and fens, where they remain even to this day as Elemental undines.

The salamanders are the strongest and most powerful of the elementals. Their ruler is a magnificent flaming spirit called Djin, terrible and awe-inspiring in appearance. In both animals and men, the salamanders work through the emotional nature by means of the body heat, the liver and the blood stream. Without their assistance there would be no warmth. Philosophers were of the opinion that the most common form of salamander is lizard-like in shape, a foot or more in length, and glows fiercely as it twists and crawls in the midst of the fire. Another group was described as huge flaming giants in flowing robes, protected with sheets of fiery armour. One important subdivision of the salamanders was the Acthnici. These creatures appear only as indistinct globes. They float over water at night and occasionally appear as forks of flame on the masts and rigging of ships (St. Elmo's fire).

The sylphs are composed from the finest ether of the four elements. Female sylphs are called sylphids. Among their many appellations, the sylphs are the riders of the night, the wind-born, the storm angels and the air-devas. Their leader is Paralda who is said to dwell on the highest mountain of the earth. To the sylphs were given the eastern corner of creation. Their temperament is mirthful, changeable and eccentric. They have no fixed domicile but wander about from place to place in the manner of elemental nomads, invisible but ever-present powers in the intelligent activity of the universe.

They move from castle to castle built out of the ether of the air element, which is the reflection of the mental plane. The sylphs sometimes assume human form but for only short periods of time. Their size varies but in the majority of cases they are no larger than human beings and often considerably smaller. It is said that the sylphs have accepted human beings into their communities and have permitted them to live there for a considerable period. They are always busy and work with the thoughts of living creatures. They work directly with the airy elementals of man's body such as the gases and ethers that have gathered within the body and indirectly with the nervous system. To the sylphs the ancients gave the labour of modelling the snowflakes and gathering clouds, accomplishing the latter with the help of the undines who supply the moisture. The sylphs are the highest form out of all the elementals, their native element being the highest in vibratory rate. They live hundreds of years, often attaining to a thousand years and never seeming to grow old. The Greek Muses are believed to have been sylphs for these spirits are said to gather around the mind of the dreamer, the poet and the artist and inspire one with their intimate knowledge of the beauties and workings of Nature. The peculiar qualities common to men and women of genius are supposedly the result of the cooperation of sylphs. The sylphs wield a powerful influence over things where the air is an important factor. Hence, during the air-age of the next 2,000 years their influence will be keenly felt.

*

… and now for the last brook, and to be a Queen! How grand it sounds!' A very few steps brought her [Alice] to the edge of the brook. 'The Eighth Square at last!' she cried as she bounded across and threw herself down to rest on a lawn as soft as moss, with little flowerbeds dotted about it here and there. 'Oh, how glad I am to get here! And what is this on my head?' she exclaimed in a tone of dismay, as she put her hands up to something very heavy, that fitted tight all around her head. 'But how can it have got there without my knowing it?' she said to herself, as she lifted it off, and set in on her lap to make out what it could possibly be. It was a golden crown.

— Lewis Carroll, *Through the Looking Glass and What Alice Found There*

It appears that Lewis Carroll either had a personal insight into the elementals, especially the sylphs, or he was guided unconsciously by the forces of living Nature to sew a seed of insight in his stories. British seeress Grace Cooke (1879-1979) used her gifts to demonstrate evidence of life after death. She was assisted in her mediumship by her spirit guide, "White Eagle." During a discourse on nature spirits, White Eagle said:

> Did we tell you of the ability of... elemental creatures to grow to
> a great size if necessary, or to diminish their size? This is one of
> their attributes. That remarkable book *Alice in Wonderland* deals
> with this happening. Do you think that book came only from the
> mind of its writer? Do you not see that such a story originated
> from the sylphs trying to teach humans great mystical truths? If
> you want to learn mysticism... read your fairy stories again. You
> will learn some beautiful truths if you ponder on what they have
> to tell you.

One is never too old to read fairy stories. One may be surprised by what they reveal.

Carroll's Alice stories also reveal close correspondences with the Greek myth of the Rape of Persephone, in which the violation of Persephone is symbolic of the divine nature defiled by the animal soul and dragged downward into the darkness of Hades, Pluto's material realm of consciousness.

In the nine days required for the enactment of the Greater Eleusinian Rites in ancient Greece, those to be initiated were questioned about their qualifications; took part in a procession to the sea for the submerging of the presiding goddess; participated in the sacrifice of a mullet; witnessed a mystic basket containing sacred symbols brought to Eleusis; ran a torch race; took part in an athletics contest; and, finally, witnessed the exhibition of a sacred urn or jar, an item of supreme importance in the ritual with which to celebrate the deepest truths of the mysteries.

In Alice's adventures we read of her being tested on her arithmetic; swimming with mythical creatures in the salt pool of tears; listening to the decidedly Innana flavoured story [" seven maids with seven mops "] of the Walrus and the Carpenter tricking and eating baby oysters; running a bizarre Caucus Race; and running the Red Queen's race ["Now, here, you see, it takes all the running you can do, to keep in the same place. If you want to get somewhere else, you must run at lea st twice as fast as that!"]. Carroll's stories are also littered with references to bottles and jars. Plenty of food for thought in Carroll's bottles and jars....

Alice, Goddess of Wonderland and the Looking-glass World

Chapter 16

Earth, Fire, Air, Water and Man

"Now hear the fourfold roots of everything: enlivening Hera, Hades, shining Zeus. And Nestis, moistening mortal springs with tears."

—Empedocles

The information in this and the following chapter is of metaphysical origin. Principally, it derives from transcripts of workshops in the USA and in Europe from the early 1970s to the late 1990s On these occasions, energies from a higher world transmitted te achings concerning the Ancient Wisdom to small circles of students, the means of transmission being the throat chakra of a medium in deep trance. It is not something taken from textbooks. It follows that because of their esoteric nature, if the teachings are to be accepted as having an essence of truth, it is more likely that one will arrive at that realisation or understanding through a belief that it feels "right," rather than through a purely intellectual or mental process. Above all, one must be open to the metaphysical axiom that says, 'Things are never what they seem.'

There are phases and energy changes that are a part of the "forces of living Nature," and which are felt best when one is in a neutral state of mind. For many centuries humans were very close to Mother Nature. They ate only what they needed; they hunted like any other creature; they discovered the healing power of plants and flowers and they were aware of the power of the seasons. The spirit of Mother Earth has been described as the "anima mundi," a sort of super memory in which is recorded all the experiences undergone by living creatures since earth was created. The Ancients taught that hum ans have within their higher self the electro-magnetic communicating system of all living things, of all energy within Mother Earth. And so, when we project in this visual element and the higher self works, it does so with recognition and empathy with the birds, with the elements, with all things because it has been all things.

Man, the Seasons and his Element(s)		
Season	**The Season's Element**	**The Season's Period**
Winter	Fire	December 21-March 21
Spring	Water	March 21-June 21
Summer	Air	June 21-September 21
Autumn	Earth	September 21-December 21
Element(s)	**Period of Reincarnation**	
	Northern Hemisphere	**Southern Hemisphere**
centre-Fire	January 21-February 21	July 21-August 21
Fire/Water or Water/Fire	February 21-April 21	August 21-October 21
centre-Water	April 21-May 21	October 21-November 21
Water/Air or Air/Water	May 21-July 21	November 21-January 21
centre-Air	July 21-August 21	January 21-February 21
Air/Earth or Earth/Air	August 21-October 21	February 21-April 21
centre-Earth	October 21-November 21	January 21-February 21
Earth/Fire or Fire/Earth	November 21-January 21	May 21-July 21

We come now to a rarely referenced component of the teachings of the Ancient Mysteries—Man and his elemental make-up. We are the grass, the tree, the four roots of Empedocles' philosophy: air, fire, water and the earth. We, our body, it is water, it is earth; it has minerals and chemicals within it. It is air, for it cannot live without breathing. It is fire, for it is warmth and without the sun it could not live. The fire we feel is a recognition of the intuition and instinct that has been somewhat dormant within us and the genes we inherited. It is coming back to life and burning away the bridges connected to the "human cocoon."

We are all things but, ignorant of the workings of the subconscious mind, we let the water, air, fire and earth rule our lives. We let every situation with people, with plant s and flowers, organise and direct us. Man is like nature. The Ancient Wisdoms taught that he is but a cycle, as our world is a cycle. Each thing has its seasons, as man has a cycle of the seasons. This is not only within man but within the history of mankind.

A spirit incarnating into this physical world can choose the moment of its reincarnation. This "time window" is from conception to eight weeks after birth. Very seldom does the reincarnating spirit choose its new body at conception; it usually observes the development of the body it will assume. This is to make sure that all the genetics, mother's nutrition and psychological behaviour, as well as the environment around her , is in line with what the incoming spirit needs for the physical experience and the lessons ahead to be learned.

In making these choices , the spirit also chooses the period of its reincarnation—in winter, spring, summer or autumn. Those that are reincarnating into these periods are influenced spiritually by their choice throughout their lives, regarding their personality, their character, their psychological makeup, their spiritual evolution, and that which will be the hardest things they will have to deal with and the highest things that they can obtain. Unlike astrology and all of the occult essences a person's elements show the destiny, or the outline, but it also shows the areas that man can step beyond to attain that control of free will.

Among the many conditions for appropriate reincarnation that the spirit considers is in which season to reincarnate: Northern Hemisphere, *Winter* December 21-March 21; *Spring* March 21-June 21; *Summer* June 21-September 21; *Autumn* September 21-December 21.

Each season has an element correlating with it: *Winter*-Fire; *Spring*-Water; *Summer*-Air; *Autumn*-Earth. In these are the cycles of Na ture incorporated: the Fire of the winter as the sun begins to shine more; the Water of the seas, rivers, lakes and streams as the spring unfolds; the Air of the summer as the harvest manifests; and the Earth of the autumn as things return to what they have been. Water and Sun are the "seen" Life-forces of this planet; Air and Nature are the "unseen" Life-forces.

The child born in any one these periods does not have any physical attributes that would indicate what element they are. This is similar to astrology in that there are no physical attributes to indicate what sign one is. Nevertheless, there are some key aspects of each season-element which each reincarnating spirit needs in order to complete its learning experience on the physical plane. Awareness of these "essences" would provide the individual with some very powerful tools to make life and living a bit easier.

An individual first reincarnates as Earth and experiences Fire last. Earth, basically, is what one might call the going-to-sleep, the relaxing. It is the time of relaxed motion. So, in the first existence, an individual coming into that element does not have to go through the intellectual, the emotional, or the energy-outwardness of Fire; they can have a slower, sedate life. After that, they return to the element that is hardest for them; and almost inevitably it is not the same, because one is dealing with an electro-magnetic negative-positive and a positive-negative. In those first four existences they are identical in their experiential pattern.

The wise men of old taught that man evolves through many lifetimes: nine to twelve. In the first six lifetimes man has no spirit guides, only angels with him. In these lives he is learning the essence of sex, of living in a material world, of poverty, wealth and disease without any ability to step beyond them.

After the sixth lifetime comes the ability and the enlightened attitude to be able to go within and find the Godforce, whether through Christianity, Islam, Buddhism or any other faith or belief; the ability is there.

A person who is living their last lifetime will not feel that it is. They will be too busy enjoying and exercising their accumulated knowledge and wisdom, loving every moment and relishing every element of beauty in this magnificent world. They see only beauty. They do not see war or poverty or famine. Theirs is an unlimited consciousness that they maintain without difficulty. Beauty becomes one with them. In essence, their higher self says, 'You have finally seen what has always been there. It is now time for you to see new things.' Most do not see the beauty around them. They get involved within the swamps but once a person becomes a magnet for beauty and positivity, day in, day out, every step of the way, fear within their life is eliminated.

A major part of this pathway to consistent beauty is that as a person unfolds and goes forward on their journey, they gradually understand that they are not only a part of mankind, of the animal, mineral and plant kingdoms but also of the elements, and that these are influential.

Fire is the element in charge of man. Water is the element, basically, of the plants. Air is in charge of the animals. Earth is in charge of the minerals. These things, in regard to their evolution and their strength, allow man to understand a little more of *his* evolution, not only within this plane but within other dimensions that interrelate; not only through the elements but through the mystical experience that they can allow man to have beyond his subconscious experience. The fifth element is Ether, an etheric energy and the strength or the connecting point to the oth er four.

The spiritual evolution of an individual allows him to understand the path that he is on. He is not looking to the horizon for his shoes; he realises that they are on his feet. And in so doing, he can project and be able to feel himself along his path so completely and fully that his path becomes not only a delightful sense of livingness, but it also becomes a creative evolution of his individual projection of his reality and spiritual growth. He that knows and can look at another man in regard to his element, and is able to interrelate that way, is taking the next step towards his own spiritual evolution of stepping above the destiny patterns set down at reincarnation. The destiny patterns, the lines upon our hand, our astrological sign; graphology, phrenology, the place we were born in, the people we were born to ; understanding the element, working with it, dealing with it in its highest perspective, will not only allow one to grow but will give one an essence of peace, an essence of understandin g why we are here and where we are going from now.

Each element has a tendency to have an acidity in its own right. A fire element's acidity is his openness to other people. In essence, when people knock on the door, the fire element does not open the door, he takes it off its hinges and allows them to come through as though he was a depot or a train station. That is the acidity that works within them: the openness, the involvement, the people area. As the fire element allows too many people come through, they lose what they are, they become just another being, they have no identification of self, they are in essence just another person.

A water element's acidity is in regard to their energy, which in essence is a holding onto, a not wanting to let go. There is emotion here, but they do not want to open the door. They want to keep everything within and when someone knocks, they are threatened. Therefore, there is not a freshness in the household, there is not an energy that allows newness, and it begins to cause the inside not to have the life it should.

The centre (100%) air element is constantly changing within his house. They want the walls to be different, the windows to be here and there. They want this and that to change. They want this form, that colour. They are scientifically altering, and no one w ants to come in because it is always in a state of confusion and a person will knock and they will open the door freely, but when they see the disarray, the person will back off because there are usually one thousand things going on and not one completed.

The earth elements will bring everyone into their house and shut the door. They want to live with everybody. They want to have the feeling of a lot of people around, but at the same time they want to be able to hit them and knock them through the windows and doors. They want to have that physical contact, that motion, that sexuality, that sensuousness.

But how does one balance these situations? How does one find the alkaline, the balancing force?

Within the fire, it is to keep the door open, but on. Within the water, it is to keep the door on, but open. Within the air, to clean up what is inside so you can open the door. And for the earth, to allow that which is inside to get out on a consistent base, on a thorough base, not through the windows, but walking. This means general changes within individuals. They begin to understand that everything they are, every essence, every power, every feeling is like a greasy stone; you do not hold on to it very long. It slips through your hands.

Each element has a specific colour or colour combination. A water element understands that blue is their key, as an air element understands that yellow is their key, as an earth element understands that green is their key, and as a fire element understands that red or energy is their key. A true Air will be yellow, and they will be drawn to the browns. You will find them usually in khaki or light brown. They will be drawn also to yellow itself but to the drabber shades, the greys. However, in reality the centre Air individual does not really care what they wear but for balance the best colour for them to wear would be a pastel yellow, or a pastel blue, or a pastel red, not pink, more of a salmon hue. Now, one who is an Air over Water combination will be drawn to greens: emerald, mint, the many colours of turquoise. Air over Earth will be drawn to the reds: the reds, dark, even to the burgundies, are excellent.

Equally, each element has one particular chakra that is developed more than another. The Air Element usually has the etheric web to the throat more developed. They usually have the ability to talk you to death, or dealing with the verbal, or the concentrated energy of voice, or what they hear. Fire deals, specifically, with the etheric web to the crown; Earth—clairvoyance, seeing the beauty of the Earth—is the seeing eye, the brow chakra. Air is the chakra to the throat; Water—clairsentience, feeling—to the heart.

How is it possible for one to recognize the element make-up of a given person? There are rules of thumb. Number one, the starker, say to them, 'You are the ugliest thing I have ever seen,' and watch their reaction. A true Fire will look at you like you are out of your mind. A Water would react, usually fight back in a flood of tears. An Air will tell you logically why they are not, and Earth will lash out physically and may beat you to a pulp. This is the first way. The second way is the subtleness. As one becomes familiar with the elements, one will be able to see the reactions of people and get an intuitive feel. If one wants to figure it and get fairly close to the astrological base, one should be looking at the mood—power, emotion, logic, and physical reaction —as related to their sign's ascendant.

The Fire Element, Winter

The Fire Element is the individual that reincarnates into their body between the 21st of December and the 21st of March. This individual has the ability to reincarnate from conception to eight of weeks after birth. The individual choosing this period of time is choosing a high strength element and power. Of all the Fire Elements, approximately seventy-five percent of them are men.

In terms of spiritual growth, a man growing within the Fire Element has one of two ways to go. There is no grey within the Fire Element It is either a strong, powerful, positive, projecting individual, or an individual that uses the Fire in the negative element to bring chaos and ruin to all he touches. So, the Fire Element can be the most fearful, especially within the male. But at the same time, it can be the most charismatic; for that amount of energy, used in the higher sense, brings warmth to all that come around them; brings an energy; brings the sun after a long autumn. Water, Air, and Earth are automatically pulled towards the Fire Element, either out of respect or out of a deep fear, not ever out of nonchalance.

The Fire male, using the energy he has, can melt all negativity in front of him. He has the ability of the sun, or the burning fire within the winter, to melt, to heat, to warm, to bring strength. He has the ability to see not only warmth within all things but to humidify and to make water less flooding; in essence, to make the air or the wind less terrifying and to bring things from the earth by its energy. Without the Fire, without its energy, Water, Air, and Earth could not survive. If, today, all Fire Elements were elim inated from Earth, we would have chaos. No one could lead, no one would be able to give a strong projective energy.

If the Fire male puts forth an energy in the negative sense, that is equally as terrifying upon the opposite scale. Instead of basically projecting the Fire outward, they pull it in to a depth that is within them.

They create what has been known by the biblical and the Ancient Wisdoms as Hades—the hell within. You go to Hades within, you go to hell, because it is within an individual. A positive Fire Element brings it out into the world, and it is not within. It is evident for all to see. A negative Fire Element pushes it so deeply within that it becomes chaotic, masochistic and terrifying. It is equally strong because within our world, people are pulled to fear; they are pulled to negativity. If you say, in a brief moment, 'Go down this street, there is a positive man talking of the beauty of spring; but go down that street and there is a man talking of death and killing,' there will be a horde going to the negative and very few to the positive. Because of that, the negative is powerful in this world, but never as powerful as the sun. The weakest point of the negative Fire Element is at the Summer Solstice when, in essence, the sun is the highest and the moon is the lowest. One of the reasons that it is said that things happen difficultly at the full moon is because the negative Fire Element uses the coldness of light, the reflection of the sun as, in essence, their energy; and it manifests then. Positive Fire Elements get along well together if they have the equal balance of Water, Air, and Earth working with them,

The female Fire Element has a great difficulty in this world. She usually comes into it to deal specifically with understanding her femininity because she is coming from a lifetime or lifetimes that have been extremely degrading to others. She is having to express her femininity in the hardest way. A positive Fire female becomes beautiful as the sun, but soft. A negative Fire female becomes the darkness on wheels, meaning, specifically, that the female negative element uses the energy in a more secretive way. Because of that, it is more terrifying and usually they will support a negative male element. But because there are so few of them, there are not usually too many problems.

The attributes of the strengths of a male Fire Element are that they are the leaders; they have the strength of society. They have the rapport; they have the ability to lead; they have the ability, in war, or in peace. Dealing with the Fire Element male, you must know these things: at times, his energy is like the sun and can come so that it is overpowering. His energy, his insistence that things, basically, must continue to go along, asking for no rest, is very tiring to those who need relaxation and repose. He usually does not need long hours of rest but consistently wants to put the energy forth. They will deal with people usually very curtly and very straightforwardly. If you say to a Fire Element, 'Am I doing the right thing?' they will usually say, 'No.' If you say that to a Water Element, they will cry and probably in one way say, 'No,' in a long explanation of emotion. To an Air Element, they will try to explain it, in depth, why it is 'No,' and usually put you to sleep, An Earth Element will usually not know which way to go, or will not have the strength and will say, 'Wait a minute, while I consult someone else.' But a Fire Element will say, 'This is the way we are to go.' Sometimes, when they are doing this and are not in tune, they go where they should not go, too fast.

They interrelate very strongly, in the male energy, with other male Fire Elements, as long as there is a balance. If two male Fire Elements are to work together, there has to be at least two female Water Elements to balance it, or three Air Elements, or a whole legion of Earth Elements, it is because of the powerful energy.

The Fire Element male, basically, does not get along too well with the Water Element male. This is not saying they cannot be friends, but to work together is very difficult. It is not that the Fire does not need that emotion, that softness to balance, that intuitive point but the male Water Element, because of the masculinity, will have a tendency to be a little draining and the Fire Element will usually not deal with them. The Water male will usually turn it into intellectual projection, and the Fire Element does not like to get into intellectual games. The Air male can get along with a Fire Element male if the Fire is a strong one; if he has the patience to listen to all that the Air Element wants to say and then can go ahead, no matter what has been said. The Air Element and the Fire male can have a deep relationship if there is mutual understanding that they are sounding boards for one another.

The Fire Element and the Earth Element can work together. The Earth Element usually becomes attached, or a follower, or a very strong supporter. A Fire Element male dealing with other males deals best with an Earth Element; secondly with an Air; third with a Water; and with a Fire Element last, because they are so much alike in energy.

The Fire Element male dealing with a female deals best with the Water female. The reason for this is that fire has a tendency to humidify, or to dry up water when it gets too deep; and water has a tendency to keep fire from getting too brilliant. But in dealing with the male/female relationship, it is sometimes difficult for the Fire Element will find it hard feeling emotion and the Water female will be all emotion. There will be emotion in times when, logically, there should not be emotion; and the Fire will not understand that. So, the Water female, in understanding this one point, can have strength with a Fire if, within their emotion, they do not try to manipulate him but use it as their release, so the Fire Element can see and react to it positively. But if it is aimed as a wily game to the Fire, he will just walk away. Too much water puts out fire and it will withdraw. But if water is used correctly within itself, fire can then take its energy and use it.

Secondly, a Fire Element dealing with a Water Element must also understand that the energy that is going to the Water is sometimes misunderstood, because the energy is projecting outward. Because it is so strong, the Water dealing with emotion will have a tendency to blow it out of proportion and will say it is this, and this, and this, and it will sound like Armageddon when it is actually a birthday party! It is natural for energy against emotion to have that reaction. The Fire Element male dealing with the Water female must understand that if they want to have a good balance, they must listen. The female Water will flow and flow and flow, if the male listens and, within the listening, will see and get the point. If they do not, there will be stagnation.

A Fire Element projecting to a Water must understand that the Water will pull from them at all times of day and night. Because Fire is what is basically called a strengthening, positive energy, when it is pulled away from the Water it will, in essence, react more than any other element. Earth can hold warmth longer than water can hold warmth. Water needs to feel that warmth at all times. The greatest difficulty comes because the Fire, needing the rest of night, takes that time to withdraw; and it is at night that the Water Element has great difficulty. The Fire must know that if he wants his Water Element to be strong through the night, or through the darkness, that he should be with her just before the darkness so that she will relax through it. A Water Element needs that energy.

A Fire will understand that in dealing with the female Water Element, the combination can bring forward a strong partnership, a strong family, But the female will have a tendency to be very inward, within the family, very protective, as the Fire is the outer energy. The Water will always try to bring the Fire back, concerned about the family; and the Fire must know that and give the energy consistently. The Fire Element male in reacting to a Water female will, as a positive element in the face of a negative element, withdraw immediately. This is not only psychic protection; it is elemental protection.

Because the Water female deals with the four elements or emotions of Water—fear, judgment, anger, frustration—the Fire Element has a tendency to pull away, especially if that emotion is negatively projected to the Fire. The Fire is dealing with energy, the strongest energy within our world; and if the Water female is projecting negative energy, the Fire energy will withdraw. This will usually cause problems for the Water female who will want to know if they could have the Water rejuvenated by the Fire.

Fire to the Air female partnerships is not often found. They usually do not come together. When the air female is the scientist, they spend more time indoors than they do out. They are the logical ones; they are the ones that think. Fire does not use that faculty very much and so seldom is there an energy pattern towards them. When there is, it is usually a marriage of convenience, and they are usually working together with very little sexual energy, very little emotion at all.

In Fire to Earth, the Earth female pulled to the Fire Element will, in essence, be somewhat of a servant but will be, in many ways, a good strength. The Fire male dealing with the Earth female must understand that, in their strength, they have to be not too demanding, too energetic, or too moving; for the Earth female will want to be in one place as long as she can, be somewhat sedentary. The Earth female and the Fire male work well together in business, or in energy patterns of that way.

Dealing specifically as a mate, it usually is a very physical relationship, which has a tendency to drop the energy of the male. It raises the energy of the female and will make them more creative. The Fire energy living with this situation must understand that their energy can bring out creativity of the female Earth; and so, if they will concentrate it to help them stop beyond material and sexual energy, they will become creative energy. They will become great artists. They will become great musicians, great dealers with the earth, with the animal, mineral, and plant kingdoms.

The Fire female can find a good match with a Fire male; and many times, the communicaion, or the togetherness, will be a companionship but a very strong one, a very overpowering one, one that will get things done, no matter who stands before them. It will be one of dedication, one different from the Fire male and the Air female relationship but it will be one of love, mutual strength, and sexual energy. They will not be dealing with emotion, so they have a tendency to be overpowering in groups. They can make a very good alignment but a Fire female dealing with a Fire male needs to project themself a little softer, for they wll be learning to be soft. The softer they become, the more powerful they will become, and the stronger will be the relationship.

The Fire female dealing with a Water male will be difficult, for the Water male will try to be emotional, to be *in* the emotion, but will be trying to be the male image. Where the Fire female has that image, the Water male will usually be dealing with spiritual evolution. The Fire female will be dealing with a very positive, one-minded evolution, and will usually direct the energy, even though she basically wants to have the support of the Water male. She will not usually be too spiritually involved through a Water male, even though he will be deeply spiritual; and she will be deeply involved with him. The Fire female in dealing with that must learn that she must help the Water male in allowing and working with him in the spiritual attitude, for if they do not, the relationship cannot last. They cannot be directive; they must be supportive with the Water male. It must be a supporting relationship— they cannot be the leaders: it must be supporting; it must be a team. But the Fire female has a tendency to be the leader, to direct, to say, 'This is where we go.' They must learn to be supporting, to bring out the strength of the Water male.

The Fire female can get along fairly well with an Air male: in fact, they can be pulled strongly together. The Air male, being intellectual, will need energy; and there can be a good strength, a mutual energy return. The only difficulty is that the sexual energies will not ever be too strong, and it will usually be for producing children because it is the thing to do, not because it is a deep emotion. The Fire female pulled to the Air male can make a strength. If the Air male is getting into metaphysical learning, then it can have a strength for it brings out the height of metaphysical teaching, which the Air male can do in its highest form. If the Fire is pulled to that, it is the best match for there will be mutual support and mutual strength. In dealing with that she will have to learn that the Air will have a tendency to be logical about his approach, while she will have a tendency to be very moving. There will have to be compromises in the partnership. The Fire female with an Earth male usually is common. Fire looks for something that will, basically, allow them to use their strength, to be strong, so they are pulled to an Earth male, who is physical. One will find that the Earth male in the physical form—that is, what one would call rough, a typical Earth male, very sexual, very energetic, very pushy—will pull the Fire female. The sadness is that often the relationship does not work. The Fire female dealing with an Earth male, who is creative in the art form, will usually help their creativity; but the Earth male will not need the Fire female after a while, so it is not a very good strength. If they want to make it, the female must know that her energy can bring the creativity out, but they have to deal with the softness to help the sexual energy. They cannot deal with just a positive energy pushing forth.

The Fire Element female is extremely strong. Learning the beauty that they have within them is their greatest spiritual endeavour; learning to express this softly and warmly. The Fire male uses his energy to warm all the time, to be positive to them, accepting and listening.

The Fire element, both male and female, in the spiritual highest, can use either a clear crystal or a rose crystal for their strength. They can use gems and other stones that deal with the darkness of reds, but the effect will not be as strong as working with the power of clear crystal or diamond.

The Fire male and female are very sexual. The males are very energetic in this way. If their energy is not being used, if they are not going forward, they will have a tendency to be pulled to a very sexual relationship, usually Earth, or a female in the Water Element that is trying to understand their emotion, the same with the Fire female.

Musically, they are pulled to the music of earth, of air, of water, not of fire. They need emotion within music. They need the strength of air, the baseness of earth . They need all three, but not the strength of fire. That only causes them to be a little more difficult to deal with. They are cautioned against dealing with artists like Wagner, Tchaikovsky, Stravinsky and Khachaturian, and instead listen to those like Mozart, Beethoven and Handel. In today's music, they get on better with Country and Western. Fire basically will be pulled in reading to those things that can relax them and take them away from their energy, not getting them involved in more energy. They will be travellers; they will be a strength in this world. The Fire Element is the light but, used negatively, they are the darkness that we see daily.

The Water Element, Spring

Most water elements are female: at least seventy-five percent. A Water Element female is aware that in the electro-magnetic sense their inner is positive and that their outer is negative. They are dee ply conscious of their inner garden; it is a beautiful place for them to go, spiritually. The reason so many women are Water Element s is because of th is positive-negative energy, of the pulling together and the creating of strength. This is unique. Man does not have this, but water does. Man dealing with this reacts differently as a Water Element than does a woman.

The Water Element womanreincarnating in the first fifteen days after spring is Water over Fire, meaning that they are dealing with the emotions, dealing with expressing self, but have the ability to have that silence within, thatstrength within to go a little further. They do not react to emotion as much. They are the empathetic, loving, feminine woman that will very seldom cry. They are strong but they are cent red around family. They are powerful and have great inner beauty, but they have the ability to express their ability verbally; they have the in trovertish-extrovertish combination. In dealing with that, they need an extreme ly strong Fire Element male as their energy force, a Fire Element male that is in the centre of the season. The reason for this is, in essence, to allow more energy to give their water the balance; but the male that is Fire over Water can also be a good balance with them. Within it, if they work together and develop a spiritual essence together and work as a team; they can have a good balance.

The Fire Earth male to the Water Fire female has strength also but he will be dealing with the material and the physiological, and the Water Fire female will not want to be dealing with this. They will not want to be bothered materially or physiologically. They will want to be able to express their emotion stoically and with strength; not in the essence of softness, as a bud, but in the strength of a tree that comes forward powerfully, not with fear of not being loved or lovable.

In a Water Element reacting to the Earth Element, they will, basically, have to be very withdrawn with their emotion, more so than with any other, not releasing it orally. They will have to be cautious in all areas, not overpowering in emotion and directing within their creativity, allowing them to be individualistic in the area that they are dealing with. The Earth Element, using their creativity, will have a tendency to be what one may call fanatical within cleanliness or within orderliness; and a Water Element may be a little upset with that.

The Water male with a female Fire/Earth has the best advantage: they can release their emotion. It can be reacted to by Earth and by Fire, and they can get the balances of both. However, the Water male can get along well with the Air female. Within their emotion, the female has a tendency to be a little more relaxed and not as outward, a fairly good aligning.

One can imagine what one will see in a Water/Water relationship: a Noah's flood. A Water/Water is catastrophic. If one is dealing with fear, the other has anger; if one has anger, the other has judgment; if one has judgment, the other has frustration. They are water, water all around them. They are usually pulled to the ocean, where there is more water and more emotion. Not a good alignment, very difficult, unless it is a Water/Fire male and a complete Water female, or the other way around,

The Water male has the best alignment with an Earth female, for within their emotion the female's natural tendency is to absorb that, even though they are Earth; and there can be a balancing. The Water will be creative and warm and loving; the female Earth will want that loving physically, will have creativity, and so will Water male. They will exceed in creativity and all forms of art.

The totality of all of these is that the Water female has beauty within family and expresses emotion and is clairsentient. The Water male is creative, artistic, and has the ability of expressing but does not deal as much with clairsentience as with expressing their inner source as an art form, outwardly, rather than through someone else, as the Water female does. The Water Element is the spring; is the beauty of the flowers; is the fertility. It is a time of creativity, of warmth and loving. Utilized in the highest sense, the Water Element can give a balance of unity, warmth, and loving to people that will be drawn to them from Earth, Air and Fire because of their femininity, or their creativity as a male, and the strength within that.

Of the four elements, Fire is the strength, is the energy, is the pattern of outward pushing; is the sun. Fire has strength, and against it nothing can stand if it is positive. If it is positive and uses its energy for the highest good, there is nothing Fire cannot do. Water, however, is the most spiritually oriented of all the elements. Those tha t are pulled to be with Water, reincarnate with the ability not only to grow but the ability to develop a spirituality of self, a spirituality that no other element can do as easily. They are naturally thos e unifiers of family, of commun ity, of individuality projecting a spiritual perception. The Water Element in this way, has great advantages over the others: easily to become spiri tual, meaning the ability to perceive, to be a medium within the area of their service, of working with people more easily, having more empathy and understanding for children and elders. Because of these things, they come with the hardest spiritual objective of them all—to deal with emotion. If it were not for the spiritual potential of the Water Element, they would not have to deal so readily with emotions. People are pulled to Fire; they are pulled to the power of that energy, but they cannot get too close, or they will be burned. They will find at times, the energy is overpowering, and they will stand away. But everyone has a tendency to be drawn to Water: to drink; to wash; and to help flush and empty away the emotions. Water Elements pull emotional beings of all the elements who have a difficult time following their path.

Consequently, these emotions—fear, judgment, anger, frustration— are not only felt by the individual Water Element, but by those that bring it to them or those in groups and even nations that are drawn to them . Everyone in this world, at one time or another, is drawn to Water. Water is the spiritual energy. Fire, of course, is needed for growth, for warmth; but all are pulled to Water, almost in a fanatical way. There will be those that would do without Fire, but not without Water.

Emotions within a Water Element are just what one may call the balance to the spiritual self. The reason they feel that it is so agonizingly overwhelming is that it is easy to overwhelm Water. Consider the element. A drop of oil can make it undrinkab le. So, fear of being loved, or lovable, or loving, or fear of being accepted as individual, is the same as fear of having the waters muddied so you could not see and be refreshed by them. Anger is the same as the torment, as the raging waters, as the energy that comes from a tornado, typhoon, or hurricane, and the water is unable to be used. Frustration is when the Water is, basically, not being used correctly; it is not staying in one place; it is flowing here and there. It is like a great dam that has burst in many places, and you do not know where to patch first. Judgments, basically, come by a Water Element in regard to what they are dealing with. If someone throws to them the fear, or oil, or pollution, they will judge them easily because they affect them quickly.

On the opposite end, the Water is the most spiritual, the most clairsentient. There are more spiritual mediums dealing with spirit communication in the Water Element within this world than any other. There are more Water Element females that are dealing with the social aspect of individuals than any other element. There are more Water Element people dealing with the specifics of the individual's flowingness, not psychiatry, but their flowingness, their understanding, their teaching. These are important things to know for the Water Element deals with spirituality on the tip of their cuff. But upon the tip of the other cuff is emotion which they deal with each and every day. A Water individual will have a tendency to overreact on things that are coming forward. First, they do not like authority of any kind. If they are surrounded by authority, their physical bodies will be absorbed with water, hard digestion, difficulty. Authority can take many forms; it can take the form of a male, of a nation, of a society, of a physical plant, of spiritual guidance. The Water Element would react to these because they want to be appreciated, but they do not want to feel this power, and they will rebel against it in the fear of not being loved or, in essence, a judgment, or anger and frustration. They will react in many ways to these things.

They will need to have solidity around them. They will be the ones that are the cleaners, that must have things in comparative order; and if it is out of order, they feel their life is out of order, and they will be frustrated. It is like keeping a clear lake. They will constantly skim, most important for their physical and emotional being. The Water Element specifically will deal with expressing themselves, and they will do this outwardly. And if an individual does not accept that expression, or they feel that someone does not like them, they will react, usually withdraw, or go within a place by themselves. This is because they are dealing with emotion. These projections are strong, powerful, and they need to work with them at all times.

The Water Element says, 'How do I deal with emotion?' The greatest fear of all, in a Water Element, is not being accepted for what they are. If someone says something to them, or is in contradiction to what they are believing, or feeling of self, it will have a tendency to cause them to react very sharply. They must know that, basically, there is nothing within the world that someone should throw to them, or project outward to them, that they cannot stand above. If someone says to them, 'What you are is wrong,' or they hear that that person is saying, 'You are not loving,' or they hear that they are not accepted for what they are, they will get mad at the individual for passing these untruths, or comparative truths. They should not, for the individual that projects any kind of gossip, any kind of word analogy to someone else, has a negative essence that, basically, is projected to hurt or to cause some kind of agitation.

Now, the female Water Element is learning to deal with their emotion, and they have to learn, with fear, whatever it is, in any area — they can be afraid of the authority of money, or the authority of poverty, this essence—they have to realize that they have the ability, through non-recognition, to be spiritually in charge, more than any others. Secondly, in judgment, they have a tendency to judge themselves , for they are always looking at themselves, more than the others who have a tendency to throw themselves together. But the Water female must be intricate, must be exacting, must work with every detail. Not because they want to

flaunt but because they want the water to be clear, that people will drink and that they can see themselves. That is important. The Water male will be somewhat of the same kind, but will have a tendency, in many ways, to be not as exacting with their presentation but be more exacting with their relatedness. The Water male will have more difficulty with interpersonal relationships than the Water female. One reason is that the Water male does not take as much care of their physical presentation. The female has— and it is good—a seemingly

The Beauty of Nature

253

positive façade around them to be able to strengthen them. The Water male, of all the things they deal with, they deal not so much with the emotions of fear, anger and judgment but with frustration. In frustration comes the sub-headings of jealousy, having a tendency to be anxious, to worry, always to wonder where things are going to come from. They will have a tendency to see a situation and, if it is a gusty wind, they will see it as a tornado. They, basically, deal with frustration, trying to get things aligned. They will have a harder time of consolidating their energy than the female Water Element: but, in strength, the Water male has the ability to give a great amount of spiritual energy in the mediumship. In the higher sense, the Water male can do things in intricacy, more than the Earth. They have abilities in intricate and long, exacting chores. They will take hours and spend hours on a project that a Fire Element would give up in minutes. They are long-suffering; they will be frustrated, but they will stay in a situation. In creativity, they are strong. They can express empathy strongly.

There are very few true centre Fire males: meaning that they reincarnated in the centre of December 21-March 21. Most Fire males are on the fringes. A Fire male that is on the fringe of Earth has a tendency to be like an Air male. A Fire male on the fringes of Water has a tendency to be like an Earth male. And so, a Water female must know that if they are dealing with the Fire/Earth male, they will be dealing with an intellectual who tries to think and wants to think things for them, does not like to do things too fast, is a very slow individual and usually smokes a pipe! They have a tendency towards this energy. The Water/Fire deals specifically with their sexual energy and with material matters. They will not have the confidence that things will be taken care of financially. They will have a tendency to worry a little too much of where the money is coming from, and of their sexual prowess.

The Water Element dealing with these two fringe areas can understand them in regard to these concerns. But with the true Fire male, the Water female will have things that they must know. First, the Fire male in the centre can deal with energy in any area. They will have, initially, no fear. If someone calls them a bad name, they will look at the individual as if they are right. They will go any place on the planet. There is no fear. There is usually not much judgment, hardly any frustration, and the only anger usually comes to the Water female herself, not to anyone else, and it is because of this projection of emotion. The Water female will feel that she is not being loved adequately by the centre Fire male, and she will press, will want to have some kind of recognition. The Fire male gives the recognition by the total energy. The Fire male will be pulled to the Water female, and the other way also, because, together, working as a team, they have the greatest abilities; but, because they have the greatest abilities, they will have the most difficult time.

The Water male dealing with a Fire female will find that, basically, they will be dealing with an energy that they will have to do what the Fire female wants, and their life will be regulated along that area. They will find that their Fire female, if it is a Water male in the companionship, will have a difficult time spiritually projecting. To the Water male, it will be easy, and they will be torn between their individual growth and staying and steadying the relationship. The Fire woman, in relationship to the Water male, will try to regulate and str engthen them through physical action; through disease of the body; through feeling badly; through feeling, basically, that they are being subjected, or not liked, because the Water male is growing in other ways.

The Water female in relationship to the Earth, dealing with the Earth male, will be dealing with an individual that is dealing materially and physiologically, sexually oriented, having a tendency to have difficult times with interpersonal relationships, being introvertive and very creative. The Water female will be drawn to them in this way; they will be drawn to the creative Earth male, to the one that can project themselves through the fine arts, or music, and want to be around them. They will want to feel that creativity, that energy, that power. But they will find that, within it, they will be the major strength and that there will be slowly a draining of what they are, even though there can be excitement within what they are doing. If they stay, or they match, then, the Earth male will have to d eal with his creativity in the highest level, meaning that everything that they do is a creative art. The Water female can deal with that. Very seldom will you find an Earth male or an Earth female that will be what one may call a one-person man or woman. They will have a tendency to need the physical satisfaction and review of what they are from many people. The Earth male will be pulled to the Water female; the Earth female will be pulled to the Fire male.

The Water male cannot stand—and usually will have great difficulty with—an Earth female. The Water male has a tendency to be soft, loving, warm, emotional, and to cry at the drop of anything. Whereas the Earth female, who has a tendency to deal sexually and materially, will tend to wear out the Water male. If the Earth female is creative, dealing in fine arts or the creative form, in the higher sense, a Water male can work with them. But it would be most difficult and, over long term, most unlikely,

Water/Air: what does Air do to Water? It churns it up, blows it away, it does not allow it to fall where it wants to fall. One thing you should learn about a Water person: don't push them away from where they are going, and wind or air does that. If it is raining, the wind will push the rain away; they will push the water someplace else: Water and Air.

A true Water female and true Air male will have great difficulty: not being able, in the true sense, to have any lasting relationships, because the Air male will think so deeply and be so deeply involved in the scientific, the logical, the political, the psychological, that they will be, in many ways, intellectually above the Water female; but not in the dealing with feelings, where the Water female is way above, A most difficult interrelationship, if it is true Air and true Water. The Air person will deal in a lot of insecurities; and a Water female will have a tendency to bring out these insecurities in an Air male. The Air male will say, 'We cannot do that because it costs two ninety-five,' and the Water female says, 'But I feel we can do it,' and the Air male will not be able to fathom that. It is that conflict. The Air male will have a tendency, in the metaphysical line, using their highest point, to be able to deal with a Water female, but as a working companion, not as a mate.

The ideal crystal for Water is amethyst. In the female especially, it has a tendency, when worn, because of the hues of the blue-violet spectrum, the spiritual energy, to calm the emotions. It works well in a dedication sense. The female can say, 'I will wear this to rid me of my fear,' and it will; it will absorb and then discard it. Clear white crystal will also help but more so in dealing with a range of emotions, whereas amethyst subdues strongly in one area more effectively than the white stone. Lapis is also a strong support for Water. From there, any of the blue minor gems will be of crystal healing value. The ideal music for Water is Chopin, Schubert and Handel, dealing specifically with organ, piano and harp

Water is the spiritual. It deals with family, with home, with consolidation of our world and its spiritual projection. Find a community, a group, an organization, a religion, a creed, a philosophy, a teaching, a guru, and you will find more Water females and Water males than any other element.

The Air Element, Summer

The Air Element is the one that deals with the earth plane in a karmic sense, with their mentalness and their intellect. This element, more than any other, is in constant conflict with the logical, the scientific and the subconscious. Liking, and many times marrying, the subconscious or the ego, they delight within the energy force that is created.

One of the things that the Air Element does is see and feel. They are, in essence, wanting to see why something works —but to see why it works to its *nth* degree, having great difficulty of accepting that it just works. They are always in the midst of decisions and experiment.

They are your debaters. They are the ones that have a tendenc y to overshadow your political scene. They are the ones that i ntellectually must project themselves and, in any way, will seek and a form of following. They are the ones that find the cause, hold on to it, and take it for the rest of their lives, whether it is politics or prisons or sex. They are those that have to think and not feel. They say they are against poverty because it is notgood, but they think it out, they logicalse it. They cannot deal with the feeling.

Very few of the true Air Element ever meet a spiritual project. Many are involved within science, within psychology and the medical field; most that deal in these areas you will find are Air Element. If they are not a Fire, they are an Air. They find themselves rooted in to patterns that they cannot get out of. Of all the elements, it is easier for them to become conservative, to believe something from the time they are taught it to the time they die,

Very very few within the world are true A ir, in the centre. Most are fringes, Air/Water or Air/Earth. Not many in the centre for there are not many who are, in essence, succinctly and fulfillingly in the logic to the nth degree. But there are some, and those you w ill find will be rec luses and hermits, those that cannot express themselves, those that, basically, withdraw, to think, to read, to write.

Even though the world has many monks and hermits, it is almost impossible at this time within the world to be a mystic or a recluse and not be an Air Element. They have a tendency to think rather than feel. Because of that, you find that these orders are lacking in the freedom of self-discipline. Today in the Western tradition —in the Americas, the European continent, the Asian or Russian area—most men are Air Elements. And it is the Air Element that has a tendency to rule, to influence, because people are afraid of the logical: or, basically, of the individual who can prove and throw words time and time again; or who tries to prove their point through argument.

The Air Element male centre can only get along with a Fire female; perhaps a little, to a degree, with the Air female. The centred Air female is exceptionally rare. One will be very fortunate to meet one in their lifetime. But those that you would meet could only marry an Air Element male—if they marry at all. The Air Element is, basically, dealing with the fringes, with water and earth. Consider, the Air Element that is dealing with Water: Air is yellow, Water is blue, which makes green.

They have many of the same reactions of the Earth Element.

The Air Element male with Water will be dealing, basically, not only with their thinking, but will be thinking to death how to correct their material and their sexual life. And because they will think about their sexual life, it will be sparse and there will be great difficulty in interrelating. The female within this area will, basically, be a female that is extremely strong, but is dealing a lot with materialism—dealing, specifically, with always hunting money, trying to find it, trying to think of a way to get more of it. Not necessarily aligned with the physical, or great difficulty in physiological, maybe using it to get money; but basically, that is their area.

The Air Element male over Water, in a highest perspective, can have a metaphysical view and deal within metaphysics: going beyond science, the logical, the written form; being able to see and perceive because of their technicality, the beginnings of the universe. But it is sad, again, that those that you find, within our world, that are Air Element males, that learn to use the metaphysical and to go beyond it, are also very rare. Those that are Air over Water can begin to work with their scientific approach, but dealing with the elements of earth, mineral, and animal in a scientific, or in a logical, way. They are able to involve and to work within the livingness of that element, putting some of the softness of water, some of the feelings of water, out. The Air Water male can deal a lot with the Water Fire female. There is good strength there. The Air/Water male can deal a lot with the Fire Earth female, basically needing that balance, that strength, but that earthiness. They have the ability, within the fulfillment, to understand. The great alchemists were Air over Water, for they used the earth, the minerals, the metals.

The Air over Earth becomes Fire in their feelings, much like the Fire Element. They will be always concerned with people loving them and not feeling loved, more so than the Fire Element. They will not have the confidence. They will be, basically, concerned with what other people think of them, A part of the Earth feeling, but with the addition of the logicalness. Someone can say they do not like them, and they will be able to logically figure out why they do not like them and why no one else would like them. But the Fire part would bring obstinance, will make them hard, and make them stick to something, even to the point of ridiculousness. They are the ones that you want to lead armies, for they will stay at the head, no matter what is fighting them; but they usually would not be found there. The Air over Earth deals specifically with beginning to learn their energy and their strengths too.

The Air over Earth male—here is where we find our politicians. Here is where we find those that are dealing with the great controversies of your world. Free the world from disease, from poverty, from the negativity, and they will carry it and they will lead it. They will seem Fire but they will have the stick ability, or the mental capacities, logically thinking and trying to scientifically prove every step they make. The true Fire Element will not care if it does not scientifically prove. He knows he is right anyway. And the Earth that is, basically, more Air is constantly trying to prove what they are doing. The Air that has Earth has abilities to deal with leading, but not as the forerunner. They are supporters. They are the ones that can do what needs to be done. They are the best supporters for a Fire Element. You will find them as the assistants, as the second or third in com mand. They will, basically, be the organizers or the generators behind the scenes.

They deal consistently with learning to be accepted by people and try to project themselves there. Most female actresses are in this line. Dealing with this as a male, their highest perspective will be a supporting role; or they will be an actor, giving forth energy, entertaining. They will be those that are al ways known as the serious actors, as the serious projectors, as the serious entertainers; the female in this, the same. The seriousness, dealing with the vanity of self, but being the entertainers, they are the ones that can bring escape to others, into worlds that are real, or unreal but have reality. Those that are involved in this can be a part of one, or two, or three, and they are good balance, for they bring humour; but they bring to it a flair that not many have.

In their mating they deal well, the female with the Fire Element male, the male with the Fire Element female . They deal fairly well with the Water/Fire female, the Earth: but the female will usually deal with every male within a lifetime, never usually being monogamous.

The Air Element is the most misunderstood. It is the hardest. It is the individual that has the most to give, and they will try to give it forth for others to live off. They are the individuals that, basically, stand up but do not know how to use their power in the higher, p ositive way. They will struggle with that. The female Air over Earth will have a tendency towards hypochondria, as will the male Air over Water. They will find things wrong with them that no one has even thought could be wrong with a human being. The male Air/Earth will not be hypochondriac; they will usually not have time for that. The fe male Air over Water will, basically, be dealing with difficulties with the female organs, physiologically. They will also have malfunctions of the thyroid that will lead to dryness and toughness of skin; and are the ones that are very wrinkled in older age.

The Air Element is the hurricane; it blows a great wind, will cause great damage to all areas. They will tear and rant and rave, because no one would listen to them. Like hurricanes, or typhoons, or tornados, one can warn people that they must protect themselves, that they must be in tune and they will not listen. So, a hurricane will come, and an Air Element will come and cause chaos in their life. They will wonder, 'Why is this person trying to think me to death, trying to, basically, deal with me in the way they are?' Those that deal with Air, deal with a heavy spiritual karma, for they are the most misunderstood: and, because of that, they are the most destructive in the way they deal. It is the Air Element that created atomic energy. It is the Air Element that is a logistic, that creates the plans of war; that creates machines; that invents and is the scientist; that dissects the subconscious mind; that does not believe in mysticism and, in religion, is very difficult.

The music of the Air is forceful. It can be like a breeze; but it can be like the thunder of Wagner, Khachaturian, Tchaikovsky and Liszt. Or it can be a softness of Handel, or Mendelssohn, or Debussy. But they will not deal with these consistently. They will seek the classical; and if they are pulled to one musical instrument, it will usually be the reeds, organ, flute: those that use air. They can find great energy within the organ or within the flute or the air or wind instruments.

Their stone is clear crystal or champagne crystal (very uncommon), or amber interlaced with moonstone, which can calm them more than any other.

Air Elements are interspersed throughout the world. They are the thinkers, the scientists, the logical ones. Their strength is not in all one area. There is not one country that is strong in what they are. There is not one that is overstrong. Britain is very strong within Air Element, extremely strong. France is another—France with a little tinge toward Earth, but it is there. America, it has a lot of it, but it is offset by much Earth. The Air Element becomes prominent and there are many of them at the end of a cycle, just before the fall, the retiring and the renewal.

The Earth Element, Autumn

The creativity of the Earth Element is always held in awe, for they bring forth most of the beauty of the world and many like what they see. They are pulled and drawn to it. But within it, they find depression, and many times they will find that, if they get involved within the artist, it is the artist's life that sells his art, more than the art itself. Because of the evolution of the trials and tribulations that they are going through, their leaves are falling consistently. They are cutting away old wood, but most do not cut away any. Financially, they deal with great trauma, great difficulties within the physiological and sexual sense, having problems in regard to sexuality and identifying themselves mostly with the creativity. The greatest artists are able to find a balance of materialism, and their sexuality usually becomes a celibate element within that area. They find that within their creativity they can replace the male, or the female. They can have an orgasm within the creativity that they place forward, whether music, whether art, or whether plant or animal; and they find their life involved within a fine art creativity. There have been many of those; and they not only feel and see what you are, but they are able to express it from beyond our perception, no matter what element one is.

They have the ability to work with plants. Plants will respond; plants will find beauty with them. Plants will feel not only their warmth and loving but will respond completely and fully. And, in many ways, as a young child would respond to the mother, a plant responds to an Earth Element. The same with animals. They would feel the affinity of the Earth Element and be drawn to them because of their strength and because of their alignment. The mineral kingdom would feel it also. The gems, earth itself, would renew upon their hand. Horticulture, biology, botany—all of these areas can exude their creativity.

Within music, they have the ability to use music and play the seasons play the music of the fall, of the winter, of the summer and spring. They have the understanding of the livingness of things and can bring the flow within it. They have the gift of basically being able to bridge the gap of the three lower kingdoms. Without the Earth Element, this world would be very boring. There would be great difficulty in feeling a baseness, or creativity itself. This does not mean that the other elements do not have it; but it means that this element deals with it the most. But, because it does, its greatest sorrow is sexual, physiological, and material.

The Earth Element over Air deals with creativity but deals with it very logically. They will have a tendency to have the ability with good finances. They will have the ability to see it and be very money-oriented within their creativity. The true Earth Element will create no matter what, and not care; but the Earth/Air will create, wondering where the money is coming from and knowing where every cent will be. The Earth/Air will also be dealing in the physiological sense with how to deal with their own energy how to deal with it in regard to others. They can tend to be scrooges; money can be their greatest difficulty.

The Earth over Fire deals specifically with sexual, having difficulty with their sexual self—having a tendency, whether male or female, of feeling that everything within this world is fertile for them, They will treat it that way, seeing not only what is called double standard, but triple and quadruple, They will be dealing with the physiological and sexual self, all the time in great quantities, but it seems never to stay for very long. Their strength deals with the ability, in the highest part of this creativity, of bringing the strength of the creativity of the earth, of the plant, and of the animal. They have an ability in a spiritual sense to communicate to those elements. They have the ability of mediumship within that area, of communicating a spiritual idea.

They are Water in the opposite: they can deal with emotion. They can be greatly overwhelmed but it is usually dealing specifically with anger—very difficult for them—anger of things that are around them and the way things do not go. They will have a tendency to be very outward and, in many ways, be very violent. The Earth Element can be a violent individual. They are the ones that, in regard to expressing themselves, can exude violence. Rather than withdraw, they will hit. They are the ones that are usually in the midst of a fight. They are the ones that you will find in those areas of great accident and great catastrophe. They are your boxers. They are those that deal with the cruelty of some sports, of those sports that men get together in to see how much harm they can inflict upon the other, or even on women.

These are the Earth Elements, dealing specifically with the baseness, with the foundations, with the roots. And you will find within them more fundamentalism, religious and faith-believing. They will believe some thing and they will die believing it, no matter what. And everyone who does not believe it is going to go someplace where it is very warm or is not going any place at all! They will have a tendency to project that fanaticism within religion so much that others cannot stand to be around them. But within that, they create a strength of those that are with them, a strength that allows them to evolve from that pattern. As they deal later on, they can step above that fundamentalism into a creativity of self; but that step is hard.

The true Earth Element is dealing with the Fire in the male sense; the Earth Element female will be drawn to the Fire Element male because of the strength and the power and the leading, being able to tell them how to do it, when to do it, and when they can. They are the epitome of a servant-type situation.

The Earth Element male, pulled to a Fire female, will usually be developed within great creativity, and the Fire female will be their manager, or the person that is pushing them for greater creativity and greater beauty. This can be a good matching.

Earth to Earth: they usually wear themselves out either in getting money or in sexual relationships. One sees many Earth-to-Earth individuals that marry within this world. They are the ones steeped in poverty and famine, a part of their experiential pattern in the evolution of this plane.

Earth to Water —an Earth female to a Water male can have some strength. Water male will be trying to play down their emotion, and so the Water can bring life to the Earth female. And they will be drawn to that energy or that sort, but they will have a tendency to rule the situation, even more so than the Fire female, for they will rule it by the use of sex, or the misuse of money.

The Earth man and the Water woman will have great difficulty for the Earth man will not be able to stand that water in the flooding of his earth. Very seldom does this link work because a female will be dealing with the emotion of water, and th ey will also be dealing with trying to maintain a balance spiritually ; the Earth Element is not concerned with that in the beginning stages. They are more concerned with the plant, the animal, and the mineral, not within ethericness.

The Earth female to the Air male can be a good relationship. This can have strength in this one way: where the Air male is so involved with inventiveness and creativity that they do not know what they are doing half of the time. The Earth female can be the grounder and keep them on the ground. A Water female would have a tendency just to withdraw and cry a lot because they could not communicate with them. The Fire Element would basically let them do their own thing but would not find any stability. They would find that the Earth Element would be their home. They would have a tendency to take them for granted. The Earth Element would develop a home and would be, in many ways, be somewhat slavish. If it is an Earth male and an Air female—one will find very few of these, fo r the Air female does not want to have that kind of base. They do not want to have that kind of servitude. They will usually be celibate, or very deeply involved within their own maidship.

The Earth Element is a diverse element because they are the rejuvenators; Fire being the birth and creator of new life ; Water being what you may call the fertilizer, the refreshment ; the sprin g; Summer, Air being the es sence of new life, of harvesting ; Autumn, of pulling things together, of getting rid of the old, of letting the dying go.

Each of us has lifetimes within the Earth Element. It is not an easy life, physiologically. The Earth Element, in the female sense, very seldom will have what you may call an average weight. They will either be very slim or the opposite—very few in-betweens, for they are dealing with their physiological body. The male will be dealing with slenderness, physiologically. Their problems will come with their feet and with the spinal cord. The female will be dealing with the inner organs and glands.

The mineral of the Earth Element, being green, is specifically different from the others. Its strength is the smoky crystal to wear—not to use, but to wear—because they are so earthy. They do not want to project that earthiness, and the smoky crystal keeps that in. They can wear the emerald. If they do, they are usually dealing with a lot of creativity, the ceativity in art or art form. They should not wear blue. It will cause them difficulties within the stone element,

The Earth's music has two phases. First, is the area of earthy-type forms such as soul, R&B, rock and blues and folk. Within the classical, it deals with those areas of Mendelssohn, of Telemann, of Handel, Liszt, Tchaikovsky, and Khachaturian. The Earth Element can be an excellent pianist.

There is one further element type—the Etheric. The Ancient Wisdoms taught that those who have stepped into the element of Ether are in the dimension of the positive. They see only the positive and the beauty in each individual. They see the negativity, but they do not react on it, or, basically, judge it. They are observers and they react that way. They can be pulled, or one can be around them, and one will have a tendency to see only beauty. One can speak with them about the negativity of the day; they will listen, but they will not respond.

Chapter 17

Man and the Subconscious Mind

Spiritual development is the discovery of self. You will not
evolve from this plane by following a particular religion, creed,
philosophy or guru. You will do so by following the inner self,
by relaxing the subconscious and by being a projection of the
Godforce, the higher self, or the spirit library, which is the same
as the higher force.

—an old sage

At the human level, a majorpart of the forces of livingNature is the brain
and its conscious and subconscious dimensions of reality.

When Brad Pulaski[52] had reached his lowest ebb, utterly bored with
sawing logs for little pay and feeling no excitement in life, he discovered
one morning while riding to work an old Flying A gas station   that had
magically come to life. Inside he was welcomed by   an old man with a
twinkle in his eye who introduced himself as the   Gatekeeper for the
Flying A, a dimension of higher learning. The Gatekeeper explained that
there were many such places in the world but that very few encounter
them in the way that Brad was doing. The Gatekeeper explained that he
and others like him are   the unseen guides that are available to anyone
who has the capacity to truly believe that there is another way.

He told Brad that each individual life creates its own dimension of
awareness, a different attraction and a different group of people with
which to interact during a period of existence. Basically, the Gatekeeper
taught that each life allows one to express different energies andpatterns,
and so an individual is a multiplicity ofdimensions that interweave, both
around and within the individual.One's capacity to see and perceive them
is limited by imagination and by the boundaries of our physical senses.

The Gatekeeper explained that the shroud over clear-sighted
perception is the psyche,   one's subconscious mind, and its relation to
time, a concept, he said, that was created by man in the far distant past to
separate the past from the present and future   in an attempt to exercise

---

[52] ibid

some form of control over the arduous and complex processes of living in a physical world. As long as we allow our psyche to remain influential with regard to our projections concerning what we are and what we feel we are, we remain shrouded by the time in which we live.

The Gatekeeper said that the Earth is interlaced with other realms of existence but explained that the concept of dimensions is not as confusing as it may seem. He told of the dimensions of the senses, feeling, sound, healing, colour, music, harmony and many more. He said that even when one is in a populated area such as a theatre, museum, art gallery or shopping mall there may be those present that are not visible to the human eye. These energy forms, he explained, are of the earth plane but not seeable due to the dimension of positivity that they inhabit. One may have a feeling that someone is walking by, and it is that sense or feeling of knowing that characterises the nature of dimensions. They are aspects of awareness: awareness within an evolutionary stage, the awareness of a particular evolvement within the cycle of existences that one spends on the earth plane.

The Gatekeper told Brad that the "I AM" is a separate energy from the body. We are not our body, our emotions or our mentality, he explained. We are above these; they are merely one's vehicles, the essence of this physical plane. We have used and are continuing to choose these essences, or body, or emotion, or mentality to express all of what we are and all that we have been in order that our tomorrows offer the highest levels of fulfilment. All of these elements are within our bodies. In its totality it is called the I Am and the All Seeing but because we see only that which can be perceived by the five senses, our subconscious mind, we find it difficult to imagine our greater self: that part of us, which is infinite, immortal, eternal and universal.

After making Brad a tasty breakfast and strong coffee, the Gatekeeper spoke at some length on this phenomenon of the subconscious mind and how one can learn to control its influences.

'How strong is your subconscious, Brad? How important are you? What are you doing? What are you feeling? Your subconscious controls you in more ways than one. But you have the ability to rebuild your whole life, to heal yourself, no matter where you are. But, first, you must start to think only positively. To that you say, "Gatekeeper, what is there positive to think about? The world is in a terrible condition." We "on the other side" hope it is in terrible condition, for that is why you are here: to learn to step above that terrible condition and have peace within yourself.

'The subconscious does not see what is going on; it relies only upon the demands of the conscious. An analogy is that of a king commanding his army. From his command post on a high hill, the king issues orders to his army in the valley below. He can see where the battle is to be fought and where and how to deploy his troops to ensure success in b attle. The battle goes on for hours until eventually the king sees a weakness in the opposing army's strategy, sends in his troops and gains victory.

'In the analogy you are the king who has a three-hundred-and-sixty-degree viewpoint on what is going on. Your subconscious, personified by your generals and the troops in the valley, does not see so clearly and can only respond to directives from the king, your conscious mind. Whether it is through hearing, sound, touch, taste or smell it will blindly go here and there. It works on demand only. Everything that is put into it, it will do in accordance with the strength of confidence behind the directives. However, if the conscious self says, "Go this way," and the subconscious begins to go but sees that it has not been that way before, either in thought or in action, there will be resistance and progress will be very difficult.

'When you reincarnate into the body that you occupy now, your subconscious is brand new. It is a clean slate, a new book that you begin to write on from the moment you draw that first breath. Your five senses constitute the pen that will write the book of your new life. Everything of which your senses partake or are involved in goes into the book. At the end of your life, when the body an d soul or subconscious mind are separated, the book goes to the library, which some call the akashic record, your higher spirit self.

'In most lifetimes, individuals react and work almost entirely because of what the subconscious mind puts forward. They ae wholly subconscious driven, responding solely to all that the subconscious has recorded from the input of the five senses, even those experiences that glimmer at the periphery or in the distant background. It records them and makes a permanent note of them. In this way you become subject to reactions, becoming bound by past experience or precedent such that the subconscious will always seek to operate in its comfort zone in accordance with what has been written in the book.

'Let us say you are the genera l in the king's army. You are the subconscious. The king commands you to "Attack to the left," and you come to a deep ravine, and you remember that in the last attack to the left in the ravine you met opposing forces that inflicted heavy casualties on your troops. So, when you come there in compliance with the king's new command you retreat, even though the ravine is empty.

'You may have certain likes and dislikes. You can say to yourself,"I do not like beetroot," and it will go into your subconscious. Or someone will say, "Beetroot is not good for you," and because you trust in their judgment you believe they are telling the truth and their words are recorded. And then in a group of vegetables mixed together like a bistro salad, you eat beetroot. Subsequently, there is a reaction to the nerve endings in the stomach, the subconscious mind goes back to the point where it said, "I do not like beetroot, it is not good for me," and even though you are not aware of eating the offending vegetable, you get an upset stomach. It is important to understand that everything that is within your subconscious mind, you are responsible for it because you have put it there.

'Pythagoras taught that the incoming spirit chooses the parent that you reincarnate through, and therefore chooses them in regard to what they would place in your subconscious through education and teaching.

'How many times has a parent said something like, "Make sure you put on a coat before going out in the rain or you will catch a cold or the flu." And so, children do this each and every day, following the dicta imposed by the parents. Years later, after the offspring have grown and you are living away from the parents, they walk outdoors, and it is a beautiful day. Along their path they meet someone who says contrarily, "Isn't it cold today?" and the subconscious throws it forward: "Cold days without a coat bring forward the flu," and they begin to feel ill because they weren't wearing a coat on a beautiful warm day.

'Ninety-eight percent of your life is run on subconscious projection and instant replay of what has been placed there before. In this way individuals become slaves to what they have placed within themselves, saying they cannot get out of them no matter how hard they try. There are so many negatives within the world that don't allow you to grow: "I will do that" is negative because you are putting it off to tomorrow. Consequently, the subconscious mind says, "He will do that sometime. In the meantime, let's act and behave like we always do."

'There are commonly expressed negatives. Your mother said, "You have been bad. Go to your room, you are forbidden from seeing your friends." Years later, you are in an important business meeting, and someone says, "That was a bad and ill-considered thing you just did." The subconscious throws out, "Bad, isolation," and, reacting to an old embedded thoughtform, you say to yourself: "I must be alone. I must run away, I must escape."

'Pscyhotherapists and psychologists feel that you must go to the depths of the subconscious and relieve all these things, basically get them out and lay them in the open. What good would that do? So, you can understand why you get a cold on a hot summer's day when someome

268

says it is cold? But then what do you do about it? Do you laugh about it? Do you catch another cold?

'The subconscious mind works in a very intricate fashion, through suggestions of other people, through feelings, especially from those people you respect deeply for what they say. All you have to do is to believe them…and they will be established in the subconscious. All you have to do is to have faith in their words and they are indelibly imprinted in the subconscious. Thereby you become a slave to the things that lie within you. You are a slave to the elements of those things that hold you in constant stress and negative force, of poverty, of having other people move and push you where they want you to go, rather than where you feel you should be.

'Ninety-eight in a hundred never get beyond the subconscious mind in their daily dealings, even those in a seemingly strong religious or other faith-based framework of living. They never get to the realisation that there is a higher self even further. They say if you do this or that, it is a sin punishable by death or hell. And so, the mind takes upon these things. You commit what the world moralistically says is a sin and you feel that you are going to hell. And because it has been imprinted within your mind since early childhood, you feel your life is not worth anything anymore and you end up in the gutter.

'Very few know how basically to go beyond the subconscious mind and allow the inspiration of the spiritual self to come through. The reason why you hit your wife or husband is not because you hated your parents. The reason that you dislike this or that is not because you have sexual tendencies that will cause great difficulty. Everything that you have received in the first thirteen years, in essence, you knew was going to be put there.

'Before reincarnation, your higher self , along with the spirit guide that works with you through most of your lifetime, chooses the parentage for genetic, national, international, personal and interpersonal relationships and environmental influences; pulls them together and allows the reincarnation to take place. And so, what happens in the first thirteen years is foreseen, and it is almost always —with perhaps one or two exceptions every one hundred years—known completely the details and circumstances of inter-reactions, divorce, separation, life, death and prolongevity.

'And so, the things that you pick up through your parental pattern are not necessarily instrumental in subconsciously establishing what you are, since you already knew this; it is basically *balancing* it. It is from the age of thirteen that you begin to utilise what has been placed there, and what you need.

'Between the age of thirteen and eighteen, you get to see what you have created. And you will say, "Oh, the teenage years are terrible, the worst years of my life!" The reason you will say that is because you are looking at yourself. In essence, the thirteen-year-old is a programming of what you have placed there or allowed to be placed there. And so, you see yourself.

'Now each of us has the ability to relax the subconscious, to re-programme it so that you can receive the energy of the higher self, so that you no longer have to rely upon cheap spiritual experiences that have a tendency to nag and egg you on, because they *reek* of the subconscious mind. Very few people understand the higher self coming into their life, for most of them allow it to come through the subconscious, which is liking walking through a dense woodland blindfolded and not hitting a tree. Those that say, "Everything must be proven and thought out, each thing must have a logical end," are basically centering their whole projectivity on the subconscious. Very few allow their higher essence to come through them or come around the subconscious, to enlighten and beautify their life through consistency.

'Religious figures say, "If you do not do that, you will go to hell or you will receive nothing good in your life." It is interesting that none of the great Masters said anything like that; only their followers who, having none of the charisma of the Master, had to put the fear of God into people so that they would submit to their authority.

'There has never been in the next generation after a Master, after Lao Tze, Buddha, Confucius, Pythogoras and Zoroaster, a true teaching of what they were. Only many people running around trying to project the magic and what went on in the Master's time. This is why the teachers of old considered it important that individuals come into contact with the Godforce within themselves, so thay they do not need to rely upon a particular system, way or pattern. They develop that pattern with themselves, finding the divinity, universality, immortality and eternity within their *own* self.

'How many times have you sat down to meditate and instead of centering and focusing, all you can think of is what you did yesterday, what you hope to do the next day, what to cook for dinner, fixating on the colour of the new car you plan to buy in two years time. And so, you throw up your hands, saying, "I can't meditate, things run in and out of my mind, it's all too difficult." The subconscious mind is like that: if the king does not excercise his troops they grumble, they move and mill about, they do not like to be relaxed and resting. The only way that the

270

king can ensure his troops achieve rest and relaxation is to practise with them or to teach o r centre them on their main pr oject of work. And this is the way, Brad, that you can relax your subconscious and reprogramme it. You reprogramme your subconscious by making it work for you.

'And so, the things that cause one lack, difficulty, pain and agony; the things that make one seek a religion, philosophy, faith of creed, are programmed elements within the subconscious and make one reliant upon certain things. A person that you respect can say that if you do this and this, you will not have a good life and that's just how it will turn out. Your parental pattern will say, "You don't have a musical bone in your body so don't bother trying," and you will not have a bit of music in your life.

'So, what to do with this monster, the subconscious mind that you have lying deep within you in the area of the pineal gland? How then do you begin to utilise the subconscious in strength for the betterment of your life and not be enslaved by it day in, day out? It's a very thin line but you have the opportunity to step and learn, to make full use of the unlimited resources at your disposal and go beyond it.

'How do you do it? You do it the way the king did with his soldiers. You keep it busy while reprogramming it. Let us say that you are concerned about certain things in your life. You take the subconscious mind and visualise or see those happenings or see yourself doing something within them. You breathe in and say, "I am in control of this situation, and I will always be in control." Slowly, the subconscious mind replaces the old programming with a new one that says, "I am in control. I will jump into the valley even though it is filled with fifty   -thousand soldiers armed to the teeth." And because of your determination to make the changes in your life you will probably be able to walk above the valley instead of jumping down into it. It is only through the ability to replace fear and the thousand and one things that you deal in each and every day, of the negati vity, of the days that look so very hard to bear, through very systematically working with the subconscious, that you will gradually bring forth the higher self.

'Understand, though, that if you are getting energy from the higher self, it *will not record* on the subconscious mind. There will be those that say, "I had a high religious experience. I walked with the Masters in the cosmic spheres." Such individuals had orgasms of the subconscious mind. They tasted every taste they ever tasted, sniffed every sme ll they ever smelled and, in truth, were ravished by their own perceptions. If what comes from the higher self is recorded on the subconscious mind, it means that you wanted it recorded there for you want to see the good works that you do.

'The higher self or the Godforce is a pure projection, not one that is relying on proving self. Have great caution concerning those who proclaim they are great healers or great teachers, for a teacher will truly not know what he is teaching, and a healer will not know what he is healing. If they did, the energy force was going through the subconscious mind and, like the figure that walked into the forest blindfolded, it would come out black and blue and you would not recognise it.

'So, the higher self *does not record*. You can get *intuitive feelings* in regard to it. It is like standing on a mountain and as you stand there the wind comes around you. You *feel* the wind, but *you do not see it*, you do not grasp it, but you have the feeling. It is the same with the higher self. You have a feeling as it goes around the subconscious, but you will not see it, you will not be able to identify it, but will feel that is going out and working for your highest good.

'What are the practical steps in a visualisation process to go one step beyond? Let us say that you are dealing with a person in your work that is causing you difficulties, just like the situation you are confronting with your boss at the lumber camp, Sam Carver. You are frustrated by his apparent disregard for the efforts you put in your work, often doing extra hours without being asked and volunteering to do tasks unpopular with the other loggers. In truth, Carver is jealous of your abilities and seeks to mask those feelings by treating you negatively.

'To redress the balance, you sit down and begin to train the army of the subconscious. You picture Mr Carver, you breathe in, pulling him towards you on the in-breath, holding your breath while counting slowly to seven, and then exhale and release. This will get you within the gravity element of your earth and synchronise your heart in the breathing sequence of the waves upon the seashore, which is the physical manifestation of the physical body. In these visualisations you say, "Sam Carver is positive and powerful and is in a strength projection. We are in harmony one to another " On saying this, the higher self comes around like the breeze; you *feel* it. And as it comes around, it picks up the sensory accents of Mr Carver; its energy, a pure energy, goes forth and surrounds him. When you come out of the relaxation period you will not be aware that anything has happened. But the person, in this case Sam Carver, has a different feeling. Doing this each and every day, the person will be so *incensed* with positiveness that as the two of you come together daily you will see the difference within them.

'The subconscious mind is what you are right now. The higher self is is what you can project and pull to you. Right now, Brad, your subconscious is working as normal. However, your higher self is glittering and filtering through and around it like a flower emerging from a swamp. However, you will find that as you work to train the subconscious to respond to reprogramming efforts, the work rate of your higher self will increase sharply because it is harder to be harmonious in the mass conscious world than it is to be inharmonious. If you should meet someone who says glibly that, "it's beautiful being so spiritual, I have so much new-found energy, strength and great health," then I suggest you climb a mountain and watch them from there. For the more finely tuned you are, the more receptive you become to outside negativity, disease and all the unwelcome thoughtforms from a world filled with so many inharmonious people.

'The challenge will be that as you begin to pull away from them you will experience profound aloneness and a feeling of being a fish out of water. Ultimately, there is a point of arrival on your spiritual quest that, no matter where you are, the people that you pull around you feel immediate harmony. But getting to that point can make you   wonder wouldn't it be great to eat all that crud again, like everyone else.

'The world we live in is the university of the physical experience. The curriculum that every student must follow consists of four core subjects: war, poverty, famine and negativity. It is through positive progression of one's own life that one eventually has the opportunity to achieve a state of inner peace through stepping above these four areas of test and challenge, which will always be compone nt parts of the university of the physical earth.

'More coffee, Brad?'

*

'Believing is the wand of the true magician. Believing in self opens the many doorways that are always around you.'

—the Flying A Gatekeeper

Mother Earth and her Crystal Power

Chapter 18

Metaphysical Crystal

The Earth is charged with an invisible flow of electro magnetic energy, its field subtlely influenced by many factors, including the gravitational influence of bodies in our solar system, and by ground level factors such as the shapes and contours of landscape features, which also influence the character of minerals deep underground.

Free thinkers and philosophers in the distant past, notablyPythagoras and, later, Plato, believed that the physical universe is composed of geometrical figures, among which the pentadodecahedron is identified as the "hull of the sphere. " Plato refers in the *Phaedo* to a belief that the construction of the world is likened to the building of a ship by the use of geometric shapes. Consider the common saying: "the four corners of the earth," a reflection of the ancient belief that the earth is a vast stone.

Scientific research appears to indicate that the earth does resemble a gigantic crystal supported by a rigid skeletal structure beneath its surface. German scientist Siegfried Wittman [53] claimed in 1952 that he and his study team had concluded that the earth has upon its surface a grid system consisting of a checkerboard pattern of positive and negative poles. The squared pattern has a centre pole surrounded by smaller poles within each section. The main pole concentrates energy through eight supporting poles. Four send pulses of energy skyward while the others send energy to the four points of the compass.

Ten years later, biologist Ivan Sanderson and colleagues, intrigued by geographical anomalies such as those portrayed in the Piri Reis map of 1523 and the Buache map of 1737 which suggest that pre -Egyptian civilizations possessed advanced mathematical and astronomical skills, set out to "pattern the mysteries." Sanderson's 1972 article, *The Twelve Devils' Graveyards Around the World*, plotted air and maritime disappearances worldwide. It focused attention on twelve areas, equally spaced over the globe, in which magnetic anomalies and other aberrations were linked to unaccountable physical phenomena.

---

[53] *Die Welt der geheimen Mächte* (*The World of the Secret Forces*)

Sanderson's investigations were the impetus for others to make a contribution to the study of electromagnetic aberrations upon the "planetary grid," the term coined by Christopher Bird writing in the *New Age Journal* of May 1975. Here, Bird refers to the work of Russian researchers: historian Nikolai Goncharov, engineer Vyacheslav Morozov and electronics specialist Valery Makarov who had published in *Khimiya I Zhizn* (Chemistry of Life) in the *Science Journal of the USSR Academy of Life* an article: "*Is the Earth a Large Crystal?*"

The Russians' paper, which supports and builds on Sanderson's work, explores an idea that visualises the core of the Earth as a growing crystal that influences what occurs on the planet. The authors postulate that the earth projects from this inner crystal a dual geometrically regularised grid. The first grid layer consists of Sanderson's twelve areas that lie over the surface of the earth, which the Russians describe as pentagonal slabs (a dodecahedron), while the second is formed by twenty equilateral triangles (an icosohedron). The writers stated that the superimposition of the two grids over the globe's surface reveals a pattern of the earth's energy network. The lines tracing out the dual grid coincide with zones of active risings and depressions on the ocean floors, cave faults and mid-oceanic ridges such as in the Bermuda Triangle. The paper refers to twelve such areas.

In esoteric teachings these principle nodal points are described as the earth's etheric web points—Gateways to other dimensions. The Russians theorised that these forms and their apexes possess qualities that can explain many unusual phenomena. They claimed that in these areas, viewed in conjunction with Sanderson's work, are to be found regions of seismic and volcanic activity, while magnetic anomalies are located at the vertices of the polygons. The grid nodes are said to denote centres of great changes in atmospheric pressures; hurricanes, for example, take shape in these areas. Prevailing winds and ocean currents also fit into the network as well as paths of migratory animals, gravitational anomalies and the sites of ancient cities. The Russians' paper claims that if the grid was lined up on the surface of the globe so that all of the many factors could be correlated, the exact centre point is found to be Giza in Upper Egypt, the key being the "measure of Light."

Researchers at the Earth-Life Science Institute at the Tokyo Institute of Technology similarly suggest that the power source for the Earth's magnetic field is the presence of crystallisation in the Earth's core.

Roy Snelling brings consciousness into the equation when he describes the powerhouse of the Earth as the presence of huge psychic crystals within its etheric body. Accordingly, our planet's true form,

Snelling suggests, *is* its geometrical grid, the physical earth being a visible manifestation that could not exist in the absence of its etheric counterpart. This idea mirrors the esoteric belief that an eth eric body is the magnetic field of a physical body (an example being the human aura) which contains a template of its idealised outer form. Snelling writes:

> The laws of physics and nature.. are part of a broader spectrum of Cosmic laws, some of which relate to other dimensions, parallel universes, anti-matter, and also a universal energy field where science claims that there is only empty space.[54]

Snelling suggests that the planetary matrix is defined by the perfect geometrical relationship of t he five Platonic solids that constitute its geometrical form. In accordance with mathematical law, these five solids may be contained perfectly inside a sphere. Energy in the edge -lines of all five within the Earth radiates upwards to form lines of force o n the surface: a projection by the Cosmos from its own substance,one of many levels of creation, each one descending in order of vibration -rate and coarseness of matter so that each level interpenetrates the level above and below without affecting the higher or lower levels.

Moreover, each form can transition into any other through a series of movements, including twisting, truncating, expanding, combining or faceting. Snelling speaks appreciatively of the mathematical beauty that binds the Platonic solid s in a state of etheric perfection, the motivating power behind the earth's dynamic energy system.

The five Platonic solids are the only shape s with equal side lengths, equal interior angles, faces made of the same regular shape which look the same from each vertex (corner point), and, crucially, all fit perfectly in a sphere with all points resting on the circumference.

Information about the Platonic solids has been taught since ancient times, particularly since the period of the Greek Mystery Schools approximately 2,500 years ago. They are called "Platonic" after Plato (427 – 347 BC) who, in the *Timaeus*, outlined a cosmology through the metaphor of planar and solid geometry. He associated the four elements with four of the Platonic solids: the tetrahedron as fire; the octahedron as air; the cube as earth , and the icosahedron as water. The dodecahedron represents the "fifth" element—the invisible ether.

> Hence between fire and earth the god placed water and air, and he made them all stand in the sameratio to one another... so that as fire is to air, so air is to water, and as air is to water, so water

[54] Snelling, R., *The Planetary Matrix*, Spiritual Genesis Books, 2013

is to earth, and so he bound together and structured the visible and tangible universe.

—Plato, *Timaeus*

Plato ascribes intelligence to the solids when he refers to the ability of the four elements to "transmute into each other" and how "they must be dissimilar to one another but capable of arising out of one another's disintegration." Cosmic Core, a web-based group that explores sacred geometry and the concept of twinning science with spirituality,[55] builds on Plato's ideas of intelligent design in describing the Platonic solids as not five separate shapes but five aspects of the same shape—the spinning torus. Cosmic Core views the torus as the embodiment of a principle of "Mater into Matter," in which Consciousness forms into Light, Light into Geometric Form, and Geometric Form into Matter.

The process begins when a sphere representing undifferentiated light polarises into opposites symbolized by two intersecting circles: the Vesica Piscis. The two poles swirl in opposite directions in rhythmic energy patterns, creating a toroidal flow. The building block of the torus is an "Aether Unit," a manifestation of the fluctuations of Consciousness. These units, Cosmic Core claim, are not "things" but an intelligent energy flow process that characterises and defines the planetary grid.

The planetary matrix comprises a network of 90 edgelines of all five Platonic solids. Snelling calls this the planet's Primary Leyline. At points on the Earth where some of these lines meet or cross at the apexes of the Platonic solids (which are all at the surface of the earth anyway), one is likely to find powerful vortices of energy. This was recognized long ago by our forebears. Many such sites became sacred and on them were built stone circles and other similar power structures.

The 5-Platonic Solids and their Elements, Faces, Apexes and Edges			
	Faces	Apexes	Edges
Cube - earth	6	8	12
Icosahedron - water	20	12	30
Octahedron - air	8	6	12
Tetrahedron - fire	4	4	6
Dodecahedron - ether	12	20	30
	50	50	90

---

[55] https://www.cosmic-core.org

The life of a region depends ultimately on its geological substratum, for this sets up a chain reaction which passes, determining their character in turn through its streams and wells, its vegetation and animal life, that feeds on this and finally through the type of human being attracted to live there. In a profound sense also the structure of its rocks gives rise to the psychic life of the land.

—Ithell Colquhoun, *The Living Stones*

Snelling asks how our forbears were able to create the secondary and tertiary ley-line networks from the primary-network defined by the Platonic Solids. He suggests that various topographical and geo logical features came into play such as fault lines in the Earth's crust where magnetic energies would be more concentrated, underground watercourses, and mountain tops. By using standing stones where the qualities of the crystalline structure of the stone is known, together with dolmens and "burial" mounds that act like electric accumulators, energy could be siphoned off from the primary -network to psychically irrigate the land for the benefit of humans, animals and crops.

In earlier pages we learned of sci entists' cutting-edge work to create exotic "time crystals." According to *Popular Mechanics*,[56] time crystals incorporate spots at thei r edges that look different from others, thus breaking the symmetry of time. Scale this up and one sees remarkable correspondences with the properties of the Earth's Platonic crystals and their ninety edge lines.

At the microcosmic level, there is emergi ng evidence that the crystalline energies that flow from the earth's toroidal geometry communicate at the cellular level in humans and in other living organisms. As we have seen, a singular characteristic of the mineral world of crystal in all its forms is its pervasiveness throughout all parts of our physical earth. This ubiquitous crystal lattice structure provides great stability of structure and regularity of flow of any kind of electromagnetic energy that move s through it. In particular, when one factors in the piezo -electric effect in quartz crystal, it does not take too many mental leaps to visualise that crystals may be capable of transforming or amplifying other energy forms not yet detected by scientific instruments, but which human consciousness can detect, especially when facilitated by an appropriate form of crystal.

The structure of DNA reflects t he essential crystallinity of living

---

[56] https://www.popularmechanics.com/science/a30755983/time-crystals-time-travel/

organisms. Each cell of a living organism contains a hexagonally shaped crystalline molecule of DNA, approximately ten atoms wide and six feet in length. If the entire DNA in the human body was unfolded and strung together, its length would be 125 billion miles, equivalent to seventy round trips between Saturn and the Sun. Yet these infinitesimally thin crystal lattice threads, too narrow to reflect light, are so strong that they have effectively carried the codes of life through billions of years of evolution.

Biophysicists are now suggesting that the physical bodies of human bodies and other organisms are so dynamically coherent at the molecular level that they appear to behave like liquid crystals. The component particles (atoms or molecules) of liquid crystals tend to arrange themselves with a degree of order and exactitude far exceeding that found in ordinary liquids and approaching that of solid crystals. Consequently, every part of the organism is in communication with every other part through a dynamic, tunable responsive crystalline medium that pervades the whole body.

Anthropologist Jeremy Narby[57] explains that these living molecules of DNA emit light photons at regular intervals in a coherence strong enough for them to be compared to an "ultra weak laser." This property is mindful of crystal radios and their energy-transducing properties. Narby has developed a hypothesis that DNA has its own consciousness, which he describes as the "mind of the biosphere" and that it is is related to crystals.

Dwelling on these startling new ideas and theories, crystallographers are posing the question as to whether our human cells each incorporate an actual laser, and if excitation of the light-producing qualities of DNA account for the phenomenon of the human aura. May exposure to certain crystals provide the necessary energy for influencing, altering and/or enhancing the human energy field? These incredible crystal properties reveal that we are not so very different from both the physical kingdom of minerals and the realm of the invisible forces of living nature. We ourselves are in a very real sense crystals composed of coherent structures approaching that of solid crystals yet retaining the superior flexibility of liquid crystals. Consequently, it is not hard to imagine how an energy flow from a very large size energy source—the Earth's invisible planetary-wide crystal structure, for example—could be received and interpreted by one's own mind and body, analagous to the reception of signals from a broadcasting tower by a crystal radio set.

---

[57] Narby, J., *The Cosmic Serpent*, Weidenfeld & Nicholson, 1999

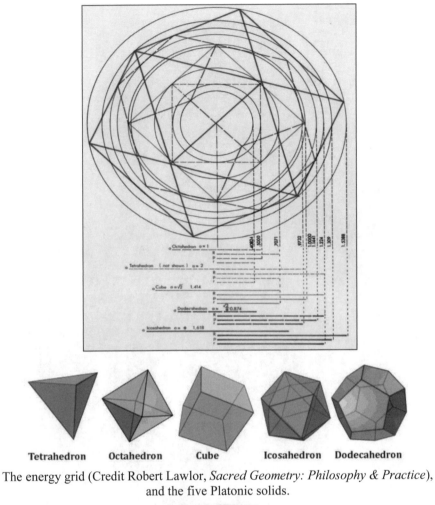

The energy grid (Credit Robert Lawlor, *Sacred Geometry: Philosophy & Practice*),
and the five Platonic solids.

The spinning torus in which Mater ("Mother") becomes Matter

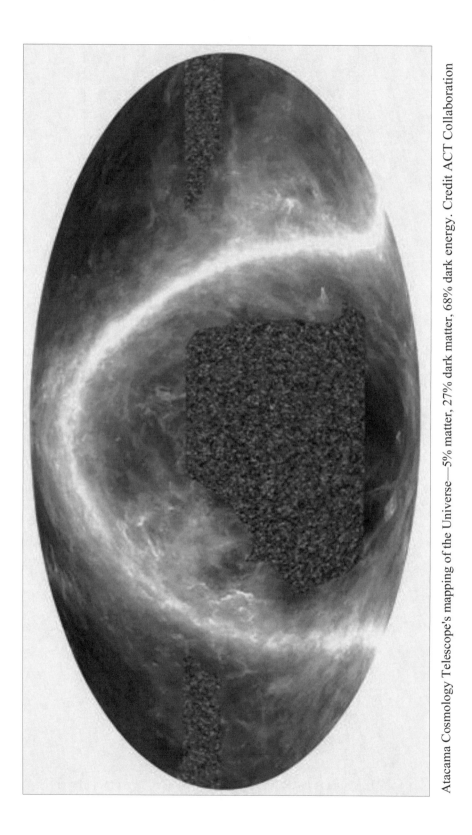

Atacama Cosmology Telescope's mapping of the Universe—5% matter, 27% dark matter, 68% dark energy. Credit ACT Collaboration

Chapter 19

Crystal Healing

There are many reasons to want to work with quartz crystals. Do we want to use them for healing oneself and others, empower our meditations, our affirmations and our thoughts? With crystals, one can energize and balance the body, develop psychic abilities. One can use crystals to change many unwanted circumstances in one's life and create new ones.

Most people beginning crystal work have these kinds of goals in mind. However, a curious thing starts to happen as one works with crystals. One may become aware of an energy or force or a "potential" higher than oneself, and gradually begin to interact with something very powerful and wonderful. Some call it Spirit, or a Higher Order, or God. Whatever name we call it, it is Universal and it transcends our limited self. We may find that we experience unlimited potential flowing around us as our prior self-imposed boundaries, limitations and ideas of who and what we are begin to crumble. Unlimited energy, vision, love, creativity, contentment and wisdom begin to flow through us as we open to this.

What things do we need to know? Because we are interacting with subtle energy or vibration when working with quartz crystal, we need to learn about energy systems as a whole, both inside the body and in the environment which surrounds us.

There are chakra systems or energy matrixes in the body that become activated as one works with crystal. Because the work one will be doing is on the subtle planes, one needs to know about the astral and mental planes and how to work with them. These levels are involved whether one is conscious of them or not. The more conscious one becomes, the more effective one will be.

Because one begins drawing tremendous forces of energy through the body as one works, one must learn how to build up and maintain the strength of the nervous system, and how to maintain the strength and health of the physical body. In short, one needs to expand one's consciousness beyond the physical body, beyond the environment and into other realms.

Crystal work concerns transcending one's limited self and limited ego. Quartz crystal is a combination of the mind, the will, the crystal and the guiding, empowering spirit. To work effectively, one must be in a state of surrender, becoming a channel through which, the creative force or spirit can do its work. One is merely the vehicle.

One becomes like a hollow tube through which this spirit can flow without impediments of doubt, ego, excess intellectuality, fear, physical weakness and a cluttered mind. To become this channel, one needs to learn to become centred and attain a calm, focused mind.

There are many ways that crystals and stones can be used for healing and consciousness-raising. They will work whether or not we believe they work and will bring more beauty and light into our environment.

Any healing stone or crystal may be used, either held or worn during meditation. They may be placed on the heart chakra for emotional balance or on the brow for mental clarity. Experiment with the various ways that different stones affect one's meditation. Clear quartz may be held at the crown centre to vibrate the higher consciousness centres and to achieve greater awareness. An amethyst placed at the brow would still the mind, and a citrine at the navel would ground the experience into physical reality.

A crystal may be programmed by directing a thoughtform into it. Project whatever quality one desires, perhaps health, mental clarity, dream enhancement, protection, or love and harmony. Insight into problems may be obtained by placing one's crystal over the third eye. Loving thoughts and prayers projected to someone will be amplified by placing the crystal over the heart chakra. Crystals should be treated with respect and love and kept in a space worthy of their presence. They respond to sunlight and being refreshed occasionally in the rain or under running water. Newly acquired crystals should be soaked in water for about twelve hours, then rinsed thoroughly and dried with a soft, clean cloth. For travelling purposes, they should be wrapped in a natural fibre cloth such as cotton, silk or wool to prevent chipping.

The unique properties of clear quartz crystals demonstrate that the material plane can and does reach a state of physical perfection capable of containing and reflecting pure white light. They are a symbol of coming into alignment with cosmic harmony. They radiate with divine white light and by seeing, touching, wearing, using or meditating with these crystals one can actually work with that light in a physical form.

To unawakened minds, they will work subliminally through the subconscious. For aware souls, crystals will be like beacons that will add more light and positive energy that can be channelled into daily thoughts, feelings, words and actions. They stimulate the finer, more subtle realms of our being which can then be integrated and manifested into our lives.

The Hypothalamus

The hypothalamus is found in a protected part of the skull. It lies under the thalamus, located under the left and right brain in almost the centre of the head. The hypothalamus serves as what Frank Dorland described as the telephone switchboard for the en tire body. It monitors all vital signs and orders any corrective measures to keep the system running smoothly. It governs the basic human drives of hunger, thirst and sex, and is responsible for broadcasting signals for fear or anger. It contains neurosecretions that aid in the control of metabolic activities. It regulates the body temperatures and their swings, and it controls the secretions of the endocrine glands. It is also the main subcortical area for the control of the sympathetic and parasympathetic nervous systems.

The pituary gland is beneath and connected to the hypothalamus. The hypothalamus sends its messages to the pituitary, which controls hormones, general metabolism, chemical balance, blood pressure, body-fluid levels, ovulation and sexual desires. Control messages are sent throughout the body by both electrical and chemical activities. The release of chemicals by neurons in the electrical transmission fro m one cell to another. The hypothalamus is an essential gland and is influenced by the tiniest electrical impulse. It contains within itself a complex communications network to send messages thoughout the ent ire body system and the brain. It is known that it is stimulated by exterior vibrations received by the five senses. It also receives oscillation energies radiated by electronic quartz crystals.

By exposing the subconscious mind to pure vi brations, it can be influenced to balance body chemistry, to heal and to achieve new goals, as well as to change old ways and habits. Whatever the vibrational message might be, the hypothalamus is believed to receive these impulses and send them throughout the body.

This is one of the secrets of past ages from our mystical forbears, who stuck a tiny piece of quartz crystal on the end of a stick and made it into a magic wand. The wand was used to gain divine guidance for decision-making. In use, the quartz crystal sent a signal via the body cells into the hypothalamus and out through the nervous system, which developed into the answer sought by the enquirer.

Electronic Quartz Crystal

Dorland describes how millions of years ago a live electronic crystal was born deep in the earth from the forces of fire and water. The ancients called it "Holy Ice," frozen holy water spilled out of heaven.

What is simply a chunk of common quartz to people today, in the past was to the initiated an original solid-state device: a natural semi-conductor and amplifying reflector that serves as an advantageous tool. The ancients secretly reserved the crystal for use by the religious herirarchy, royalty, military leaders, and the secret brotherhoods. They were used as natural amplifiers to cultivate the mind and sharpen the instinctual and intuitive processes.

Dorland was of the opinion that if the crystal and all knowledge derived from it were obliterated, the world would be plunged backwards into the dark ages of isolation.

The natural quartz crystal as found in the ground has been largely regarded as the supreme crystal. It is undoubtedly true that sensible use of a good working crystal can result in many benefits. However, it is unfortunate that the natural crystal point with its six sides converging to a pointed, pyramid-shaped top is simply not efficient for metaphysical or psychic use. A crystal, like a radio receiver, must be turned on to use it. A crystal user can do this by wearing it next to the body or, better yet, by grasping it in the hand.

By wrapping the fingers around a crystal, it starts reacting to energies received from the living cells and the mental output of the brain. The crystal then starts vibrating on a frequency compatible to and in hamony with the body and brain. Upon receiving pulsed messages from its energy source, the crystal then amplifies and broadcasts them outward in spiral waves of energy information. Electronic engineers have called this an amplifying reflector.

If the crystal is efficient, these messages may be received by the body cells, the subconscious and the conscious mind of a good crystal user. Much of this may be subliminal and received mostly by the subconscious and body cells, which may or may not relay it on to the five-sense mind. A knowledgeable crystal user can usually get the subconscious to cooperate and deliver the information.

Dorland described taking a mental journey into the centre of a crystal point for a good look around. In doing so, we find ourselves in a hall of mirrors with six flat sides ascending to a point. This creates an array of dazzling reflections reflecting and re-reflecting countless shadows and lights from the mirrors. When the crystal is activated to receive outside energies, the observer from within the crystal structure would see, as these energies were being received, a rotating spiral ball of electronic forces which would grow and fill the interior. These spiral waves would then start hitting against the flat sides where they would ricochet to another flat surface and then another again, and again and again. Most of these energies are being dissipated and shattered into thousands of weak, ghost images. The outward escaped broadcasts are very weak and often garbled.

Many thousands of years ago crystal workers found that river-tossed quartz crystals eventually became rounded, much like cobblestones. This is how the first crystal balls came into existence. The crystal workers discovered that these rounded forms were much more active than the crystal points they had been using. When some of the balls were polished, they discovered that the activity was once again greatly increased. From that time on the initiates would use only the rounded and polished quartz pieces.

Single point crystals are indeed very beautiful and may well have been the original inspiration for the science of faceting gemstones to increase their glitter. The single crystal's point's best usage lies in the physical world. For usage in mind control and development , plus achievements both physical and mental, the crystal with carved, rounded and polished surfaces is the one that really does the work. Its reponse to mental activities is remarkable.

Crystal Divination

The best crystal working tools may be carved in a great variety of shapes with the major consideration that all surfaces must be smoothed and rounded. There must be no sharp angles, edges or points because the crystal is a working piece designed to be held in the hand or worn close to the skin. When the crystal is energised, it broadcasts outward in spiral waves both clockwise and counterclockwise in a ll directions simultaneously. This energy is believed to flow unimpeded through carved surfaces, but flat and faceted surfaces tend to ricochet the energy waves from one flat surface to another , an action that dissipates the energy inside the crystal much like a spent pool ball so that most of the "broadcast" cannot get out.

The oldest known round crystal ball was found in France in the tomb of the Merovingian ruler, Childeric I, King of the SalianFranks (437-481 AD). A most unusual ruler, Childeric's long and successful reign abounded with magical mysteries and the supernatural.

During the French Revolution, the people sacked the royal tombs in the Bastille hoping to find royal treasure. Imagine their disgust when all they found among the royal bones were small, personalised crystal balls, evidently items held in far greater esteem than adoring gemstones. Napoleon Bonaparte understood it, though. He commanded that his coronation robes be studded with tiny gold figures of honeybees taken from Childeric's tomb.

A crystal ball will not work by itself sitting on a stand; a person must hold it or cup their hands around it. For a higher-level reading, when gazing at a crystal ball one must project the mind deeply inside it rather than just stare at it. In this way, the gazer enters the crystal itself, concentrating only on the single purpose at hand. Here, the five senses are subdued sufficiently to allow the psychic portions to communicate with the crystal cells. These cells transmit radio-like waves to the cortex cells in the gazer's brain, which unscrambles and composes them into meaningful signals that are recognisable as pictures, impressions, words or just a sense of knowing in the conscious mind. The size of the crystal is not too important because the energy comes from the crystal gazer and not from the crystal. The gazer is aware that impressions from the crystal are not seen by with the two physical eyes but are interpreted by the third eye, the eye that "knows" in the brow chakra.

Crystal Talismans

A talisman, distinct from an amulet which is a form of lucky charm such as a rabbit's foot, is a potent object that confers supernatural powers and protection to the user. One should remember that once supernatural forces are understood, they become applied natural laws.

Talismans have been made by a great range of materials. Besides gemstones, there were metals, fabrics, woods, grains and hides. Common shapes were all styles of crosses, astrological symbols, animals, fish, divinities and mystical figures, many engraved or lettered with magical texts.

Talismans fashioned from electronic quartz crystals are potent forces, because they have thir own intrinsic magnetic energy field and they do react and respond. The Chinese refer to a quartz electronic crystal as a "living stone" because the crystal is in a constant state of oscillation through its unique latticework structure designed by Mother Nature and constructed during its growth from individual crystal cells.

Out of the innumerable shapes in which talismans have been traditionally constructed, almost all are primarily based on the cross, the circle and the triangle. In modern times, the majority of crystal talismanic crosses are carved in one of three basic styles—the mystic, the ankh and the Latin cross. Talismans are to be worn and must be safe and easy to work with. A properly carved talisman should feel good in the hand and anywhere else on the body.

Talismans and the Chakra Centres
During the Piscean Age the psychic receptors were located mainly in the solar plexus area. A seer might say, 'It's a gut feeling, I get it right in the pit of my stomach.' In this new Commmuni cations Age , the receptor centre is expected to elevate itself to the heart or even higher. This means that the favoured location for wearing a crystal talisman would be anywhere between the solar plexus and the heart chakra.

The word "chakra" means the "circle of Vishnu "—a spinning dynamo-like wheel. Chakras are usually illustrated as round, spinning discs of colour but they are also symbolically sh own as a lotus blossom with a varying number of petals There are seven beneficial chakra centres of energy.

1.   The root chakra is located at the base of the spine and is called the sacred ganglion and known as the coiled sleeping serpent, the Kundalini power. The colour is fiery red; the sound is   the chirping of crickets. The symbolic lotus has four petals. Its function is regenerative power and is an earth sign.

2.   The spleen chakra, or prostatic plexus, is located over the spleen. The colour is yellow -orange, and the sound is the buzzing of bees. The lotus has six petals. The fuction is the utilisation of natural energies. It is a water sign.

3.   The solar plexus chakra or the navel ; its colours are reds and greens. The sound is a heavy drone, deeper than bees. The symbolic lotus has ten petals The function is the emotions and control over interior cells. It is a fire sign.

4.   The heart chakra or cardiac plexus; the colour is golden sunlight, and the sound is that of a pleasant flute. This lotus has twelve petals. This air sign's function is control over the winds.

5.   The throat chakra or pharyngeal plexus; its colour is silvery blue, and the sound is a medium-pitch bell note. This lotus has sixt een petals. The function is the control over the etheric elements, and hence it is a n ether sign.

6.   The crown chakra or cavernous plexus; the colour is golden yellow and purple, and the sound is that of a deep, temple gong. This lotus has ninety-six petals. Its function is mastery over all elements, and the sign is that of the mind.

7.   The crown chakra is located in the centre of the top of the head. It contains all the colours and approaches pure white light. The sound is

the steady roar of the distant ocean. This symbolic lotus has 972 petals. Its function is mastery of the gift of complete understanding. The sign is that of total refinement into eventual perfection.

Colour and Crystal Reference Guide

As a guideline, Dorland provided standardised symbolic meanings of the basic colours for reference. As in most most therapies, the colours may be custom mixed. For example, a crystal may be wrapped in a green cloth to give independence, and then both crystal and green cloth wrapped in a yellow cloth to give hopefulness and understanding.

Grey	Protection, quiet, avoidance of conflicts, peace-making, placidity and serenity
Black	Neutralising, simplification, reduction to basics, and subdued emotions
Blue	Harmony, tranquility, intimacy, spiritual satisfaction, forgiveness and peace
Red	Vitality, strength, excitement, physical satisfaction and enthusiasm
Green	Achievement, success, independence, resilience and control
Yellow	Ambition, hope, understanding, warmth and affection
Violet	Sentimental, romantic, idealistic, tender, spiritual strength and fantasy
Brown	Safety, security, indulgence, restfulness, tranquility and conservativeness
White	Purity

The Crystal Divining Pendulum

Tiny crystals are preferred because heavier ones are sluggish. The string used to suspend the crystal should not be too long because the pendulum must hang close enough to the aura to receive energy from the magnetic flux surrounding the body, but long enough to swing freely. Generally, 3-4 inches of string is more than adequate; silk or cotton is the preferred material.

One should hold the thread with one's fingertips, leaving about two to three inches between the top of the pendulum and the fingertips. One might consider using a circular pendulum card. The pendulum swings back and forth over the card, answering questions by swinging to its letters, numbers and other features. Dorland stresses the importance of making adequate preparations prior to embarking on crystal pendulum use. To comply with the laws of checks and balances in the universe that keep everything in order in the correct proportions of positive and negative, Dorland suggests that users develop a   strong foundation of morality, integrity and responsibility.

This is advised because when one uses a pendulum one is not only speaking with the five senses but also with one's superconscious, an elevated level of communication that demands great care because if one pursues a subject, one will probably get an answer, and so scrupulous integrity is required.

Dorland's method was firstly to address the pendulum, asking out loud, 'Would you like to work with me today?' The pendulum will answer either 'Yes' by swinging forward and backward as one would nod the head or signify 'No' by swinging sideways back and forth as if shaking the head.

If 'yes,' the question is then asked out loud because it is easier to audibly talk to the crystal than to silently think. In fact, it is necessary to talk to the crystal constantly as it swings in order to keep up the vibrations and energy flow. Thank it for each answer. The crystal powers appreciate good manners!

A pendulum divination board

When one first uses a crystal pendulum, one should write down the letters and numbers. Obviously, each swing is going to point to two letters or two numbers, one at each end of the swing, so it is a good idea to write two lines of messages. With practice it will become apparent to the user to distinguish the correct message that the crystal is conveying. One should not be too hasty to discard seemingly unintelligible messages; sometimes a crystal will transmit a message in a foreign language. Latin is a favourite.

Clear and Coloured Crystals

The finest transparent gem grade of pure quartz crystal is inherently colourless. Most pieces discovered have this characteristic, but they are also commonly found in innumerable shades of of smoky, yellow, amethyst and rose colours. Whenever this occurs, it means that an impurity has found its way into the quartz structure.

Sometimes clear quartz is cloudy or milky at the base and gains more clarity as it reaches the terminated point. This symbolises a growth pattern in which the cloudiness and dullness of consciousness is cleared as we grow closer to the point of union with our inner self. Clouded areas or inclusions in clear crystals show us that worlds exist within worlds and that creation is limitless and unfathomable. Some of these crystals may actually clear as they evolve and grow, along with the consciousness of their owner.

Milky quartz crystals represent the female or "yin" aspect. They are gentle, calm and serene, inspiring peace and equanimity. They have quite remarkable healing qualities in their ability to "draw out" pain and disease. They soothe and sedate and promote relaxation on all levels. They help release old negative belief systems and open us to more beneficial growth patterns.

Rutilated quartz, a clear quartz threaded with needle-like forms, adds even more intensity and transmission power because they bear cross currents of electrical charges that amplify healing, thereby aiding in the building of healthy cells and tissue. It may be used in the area of the solar plexus to relieve anxiety and fear or to aid in giving it equilibrium and power. It may also be used to counter unwelcome feelings of the heart or of sadness. It is an exceptionally good balancing and healing agent.

Smoky quartz is caused by traces of aluminium present in the crystal. If the crystal has grown in a spot where there was absolutely no natural radiation of any strength it would be clear rock crystal. However, if the growth area had deposits of radioactive ore such as uranium, the gamma radiation present would colour the crystal and make it "smoky."

The smoky colours range from a very pale smoke to practically coal black, depending on the amount of radiation, length of exposure time, and quantity of the accompanying aluminium impurity. In addition, the colour may be a very warm smoke or a cold tone smoke. Smoky crystal is the one to use to receive energy, and to begin to feel it, in a large amount. The energy disseminates from it slowly, because of its dark colour; and so, it becomes a pulsating element, not a very projecting one, as with clear crystal. One can sit with it and put one's hands around it, not touching it. One can close the eyes and it will pull energy in and one will feel the energy; the picture will not be within the crystal, but within the mind. Crystal is a bringer and a transmitter. The smoky crystal can be used the best way in that form.

Smoky quartz assists the root or base chakra to become radiant with light, a strong foundation upon which the spiritual force is manifested in the physical body. It is one's connection with the earth and inspires one to change the quality of one's life here by attuning to Nature and the treasures of the earth. It helps one to realise that only by living within the natural laws will Nature support us. Because of its grounding abillty, smoky quartz helps one to come to terms with one's body, heart and life. It will benefit anyone who is depressed, fatigued, spaced-out or unable to live up to seemingly unattainable standards. It will dissipate and purify negative energy and enable one to assimilate more in life by teaching how to let go of what is no longer needed for growth.

When a crystal has traces of ferric iron instead of aluminium and has also been subject to irradiation, the resultant colour could be many shades of yellow, orange or amethyst. Some crystals are citrine yellow on one end and amethyst on theother. Rock hunters have dubbed these ametrine. The change of colour from amethyst to citrine was caused by a change of the location of the ferric iron impurity from one end of the crystal to the other. Every quartz crystal structure contains within itsef a colour centre. When the ferric iron impurity is located in a certain spot in the colour centre, the crystal is coloured amethyst; if located in a different position, citrine, which ranges in colour from yellow to brown.

Citrine's gold ray energy is like that of the sun, warming, comforting penetrating, energising and life-giving. The consciousness associated with the navel centre is one of physical and material power. When this centre is evolved it is possible for us to attract towards us all necessary material wealth. Citrine can be used to build up light force and integrity of mind so that by channelling pure crown energy into the navel centre, conscious manifestation for creative purposes can occur. Citrines placed upon the navel centre or over affected areas can alleviate poor digestion, kidney and bladder complaints and constipation.

Citrine also breaks up and dissolves the psychic and emotional correlations that create these physical problems. It is for psychic digestion and assimilation so that one can flow with life instead of hanging on to it. Citrine increases the protective light in the aura and protects overly sensitive people against negative outside energies and influences. It increases self-confidence and inner security and is the best stone for use in matters of earthly experience, such as business, education, personal relationships and family matters.

It should be noted that heat treating coloured crystals can either change the colour or in some cases completely eliminate it. Certain grades of amethyst (not the highest quality) are commercially heat treated which changes the colour from amethyst to yellow-brown, brownish orange or "topaz" colour. If the resultant colour is not satisfactory, the amethyst colour can be restored by bombarding the heat-treated crystal with gamma rays.

Rose and amethyst crystals have an exceptionally wide range of both colour and quality. The rare ones are perfecly transparent with an even colouring of clean rose or deep royal amethyst, while thousands of tons of lesser quality contain chemical impurities of many types, which are desirable for electronics.

The soft soothing pink of rose quartz heals the heart. For people who have been unable to experience the joy of living through deprivation of love, rose quartz brings dynamic energy and healing power. It teaches one the powers of self-love and forgiveness and shows that the source of infinite love comes from within oneself, no matter how deep the emotional wound.

Amethyst, a beautiful form of quartz, has been employed in practical and mystical healing since ancient days. We can see in the quotation below that it was one of the twelve stones chosen for the breastplate of Aaron in Old Testament times. The early Greeks, Romans, and Egyptians employed the amethyst widely as a protective stone, favouring it especially for amulets and talismans. Its shades range from deep purple to palest violet, the result of iron and manganese oxide which make up the stone's composition.

And thou shalt make the breastplate of judgment with cunning work, and thou shalt set in its settings of stones, even four rows of stones, and the third row shall be a ligure, and agate, and an amethyst.

—Exodus 28:19

The deep rich viol et which is found in many specimens   probably gave rise to the ancient belief that amethyst protects men from excesses of alcohol. In fact, the word "amethyst" stems from a Greek word which can be translated as "without alcohol" or "without drunkenness, " the stone not only allege dly being an effective antidote against alcohol but also as a crystal to counteract the fumes given off by all spirits and wines. There are lots of old tales about the amethyst and the drinkng of wine or spirits. For instance, an amethyst placed under the tongue enabled the person to quaff several glasses of strong wine without intoxication.

Aristotle knew and admired the beautiful amethyst and tells a pretty story about it. A nymph appealed to Diana to save her from the importunings of the god Bacchus. To aid her, the goddess turned the maiden into a jewel, whereupon Bacchus, mourning his lost love, gave to the stone into which she had been metamorphosed its glorious wine-like hue. The legend became that the amethyst forever afterwards would protect all who wore it against over-indulgence through drunkenness.

What is certain, however, and more potent in the story of healing, is that ever since man first mined the   amethyst it has been valued for its calming and soothing influence when worn upon or applied to the physical body. Some of the stone's reputation for bestowing tran quility and peace must be due to the glorious light it radiates, since all shades of purple and blue are known to exercise therapeutic effe cts, being especially beneficial to sufferers from nervous or tense conditi ons, in states of fever or inflammatory diseases.

In medieval times, healers and alchemists believed very strongly in this calming power of the   amethyst; doctors frequently wo re it themselves upon their per sons, as well as employi ng it in medicine. Amethyst amulets were recommended for the cure of gout. Pieces of the stone were placed under the pillow upon retiring, when they were said to allay insomnia, inducing pleasant and healing dreams. For sufferers from nervous headache, it was recommended that the stone be warmed first in the sun's rays or by artificial heat. Wrapped in silk or fine cloth, it was then bound about the temples of the patient, where it reduced throbbing and relieved pain and tension.

Particularly valued as a protective stone not only against excesses of alcohol or wine, the ravages of fever, or circulatory disorders, the amethyst was always a powerful talisman in an occult, mystic sense. The ancient Egyptians believed its rays warded off the "Evil Eye." If a wearer of an amethyst was in danger of treachery or any kind of personal danger, the crystal's colour and lustre faded, and the person was thus warned in advance.

It was especially potent as a charm against witchcraft and black magic. Symbols of the sun and moon were often carved upon the surface of these stones. Placed then around the neck, they warded off all evil influences of an occult nature and confounded the most secret plots and machinations of sorcerers. Some students of the occult highly prized the amethyst because they held that it conferred "Second Sight," opening up the psychic centres. It had remarkable effects upon the brain, inducing mental clarity and pre-vision about material things, so that businessmen often wore it as a kind of talisman to make their affairs prosper.

Another of antiquity's claims for this beautiful stone's virtues was its alleged faculty of changing colour when placed in the vicinity of any kind of poisonous substance. For this reason, it was particularly valued by persons of high rank and those holding public office, who tested their food and drink by holding amethyst rings or amulets close to see whether enemies were attempting to poison them.

Physical changes, too, in the body of the wearer were reflected by the amethyst, which grew pale and dim at times of threatened sickness, either of the mind or body.

In a deeply spiritual, mystical sense the beautiful colours irradiated by the jewel contribute to healing. They induce meditation and lift the spirit. Often in religious ceremonies it is seen in altar cloths or priestly vestments. It was also used for rosary beads and for episcopal rings, in this latter regard sometimes referred to as the "The Bishop's Stone." Everywhere it seems to have been accepted as a symbol of piety, spiritual wisdom and humility, and to be capable of invoking these qualities when contemplated. It was probably for this reason that amethysts were set in temple vessels in ancient times, as well as in as priests' regalia.

Amethyst is still a favourite gem for lovers, probably because of its wonderful colour, which symbolises the depth and the constancy of true love. It was credited, in medieval times, with the ability to soothe violent and angry passions. People who habitually suffered from these kinds of emotional attack attacks of these were quite often given an amethyst in some form to wear so as to make them more amiable and gentler.

Though giving warning against treachery, misfortune and sickness, amethyst seems not to attract these things to those who own or wear it, for the amethyst is a bringer and a giver of light, waging mystic battle against evil forces, yet remaining curiously untouched and unharmed itself.

Amethyst reflects the purple ray of the brow chakra which symbolises the change of consciousness from the normal waking state to the inner planes of altered awareness. It is thus the very best stone for meditation as it can temporari ly still the mundane thought processes so that inner tranquility, deeper understanding and higher states of consciousness can be realised. Only when the mind realises its limitations and perceives glimpses of the ultimate reality during medit ation can it surrender its self-centred thought patterns.

Amethyst initiates deep soul experien ces, wisdom and understanding. It i s comforting in times of grief and sorrow. It has a calming mental effect on people who are overstressed, overworked or easily angered. It eases mental anxieties, tension and migraine headaches, and can transform recurrent ni ghtmares into peaceful sleep and sweet dreams. Hold an amethyst in your left-hand during meditation to relax the physical system and encourage deep meditative experiences.

Crystals and Gaia's Light Energy

Respected crystal practitioner Robert Simmons[58] has drawn fascinating parallels between the forces of living Nature in the Earth's Gaia body and the corresponding microcosmic forces at work in the human body. Gaia has a field, or aura, that consists of ele ctromagnetic energy-Light. Equally, humans have an energy field that surrounds their bodies. The Earth's continental plates constantly shift and move to balance Gaia's body. This densest aspect of Gaia represents the energy of the Earth element.

In our bodies, this movement is mirrored in our densest components, muscles and bones. Gaia's fiery core continually recycles Earth by melting rocks and minerals and releasing energy through volcanoes and geothermal activity. Similarly, this Fire element finds correspondence in our digestive processes that transform nutrients into energy and heat. Gaia's circulatory system shifts and moves through the planet's water systems: oceans, tides, rivers, streams, springs and ponds that carry nourishment to every part of her and carry away waste. This is the Water element, which, in the human form, is reflected in our circulatory and lymphatic systems.

The breath of Gaia circulates around and through her body in the form of air and gasses; in humans the Wind element is pres ent in our breath and bodily gasses. The element of Storm -Thunder-Lightning is created when all four elemental forces are empowered at once.

The Storm energy is a dynamic force that helps Gaia correct imbalances within her energy field. We experience the energy of Storm in the form of continual massive cleansing, spiritual awakening and the

---

[58] Simmons, R., *The Book of Stones*, Heaven and Earth, 2005.

correction of vibrational imbalance. In the same way that crystals and stones act as regulators and distributors of electromagnetic (Light) energy throughout the Earth, they are especially helpful in balancing these elemental forces within the body.

A Crystal Healing Affirmation

I have found this crystal affirmation to be very beneficial and restorative. Lie or sit in a comfortable position. Surround yourself with crystals of your choice: those that you are personally drawn to, or simply hold a palm-sized small clear quartz crystal ball. Perhaps put on some soothing music. I usually choose deeply relaxing pieces by artists such as Ennio Morricone, Vangelis, Constance Demby, Marcy Hamm, Sarah Hopkins, Ray Lynch and Tony O'Connor. Breathe deeply, focus, and mentally say:

> *I am surrounded by the healing power of crystal. Its magic vibrates its healing essence through the air and is absorbed by every pore of my body.*
>
> *My body is relaxed...I breathe deeply, and I know I am free.*
>
> *The crystal energy begins to make my body as light as a feather...every pore and nerve, every bone, every artery, every part of me is filled full of the magic of crystal healing.*
>
> *I am now filled with the highest healing power known to man.*
>
> *It is vibrating, pulsating within my body. It caresses and strengthens every part of me. I feel the acidity being freed from my body. Only positive thoughts are dwelling there.*
>
> *The crystal is filling me, is filling me, is filling me more and more and more with the power to be free, totally, unconditionally free.*
>
> *There is strength in the rebuilding vibration circling through me.*
>
> *Abundance begins to appear. I begin to feel abundantly with my health, in my interpersonal relations, in my work, in my home, in my whole life.*
>
> *Abundance is a tool, it now flows through my body, strengthens my mind and stabilises me for the future.*
>
> *As my body begins to be new, my thoughts take on new challenges, there isn't anything I cannot do: love, be a friend, see beauty, be free.*
>
> *The energy of the crystal is now blowing through me like a fresh wind. It blows all the disturbing memories from the subconscious*

mind. It moves and blows away anything within my body that causes discomfort or imbalance.

I am now timeless, and I am now in the centre of the crystal healing power.

I relax and give myself completely up to be whole and free once again.

The greatest healing power in all the world is my subconscious mind. The magic of the crystal has relaxed and centred it.

It is now sending out messages to every part of me. I am fine, I am well, I am powerful, I am free.

I relax and breathe deeply. My life is just beginning.

May peace be in my every breath, always.

A Solstice Celebration of the Forces of Living Nature

During the Solstices, we celebrate the creation and evolution of the forces of living nature and the divine crystal seed within us as simple gardeners:

'I am the power in my life.
I am in control of my life.
I am unlimited and free of all imbalance.
My power is fresh, honest and in harmony with all of life.
My control is centered and directed toward a positive end.
My balance is filled with a sense of grace.

'I am Nature. Within Nature
I am one with the God within.
I am the elements: sun, wind, rain and earth.
I am infinite, because nature is my home.
Nature is my spirit...My guardian.
As I walk it opens my path for me.
Nature's pathways are always to my spirit,
And I find peace and solace there.

'Nature and I are one, neutral and powerful.
I am not what I see.
I am more than I know.
I am Godly, seeking my home.'

Hardraw Force in North Yorkshire

Chapter 20

Colour Healing

Colours, being the visible aspect of energies that vibrate at defined, unchanging frequencies, are a product of the unlimited forces of living nature.

Every colour that we see, every colour we react to comes from the subconscious. If we do not like a col our, that reaction comes from the subconscious. For there is really no colour, only energy, and we perceive it as colour.

The vibrational energy of 460 trillion vibrations per second, or wave lengths per second, is red. The vis ible spectrum's highest frequency is violet, which vibrates at 760 trillion vibrations per second. These are wavelengths; there is no actual colour.

If we wear red and violet, people will see the red two miles before they see the violet. Put a violet light two miles away and one will hardly see it, maybe not at all. Put a red light two miles away and one will see it, because the cycle wave of the red is coarser. The finer the vibration, the less it affects and the more balanced one becomes.

In the mineral kingdom, there is that which gives light and that which takes it. Consider the colours in the context of their electro -magnetic polarity in quartz crystals : clear crystal, positive; rose crystal, positive; amethyst, positive; turquoise, positive; black crystal, because it is a crystal becomes neutral; jade, according to the colour it can be positive or negative; amber , negative. One begins to understand that there are those that take energy and those that give energy. There are those that strengthen and those that weaken. These actions are completely natural and take place to allow a balance.

Go through the home. Look at the colours that are there. Look at the lightness or the darkness, look at the excitement, what energy do we listen to? Look at the clothes we wear, the make-up, the perfume.

Most men should accentuate blue in clothing. The reason for that is that they can carry the energy, but it allows them to be in control and not controlled. Most women should accentuate with whites, greens and some of the pastels. But it is the green that a llows them to have the ability to bridge in any direction. If they over-use the other colours they will find themselves being picked out, singled out by certain kinds of energy. If you walk down the street and you have a white dress accentuated in red and yellow and orange, you will find that the energy that is reflected from red and yellow and orange is the same energy as the drunk coming out of the bar. His energy has the same vibrational wave as red, yellow and orange. You may feel a million dollars and he may feel like he is two pennies, but you have the same reflective vibration, and you might find him asking you for a drink. It is a subtle effect. You could have the most positive thought in the world but if you are accentuating a colour in too high a form you are aligning with another energy. Now your thought is, 'If I wear the colours, how can I overcome that drunk? Can my thought projection and energy force allow it to be?' Yes, but no; there is no one that can walk down the street more than three minutes and centre themselves so deeply that no one is going to react to them. They are going to hear a car screech, or someone walk by, and they are going to be pulled out of their concentration. If an individual feels that they have their diet in order, if he feels that his relationships with those around him are in order, if he is pulling abundance to him so that the world is opening, then he can accentuate a little acid so that he can continue to grow.

One can use colour to balance onself more easily than one can food or music or anything else because people react to us in that. Within the home we should have one room that is accentuated deeply within yellow, that is the room of communication. Within that room we should not have to say 'no yelling and screaming,' because that room needs to have yelling and screaming. It needs to be a communicating room.

There needs to be a room that has a softness, a green, for relaxation. There needs to be a room that has the lightness and the power healing of blues, indigos and violets. Whether it is a sleeping room or a room we come into just to relax completely. A green room is a place to bring friends so there can be no difficulty of communication, and so there will not be too much of it.

And there needs to be reds and oranges in some rooms. These would be where we iron or wash, or where we want to get things done. Within that, if we want to go on a diet, have the refrigerator painted violet, inside and out. We will find that every time we open it the colour will make us sick as we look at it reflected upon the food. It is a reflection. Take, for instance, violet lights and put them in all the light sockets in the room we are eating in, and all the food will look mildewed or decayed and we will find all our hunger releasing.

We should try to have a brilliance for the ceiling, a white. And we should try to use paper or wood for the walls as much as possible, for it has a tendency to allow a warmth and a life force.

Paint a house one has just moved into. It is important for if we paint it, we exorcise it, for we are putting paint into every corner. It is the perfect way of cleansing. If we rent a place and it has just been painted by professional painters there is a similar energy, but if it has not, one will feel the vibrations of past occupants easily and quickly. It is all energy. Each thing you have in one's house has positive or negative force.

The Aura

One's aura is unique, for there is none other like it.One's aura is what our subconscious mind sees of us. The aura deals specifically with waves of energy. All energy has waves. The waves may be hard or soft, they may be electromagnetic, but all things, from the smallest atom to the largest star, move. There is no element within the physical plane that does not have movement. Our aura is what we make it, no more, no less. It is the projection of the subconscious mind. It is the subconscious mind in etheric strength. We have the ability to change the colours of our aura. We have the ability to change the programming of one's subconscious mind, as one does the lines upon our palm, which indicate the destiny that we have come to be in.

Around the body is a white aura called a mantle. The mantle is either a shield or a protector, depending upon its development. It is the l ight force from which all colour comes. It is the energy that allows the energies of colour to be perceived. In childhood, the white aura is naturally strong.

At age thirteen, the strength begins to correspond to the individual's belief in self. As the i ndividual grows more positive, the white aura becomes stronger and there is more protection. The subconsci ous mind reacts to and has a re cording on everything within one's body: genetic pattern, bones, muscles, nerves, circulation, organs. It not only controls our body as it is, but it controls the energy that our body projects. It is not only physiologically within one, but also a physiological projection, and there will be people who will respond to it.

Upon rising in the morning, the aura is constant, it is like a flow, it is at rest. The red, the orange, the yellow, the green, the blue are th e same strength, but as the sub conscious comes to life it begins to work predominately in one specific colour. The aura shows what one's body is and what it has become.

Red is the physical. It is the sun; it is the energy; it is vibration and movement. It is the individual who is dealing with their physical body and with keeping the body in order. It is usually a person in a beginning evolution. One will know them because they are the one who goes from bar to bar, from physical experience to physical experience. They are red in their energy for the body is being used and the subconscious allows the remainder to rest. There is not much emotion in physical energy. The boxer or the sportsman who is dealing with the physical energy is not thinking much. They do not deal in emotions and is not often philosophic. If one is reacting physically towards someone, or feeling ill, the red will be the highest projection because the subconscious is projecting red. It is this way when there is pain or when dealing with the physical elements of the sexual body.

The **orange,** the emotion, are those things within the subconscious that frustrate the individual. Emotion deals with involvement in the material plane or the negative aspects of it, whether it is war, famine, poverty or disease. It deals with it not physically, but with a feeling of fear: fear of dying, fear of not being loved or lovable, fear that the body is getting old, fear that there is no friendship, fear that there is no God Force, fear that there will be no representation of loving kindness. Fear is an emotion. When it is felt, the orange is between the red and the yellow. It is not physical, it is not mental, it is in-between. Emotion is directly aligned to mental thought and the physical body. Emotion is precarious and the subconscious mind responds to it. The body reacts physiologically, and the mind reacts in emotion or nervousness.

How does emotion come about? It begins when the body reacts, and the mind thinks about the reaction. Fear is not something that one can put their finger on and say, 'This is fear.' One can look at their skin and say, 'This is scaley.' But one cannot hold back fear; it is a feeling. If someone hurts you and you have a reaction of sadness, the subconscious mind records it. If there is an indication of this action again, or if someone indicates it within their thought form, the recordings of the subconscious mind will come forward and the emotion will reoccur. Emotions are easy to get rid of, but because there is continued stimulus they also recur easily.

Yellow is the energy of the sun. It is a reflected energy, but it is also a reflection. The mind thinks and stores many things. It then goes back and reviews, compares and refers to it. 'Is this person as good as that, is that person as good as this?' The energy of yellow is a very strong energy; it is a combination of red, green and blue. But yellow as energy within the aura does not necessarily deal with pigmentation, it deals with the green that it is close to and the blue. The interrelation between philosophical and spiritual thought allows the yellow to develop. A yellow aura deals with a philosophical or a spiritual attitude. It is the last element from the physical and the emotional. The yellow is close to the bridge of philosophy. Because of that it is not, in e ssence, a colour. It is a combination. It is a little bit a philosophy and alittle bit of the religious. By not deciding which one it is, it brings forward theyellow. It is thought and it is confusion. The thinker is one who cannot decide between his spiritual oneness or the philosophical oneness.

The **green** is the bridge, the philosophic. It is softer that yellow, the mental. The energy that comes from green isnot very strong in the world in actuality. There are not manypeople who step away from the physical, emotional or mental and begin to think about life in relation to themselves. Those who pull away from religion, creed, philosophy or faith and begin to centre, have calmness, the freshness of spring and the energy of green. It is an energy of temperance and softness. It comes forward from the subconscious and deals with feelings. It is the link with the physical extending to the spiritual. The energy projecte d from the subconscious is somewhat hesitant for the subconscious begins to realise that this colour is interfering with its influence. Green is softness; green is the s pringtime; green is the summer . And the subconscious reacts to physical, emotional and mental thought. Green is a part of those evolutionary feelings. Green is an energy that notmany project regularly, for it is one of those in -between areas that is ha rd to identify. It is an energy that the subconscious can project, but it holds back. As the green becomes turquoise, the subconscious begins to lose its influence and the aura becomes deep blue, like a pool of water. The influence of the subconscious is almost gone when the green becomes blue.

The **blue** is the connection to the higher self, and it is beyond the subconscious mind. The subconscious mind cannot reactto it very much. The energy projections are not necessarily always in the blue . It can be turquoise, but the blue is theconnection to the etheric. Blue is the balance that one needs, for the blue is a vital part of each individual. The subconscious mind will reject it in most cases, because it has no control over it as an energy. Th e energy of the blue is more refined and deals with the energy projected through the etheric web points of the cent re eye, the crown, the throat and the heart. It is an outside energy, not an inside energy. Blue in the aura is not a matter of good works, f or those who are involved with good works in order to have great reward within their religion usually find themselves within the orange colour more than the blue. The blue is the connection we have with the higher self; it is the umbilical cord. It is the one colour that people want to know about because the subconscious mind cannot record it and cannot control it. Blue is a mystery.

Indigo is an energy that is projected by an individual closing down the emotional and the physical. As the physical stands aside, no longer reacting to body images and energies and as the subconscious mind is no longer controlling it, the indigo grows stronger. One is controlling their projections and meditative sense, and the emotions are as calm as a placid lake; this is indigo. The stronger it becomes, and the more strength around the aura, the more the red and the orange will go into a pattern of non-influence. The indigo is an energy pattern that allows more strength coming from the higher self because of less energy coming from the emotional and the physical. Violet follows indigo and is the closing down of the mental. Indigo is the hardest.

The **violet** is the individual that connects to all things. Because of the ultraviolet energy, it is like the rays of the sun. It is an energy that exudes through the crown, seeing eye, throat and heart. The body is there, the mind is there, but they are not in control. This individual walks with all things, can see and hear and feel, but the subconscious is centered. It is possible, within a meditative sense to get glimpses of indigo and violet.

Colour Healing and the Chakras

RED—physical ailments treated by using the colour red include problems with the bloodstream such as anemia, low vitality and poor circulation. Red vitalizes the physical body and is a powerful stimulant. It should not be used for people who are nervous and irritable. Too much red results in feelings of anger, frustration, lust, violence, destruction and so on. The positive understanding of red results in strength, power, initiative and honour.

The **first chakra** is known as the root chakra. The Sanskrit name is Muladhar meaning "root/base." Its location is at the base of the spine along the first three vertebrae. Its function is for survival and grounding. If this chakra is blocked, an individual can feel fearful, anxious, angry and frustrated. Clues to this will be tightened jaws and fists, and sometimes violent behaviour based on feelings of insecurity. Obvious physical malfunctions may manifest in problems such as obesity, haemorrhoids, constipation, sciatica, degenerative arthritis, anorexia nervosa, or knee troubles. When the chakra is open and balanced, the individual will be in balance and will act wi sely and with moderation. When working with this chakra, it is helpful to visualize the colo ur red or black.

ORANGE—this colour can be used to treat problems with the spleen, lungs and pancreas. It is helpful for muscle spasms and cramps. Orange has an enlivening effect and provides energy to deal with life's situations. This colour has been used to treat asthma, bronchitis, gall stones and menstrual problems. Negative aspects of orange energy results in aggressiveness, uncooperative behaviour, inferiority or superiority complexes and procrastination. Positive use of orange results in illumination, confidence, intellect, inventiveness and self-motivation.

The **second chakra** is known as the sex chakra, or in some philosophies the spleen chakra. The Sanskrit name is Svadhisthana, meaning "one's own place." Its location is on the genitals along the first lumbar vertebra. The function for this chakra is desire, pleasure, sexuaIty and procreation. If this chakra is blocked, a person may be restless and confused. Physical malfunctions may result in problems such as impotence, frigidity, uterine, bladder or kidney trouble, or a stiff lower back. When the chakra is functioning properly, the individual will feel emotional gratification, courage, and attraction to th e opposite sex. The colour to visualize for strengthening or balancing this chakra is orange.

YELLOW—the stomach area is successfully treated by yellow. Problems such as constipation, indigestion, bile flow, diabetes, flatulence, heartburn and skin troub les are helped with yellow. Yellow activates the motor nerves and generates energy in the muscles. Negative use of yellow results in criticism, over -indulgence, stubbornness, cowardice and being judgmental. Positive use results in joy, mental discrimination, organization, attention to detail and discipline.

The **third chakra** is known as the solar plexus chakra. The Sanskrit name is Manipura, meaning "jewel city ." Its location is in the region of the navel along the 8th thoracic vertebra. The function for th is chakra deals with developing the ego. The solar plexus is the seat of feelings and emotions. It deals with will and power. When this chakra is balanced, the need to feel important and achieve outside material identity in the world is transformed into true contentment and faith that what is occurring now is what is really needed at the moment for complete spiritual growth. An open solar plexus chakra is shown by acts of charity and selfless service. The colour to visualize while healing this chakra is golden yellow.

GREEN—this colour is used to treat problems in the heart area. It has been used for blood pressure, ulcers and headaches. Green is a very important colour as it lies midway between the two ends of the colour spectrum. Its function is one of balancing with harmony, peace and serenity resulting from it. Green quietens and refreshes the mind and body. Qualities of green lend determination, efficiency and conscientious attention to detail. Misuse of green energy results in jealousy, envy, stinginess and greed. Wise use of this energy lends enthusiasm, hope, sharing, growth and expansion.

The **fourth chakra** is known as the heart chakra. The Sanskrit name is Anahata, meaning "unstruck sound." It is located in the centre of the chest in the heart or the cardiac area, along the 8th cervical vertebra. The function of the heart chakra deals with love. It is one of the most important of the body centres. It is said that if this chakra is open, all the other chakras will come into alignment with it. The heart extends its circulation to the entire body, and all systems and tissues are nurtured with vital force. If the heart chakra energies are blocked, physical symptoms such as asthma, high blood pressure, heart disease, or lung disease may result. An open and balanced heart chakra demonstrates compassion, and the ability to see and feel through the eyes and heart of the other person without losing or betraying oneself. The colour to visualize in balancing this chakra is green.

BLUE—the colour blue is helpful in treating all throat ailments such as sore throat, hoarseness, goitre, fevers and laryngitis. Blue is very peaceful and relaxing and has the capability to draw one out of the physical world and up into the spiritual world. The negative qualities of blue are shown in depression, self-pity, fear, coldness, detachment and indifference, while the positive use of blue results in wisdom, gentleness, trust, understanding and forgiveness.

The **fifth chakra** is known as the throat chakra. The Sanskrit name is Vishuddha, meaning "with purity." It is located in the laryingeal area, at the base of the throat along the 3rd cervical vertebra. The function for this chakra deals with communication, creativity and speaking higher truths. When this chakra is balanced, the cosmic laws of God and life are understood and lived. One will have calmness, serenity, purity, a melodious voice and a good command of speech. If it is blocked, physical symptoms may manifest such as a sore or stiff neck, colds, thyroid or hearing problems. The colour to visualize with this chakra is blue.

INDIGO—this deep blue/purple colour is helpful for problems associated with the head, such as eye, ear and nose troubles. It is also beneficial in the treatment of certain nervous and me ntal disorders. It works on the parathyroid glands but depresses the thyroid. Indigo helps inflamed eyes and ears, and has been used to treat pneumonia. Misuse of energy from indigo can result in pride, separaten ess, con ceit, gossip, deceit and irritability. The positive aspect of indigo helps bring about qualities like unity, calm, balance, humanitarian and w orld service, and aspiration. Indigo also acts as a catalyst.

The **sixth chakra** is known as the brow or third eye chakra. The Sanskrit name is Aj na, meaning "command cent re." It is located in the middle of the forehead in the area between the eyebrows, along the lst cervical vertebra. The function of this chakra is clear seeing and intuitive sight. When this chakra is balanced and opened, the third eye is able to see clairvoyantly. Intuitive knowledge is available for help in making decisions. If the brow chakra is blocked, malfunctions such as blindness, headaches, nightmares, eyestrain or blurred visions may result. The colour to visualize for balancing this chakra is indigo.

VIOLET—this colour is best used for treat ment of nervous and mental disorders. It helps purify the blood and stops the growth o f tumours. It controls the pitui tary gland. Insomnia is helped with violet, as are eye troubles. It has been used to treat sciatica, meningitis and epilepsy. Misuse of the violet color can result in obse ssion, martyrdom, injustice, intolerance and restriction. Wise use of the qualities of violet reveals mercy, devotion, loyalty, idealism, wisdom and grace. Violet represents the highest element in human nature.

The **seventh chakra** is known as the crown chakra. The Sanskrit name is Sahasrara and means "thousand-petaled lotus." It is located at the top of the head, The function of this chakra deals with perfect understanding and having a higher state of consciousness. Opening this chakra results in bringing through and mani festing higher wisdom and Divine Light and love. If this chakra's energies are blocked, physical symptoms such as depression, alienation, confusion, boredom, apathy or an inability to learn or comprehend will sometimes be apparent. This chakra represents the highest level of attainment for understanding cosmic bliss while in the physical body, and is the last to be developed in an indivi dual. The colo ur to vis ualize while balancing this cha kra is white or clear, representing all colours. Sometimes violet is used.

Use of these colours can enhance all forms of healing. When possible, it is helpful to have several different coloured quartz crystals, but is almost as effective to use a clear crystal and visualize the colour needed in treatment. The crystal will amplify the thought forms and give more energy to the focus of attention.

Some healers like to begin a healing session by checking out or scanning each chakra with a crystal held in their left hand. This increases their sensitivity to feeling blocks or cold spots on these energy points. They do this by stroking the area an inch or two above the body from the top of the head down to the toes. They feel for heat, tingling, cold, or resistance. Either gently massaging the crystal on the chakra or rotating it gently above the area can be effective in opening blockages.

Sometimes it is helpful to place a crystal or gemstone on each of the seven main chakra points, or place a crystal anywhere on the body where there is pain or discomfort.

When a healer has completed the session, they will again lightly brush the body down the front and the back to cleanse and seal the chakras from any undesirable energy which may interfere with healing. A healing like this may be likened to psychic surgery; and the energy centres may be sensitive to harsh vibrations for a short while and so should be protected from unwanted influences.

The Aura

Chapter 21

One Man's Remarkable
Journey to the Andes

One fine early Autumn morning in the late 1990s, a 60-year-old man was walking his chocolate Labrador in the San Francisco headlands. The air was filled with the intoxicating smells of newly awakened flowers. The man knew that today's walk would be especially delightful for he noticed that the hills were surrounded with clouds, which would provide a foggy walk higher up the mountain. Each step he took up the winding road brought about in the walker a deepening sense of physical well-being and inner peace. The nature sounds around him were somewhat muted by the fog and he found himself being drawn onward as if pulled by an unseen force.

Smiling, stepping lightly, he stopped to catch his breath just before entering the fog. To his surprise, he heard the faint opening notes of a far-off melody. Straining to hear more clearly, he held his breath. There it was again —a distinct, mysterious melody! It was definitely coming from somewhere within the fog.

Mesmerised, he entered the mist and found himself on a narrow mountain path that he was certain he had never followed before . Each careful step required intense focus and concentration. His sense of isolation and the unfamiliar surroundings sharpened his sense of hearing as he was pulled ever nearer to the haunting sound of a flute. The enchanting melody seized all of his sense s and pulled him ever further along the increasingly precarious path.

With each step the music comforted him while he struggled to understand if he was indeed awake or else being pulled into some kind of mystical dream. He soon gave up this internal debate as increasingly his thoughts would not come clearly.

A chill passed through the entire length of his body. He felt timeless and alone as he was drawn quickly into another alternate world. Even as small rocks that crumbled under his feet fell hundreds of feet down the mysterious mountain and he hugged the cliff-face for support, he felt no fear. Moving more slowly now, he edged around a rocky outcrop and emerged from the fog into a place that was decidedly not the San Francisco headlands.

All around was fresh green growth accented by a myriad of beautiful, fragrant wildflowers. The haunting melody was stronger now, appearing to originate from the other side of a grassy knoll before him. He reached the top of the knoll and was awestruck by the scene below. Nestled in a saddle-shaped area between two small peaks was what looked like an ancient Greek amphitheatre. In the far distance were other, much higher peaks. At an altar in the centre of the arena stood a solitary male playing a wooden pan-flute.

The absorbing melody of the flute pulled the visitor into the amphitheatre. Other people were gradually emerging from the fog and filling the marble seats that circled a platform in the centre. By this time, the man's legs were no longer his own; he could only make his way into the amphitheatre and occupy a seat. He felt out of place because all those that were gathering were wearing sandals and toga. He looked down and, to his amazement, his sweatshirt, jeans and tennis shoes had been replaced by identical attire. He sat down on the highest row and it was then he noticed that the platform was constructed in the shape of a nine-pointed star. At the tip of each point was a pillar sculpted out of shiny red marble.

The seats filled rapidly; all the onlookers appeared to be transfixed by the entrancing flute music. He closed his eyes, relaxed, took a deep breath and allowed the music to saturate every cell, pore and nerve of his being. His bodily functions seemed to come alive in a way he had never experienced. By breathing deeply, he could actually feel and see air going into and out of his lungs.

He could feel every aspect of his body but, at the same time, he was also aware of a spatial distance between his mind, his body and the marble on which he was seated. Names and faces from his childhood began to appear in his mind and he felt that in some way these were an igniter for what he was now experiencing.

While the flautist's melody continued to weave a magic spell upon the gathering spectators, the man observed the entrance of nine figures in grey cowled robes. Silently, they circled the platform. Each was carrying a polished box beneath their left arm. On the second revolution of the platform, they positioned themselves one by one at their respective pillars. All the while, the echoing sounds of the flute made it seem as these nine figures had been created by the magical music.

Each figure delicately opene d their box, slid off the top, reached inside and pulled out a cloth-covered object. With great care they placed their respective treasures, still covered, on top of a pillar. Completing this task, in unison they all stepped back and the flautist finished his refrain.

As the flautist moved away from the altar, one of the robed figures removed the cover from the object beneath. The audience gasped as one, for the object was a beautifully sculpted crystal skull! One by one the remaining figures completed the same action, revealing a skull facing the pillar to its left. A subdued glow of light emanated from each, creating a luminous effect. The strength of light startled the man for it was only then did he realise that it was dusk.

Each of the nine crystal skull-bearers clapped their hands together and stretched out the left hand, face up. In it appeared a small leather - bound mallet. The closest figure touched the skull before it lovingly and struck it lightly with the hammer.

A clear, resonating tone filled t he amphitheatre as a brilliant light shot from the eyes of the first skull to the rear of the next. As if igniting it, the next skull glowed radiantly. The second robed figure repeated the action, and its skull projected its light on to the neighbouring sk ull. One by one the the projecting lights connected with each other until there was a perfect nine-pointed star around the platform. It glowed with the intensity of a sunny day.

All the man knew was that he did not want to get out of his seat. He felt no pressure, just a soft secure presence which let him know he was safe and that he was where he was meant to be. He began to feel a rhythmic pulse vibrating his seat and was aware that the light from the crystal skulls was pulsating in unison with his own heart.

One of the robed figures turned, bowed and beckoned to an individual on the second row. Rising slowly, this person walked carefully down the aisle and stood in front of the mystical figure who placed the man's hand on top of the skull. Then came a blinding flash, followed by the man's audible gasp as the power of light began to occupy his body.

Gradually, he became translucent. All those present could clearly see his bones, heart, lungs, blood vessels...everything as if one were looking through a giant X-ray. His body was vibrating from what seemed to be thousands of volts of electricity. Tears streamed down his cheeks as he eventually stepped back expecting to to find something changed. He returned to his seat.

Again and again, individuals from the audience were invited onto the platform to experience the same amazing ceremony. It was impossible to know what was happening to each person or to know why they were being singled out but what was evident was the aura of contentment and peace they exuded as each departed the platform and returned to their seat. Eight of the robed figures had pulled many people onto the platform but the ninth just stood patiently as its companions went about their work.

Our visitor closed his eyes and enjoyed the feeling of being surrounded by a great but friendly force in this timeless place, which his instincts told him was in the Andes in the far distant past, a few hundred years after the pole switch and the ensuing cataclysm that destroyed Atlantis and revitalised Mother Earth.

Suddenly, he caught his breath and felt a little faint for the ninth figure was now pointing in his direction! His heart skipped several beats as he hoped the cowled figure was actually pointing at someone else. No such luck; it was he being summoned. He tried rising but it was as if his body was hewn from the surrounding mountainside. Slowly, his body began to respond and he descended to the platform. It was not more than sixty feet away but his transition from seat to platform and the beckoning cowled figure seemed to take a lifetime.

Gently, the figure took his arm and led him towards the crystal skull, then moved his hand towards the top of the skull. Every muscle and tendon in his arm tightened as his hand was placed on the ancient crystal head. His first impression was of an exhilarating power flowing through him like the first sip of a warm cognac on a cold evening. This was followed by a strong sensation, which assisted him to relax and feel contented.

He breathed a sigh of relief and let go. Instantly, he could feel a tingling on the bottom of his hand. He closed his eyes and one by one felt the nine separate pulsating energies every few seconds. At first, it felt as if there were nine individual currents, and at the end of each sequence of nine there was about a five-second pause before the pulsating resumed. Each of the nine energies felt equal in power but separate and distinct in nature. To increase his confidence, he whispered to himself, 'C'mon, be strong!' Straightaway, his body began to vibrate, and his mind was engulfed by a deep resounding voice:

'We are the physical power of nine, the Ennead, representing the nine bonding energies of the earth experience. Together, they are the energies of CHALLENGE, an understanding of which guides one towards the totality of oneself. These energies comprise the learning experiences one must undertake as we graduate and evolve through the University of the Physical during many lifetimes. By working on them fully, consistently, and joyfully one opens that hidden door to unlimited adventure. Taking them one by one, they are:

OPPORTUNITY—the energy of unlimitedness. There are no limits in our lives.

COMRADESHIP—the energy of deep interpers onal understanding. We accept unconditionally the realities of others, embracing neutrality rather than interference.

CELEBRATION—the energy of joy, humour, and hopefulness. Through celebration we bring adventure into our lives, daily.

FORCE and STRENGTH—the energy of personal stability. This energy is not forceful but the essence of force. Through it we express our inner power while going beyond intimidation and fear.

BALANCE—the energy of rejuvenation. We renew our energies every hour, refocusing so that we move positively into the future.

TEMPERANCE—the energy of understanding strengths and weaknesses and is the companion to BALANCE. Within this energy we learn to enjoy all aspects of life. In this, we must larn to persist for the when, where, and how will be in a temperate manner.

INTUITION—the energy of instinct. We allow ourselves to listen to our inner voice more and more daily.

PATIENCE—the energy of the neutral observer. We are open and more observant each day, allowing a positive perception of all living things.

EVOLUTION is the energy of complete change, a change to the opposite pole or idea. Are you a teacher? Become a student.

Through EVOLUTION we step into a no-return energy and literally change our lives.

These are positive, patient, observant and nurturing energies available for nature and human completion. Each of the nine energies is prominent but also a part of the whole.'

The man was aware that one by one each energy bypassed the Ennead circle, went through him, and re-joined the circle at exactly the right pulsation point. He found himself counting one, two, three, four, five, six, seven and eight and gritting his teeth as the ninth energy, Evolution, charged through his body, bringing the understanding that this energy was especially important to him and also making him feel uniquely vibrant and strong. The energy emerging from the poly-dimensional nine-pointed circle began to produce in him an unusually sharp awareness of the separate powers which were passing through his body.

'Why am I here?' he asked nervously.

'To learn of the unique Ennead energy and how to apply its potentials in your life,' came a resonant reply. 'Observe your current world's many signs and symbols that are used by its religions, philosophies, governments and businesses. Ennead is also a symbol, a poly-dimensional nine-pointed symbol. Its "symbolic" strength has never been used in a negative way. It was nurtured by the wisdom and knowledge of those who knew the difficulties of living in a crisis-torn world. Those individuals sought to maintain a positive balance in a secluded-secret community...in essence to create the Utopian society.

'However, the Ennead potentials cannot be secluded in that way. Its ultimate capacity is balance, a balance which must be discovered within each person. Most of your world seeks to create peace, healthy bodies and happiness. Ennead reminds us that these things are already in existence within you. Your quest is to discover them and integrate their discovery into your life.

'Those that created that community a long time ago realised that the key to utilising the power of Ennead was an unlimited state of mind. That is why Ennead's primary energy is Opportunity. To discover this power, you must begin to think, talk and act no limits, and acknowledge no limits in your life. It is only through that recognition and acceptance that you can step into the total power available in Ennead.'

As if sensing the visitor's unspoken question, the figure said, 'No, you do not learn to be unlimited in Ennead; it is the key, and you must

316

have it or accept it before you can enter.

'Once you become aware of the potentials ofthe Ennead power, your life will change drastically. Each time you review and comprehend one of its nine energies, you will find increased inspiration in that area   of your life. Your unlimited attitude will intuitively let you know if that is a positive of negative experience. Awareness and application of the nine energies of the Ennead can bring balance in the most difficult of times. The balance obtained from them can heal anything.'

Immediately, he was aware of every imbalance his mind and body had experienced and accumulated over the years and what their continued presence would do to him in the future. He was fascinated as he looked through this "mystical microsc ope" into the vulnerabilities he had created in his world and at the same time faintly remembered thinking, 'I am definitely a product of my own thought...no -one brought these imbalances into my life except me. I hope I remember this.'

No sooner did he   have that thought, than the energy of Intuition spiralled through his body. He knew that , in some way, everyone in the amphitheatre were individuals, while at the same time a part of the whole energy of the Ennead power. Perhaps each of us, he thought, were apprentices to an overwhelmingly magnificent energy that we could use and bring back to our respective worlds.

The words Force and Strength began to flash in his mind like a neon sign on a cheap cafe. At that moment, the energy of Patience replaced intuition and whirled through his body.

'Ennead is one of the ultimate powers of order. The only way this power can finally expand and come to full use is though crisis or chaos.'

He was immediately reminded of the two Chinese characters that made the word balance. Separately, however, they were the words "crisis" and "opportunity."

'Know each energy and become part of the whole!' said the mysterious voice as Opportunity took over from Patience.

The visitor seemed to explode into millions of pieces and he was no longer a physical being...just a part of an unexplainable whole. He knew he was still very distinctly an individual, not a body, but a definite individual who was a part of everything that his mind could imagine.

Opportunity opened amazing pathways! He began to experience intimate details of past times and places and how they bonded with his current life situation. He felt a part of every colour available. He enjoyed the tastes and scents of all his favourite delights: hot rhubarb and apple pie, freshly popped corn, pine needles after rainfall, freshly mown grass, and the ozone-rich ocean air after a storm. He was suddenly infused with all the energies of Ennead and then...silence.

Instinctively, he knew that within him was being planted some kind of esoteric seed in relation to order and balance within each of the Ennead energies.

The tingling in his hand increased and a surge of power made its way through his hand and up his arm. He felt as if he was going to explode at any moment and that these energies were the dynamite. Everything seemed to elasticise as in one final surge the energy of Evolution planted the seed of the death of the visitor from the San Francisco headlands.

He understood that at an appropriate time in the future he would no longer be himself but a part of something else...but not sure exactly what. Somehow, making this realization induced in him a feeling of ecstasy. Perhaps his perceptions were limited by the mind tools with which he was confined or, perhaps, he would always be unable to perceive all that there is because of what he thought he was. Rebirth would come slowly and probably take years.

The Ennead energy of Opportunity began withdrawing from his body and he was once again influenced by the figure who had called him to the platform. His hand was removed from the skull and he was directed back to his seat.

On the platform the robed figures stepped to their respective skulls and turned to face the centre. Nine beacons of light merged in the centre, creating a giant axle that beamed straight up to the heavens. This magnificent radiance of light now illuminated all the surrounding area as if it were midday. The nine beacons of light were spokes in a star-wheel whose cosmic axle was projecting its energy infinitely.

Our visitor was so entranced by the spectacle that he almost missed seeing the nine figures take their small leather hammers and, one by one, tap the top of their skull lightly.

The light began to fade and completely withdraw. All the energies faded until only Evolution remained. Its guardian figure put its hand on top of the skull before him and in a fast wrist action gave it a spin on its dowelled stand. As the crystal skull spun, one by one the eight cowled figures disappeared. Gradually, the skull's spin slowed and at the same time its light became fainter. Finally, it stopped, and the amphitheatre was plunged into total darkness. The flautist resumed his playing, as if saying, 'It's time to leave.' Slowly, the audience members rose from their seats and retraced their steps along the many pathways by which they had arrived at the Andean Mountain amphitheatre thousands of years in the past.

Soon, the fog was around him and the music of the flute began to fade. Without hesitation, he stepped onto the road in the headlands that he walked each day. Moving very slowly, he stopped to let his companion lab catch up with him.

He said to him, 'Prince, did you know that we can experience anything within our minds?' The lab cocked his head and gave him a puzzled look.

The man laughed and said, 'Don't worry, I haven't gone crazy. It's a beautiful morning, Prince, let's enjoy it to thefull.' He fished a tennis ball from his pocket and tossed it in the air. As Prince dashed forward in full retrieval mode, barking excit edly, the man suddenly retrieved a distant memory.

He had observed that the flautist was wearing an unusual silver medallion enamelled with a beautiful white rose and now, as Prince was chasing the ball, he suddenly realised that he had seen an identical o ne before! Immediately, he experienced a strong sense of déja vu and a distant memory rose to the surface.

He recalled being pulled down a powerful shaft of light. The next thing he knew he was with a group of people who seemed to be friends but whom he did not immediately recognise. Mysteriously, he was able to perceive himself as a twentieth century American, but he was also completely aware that he was someone else from a time ten thousand years in the past.

His surroundings were primitive, wet and h umid. The sunless sky was filled with an unbroken blanket of grey cloud. It looked as if it might rain at any moment. As he sought to get his bearings, he looked around. It was all very eerie, almost indescribable. For the first time, he felt fear.

Just as he was on the verge of panic, a calm, sturdy voice held his attention. As if by magic, he felt himself being drawn toward a very unusual man. His dress was bizarre, but this was offset by his warm and charismatic energy. Soon, along with four hundred other people, he found himself gathered round this magnetic figure. He also noticed that everyone in the gathering w as wearing the same clothes as the lead figure. It was then that he looked down and saw that he was similarly dressed.

A hush came over the crowd and the unusual man in a clear crystal-clear voice said, 'Welcome to the earth reincarnated.' The gathering listened to this magical man as he began to give instructions and to explain the reason that they were not able to bring anything with them from the earth as they had once known it. This was to allow nature to have the time for rebuilding the natural resources that had been stripped from it by an unfeeling and uncaring populace. Surviving humans were in a new world with only their minds and bodies as tools for starting anew. Anything that they used to help themselves now had to be created by hand with the resources that were currently available.

The visitor was fascinated by the warmth and sincerity of this man and entranced by his power to create calm. The teacher went on to explain that the earth would probably be covered by a thick cloud layer until the sun could burn off the tremendous amount of humidity that had been created by the vast movement of all water masses in the polar shift. This process would take around three hundred years. The land they now occupied, about two hundred square miles, would eventually be called Coyhaique in Patagonia. As the centuries went by the water would recede and the earth would re-adjust through a series of earthquakes and volcanic eruptions. Man would spread throughout the world.

Firmly, the teacher said that their first task was to construct shelter and then secure food sources. The visitor was assigned to a group that was assigned for scouting purposes. It began making its way over the soggy terrain looking for any type of edible life-form. In one area they found a lot of timber that was heaped in a huge, dishevelled pile. This would be the foundation of shelter, firewood and the material for rudimentary tools.

They came across animals that had managed to survive. More surprisingly, they seemed to have come from different parts of the former ten continents and been relocated into a new environment. The leader later explained that animals of different species would mate with each other and so create new life forms that would have names such as Tapir, Llama, Jaguar, Sloth, and a myriad of new species of birds.

There was an unusual sense of excitement among the survivors and at the same time a strong feeling of peace, cooperation and positive communication on every level. Slowly, the new community began to construct crude houses out of wood, stone and mud. Fire was built from sparks. People began acquainting themselves with one another. Food was abundant and only clothing presented a potential problem. The teacher explained that each community would face different challenges and obstacles, but all would have the same opportunities.

'You were taught before the cataclysm that you must function only in companionship with nature and never in opposition. A community that tries to alter or infringe upon the forces of living nature will find itself diverging from the noble plans and goals it had before the poles switched. If the wind blows...it blows. If it rains...it rains. If the tides rise...they rise. If the earth shakes...then it shakes. If it snows, sleets, freezes or if the winds rage...then so be it. Nature and man are one, ' he emphasised. 'Nature and man are one!

'As time goes by, some communities will worship their leaders; some will construct images which they remembered from before ; some will worship nature. In all of this, it is important to remember that man and nature are one.

'Within man are all the powers and weaknesses of nature. It is through observing and living side by side with nature's neutrality that we learn of our infinite continuance. The trees will fall and return to the ground...then grow again. Man will physically return to nature but will come again.

'Each of you will live many times on this planet and experience many different types of lives. Some will be difficult while others will flow evenly but, like nature, you cannot change the cycle. It is within that cycle that we, in harmony with the forces of living nature, exper ience everything that this world has to offer, and I mean everything. If you fight or try to change the natural flow of your Nature -Self, you will have an inner cataclysm and have to start over.

'There is a natural order in all living things. Within you , it is called the spirit. Within that natural order, you slowly gain the power, poise and majesty that we feel in tidal waves, earthquakes, hurricanes and blizzards. These energies are naturally within us but, sadly, we spend many lifetimes learning this.

'You may be thinking, why cannot we take what you say and apply it now...forever? You can. You can heal yourself through nature You can feed and clothe yourself from nature. You can relieve all tensions through nature. You can have abundance from nature.

'Remember, it is in nature that you will be free a nd find the answer to any problem that confronts you. These are things you can see. Just understand that you also have all of this within you.'

The teacher paused before slowly and emphatically concluding, 'Every day is a new life, and every life is your nature -self growing, expanding and eventually evolving to other existences. Each of you have *your* time to feel that Nature-Self merging with something unexplainable.'

Volcano erupting, Calbuco, Chile

Bibliography

Andrews, C., *The New Circlemakers: Insights into the Crop Circle Mystery*, Virginia Beach, VA: 4th Dimension Press, 2nd ed., 2009.

Andrews, C. and Hein, S., *Crop Circles: More than Exotic Designs in the Field.* Presentation to the International UFO Congress, Laughlin, Nevada. Sept. 20, 2001.

Andrews, C., with Spignesi, J., *Crop Circles: Signs of Contact*, Franklin Lakes, NJ: New Page Books, 2003.

Baring, A., and Cashford, J., *The Myth of the Goddess: Evolution of an Image,* Penguin, 1993.

Bartholomew, A. (Ed.)., Crop Circles: Harbingers of World Change, Gateway, 1991.

Bohm, David. *Wholeness and the Implicate Order*, Great Britain. Routledge, 1980.

Bond, F., *The Company of Avalon*, Oxford, Blackwell, 1924.

Bonewitz, L., *New Cosmic Crystals,* Thorsons, 2000.

—, *Rocks and Minerals*, Dorling Kindersley, 2005.

Bord, Janet. *Mysterious Britain*, St. Albans. Granada Publishing Limited, 1974.

Bowen, S; Nocerino, F; Shapiro, J., *Mystery of the Crystal Skulls Revealed*, J & S Pacifica, 1988.

Campbell, John. *The Gaelic Otherworld*, Glasgow. James Maclehose and Sons, 1900.

Camphausen, R., *The Ka'bah at Mecca,* Bres (Holland) No.139, 1989

Carroll, L., *Alice's Adventures in Wonderland*, Macmillan, London, 1865.

—, *Through the Looking Glass*, Macmillan, London, 1872.

Cathie, B., *The Energy Grid*, Illinois. Adventures Unlimited Press, 1990.

Childress, D; Mehler, S., *The Crystal Skulls: Astonishing Portals to

Man's Past, Adventures Unlimited Press, Illinois, 2008.

Coats, C., *Living Energies,* Gateway, 1996.

Cohen, M., *Lewis Carroll: A Biography*, Alfred A. Knopf, 1995.

Colqoun, I., *The Living Stones*, Peter Owen, 1957.

Conan Doyle, A., *The Coming of the Fairies*, Hodder & Stoughton Ltd., London, 1922.

Cooke, Grace. *Sun-Men of the Americas*, Liss, Hampshire. The White Eagle Trust, 1983.

—, with Cooke, I., *The Light in Britain*, Liss, Hampshire. The White Eagle Publishing Trust, 1971.

Cotsworth, M., *The Need of a Rational Almanac*, Forgotten Books (reprint), 2018.

Crop Circles: Harbingers of World Change, ed. Bartholomew A., Gateway, 1991.

Devereux, Paul. *Earth Lights*, Wellingborough. Turnstone Press Limited, 1982.

—, *Places of Power*, London. Blandford Press, 1990.

—, *Spirit Roads*, London. Collins & Brown, 2003.

—, *Symbolic Landscapes*, Glastonbury. Gothic Image Publications, 1992.

Devereux, P. & Pennick, N., *Lines on the Landscape*, Robert Hale, 1989.

Dorland, F., *Holy Ice: Bridge to the Subconscious*, Galde Press Inc., St. Paul, MN, 1992.

Elder, I., *Celt, Druid, and Culdee*, London, 1962.

Farndon, J. and Parker, S., *Minerals, Rocks & Fossils of the World*, Anness Publishing, 2012.

Finkelstein, David. *The Space-Time Code*, Physical Review, 5D, no.12 [15 June 1972]: 2922.

Furlong, D., *Illuminating the Shadow: Transmuting the Dark Side of the Psyche*, Atlanta Books, 2016.

—, *The Keys to the Temple*, Piatkus Books, 1997.

Gardner, E. *Fairies: A Book of Real Fairies*, London. The Theosophical Publishing House, 1945.

Garvin, R., *The Crystal Skull: The Story of the Mystery, Myth, and Magic of the Mitchell-Hedges Crystal Skull, Discovered in a Lost Mayan City During a Search For Atlantis*, Doubleday, 1973.

Gienger, Michael. *Crystal Power, Crystal Healing: The Complete Handbook*. London: Blanford, 1998.

Glickman, M., *Crop Circles*, Glastonbury, Wooden Books, 2005.

—, Crop Circles: *The Bones of God*, Berkeley, CA: Frog Books, 2009.

Godwin, Joscelyn. *Atlantis and the Cycles of Time*, Raoulster, Vermont. Inner Traditions, 2011.

Graddon, N., *Otto Rahn and the Quest for the Grail*, Kempton, Illinois, Adventures Unlimited Press, 2008.

—, *The Landing Lights of Magonia: UFOs, Aliens and the Fairy Kingdom*, Adventures Unlimited Press, 2018.

—, *The Gods in the Fields*, Adventures Unlimited Press, 2020.

—, *Pythagoras of Samos: First Philosopher and Magician of Numbers*, Adventures Unlimited Press, 2021.

Grosso, M., *"UFOs and the Myth of the New Age,"* in *Cyberbiological Studies of the Imaginal Component in the UFO Contact Experience*, ed. Dennis Stillings [St. Paul, Minnesota Archaeus Project, 1989].

Hall, J., *The Crystal Bible*, Godsfield Press, 2003.

Hall, Manley P. *The Secret Teachings of All Ages*, Los Angeles. The Philosophical Research Society, Inc., 1928.

—, *Unseen Forces: Nature Spirits, Thought Forms, Ghosts and Specters, The Dweller on the Threshold*, Philosophical Research Society, 1978.

Haselhoff, E., *Dispersion of energies in worldwide crop formations*, Physiologia Plantarum, vol. 111, 2001, pp. 123-4; Haselhoff, 2001, pp. 71-81.

—, T*he Deepening Complexity of Crop Circles: Scientific Research and Urban Legends*. Berkeley, CA: Frog, Ltd. 2001.

Hein, Simeon. Electromagnetic Anomalies and Scale-Free Networks in British Crop Formations." The Circular 38: 35-8. 2000.

Hesemann, Michael. *UFOs: the Secret History*, New York: Marlowe and Company, 1998.

—, *The Cosmic Connection: Worldwide Crop Formations and ET Contacts*, Bath. Gateway Books, 1996.

Hesemann, Michael, and Philip Mantle. *Beyond Roswell*, London. Michael O'Mara Books Limited, 1997.

Howe, L., *Glimpses of Other Realities, Volume II: High Strangeness*, New Orleans. Paper Chase Press, 1998.

Jeans, James. *The Mysterious Universe*, New York. E.P. Dutton, 1932.

Jung, Carl. *Flying Saucers: A Modern Myth of Things Seen in the Sky*, London. Ark Paperbacks edition, 1987.

Keel, John. *Operation Trojan Horse*, San Antonio. Anomalist Books, 1970.

—, *Haunted Planet*, West Virginia. New Saucerian Books, 2014.

—, *The Endles Procession*, Pursuit Magazine, Third Quarter, 1982.

Layne, Meade. *The Coming of the Guardians*, San Diego. Inner Circle Press, 2009.

Lemesurier, P., *The Great Pyramid Decoded,* Element, 1996.

Levengood, W. & Talbott, N., (1999). *Dispersion of energies in worldwide crop formations*, Physiologia Plantarum. 105 (4): 615–24 Physiologia Plantarum. 92 (2): 356–63.

Michell, J., *City of Revelation*, Abacus, 1973.

—, *New Light on the Ancient Mystery of Glastonbury*, Thrift Books, 1990.

—, *The Dimensions of Paradise*, Inner Traditions, 2008.

—, *The Earth Spirit: Its Ways, Shrines and Mysteries*, Thames and Hudson, 1975.

—, *The Face and the Message*, Gothic Image Publications, 2002.

—, *The Flying Saucer Vision*, London. Abacus, 1974.

—, *The New View Over Atlantis*, London. Thames and Hudson, 1983.

Miller, H. & Broadhurst, P., *The Sun and the Serpent,* Pendragon Press, Launceston, Cornwall, 1989.

Mitchell-Hedges, F., *Danger My Ally*, Elek Books Ltd, London, 1954.

Narby J., *The Cosmic Serpent*, Weidenfield & Nicholson, 1999.

Neal, J., *All Done with Mirrors*, Secret Academy, 2016.

Oulette, J., "Seeing the Future in Photonic Crystals." The Industrial Physicist (December2001/January 2002).

Pennick, N., *Celtic Sacred Landscapes*, Thames & Hudson, 1996.

—, *The Ancient Art of Geomancy*, Thames and Hudson, 1979.

Persinger, M; Lafrenière, G., *Space-Time Transients and Unusual Events*, Burnham Inc. Publishing, 1977.

Pringle, L., *Crop Circles: The Greatest Mystery of Modern Times*, London: Thorsons, 1999.

Qualls-Corbet, N., *The Sacred Prostitute: Eternal Aspect of the*

Feminine, Inner City Books, Toronto, 1988.

Raphael, K., *Crystal Enlightenment,* Aurora Press, 1985.

Reiser, O., *This Holyest Erthe: The Glastonbury Zodiac and King Arthur's Camelot*, Perennial Books, London, 1974.

Roberts, A. (Ed.)., *Glastonbury: Ancient Avalon, New Jerusalem*, Rider, 1978.

Sarfatti, J., *Implications of Meta-Physics for Psychoenergetic Systems, in Psychoenergetic Systems*, Vol. 1, London. Gordon and Breach, 1974.

Silva, F., *Secrets in the Fields: The Science and Mysticism of Crop Circles*, Hampton Roads Publishing Company, 2002.

Simmons, R., *The Book of Stones*, Heaven and Earth, 2005.

Snelling, R., *The Planetary Matrix*, Spiritual Genesis Books 2013.

—, *The Atlantis Line*, 2017.

Spence, L., *The Mysteries of Britain*. London. Senate, 1994.

Talbot, Michael. *Mysticism and the New Physics*, London. Arkana, 1993.

—, *The Holographic Universe*, London. HarperCollins Publishers, 1996.

Underwood, G., *The Patterns of the Past*, Abelard-Schuman Ltd, 1973.

Vallée, Jacques. *Passport to Magonia*, Brisbane. Daily Grail Publishing, 2014.

—, *UFOs: The Psychic Solution*, St. Albans. Panther Books Ltd, 1977.

Walker, E., *The Nature of Consciousness*, Mathematical Biosciences 7, 1970.

Walsh, J. and Topping, B., *The Man Who Invented the Aztec Crystal Skulls: The Adventures of Eugène Boban*, http://berghahnbooks.

White Eagle Publishing Trust, *White Eagle on Divine Mother: the Feminine & the Mysteries*, 2004.

Woolf, J., *The Mystery of Lewis Carroll: Understanding the Author of Alice in Wonderland*, London: Haus Books, 2010.

Get these fascinating books from your nearest bookstore or directly from:
Adventures Unlimited Press
www.adventuresunlimitedpress.com

COVERT WARS AND BREAKAWAY CIVILIZATIONS
By Joseph P. Farrell

Farrell delves into the creation of breakaway civilizations by the Nazis in South America and other parts of the world. He discusses the advanced technology that they took with them at the end of the war and the psychological war that they waged for decades on America and NATO. He investigates the secret space programs currently sponsored by the breakaway civilizations and the current militaries in control of planet Earth. Plenty of astounding accounts, documents and speculation on the incredible alternative history of hidden conflicts and secret space programs that began when World War II officially "ended."

292 Pages. 6x9 Paperback. Illustrated. $19.95. Code: BCCW

THE ENIGMA OF CRANIAL DEFORMATION
Elongated Skulls of the Ancients
By David Hatcher Childress and Brien Foerster

In a book filled with over a hundred astonishing photos and a color photo section, Childress and Foerster take us to Peru, Bolivia, Egypt, Malta, China, Mexico and other places in search of strange elongated skulls and other cranial deformation. The puzzle of why diverse ancient people—even on remote Pacific Islands—would use head-binding to create elongated heads is mystifying. Where did they even get this idea? Did some people naturally look this way—with long narrow heads? Were they some alien race? Were they an elite race that roamed the entire planet? Why do anthropologists rarely talk about cranial deformation and know so little about it? Color Section.

250 Pages. 6x9 Paperback. Illustrated. $19.95. Code: ECD

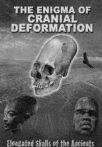

ARK OF GOD
The Incredible Power of the Ark of the Covenant
By David Hatcher Childress

Childress takes us on an incredible journey in search of the truth about (and science behind) the fantastic biblical artifact known as the Ark of the Covenant. This object made by Moses at Mount Sinai—part wooden-metal box and part golden statue—had the power to create "lightning" to kill people, and also to fly and lead people through the wilderness. The Ark of the Covenant suddenly disappears from the Bible record and what happened to it is not mentioned. Was it hidden in the underground passages of King Solomon's temple and later discovered by the Knights Templar? Was it taken through Egypt to Ethiopia as many Coptic Christians believe? Childress looks into hidden history, astonishing ancient technology, and a 3,000-year-old mystery that continues to fascinate millions of people today. Color section.

420 Pages. 6x9 Paperback. Illustrated. $22.00 Code: AOG

JACK THE RIPPER'S NEW TESTAMENT
Occultism and Bible Mania in 1888
By Nigel Graddon

This book offers evidence, for the first time, that those responsible for the Whitechapel murders were members of a hit team associated with a centuries-old European occult confederacy dedicated to human sacrifice. This was corroborated in the private papers of a Monsignor who carried out intelligence work for Pope Pius X in the run-up to the outbreak of global conflict in 1914. The priest told of the existence of a Vatican-based cabal of assassins formed by the infamous Borgias that is in alliance with a Teuton occult group formed in the 9th century. It was from within this unholy alliance that assassins travelled to London to carry out the Ripper murders to "solve a sticky problem for the British Royal Family"

302 Pages. 6x9 Paperback. Illustrated. $19.95. Code: JRNT

SECRETS OF THE HOLY LANCE
The Spear of Destiny in History & Legend
by Jerry E. Smith

Secrets of the Holy Lance traces the Spear from its possession by Constantine, Rome's first Christian Caesar, to Charlemagne's claim that with it he ruled the Holy Roman Empire by Divine Right, and on through two thousand years of kings and emperors, until it came within Hitler's grasp—and beyond! Did it rest for a while in Antarctic ice? Is it now hidden in Europe, awaiting the next person to claim its awesome power? Neither debunking nor worshiping, *Secrets of the Holy Lance* seeks to pierce the veil of myth and mystery around the Spear.

312 PAGES. 6x9 PAPERBACK. ILLUSTRATED. $16.95. CODE: SOHL

THE CRYSTAL SKULLS
Astonishing Portals to Man's Past
by David Hatcher Childress and Stephen S. Mehler

Childress introduces the technology and lore of crystals, and then plunges into the turbulent times of the Mexican Revolution form the backdrop for the rollicking adventures of Ambrose Bierce, the renowned journalist who went missing in the jungles in 1913, and F.A. Mitchell-Hedges, the notorious adventurer who emerged from the jungles with the most famous of the crystal skulls. Mehler shares his extensive knowledge of and experience with crystal skulls. Having been involved in the field since the 1980s, he has personally examined many of the most influential skulls, and has worked with the leaders in crystal skull research. Color section.

294 pages. 6x9 Paperback. Illustrated. $18.95. Code: CRSK

THE LAND OF OSIRIS
An Introduction to Khemitology
by Stephen S. Mehler

Was there an advanced prehistoric civilization in ancient Egypt? Were they the people who built the great pyramids and carved the Great Sphinx? Did the pyramids serve as energy devices and not as tombs for kings? Chapters include: Egyptology and Its Paradigms; Khemitology—New Paradigms; Asgat Nefer—The Harmony of Water; Khemit and the Myth of Atlantis; The Extraterrestrial Question; more. Color section.

272 PAGES. 6x9 PAPERBACK. ILLUSTRATED . $18.95. CODE: LOOS

VIMANA:
Flying Machines of the Ancients
by David Hatcher Childress

According to early Sanskrit texts the ancients had several types of airships called vimanas. Like aircraft of today, vimanas were used to fly through the air from city to city; to conduct aerial surveys of uncharted lands; and as delivery vehicles for awesome weapons. David Hatcher Childress, popular *Lost Cities* author, takes us on an astounding investigation into tales of ancient flying machines. In his new book, packed with photos and diagrams, he consults ancient texts and modern stories and presents astonishing evidence that aircraft, similar to the ones we use today, were used thousands of years ago in India, Sumeria, China and other countries. Includes a 24-page color section.

408 Pages. 6x9 Paperback. Illustrated. $22.95. Code: VMA

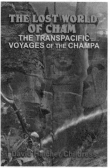

THE LOST WORLD OF CHAM
The Trans-Pacific Voyages of the Champa
By David Hatcher Childress

The mysterious Cham, or Champa, peoples of Southeast Asia formed a megalith-building, seagoing empire that extended into Indonesia, Tonga, and beyond—a transoceanic power that reached Mexico and South America. The Champa maintained many ports in what is today Vietnam, Cambodia, and Indonesia and their ships plied the Indian Ocean and the Pacific, bringing Chinese, African and Indian traders to far off lands, including Olmec ports on the Pacific Coast of Central America. opics include: Cham and Khem: Egyptian Influence on Cham; The Search for Metals; The Basalt City of Nan Madol; Elephants and Buddhists in North America; The Olmecs; The Cham in Colombia; tons more. 24-page color section.
328 Pages. 6x9 Paperback. Illustrated. $22.00 Code: LPWC

OTTO RAHN & THE QUEST FOR THE HOLY GRAIL
The Amazing Life of the Real "Indiana Jones"
By Nigel Graddon

Otto Rahn, a Hessian language scholar, is said to have found runic Grail tablets in the Pyrenean grottoes, unearthed as a result of his work in decoding the hidden messages within the Grail masterwork *Parsifal*. The fabulous artifacts identified by Rahn were believed by Himmler to include the Grail Cup, the Spear of Destiny, the Tablets of Moses, the Ark of the Covenant, the Sword and Harp of David, the Sacred Candelabra and the Golden Urn of Manna. Some believe that Rahn was a Nazi guru who wielded immense influence within the Hitler regime, persuading them that the Grail was the Sacred Book of the Aryans, which, once obtained, would justify their extreme political theories.
450 pages. 6x9 Paperback. Illustrated. Index. $18.95. Code: ORQG

THE LANDING LIGHTS OF MAGONIA
UFOs, Aliens and the Fairy Kingdom
By Nigel Graddon

British UFO researcher Graddon takes us to that magical land of Magonia—the land of the Fairies—a place from which some people return while others go and never come back. Graddon on fairies, the wee folk, elves, fairy pathways, Welsh folklore, the Tuatha de Dannan, UFO occupants, the Little Blue Man of Studham, the implications of Mars, psychic connections with UFOs and fairies. He also recounts many of the strange tales of fairies, UFOs and Magonia. Chapters include: The Little Blue Man of Studham; The Wee Folk; UFOlk; What the Folk; Grimm Tales; The Welsh Triangle; The Implicate Order; Mars—an Atlantean Outpost; Psi-Fi; High Spirits; "Once Upon a Time…"; more.
270 Pages. 6x9 Paperback. Illustrated. $19.95. Code: LLOM

ADVENTURES OF A HASHISH SMUGGLER
by Henri de Monfreid

The son of a French artist who knew Paul Gaugin as a child, de Monfreid sought his fortune by becoming a collector and merchant of the fabled Persian Gulf pearls. He was then drawn into the shadowy world of arms trading, slavery, smuggling and drugs. Infamous as well as famous, his name is inextricably linked to the Red Sea and the raffish ports between Suez and Aden in the early years of the twentieth century. De Monfreid (1879 to 1974) had a long life of many adventures around the Horn of Africa where he dodged pirates as well as the authorities.
284 Pages. 6x9 Paperback. $16.95. Illustrated. Code AHS

TECHNOLOGY OF THE GODS
The Incredible Sciences of the Ancients
by David Hatcher Childress

Childress looks at the technology that was allegedly used in Atlantis and the theory that the Great Pyramid of Egypt was originally a gigantic power station. He examines tales of ancient flight and the technology that it involved; how the ancients used electricity; megalithic building techniques; the use of crystal lenses and the fire from the gods; evidence of various high tech weapons in the past, including atomic weapons; ancient metallurgy and heavy machinery; the role of modern inventors such as Nikola Tesla in bringing ancient technology back into modern use; impossible artifacts; and more.

356 pages. 6x9 Paperback. Illustrated. $16.95. code: TGOD

THE ANTI-GRAVITY HANDBOOK
edited by David Hatcher Childress

The new expanded compilation of material on Anti-Gravity, Free Energy, Flying Saucer Propulsion, UFOs, Suppressed Technology, NASA Cover-ups and more. Highly illustrated with patents, technical illustrations and photos. This revised and expanded edition has more material, including photos of Area 51, Nevada, the government's secret testing facility. This classic on weird science is back in a new format!

230 pages. 7x10 paperback. Illustrated. $16.95. code: AGH

ANTI–GRAVITY & THE WORLD GRID

Is the earth surrounded by an intricate electromagnetic grid network offering free energy? This compilation of material on ley lines and world power points contains chapters on the geography, mathematics, and light harmonics of the earth grid. Learn the purpose of ley lines and ancient megalithic structures located on the grid. Discover how the grid made the Philadelphia Experiment possible. Explore the Coral Castle and many other mysteries, including acoustic levitation, Tesla Shields and scalar wave weaponry. Browse through the section on anti-gravity patents, and research resources.

274 pages. 7x10 paperback. Illustrated. $14.95. code: AGW

ANTI–GRAVITY & THE UNIFIED FIELD
edited by David Hatcher Childress

Is Einstein's Unified Field Theory the answer to all of our energy problems? Explored in this compilation of material is how gravity, electricity and magnetism manifest from a unified field around us. Why artificial gravity is possible; secrets of UFO propulsion; free energy; Nikola Tesla and anti-gravity airships of the 20s and 30s; flying saucers as superconducting whirls of plasma; anti-mass generators; vortex propulsion; suppressed technology; government cover-ups; gravitational pulse drive; spacecraft & more.

240 pages. 7x10 Paperback. Illustrated. $14.95. Code: AGU

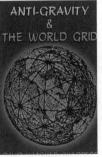

THE TIME TRAVEL HANDBOOK
A Manual of Practical Teleportation & Time Travel
edited by David Hatcher Childress

The Time Travel Handbook takes the reader beyond the government experiments and deep into the uncharted territory of early time travellers such as Nikola Tesla and Guglielmo Marconi and their alleged time travel experiments, as well as the Wilson Brothers of EMI and their connection to the Philadelphia Experiment—the U.S. Navy's forays into invisibility, time travel, and teleportation. Childress looks into the claims of time travelling individuals, and investigates the unusual claim that the pyramids on Mars were built in the future and sent back in time. A highly visual, large format book, with patents, photos and schematics. Be the first on your block to build your own time travel device!

316 pages. 7x10 Paperback. Illustrated. $16.95. code: TTH

ANCIENT ALIENS ON THE MOON
By Mike Bara
What did NASA find in their explorations of the solar system that they may have kept from the general public? How ancient really are these ruins on the Moon? Using official NASA and Russian photos of the Moon, Bara looks at vast cityscapes and domes in the Sinus Medii region as well as glass domes in the Crisium region. Bara also takes a detailed look at the mission of Apollo 17 and the case that this was a salvage mission, primarily concerned with investigating an opening into a massive hexagonal ruin near the landing site. Chapters include: The History of Lunar Anomalies; The Early 20th Century; Sinus Medii; To the Moon Alice!; Mare Crisium; Yes, Virginia, We Really Went to the Moon; Apollo 17; more. Tons of photos of the Moon examined for possible structures and other anomalies.
248 Pages. 6x9 Paperback. Illustrated.. $19.95. Code: AAOM

ANCIENT ALIENS ON MARS
By Mike Bara
Bara brings us this lavishly illustrated volume on alien structures on Mars. Was there once a vast, technologically advanced civilization on Mars, and did it leave evidence of its existence behind for humans to find eons later? Did these advanced extraterrestrial visitors vanish in a solar system wide cataclysm of their own making, only to make their way to Earth and start anew? Was Mars once as lush and green as the Earth, and teeming with life? Chapters include: War of the Worlds; The Mars Tidal Model; The Death of Mars; Cydonia and the Face on Mars; The Monuments of Mars; The Search for Life on Mars; The True Colors of Mars and The Pathfinder Sphinx; more. Color section.
252 Pages. 6x9 Paperback. Illustrated. $19.95. Code: AMAR

ANCIENT ALIENS ON MARS II
By Mike Bara
Using data acquired from sophisticated new scientific instruments like the Mars Odyssey THEMIS infrared imager, Bara shows that the region of Cydonia overlays a vast underground city full of enormous structures and devices that may still be operating. He peels back the layers of mystery to show images of tunnel systems, temples and ruins, and exposes the sophisticated NASA conspiracy designed to hide them. Bara also tackles the enigma of Mars' hollowed out moon Phobos, and exposes evidence that it is artificial. Long-held myths about Mars, including claims that it is protected by a sophisticated UFO defense system, are examined. Data from the Mars rovers Spirit, Opportunity and Curiosity are examined; everything from fossilized plants to mechanical debris is exposed in images taken directly from NASA's own archives.
294 Pages. 6x9 Paperback. Illustrated. $19.95. Code: AAM2

ANCIENT TECHNOLOGY IN PERU & BOLIVIA
By David Hatcher Childress
Childress speculates on the existence of a sunken city in Lake Titicaca and reveals new evidence that the Sumerians may have arrived in South America 4,000 years ago. He demonstrates that the use of "keystone cuts" with metal clamps poured into them to secure megalithic construction was an advanced technology used all over the world, from the Andes to Egypt, Greece and Southeast Asia. He maintains that only power tools could have made the intricate articulation and drill holes found in extremely hard granite and basalt blocks in Bolivia and Peru, and that the megalith builders had to have had advanced methods for moving and stacking gigantic blocks of stone, some weighing over 100 tons.
340 Pages. 6x9 Paperback. Illustrated.. $19.95 Code: ATP

HESS AND THE PENGUINS
The Holocaust, Antarctica and the Strange Case of Rudolf Hess
By Joseph P. Farrell

Farrell looks at Hess' mission to make peace with Britain and get rid of Hitler—even a plot to fly Hitler to Britain for capture! How much did Göring and Hitler know of Rudolf Hess' subversive plot, and what happened to Hess? Why was a doppleganger put in Spandau Prison and then "suicided"? Did the British use an early form of mind control on Hess' double? John Foster Dulles of the OSS and CIA suspected as much. Farrell also uncovers the strange death of Admiral Richard Byrd's son in 1988, about the same time of the death of Hess.

288 Pages. 6x9 Paperback. Illustrated. $19.95. Code: HAPG

HIDDEN FINANCE, ROGUE NETWORKS & SECRET SORCERY
The Fascist International, 9/11, & Penetrated Operations
By Joseph P. Farrell

Farrell investigates the theory that there were not *two* levels to the 9/11 event, but *three*. He says that the twin towers were downed by the force of an exotic energy weapon, one similar to the Tesla energy weapon suggested by Dr. Judy Wood, and ties together the tangled web of missing money, secret technology and involvement of portions of the Saudi royal family. Farrell unravels the many layers behind the 9-11 attack, layers that include the Deutschebank, the Bush family, the German industrialist Carl Duisberg, Saudi Arabian princes and the energy weapons developed by Tesla before WWII.

296 Pages. 6x9 Paperback. Illustrated. $19.95. Code: HFRN

THRICE GREAT HERMETICA & THE JANUS AGE
By Joseph P. Farrell

What do the Fourth Crusade, the exploration of the New World, secret excavations of the Holy Land, and the pontificate of Innocent the Third all have in common? Answer: Venice and the Templars. What do they have in common with Jesus, Gottfried Leibniz, Sir Isaac Newton, Rene Descartes, and the Earl of Oxford? Answer: Egypt and a body of doctrine known as Hermeticism. The hidden role of Venice and Hermeticism reached far and wide, into the plays of Shakespeare (a.k.a. Edward DeVere, Earl of Oxford), into the quest of the three great mathematicians of the Early Enlightenment for a lost form of analysis, and back into the end of the classical era, to little known Egyptian influences at work during the time of Jesus.

354 Pages. 6x9 Paperback. Illustrated. $19.95. Code: TGHJ

ROBOT ZOMBIES
Transhumanism and the Robot Revolution
By Xaviant Haze and Estrella Eguino,

Technology is growing exponentially and the moment when it merges with the human mind, called "The Singularity," is visible in our imminent future. Science and technology are pushing forward, transforming life as we know it—perhaps even giving humans a shot at immortality. Who will benefit from this? This book examines the history and future of robotics, artificial intelligence, zombies and a Transhumanist utopia/dystopia integrating man with machine. Chapters include: Love, Sex and Compassion—Android Style; Humans Aren't Working Like They Used To; Skynet Rises; Blueprints for Transhumans; Kurzweil's Quest; Nanotech Dreams; Zombies Among Us; Cyborgs (Cylons) in Space; Awakening the Human; more. Color Section.

180 Pages. 6x9 Paperback. Illustrated. $16.95. Code: RBTZ

THE GODS IN THE FIELDS
Michael, Mary and Alice-Guardians of Enchanted Britain
By Nigel Graddon
We learn of Britain's special place in the origins of ancient wisdom and of the "Sun-Men" who taught it to a humanity in its infancy. Aspects of these teachings are found all along the St. Michael ley: at Glastonbury, the location of Merlin and Arthur's Avalon; in the design and layout of the extraordinary Somerset Zodiac of which Glastonbury is a major part; in the amazing stone circles and serpentine avenues at Avebury and nearby Silbury Hill: portals to unimaginable worlds of mystery and enchantment; Chapters include: Michael, Mary and Merlin; England's West Country; The Glastonbury Zodiac; Wiltshire; The Gods in the Fields; Michael, Mary and Alice; East of the Line; Table of Michael and Mary Locations; more.
280 Pages. 6x9 Paperback. Illustrated. $19.95. Code: GIF

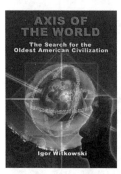

AXIS OF THE WORLD
The Search for the Oldest American Civilization
by Igor Witkowski
Polish author Witkowski's research reveals remnants of a high civilization that was able to exert its influence on almost the entire planet, and did so with full consciousness. Sites around South America show that this was not just one of the places influenced by this culture, but a place where they built their crowning achievements. Easter Island, in the southeastern Pacific, constitutes one of them. The Rongo-Rongo language that developed there points westward to the Indus Valley. Taken together, the facts presented by Witkowski provide a fresh, new proof that an antediluvian, great civilization flourished several millennia ago.
220 pages. 6x9 Paperback. Illustrated. $18.95. Code: AXOW

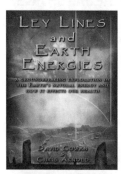

LEY LINE & EARTH ENERGIES
An Extraordinary Journey into the Earth's
Natural Energy System
by David Cowan & Chris Arnold
The mysterious standing stones, burial grounds and stone circles that lace Europe, the British Isles and other areas have intrigued scientists, writers, artists and travellers through the centuries. How do ley lines work? How did our ancestors use Earth energy to map their sacred sites and burial grounds? How do ghosts and poltergeists interact with Earth energy? How can Earth spirals and black spots affect our health? This exploration shows how natural forces affect our behavior, how they can be used to enhance our health and well being.
368 pages. 6x9 Paperback. Illustrated. $18.95. Code: LLEE

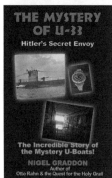

THE MYSTERY OF U-33
By Nigel Graddon
The incredible story of the mystery U-Boats of WWII! Graddon first chronicles the story of the mysterious U-33 that landed in Scotland in 1940 and involved the top-secret Enigma device. He then looks at U-Boat special missions during and after WWII, including U-Boat trips to Antarctica; U-Boats with the curious cargos of liquid mercury; the journey of the Spear of Destiny via U-Boat; the "Black Subs" and more. Chapters and topics include: U-33: The Official Story; The First Questions; Survivors and Deceased; August 1985—the Story Breaks; The Carradale U-boat; The Tale of the Bank Event; In the Wake of U-33; Wrecks; The Greenock Lairs; The Mystery Men; "Brass Bounders at the Admiralty"; Captain's Log; Max Schiller through the Lens; Rudolf Hess; Otto Rahn; U-Boat Special Missions; Neu-Schwabenland; more.
351 Pages. 6x9 Paperback. Illustrated. $19.95. Code: MU33

HITLER'S SUPPRESSED AND STILL-SECRET WEAPONS, SCIENCE AND TECHNOLOGY
by Henry Stevens

In the closing months of WWII the Allies assembled mind-blowing intelligence reports of supermetals, electric guns, and ray weapons able to stop the engines of Allied aircraft—in addition to feared x-ray and laser weaponry. Chapters include: The Kammler Group; German Flying Disc Update; The Electromagnetic Vampire; Liquid Air; Synthetic Blood; German Free Energy Research; German Atomic Tests; The Fuel-Air Bomb; Supermetals; Red Mercury; Means to Stop Engines; more.
335 Pages. 6x9 Paperback. Illustrated. $19.95. Code: HSSW

PRODIGAL GENIUS
The Life of Nikola Tesla
by John J. O'Neill

This special edition of O'Neill's book has many rare photographs of Tesla and his most advanced inventions. Tesla's eccentric personality gives his life story a strange romantic quality. He made his first million before he was forty, yet gave up his royalties in a gesture of friendship, and died almost in poverty. Tesla could see an invention in 3-D, from every angle, within his mind, before it was built; how he refused to accept the Nobel Prize; his friendships with Mark Twain, George Westinghouse and competition with Thomas Edison. Tesla is revealed as a figure of genius whose influence on the world reaches into the far future. Deluxe, illustrated edition.
408 pages. 6x9 Paperback. Illustrated. Bibliography. $18.95. Code: PRG

THE ENCYCLOPEDIA OF MOON MYSTERIES
Secrets, Anomalies, Extraterrestrials and More
By Constance Victoria Briggs

Our moon is an enigma. The ancients viewed it as a light to guide them in the darkness, and a god to be worshipped. Did you know that: Aristotle and Plato wrote about a time when there was no Moon? Several of the NASA astronauts reported seeing UFOs while traveling to the Moon?; the Moon might be hollow?; Apollo 10 astronauts heard strange "space music" when traveling on the far side of the Moon?; strange and unexplained lights have been seen on the Moon for centuries?; there are said to be ruins of structures on the Moon?; there is an ancient tale that suggests that the first human was created on the Moon?; Tons more. Tons of illustrations with A to Z sections for easy reference and reading.
152 Pages. 7x10 Paperback. Illustrated. $19.95. Code: EOMM

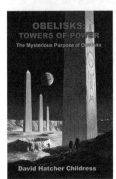

OBELISKS: TOWERS OF POWER
The Mysterious Purpose of Obelisks
By David Hatcher Childress

Some obelisks weigh over 500 tons and are massive blocks of polished granite that would be extremely difficult to quarry and erect even with modern equipment. Why did ancient civilizations in Egypt, Ethiopia and elsewhere undertake the massive enterprise it would have been to erect a single obelisk, much less dozens of them? Were they energy towers that could receive or transmit energy? With discussions on Tesla's wireless power, and the use of obelisks as gigantic acupuncture needles for earth, Chapters include: Megaliths Around the World and their Purpose; The Crystal Towers of Egypt; The Obelisks of Ethiopia; Obelisks in Europe and Asia; Mysterious Obelisks in the Americas; The Terrible Crystal Towers of Atlantis; Tesla's Wireless Power Distribution System; Obelisks on the Moon; more. 8-page color section.
336 Pages. 6x9 Paperback. Illustrated. $22.00 Code: OBK

ORDER FORM

10% Discount When You Order 3 or More Items!

One Adventure Place
P.O. Box 74
Kempton, Illinois 60946
United States of America
Tel.: 815-253-6390 • Fax: 815-253-6300
Email: auphq@frontiernet.net
http://www.adventuresunlimitedpress.com

Please check: ☑

☐ This is my first order   ☐ I have ordered before

Name
Address
City
State/Province   Postal Code
Country
Phone: Day   Evening
Fax   Email

Item Code	Item Description	Qty	Total

Please check: ☑

Subtotal ▶	
Less Discount-10% for 3 or more items ▶	
☐ Postal-Surface — Balance ▶	
☐ Postal-Air Mail (Priority in USA) — Illinois Residents 6.25% Sales Tax ▶	
— Previous Credit ▶	
☐ UPS — Shipping ▶	
(Mainland USA only) — Total (check/MO in USD$ only) ▶	

☐ Visa/MasterCard/Discover/American Express

Card Number:
Expiration Date: Security Code:

✓ SEND A CATALOG TO A FRIEND: